Unity Certified Programmer Exam Guide

Expert tips and techniques to pass the Unity certification exam at the first attempt

Philip Walker

BIRMINGHAM - MUMBAI

Unity Certified Programmer: Exam Guide

Commissioning Editor: Pavan Ramchandani
Acquisition Editor: Ashitosh Gupta
Content Development Editor: Aamir Ahmed
Senior Editor: Hayden Edwards
Technical Editor: Deepesh Patel
Copy Editor: Safis Editing
Project Coordinator: Kinjal Bari
Proofreader: Safis Editing
Indexer: Tejal Daruwale Soni
Production Designer: Alishon Mendonca

First published: June 2020

Production reference: 2020720

Livery Place
35 Livery Street
Birmingham
B3 2PB, UK.

ISBN 978-1-83882-842-4

www.packt.com

Packt.com

Subscribe to our online digital library for full access to over 7,000 books and videos, as well as industry leading tools to help you plan your personal development and advance your career. For more information, please visit our website.

Why subscribe?

- Spend less time learning and more time coding with practical eBooks and Videos from over 4,000 industry professionals

- Improve your learning with Skill Plans built especially for you

- Get a free eBook or video every month

- Fully searchable for easy access to vital information

- Copy and paste, print, and bookmark content

Did you know that Packt offers eBook versions of every book published, with PDF and ePub files available? You can upgrade to the eBook version at www.packt.com and as a print book customer, you are entitled to a discount on the eBook copy. Get in touch with us at customercare@packtpub.com for more details.

At www.packt.com, you can also read a collection of free technical articles, sign up for a range of free newsletters, and receive exclusive discounts and offers on Packt books and eBooks.

About the author

Philip Walker originally started as a 3D games artist, but then decided he wanted to combine his current skills with coding so that he could see through the majority of his games' and apps' development himself. Philip has worked in five different industries as an artist and/or a Unity developer using various types of technology and techniques.

I started writing this book just over a year ago and it definitely hasn't been easy keeping up with the pace of the deadlines. The start was bumpy but near the end, I found two particular members of staff at Packt that helped me to the finishing line, and that's what I'll remember most about writing this book. I would like to thank Aamir Ahmed and Divij Kotian for generally helping me and pushing me through the final stages of writing this book.

About the reviewer

Jeremy Luisier is a Unity certified instructor and the leading representative of the Unity Academic Alliance at **King Mongkut's Institute of Technology Ladkrabang (KMITL)**, where he also serves as the director of IAAI Virtual—the KMITL International Academy of Aviation Industry's extended reality research and design facility. He is also a Ph.D. candidate in the field of industrial innovation management at KMITL's College of Educational Innovation Research and the environmental scan lead for the VR/AR Association for the Asia-Pacific region. In his free time, Jeremy enjoys designing and developing Unity games, XR experiences, and traveling with his beloved wife, Maylyn.

Packt is searching for authors like you

If you're interested in becoming an author for Packt, please visit `authors.packtpub.com` and apply today. We have worked with thousands of developers and tech professionals, just like you, to help them share their insight with the global tech community. You can make a general application, apply for a specific hot topic that we are recruiting an author for, or submit your own idea.

Table of Contents

Preface

Unity Certified Programmer: Exam Guide will take a basic object-oriented programmer and introduce them to Unity through a creative project that stretches across the entire book, achieving essential exam core objectives that can be put toward Unity's own Official Programmer Exam.

This book will take you (the programmer) through discussing the exam itself, breaking down each of its objectives, and what is expected of you to achieve a pass. From there, everything we'll discuss relates to supporting you with potential questions from the exam. So, we'll start straight away and refer to an overview of common design patterns and even more common SOLID principles that all programs need to know. We will go through our game design brief and custom-built framework before we even touch Unity.

After installing Unity, you will begin to take your first steps in building a side-scrolling shooter game, and at the beginning of every chapter, it will be brought to your attention which core objectives you will be covering to support you. After some chapters, you will also be tested with a mini mock exam to see how you are getting on.

By the end of the book, you will have created a game that can be played on a standalone PC and/or Android device supporting a keyboard and touch screen controls, where you will fly a spaceship to fight off oncoming enemies.

As early as Chapter 2, *Adding and Manipulating Objects*, you will have coded the majority of the game and the following chapters we'll progress through will introduce you to Unity's tools and components, such as the Timeline, which is specifically built for the TV/film industry and cutscenes in games. You will cover particle effects, different materials to apply to your game objects to make them react to light, fading the sound in and out by manipulating an audio mixer with your scripting, pausing the game, storing values in your own scriptable objects, and much, much more.

Even if you aren't taking the Unity Certified Programmer Exam, you will make a game that you can continue to develop, play, and learn from.

Who this book is for

This book is for any object-oriented programmer who wants to learn more about Unity and go as far as feeling ready to go even further and take the Unity Certified Programmer Exam after completing this book.

What this book covers

Chapter 1, *Setting Up and Structuring Our Project*, introduces what is expected of you in the exam, discusses SOLID principles, and gives an overview of design patterns. You will also see how we are going to create our game by looking at its framework and version control.

Chapter 2, *Adding and Manipulating Objects*, gets you started with coding and importing 3D assets to get the basics of the game functioning.

Chapter 3, *Managing Scripts and Mock Tests*, extends the game out into menu screens, adding sound, adding a scoring system, and ending with the first mock exam.

Chapter 4, *Applying Art, Animation, and Particles*, focuses on understanding materials, animating textures, and creating particle systems.

Chapter 5, *Creating a Shop Scene for Our Game*, introduces the shop scene and making use of Unity's raycast system, which shoots invisible rays to help identify game objects, and looks at uses of scriptable objects for filling out content.

Chapter 6, *Purchasing In-Game Items and Advertisements*, covers making the shop scene have a working in-game balance to buy upgrades and introduce users to watch adverts to gain extra in-game credits. By the end of the chapter, the player will be able to make use of firing a new weapon and taking extra hits from enemies with their bought shield.

Chapter 7, *Creating a Game Loop and Mock Test*, moves through each screen until the game loops back to the beginning to create a game loop, finishing off with a mock test that has questions on the material learned so far.

Chapter 8, *Adding Custom Fonts and UI*, gets more familiar with Unity's 2D Canvas, adding polish to each screen by applying image components and custom font and animating each level's title.

Chapter 9, *Creating a 2D Shop Interface and In-Game HUD*, takes the shop scene from looking less like a prototype to more polished and functioning to support various screen aspect ratios. This chapter also introduces an in-game life, map, and score system.

Chapter 10, *Pausing the Game, Altering Sound, and a Mock Test*, covers creating a pause screen for each level of the game, which will give options to alter the game's volume controls, quit and resume the game, followed by a mock test to check your knowledge of the chapter.

Chapter 11, *Storing Data and Audio Mixer*, makes use of Unity's own PlayerPrefs and compares it with JSON and storing data in the cloud with remote settings.

Chapter 12, *NavMesh, Timeline, and Mock Test*, introduces a new enemy that attempts to escape the player with the use of AI and looks at animating a boss into the scene with the use of Unity's animation tool, Timeline, and extending its functionality to animate flashing lights. There's another mock test at the end of the chapter to see how well things are going.

Chapter 13, *Effects, Testing, Performance, and Alt Controls*, discusses making use of colliders, rigidbody properties, visual effect post-processing, global lighting, and reflection probes. This chapter also looks at further gameplay functionality to support mobile controls, building, and testing the game on PC and mobile.

Chapter 14, *Full Unity Programmer Mock Exam*, includes over 90 questions to answer and to test you on what you've learned from all 13 chapters and the answers will be found in the appendix.

To get the most out of this book

Some familiarity with Unity would be helpful but is not essential. A basic understanding of C# or any other object-oriented programming knowledge is required. At the time of writing this book, the Unity exam is based on Unity version 2017.3. We'll go through the procedure of downloading and installing the software in Chapter 1, *Setting Up and Structuring Our Project*. If for any reason, you are using a later version of Unity, that shouldn't matter unless the book mentions where things may differ between versions.

Download the example code files

You can download the example code files for this book from your account at www.packt.com. If you purchased this book elsewhere, you can visit www.packtpub.com/support and register to have the files emailed directly to you.

You can download the code files by following these steps:

1. Log in or register at www.packt.com.
2. Select the **Support** tab.
3. Click on **Code Downloads**.
4. Enter the name of the book in the **Search** box and follow the onscreen instructions.

Once the file is downloaded, please make sure that you unzip or extract the folder using the latest version of:

- WinRAR/7-Zip for Windows
- Zipeg/iZip/UnRarX for Mac
- 7-Zip/PeaZip for Linux

The code bundle for the book is also hosted on GitHub at https://github.com/PacktPublishing/Unity-Certified-Programmer-Exam-Guide. In case there's an update to the code, it will be updated on the existing GitHub repository.

We also have other code bundles from our rich catalog of books and videos available at https://github.com/PacktPublishing/. Check them out!

Code in Action

Code in Action videos for this book can be viewed at https://bit.ly/3hZHeGi.

Conventions used

There are a number of text conventions used throughout this book.

CodeInText: Indicates code words in the text, database table names, folder names, filenames, file extensions, pathnames, dummy URLs, user input, and Twitter handles. Here is an example: "A Unity package is a single file that contains various assets that can be used in Unity in a similar manner to a .zip file."

A block of code is set as follows:

```
void Start()
  {
      this.transform.localPosition = Vector3.zero;
      startPos = transform.position;
      Distance();
  }
```

When we wish to draw your attention to a particular part of a code block, the relevant lines or items are set in bold:

```
public class PlayerSpawner : MonoBehaviour
```

Bold: Indicates a new term, an important word, or words that you see onscreen. For example, words in menus or dialog boxes appear in the text like this. Here is an example: "To finally bake the lights, open the **Lighting** window by going to **Window | Lighting | Settings**. Once there, select the **Global Maps** tab."

Warnings or important notes appear like this.

Tips and tricks appear like this.

Get in touch

Feedback from our readers is always welcome.

General feedback: If you have questions about any aspect of this book, mention the book title in the subject of your message and email us at customercare@packtpub.com. You can also contact the author of the book on Twitter: @retrophilion

Errata: Although we have taken every care to ensure the accuracy of our content, mistakes do happen. If you have found a mistake in this book, we would be grateful if you would report this to us. Please visit www.packtpub.com/support/errata, selecting your book, clicking on the Errata Submission Form link, and entering the details.

Piracy: If you come across any illegal copies of our works in any form on the Internet, we would be grateful if you would provide us with the location address or website name. Please contact us at copyright@packt.com with a link to the material.

If you are interested in becoming an author: If there is a topic that you have expertise in and you are interested in either writing or contributing to a book, please visit authors.packtpub.com.

Reviews

Please leave a review. Once you have read and used this book, why not leave a review on the site that you purchased it from? Potential readers can then see and use your unbiased opinion to make purchase decisions, we at Packt can understand what you think about our products, and our authors can see your feedback on their book. Thank you!

For more information about Packt, please visit packt.com.

1
Setting Up and Structuring Our Project

For some time, Unity has been issuing exams that cover a range of different skills for people who are either graduates, self-taught, or are classed as veterans in their field.

If we check the prerequisites on Unity's website (`https://certification.unity.com/products/certified-programmer`), they tell us that this exam isn't for absolute beginners and you need at least 2 years of experience working with Unity and computer programming, including C#. This book will take you through the process of becoming as familiar as possible with Unity and its services, to the point where it might feel like a beginners course; however, I expect you to understand the fundamentals of C# programming, such as what an `if` statement is, what a function does, and what a class represents. If you don't, I would recommend reading Harrison Ferrone's *Learning C# by Developing Games with Unity 2019* book first (`https://www.packtpub.com/gb/game-development/learning-c-developing-games-unity-2019-fourth-edition`). Be aware that this exam is based on Unity 2017.3 and it hasn't been updated since it's launch, but it's definitely the best place to start if you are working with the fundamentals of Unity.

As you can imagine, it is sometimes difficult to gauge what level a programmer is at with their experience. Imagine what it's like for an employer to recruit someone. Often, a programmer is judged by their portfolio, but what happens if you're a graduate without one or you lack a large quantity of work because you've been too busy studying? Perhaps you've been a programmer for years but can't show any recent work due to signing non-disclosure agreements? Some employers might look at your CV and not even look at your portfolio as the qualifications just don't look impressive enough. The tests a potential employer can put a developer through can also be unbalanced, unfair, unrealistic, and not challenging enough; it's likely that the employer has grabbed a programmer's questionnaire template off the internet to test you.

However, having qualifications from Unity itself sends a clear message that you've been tested and covered all the fields that acknowledge you as a certified Unity programmer. Even if you have a decent portfolio showing a level of standardization and focus, having qualifications from Unity can give you the edge over someone else in a job application.

This book serves two main purposes:

- To take you through a fun, simple, side-scrolling shooter project with some downloadable art assets and sounds that will cover the core objectives in Unity's exam
- To get you as ready for the exam as possible with regular testing and reviewing

So, if you feel like you don't need to carry out the project, skip to the very end of this book to try out the final mock test—actually, I recommend you do this now. Flick to the back of the book, take the test, and if you don't do as well as you planned (that is, score over 75%), at least you know you have something to learn, and working through the project might help. Don't take the exam too soon after taking the mock test if you aren't happy with your score—you will be going up against your own muscle memory, rather than the knowledge itself.

Unity has split the necessary areas of this exam into six core objectives. We will cover what these objectives are in this chapter before introducing our side-scrolling shooter project, which will cover the majority of the objectives. We will also cover specialized subjects outside of the project, such as networking, VR, and more, in the *Appendix* section of this book.

Throughout the following chapters, we will refresh ourselves with the general practices of coding—a bit like the dos and don'ts when coding a project. Then, we will get to grips with the genre of the game and, hopefully, get you thinking about how to set up a game framework. Finally, we will download and set up our empty project in Unity and learn about Unity services.

In this chapter, we will cover the following topics:

- The six core objectives
- Overview of design patterns
- The SOLID principles
- Designing the Killer Wave game
- The Killer Wave game framework

- Setting up Unity 2017.3
- Collaborate

We won't be doing any coding in this chapter as our focus is on what Unity wants from you in the exam. We will discuss an overview of the methodology and structuring code with design patterns. You may feel tempted to skip some parts because you simply aren't interested, but remember the only reason I am mentioning the majority of this stuff is that it's highly likely it will come up in the exam. So, please don't feel like I'm punishing you on purpose!

The next section will detail the core objectives covered in this chapter.

The core exam skills covered in this chapter

Working in professional software development teams:

- Recognize concepts associated with the uses and impacts of version control using technology such as Unity Collaborate.
- Recognize techniques for structuring scripts for modularity, readability, and reusability.

Technical requirements

Check out the following video to see the Code in Action: `https://bit.ly/2VjmVtL`.

The six core objectives

The exam will mainly focus on scripting and the use of Unity's **Application Programming Interface (API)**, Animation Controller, particles, rendering, and more. The whole idea is to get you familiar with what Unity has to offer you as a programmer. Unity has categorized their exam into core sections, which is a nice way of separating the workload up for the exam.

Developing application systems

I wouldn't say that this is a core objective as such; it's more of a cluster of things Unity have tied into one bundle and labeled it "core." So, let's break this down and work out what they want from us. Developing application systems is focused on how Unity communicates with the user and stores their information. This is where a **User Interface** (**UI**) needs to contain the right guidance and information; but also, from a technical point of view, it needs to be positioned correctly no matter what ratio the screen size is. UI can also be used in-game in the form of a minimap guiding the player through a maze, showing them where enemies are. UI can also be used for advertising and displaying information from a different computer server online. When information is taken from the player, how sensitive is this information? Should it be stored locally with low security? Do we need encryption? Should it be stored in a different file format online? Finally, Unity is currently getting rid of their multiplayer network system, called UNet, and replacing it with something brand-spanking new. This means we only need to be aware of Unity's network and prepare for a few general networking exam questions.

To pass the exam, you need to know how to do the following:

- Interpret scripts for application interface flow such as menu systems, UI navigation, and application settings
- Interpret scripts for user-controlled customization, such as character creators, inventories, storefronts, and in-app purchases
- Analyze scripts for user progression features, such as scoring, leveling, and in-game economies, by utilizing technologies such as Unity Analytics and PlayerPrefs
- Analyze scripts for two-dimensional overlays, such as **Heads-Up Displays** (**HUDs**), minimaps, and advertisements
- Identify scripts for saving and retrieving application and user data
- Recognize and evaluate the impact of networking and multiplayer functionality

Let's move on to the fourth Unity exam core objective, where we'll focus again on game objects.

Programming for the scene and environment design

This core exam objective sounds similar to the first core objective, where we introduced the game object; however, this time we are concentrating more on the management of the object. When is a game object made? How is it made? How do we get rid of it when we don't need it anymore? Should we destroy it? Or, do we label it as destroyed but store it elsewhere in the scene to save memory? We can also look at less common components, such as artificial intelligence, and understand what a game object would do if, for example, it's a character that knows when to patrol, chase an enemy, or hide. We will also need to know about the audio component and mixer, how we can manipulate them, and how to create echo effects. Yet again, we have a situation as with the animation and art—we don't need to be amazing at these skills, we just need to know that they exist.

To pass the exam, you need to know how to do the following:

- Determine scripts for implementing audio assets
- Identify methods for implementing game object instantiation, destruction, and management
- Determine scripts for pathfinding with the Unity navigation system

Let's move on to the fifth Unity exam core objective, which is about knowing what to do when you've broken something and how to check performance issues.

Optimizing performance and platforms

Any programmer will encounter problems, and it's sometimes helpful to know about the problem before you have to solve it. This Unity exam core objective is about tracking and fixing your own issues. Sometimes, you will need to step through your code to find a game-breaking bug, or you might want to know why a game is stuttering at a certain point when it is played. This is where you would use one of Unity's handy tools, such as the profiler, to monitor performance. You will be able to strip back the components to see whether you're dealing with a physics issue or whether your second scene is taking a long time to load, for example. Being able to solve your own problems with Unity's tools is the key point of this core objective. Other examples of issues that Unity wants you to think about is, for example, if you are going to build a virtual reality app, where would the UI be placed, if at all? Do you need to be more aware of your frames per second? These are the types of questions we will cover in the book.

To pass the exam, you need to know how to do the following:

- Evaluate errors and performance issues using tools such as the Unity profiler.
- Identify optimizations to address requirements for specific build platforms and/or hardware configurations.
- Determine common UI affordances and optimizations for XR platforms.

Let's now move onto your sixth and final Unity exam core objective, working with people.

Working in professional software development teams

Working with others in a professional environment and sharing and working with each others' code can be tricky if a decent structure isn't in place. Things such as version control can help, where each member can book their work in and book it out. Some users might work remotely, or you could all work remotely. There are different types of version control; the most typical one used is called git. Unity also has its own version that they would really like you to use. We will be covering Unity Collaborate in this chapter, which is a program that lets you book your work in, book it out, alter it, make some mistakes, and fix it all in the end.

To pass the exam, you need to know how to do the following:

- Recognize concepts associated with the uses and impacts of version control using technology such as Unity Collaborate
- Demonstrate knowledge of developer testing and its impact on the software development process, including the Unity profiler and traditional debugging and testing techniques
- Recognize techniques for structuring scripts for modularity, readability, and reusability

That's it! If you know the content of these six objective cores, you will pass. This book will cover all of these problems and issues within the project that we will be talking about later on in this chapter. How will you know whether you've successfully met your objectives? I will be throwing questions at you every few chapters to see how you are getting on. If you fail or don't do too well, then I see that as a good thing because you'll know exactly what you need to focus on and revisit before taking the exam.

Anyway, this is all to come. Next, I want to talk about design patterns. Given that we are coding, it's a good idea to talk about structuring code, following decent methods, and not creating code that can get tangled into a mess if there isn't enough planning in place.

Overview of design patterns

At the beginning of this book, I mentioned that I will cover as much of Unity as possible, even though it is expected that you have been using Unity for at least 2 years before taking the exam. With regard to the fundamentals of programming, we will obviously be applying C# code. So, I expect that you are familiar with things such as functions, methods, `if` statements, classes, inheritance, polymorphism, and so on. I will explain what I'm doing and what you should be doing for each bit of code I present, but I won't be going through the basics of each segment of code.

Design patterns are typical solutions to problems you are likely going to come across, and if you have a pattern that can solve, then you should use it. Creating applications yourself with your own workflow is great, but if you can explain an issue to another programmer using design pattern terms, it shows that you know what you are talking about and if they are a good programmer, they'll likely know what you are talking about as well. The more patterns you know, the more flexible and standardized your code will be, and you are likely going to need more than one pattern. Otherwise, you'll be forcing your code down a structure that might not suit it and this will just cause problems.

The batch of 23 design patterns that are considered to be the foundation of all patterns was created by **the gang of four.** If you want to check out who the gang are and all of their 23 patterns, then go to `https://www.packtpub.com/gb/application-development/hands-design-patterns-c-and-net-core`. All of these patterns are divided into three categories—creational, structural, and behavioral:

- **Creational**: These patterns are designed to deal with the creation of objects—how and where an object is made.
- **Structural**: These patterns are built to show the relationships between entities.
- **Behavioral**: These patterns are designed to deal with how objects communicate with each other.

- `EnemySpawner` is similar to `PlayerSpawner` but it can manage all different types of enemies.
- `Enemy` refers to multiple enemy classes—for example, if an enemy that shoots is made, it will go in this location of the framework. If an enemy moves or acts differently, it will also be put into the same allocation.
- `EnemyBullet` travels at a set rate and removes the player after a set time or if it makes contact with the scenery.
- `PlayerSpawner` launches the player in a certain location of the screen and keeps its hierarchy in order.
- `Player` fires bullets, receives input controls from the user, and is removed if contact is made with the scenery, enemy, or enemies' bullets.
- `PlayerBullet` travels at a set rate, removes and damages the enemy, and removes itself after a set time or if it makes contact with the scenery.
- `ShopPiece` handles the content of the player's ship upgrade selections.
- `SOShopSelection` holds the data types that are used in each grid selection in the shop menu.
- `SOActorModel` holds the common variables for each class it is connected to. As an example, all moving objects have a speed setting; this includes player bullets, enemy bullets, enemy ships, and so on.
- `IActorTemplate` isn't a class but an interface. An interface works a bit like a contract to whatever it is connected to. For example, this interface wants the class connected to it to have functions titled `Attack()`, `Die()`, and so on. The class must include these functions, even if they are empty. You should, hopefully, already know what an interface is; we will be using them frequently in this book. For more information about interfaces, check out https://learn.unity.com/tutorial/interfaces.
- **Additional enemy/player behavior**: It is possible to have an enemy that might require more functionality than it has already been given. The same applies to the player. As a precaution, I have sketched in additional classes that are responsible for the extra rotation of the ship, extra particle effects, extra guns, and more.

The following diagram shows the visual relationship between each class that we have just listed. These diagrams are typically called **Unified Model Language** (UML) (https://subscription.packtpub.com/book/application_development/9781789809770/1/ch01lvl1sec12/understanding-behavioral-uml-diagrams). We could have used a more detailed diagram than the following one, but for the purpose of keeping things as simple as possible, we will just refer to the classes with boxes and names.

Some of you may find this shell-looking framework complex, but both sides mirror each other and control the responsibilities of either game object separately. Let's have a look at this in more detail:

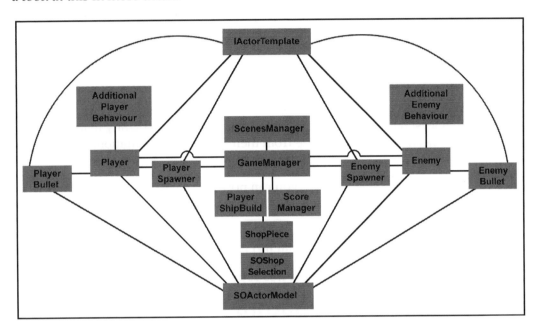

Each gray box represents a class that is mentioned in the preceding list; the lines between each box indicate the inheritance of that class. The PlayerSpawner class, for example, will need to be coupled with the GameManager class to notify it of what is happening to the Player class; the Player class will need to send and receive information such as lives, enemy kill count, and other stats to the GameManager class directly. If we want to move our score over to be stored on the device, then we can link this to our ScoreManager class. The main takeaway from this diagram is that if a line is connected to either box, there will be communication between the classes.

UMLs are not a prime focus for the exam, but they should be mentioned at this stage given that we are creating a plan for the game. I personally like creating UMLs, in a way; as long as the flow of the game is understood, we shouldn't worry about finalizing every detail.

So, now we have an idea of how the game works, how we are going to break it up into segments, and how segments are related to each other. The next step is to prepare our version of Unity and start planning how to bring the game over to this piece of software.

Load up Unity Hub and let's sign in, if you haven't already:

1. The following screenshot shows you where to sign-in on Unity Hub:

2. Once signed in, go to the **Projects** tab (denoted with **1** in the following screenshot) at the top-left of Unity Hub and select the down arrow next to **New** (denoted with **2**) to pick the version of Unity to run this project, as shown:

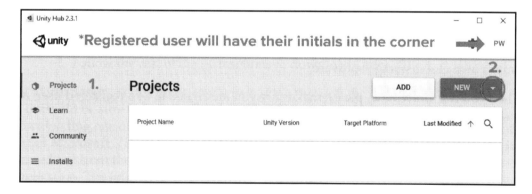

3. From the dropdown, you should see a copy of **Unity 2017.3**, which we installed from the archive link in the previous section. Select **Unity 2017.3**.

The last screen before the Unity Editor is launched is a selection between two templates:

- **3D**: The Unity editor starts in a three-dimensional view.
- **2D**: The Unity editor starts in a two-dimensional view.

Let's create our Unity project:

1. Select **3D**.
2. Give your project a name. I'm calling mine `KillerWave`.
3. Add a location where you want the Unity project to be stored.
4. Click **Create**:

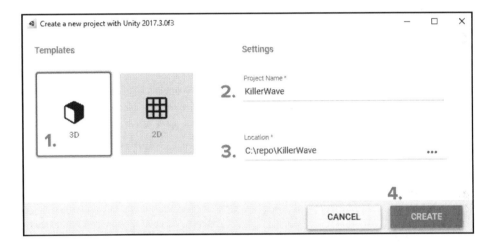

It doesn't really matter which of the templates you pick, as once the Unity editor loads, all that we need to do to change between **2D** and **3D** is press 2 on our keyboard, or press the **2D** button at the top of the **Scene** window, as in the following screenshot:

After pressing **Create**, you are presented with the Unity editor.

Next, we will talk about version control and introduce Unity's Collaborate system. Please go through this section, as it's highly likely it will be in your exam.

Collaborate

Collaborate is a form of version control, which means multiple people can work on the same project at the same time. It's similar to Git, Perforce, and Mercurial. All project files are stored locally but can then be pushed to an online server (the cloud) where all members of the project can pull your changes to their local machine and vice versa.

Similar to other types of version control, Collaborate has the following features:

- **Add**: Include your local files to the project to be pushed onto the cloud.
- **Conflict Resolution**: Change or update yours or someone else's scene file or code when work is merged together.
- **History**: Go back to a previous push to amend an issue.
- **Publish**: Push your work onto the cloud for everyone in the project to share.
- **Pull**: Pull work from the cloud to your local machine.

Collaborate also has a **repository**, which is where your project is stored.

Let's move on and set up a Collaborate project in Unity.

Setting up Collaborate

To set up Collaborate for our project, follow these steps:

1. Make sure you have signed in to your Unity account, as mentioned previously.
2. Open the **Services** tab. You can do this by clicking on **Windows** and then **Services**, or you can click on the cloud in the top-right corner of the editor:

3. Click on the **Create** button.
4. With the **Services** tab open, change the **Collaborate** option to **ON**:

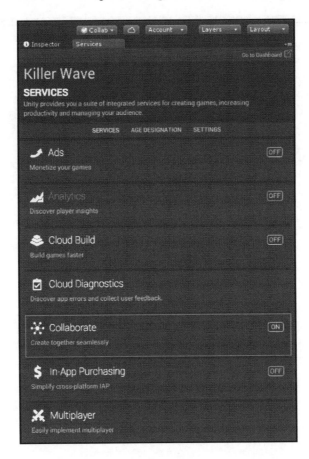

5. Notice how at the top of the Unity editor, the **Collab** tab has a green circle with a white tick:

6. Click on it and it will let you know whether you are up to date and whether there are any files that need publishing. It also tells you whether anyone on your project has published anything.
7. Next, save your scene. Name it testLevel.

8. Notice how your saved scene has a blue square with a plus sign. This indicates that you have a file that you can publish to the cloud:

9. The **Collab** tab at the top has also changed from a green circle with a white tick to a blue square with a white arrow pointing upward. This means you have a new file that can be pushed to the cloud. As with any version control software, multiple files can be published in one go; you don't need to push each file individually.

10. Click on the **Collab** tab.

11. Click in the **Describe your changes** box here and as it prompts, provide a description. Then, click **Publish now!**, as in the following screenshot:

12. The file will push to the cloud and your **Collab** tab will go back to the green circle with a white tick.

Congratulations, you have created and pushed your first change to Collaborate. This is the most common use of making a change—giving it a name and clicking **Publish Now!** to save your changes. Let's continue with the other features of Collaborate. Next, we will look at files that aren't of concern to us and can be left out of the project.

Ignoring files and folders

Collaborate creates a file that contains a list of file types and folders that you are likely not going to want to push to the cloud. For example, an `Editor` folder containing files specifically for your editor might not need to be shared with other members of the project:

1. The ignore file is located outside of the `Assets` folder. It's default name will be `.collabignore`.
2. Locate it and open it in a text editor to view the files and folders it's currently ignoring.
3. If you wish to add more file types to ignore, you can, but I wouldn't recommend doing so unless you are sure you don't want to update specific file types.
4. Close the text editor.

Let's keep going and look at what to do when we make a mistake and we need to revert the changes. We all do this!

Reverting changes

Imagine if we made a mistake in a project—for example, we deleted the `testLevel.unity` file and pushed it on to the cloud. This can be amended by doing the following:

1. Go to the **Services** tab (the cloud button in the top-right corner of the editor).
2. Select **Collaborate**.

3. Under **Collab History**, click on **Open the history panel**.

4. You will be presented with your pushes with the description you named when it was done and how many files were pushed. Also, a drop-down symbol will show the filenames that were pushed:

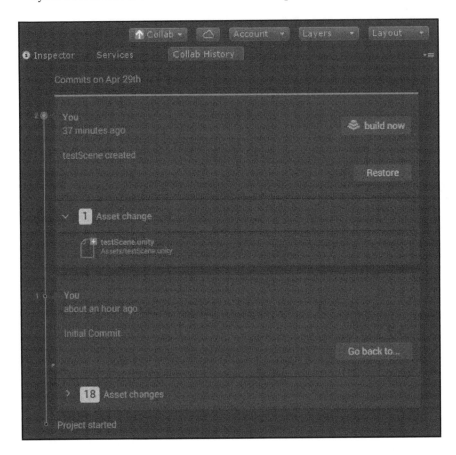

5. Click the **Restore** button to bring back `testLevel.unity`. Any changes that haven't been published will be removed.

Now that you know how to revert your mistakes, let's now go in a little deeper and check our account to find out further information about our project with the Unity dashboard.

The dashboard

With your Unity account, you have access to more information about your Collaborate account and other services, such as **Cloud Build**. In a potential exam question, you may be asked what and where the dashboard is and where you would find details about your Collaborate projects. Here is how you access the dashboard:

1. Click on the **Go to Dashboard** link in the top-right corner of the **Services** window:

2. Within the **Unity Dashboard** browser, you will be presented with a series of options and details specifically to do with Collaborate, Analytics, remote settings (in `Chapter 11`, *Storing Data and Audio Mixer*, we discuss storing/manipulating online data), cloud building (briefly mentioned in the following information box), and more:

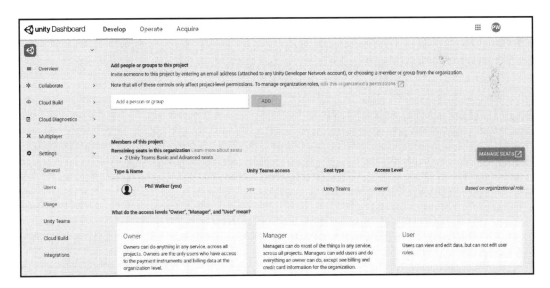

The preceding screenshot shows the **Settings** tab is open and **Users** (on the left-hand side of the screen) is where team members can be added/removed and given certain levels of access relating to the project. We don't need to go into any further detail about this, but you just need to be aware of where these extra editions are based.

Cloud Build:

Build your pushed projects online for multiple platforms (for example, Android, iOS, PC, and so on). This saves you and others in your team the hassle of switching platforms, building on a local machine, and waiting until you can start using your Unity project again. If developers in the same team are all building slightly different versions of the same build, this can be inefficient and cause issues. With **Cloud Build**, you are given a build number, which helps you keep tabs on the current version build.

Wow, we have covered a lot and it's only chapter 1! You have covered some of the most important stuff that isn't common knowledge when it comes to being a Unity developer. When I started as a developer, I thought it was just about getting cubes moving and jumping and firing other cubes then prettying them up. In some ways, it is, but we need to make sure we avoid a lack of structure in Unity projects as things can fall apart quickly without it, especially when it comes to expanding a project. We will dig deeper into all of the things we have mentioned in this chapter, but for now, let's just recap what we have covered.

Summary

In this chapter, you were introduced to the six core objectives of the exam. You may have skipped on to the final mock exam and scored well, and you may want to increase your score and carry on with the project that we are gearing ourselves up for. With regards to the project, we have an idea of a few design patterns that we can implement as the project goes on (such as **Singleton** for manager scripts) and these patterns will be built within the game framework. We know what the SOLID principles are and we mustn't forget them as our project expands. We also know how to use Unity's own version control platform, Collaborate, and we know that we can build our projects in the cloud, which is ideal for team projects and multi-platform projects.

In the next chapter, we are going to start setting up our camera and light in the testLevel scene. We'll also bring in our player ship and hook it up with some controls so that we can move and shoot bullets. The first enemy will be imported with its own wave attack pattern. We will also be looking into what scriptable objects are and how they can benefit programmers and designers.

2
Adding and Manipulating Objects

In the previous chapter, we discussed the importance of the Official Unity Programmer exam and what benefits it can produce for any developer who is looking to reassure either themselves or others in understanding programming in Unity. We also discussed the building blocks of being a programmer in general and our game's design brief.

As we are programmers working on a game engine, it is likely you will be working for a range of industries. In many of these industries, you will be issued with a technical brief/documentation (well, you should be!) for building the application. With this project, we are making a game and the game design brief is effectively the blueprint for making this game. In this chapter, we will be applying the majority of our code, game objects, prefabs, and more, based on the guidance of the brief and the game framework. We will be reminding ourselves of the brief and game framework during this chapter and will transfer specific information across into our code.

With regard to our code, we will be covering the importance of interfaces and scriptable objects to help structure and uniform our code to help it from bloating unnecessarily, which we covered in Chapter 1, *Setting Up and Structuring Our Project* with SOLID principles. We will also be getting used to the Unity editor and becoming familiar with game objects, prefabs, and importing three-dimensional models to animate.

In this chapter, we'll be covering the following topics:

- Setting up our Unity project
- Introducing our interface (`IActorTemplate`)
- Introducing our `ScriptableObject` (`SOActorModel`)
- Setting up our `Player`, `PlayerSpawner`, and `PlayerBullet` scripts

- Planning and creating our enemy
- Setting up our `EnemySpawner` and enemy script

The next section will outline the exam objectives covered in this chapter.

Core exam skills covered in this chapter

Programming core interactions

- *Implement and configure game object behavior and physics.*
- *Implement and configure inputs and controls.*
- *Implement and configure camera views and movement.*

Working in the art pipeline

- *Understand lighting, and write scripts that interact with Unity's lighting API.*
- *Understand two- and three-dimensional animation, and write scripts that interact with Unity's animation API.*

Programming for scene and environment design

- *Identify methods for implementing game object instantiation, destruction, and management.*

Working in professional software development teams

- *Recognize concepts associated with the uses and impact of version control, using technologies such as Unity Collaborate.*
- *Demonstrate knowledge of developer testing and its impact on the software development process, including Unity Profiler and traditional debugging and testing techniques.*
- *Recognize techniques for structuring scripts for modularity, readability, and re-usability.*

Technical requirements

The project content for this chapter can be found at `https://github.com/PacktPublishing/Unity-Certified-Programmer-Exam-Guide/tree/master/Chapter02`.

You can download the entire chapter project files at `https://github.com/PacktPublishing/Unity-Certified-Programmer-Exam-Guide/archive/master.zip`.

All content for this chapter is held in the relevant `unitypackage` file, including a `Complete` folder that contains all of the work we'll carry out in the chapter, so if at any point you need some reference material or extra guidance, be sure to check it out.

Check out the following video to see the Code in Action: `https://bit.ly/3i2OnW6`.

Setting up our Unity project

Things can get messy quickly in a project if we don't manage our files correctly by placing them into the allocated folders. If you want to structure your folders your own way, or during the book you decide to stray away from how I'm doing it, that's also fine. Just try and be conscious of your future self or other people working on this project when it comes to finding and organizing files.

Open the project up if you haven't already and create the following folders:

1. `Model` contains 3D models (player ship, enemies, bullets, and so on).
2. `Prefab` holds instances of game objects (these are created within Unity).
3. `Scene` stores our first-level scene as well as other levels.
4. `Script` contains all of our code.
5. `Material` stores our game object materials.

 You should know what a prefab is, as it's one of the main parts of what makes Unity so quick and easy to use. However, if you don't: it's typically your game object with its settings and components stored in an instance. You can store your game objects in your **Project** window as prefabs by dragging the game object from the **Hierarchy** window. A blue box icon will be generated following the game object's name, and if you select the prefab in the **Project** window, its **Inspector** window details will show all its stored values. If you would like to know more about prefabs, you can check out the documentation at `https://docs.unity3d.com/Manual/Prefabs.html`.

The following screenshot shows you how to create these folders:

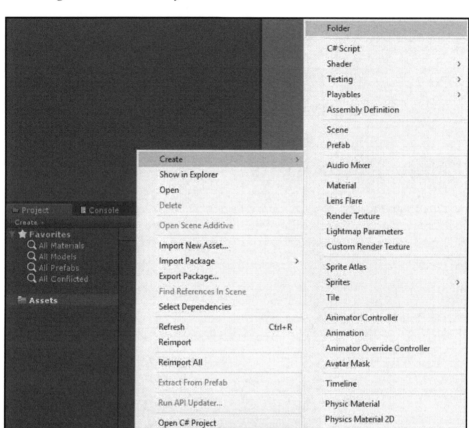

Follow the steps given below:

1. Within our `Prefab` folder, create another two folders, `Enemies` and `Player`.
2. Inside the `Script` folder, create a folder called `ScriptableObject`.
3. Create a folder in the `Assets` folder called `Resources`, and move our `Model`, `Prefab`, `Script`, and `Material` folders into it. The following screenshot shows what our folder structure should look like now:

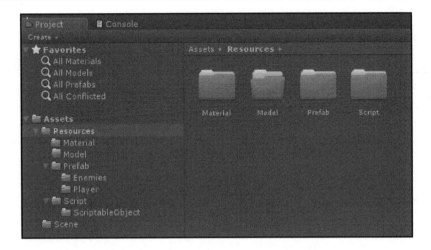

`Resources` is a special folder that Unity recognizes. It will allow us to load assets while the game is running. For more information about the `Resources` folder, check the documentation at `https://docs.unity3d.com/Manual/BestPracticeUnderstandingPerformanceInUnity6.html`.

Provided in the *Technical requirements* section is the download link for the GitHub repository of this chapter. Once downloaded, double-click the `Chapter2.unitypackage` file and we will be given a list of assets to import into our Unity project:

- `Player_ship.fbx`
- `enemy_wave.fbx`

The following screenshot shows the import window of the assets we are about to bring into our project:

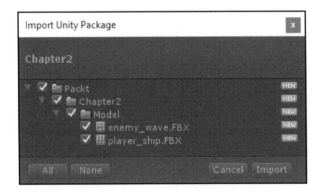

Make sure all assets are ticked and click the **Import** button in the bottom-right corner of the window. We can now move on to organizing our files and folders in the **Project** window in the next section.

Creating prefabs

In this section, we going to create three prefabs: the player, the player's bullet, and the enemy. These prefabs will hold components, settings, and other property values for our game that we can instantiate throughout our game.

Let's start with making our `player_ship.fbx` file into a prefab instance by doing the following.

Sometimes, when importing any three-dimensional file, each file may contain extra data that we might not need. For example, our `player_ship` model comes with its own material and animation properties. We don't require any of these, so let's remove these properties before continuing to import our models fully into our Unity project.

To remove the **Animation** and **Material** properties from our `player_ship` model, we need to do the following:

1. In the **Project** window, navigate to `Assets/Resources/Model` and select the `player_ship` file.
2. In the **Inspector** window, select the **Materials** button.
3. Untick the **Import Materials** box, then click the **Apply** button.
4. Now click the **Animation** button next to the **Materials** button.
5. Untick the **Import Animation** checkbox, followed by clicking the **Apply** button.
6. Select the **Rig** button next to the **Animation** button.
7. Select the current value in the **Animation Type** drop-down menu and select **None**, followed by the **Apply** button.
8. That's all of our **Material** and **Animation** information removed from our `player_ship` model.

 Throughout the book whenever we select a three-dimensional model, make sure to run through the same process, as we will not require imported extras such as the ones we just removed. This means I would like you now to repeat the process we have just gone through with the `enemy_wave.fbx` model.

Let's continue preparing our `player_ship` model for our game:

1. Click and drag the `player_ship` from `Assets/Resources/Model` into the **Hierarchy** window.
2. Select the `player_ship` in the **Hierarchy** window and set its name and **Transform** properties to the following values:

   - **Game Object name**: `player_ship`.
   - **Tag**: **Player** (easier to detect when colliding with enemies or other collisions).
   - **Transform**: All values set to zero apart from the **Scale** that is set to 1 on all axes.

   The following screenshot shows the `player_ship` values in the **Inspector** window:

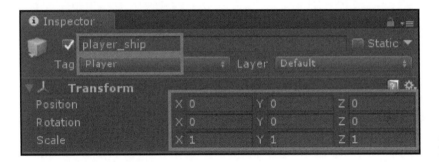

3. Click and drag the `player_ship` from the **Hierarchy** window into the `Assets/Resources/Prefab/Player` folder.

   Notice the `player_ship` in the **Hierarchy** window has turned blue, which means it has become a prefab.

4. Delete the `player_ship` from the **Hierarchy** window.

We are going to use a similar process to create our `enemy_wave` prefab, but we will also need to create its own name tag because there isn't an **Enemy** tag... yet.

Enemy prefab and custom tags

In this section, we are going to create an `enemy_wave` prefab along with a custom tag. The tag will be used to identify and categorize all related enemies under one tag.

To create an enemy_wave prefab and custom name tag, follow these instructions:

1. In the **Project** window, drag the enemy_wave.fbx file from Assets/Resources/Model into the **Hierarchy** window.
2. With the enemy_wave file selected in the **Hierarchy** window, update the following values in the **Inspector** window:

   - **Game Object name**: enemy_wave.
   - **Transform**: All values set to zero apart from the **Scale**, which is set to 1 on all axes:

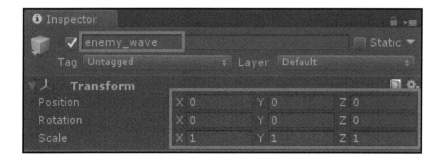

Now let's create a new tag for the enemy_wave game object by doing the following:

1. Choose the **Untagged** parameter in the **Inspector** window.
2. From the **Tag** drop-down menu, select **Add Tag....**
3. The **Inspector** window will now show the **Tags & Layers** window.
4. Click the **+** to add a new tag, as circled in the following screenshot.
5. Enter Enemy in the pop-up window, as shown in the following screenshot, then click the **Save** button:

6. Back in the **Hierarchy** window, select the enemy_wave game object to bring back our **Inspector** window details.
7. Click the **Untagged** parameter again.
8. We can now see **Enemy** in our drop-down list, so select it.
9. Drag the enemy_wave game object from the **Hierarchy** window into Assets/Resources/Prefab/Enemies.

We now move on to our third prefab creation – the player's bullet. But this time, we won't import a three-dimensional model – we are going to create one in the Unity editor, then create a prefab from it in the next section.

Creating the player's bullet prefab

Next, we are going to create the visuals for the player's bullet in the Unity editor. We will make a blue sphere and give it a surrounding light source. Let's start by creating a three-dimensional sphere game object.

In the **Hierarchy** window, right-click and from the drop-down list select **3D Object | Sphere**.

With the newly created Sphere in the **Hierarchy** window still selected, make the following changes to the **Inspector** window:

- Change the game object name from Sphere to player_bullet.
- Change **Tag** from **Untagged** to **Player**. The tag name makes it easier to identify later on in the chapter.
- The **Transform** parameters are all set to zero, apart from the **Scale** of the bullets, which should be slightly larger, with a **Scale** of 2 on all axes.

The following screenshot shows all three changes:

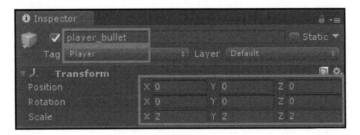

Next, we will give the player_bullet game object a new blue material.

Creating and applying a material to the player's bullet

In this section, we will be creating a simple unlit material that will not take up much of the device's performance thanks to the simplicity of the material. To create a basic material and apply it to the `player_bullet` object, do the following:

1. In the **Project** window, navigate to the `Assets/Resources/Material` folder.
2. Inside the `Material` folder, make a new folder (the same way we did in the *Setting up our Unity project* section) and name the folder `Player`. That way, any material related to the player can be stored inside.
3. Double click the newly created `Player` folder and right-click in the **Project** window (in the open space in the right section of the window) again and, from the drop-down list, select **Create | Material**.

   A new material file will be made. Rename it to `player_bullet`.

4. Select the `player_bullet` material and, in the **Inspector** window, change the material from a **Standard** shader to **Unlit | Color** by following the three steps in the following screenshot:

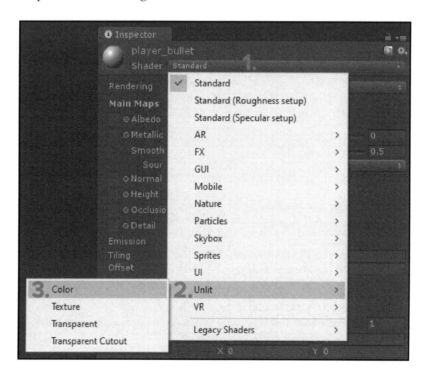

The **Inspector** window will remove the majority of the properties and strip the material back to something simpler and easier to perform on any device.

5. Still, in the **Inspector** window, click the **Main Color** swatch parameter and change it to a cyan color with the following values: **R**: 0, **G**: 190, **B**: 255, and **A**: 255.

We have created and calibrated our player's bullet, so now, we can apply the material to the `player_bullet` prefab by doing the following:

1. Select the `player_bullet` prefab in the following location of the **Project** window: `Assets/Resources/Prefab/Player`.
2. In the **Inspector** window, under the **Mesh Renderer** component, click the small round radio button to the right of the **Element 0** parameter and type `player_bullet` in the drop-down list until you see the material, then select it.

The following screenshot shows the `player_bullet` prefab's **Mesh Renderer** component updated to our new unlit material:

In `Chapter 4`, *Applying Art, Animation, and Particles*, we will return to materials and art in general, which will be of note if you found this interesting. We will also play around with particle systems to create a fleet of stars rushing past the player's ship.

The last component we will add to our player's bullet is a surrounding light to give our bullet an energy glow.

Adding a light to the player's bullet

In this section, we will be adding a light component to the player's bullet to hide the impression that all that we are doing is firing spheres. It will also introduce us to Unity's point light, which acts as a glowing ball.

To add and customize a ball of light to the player's bullet, we need to do the following:

1. In the **Project** window, navigate to the `Assets/Resources/Prefab/Player` folder and select the `player_bullet` prefab.

2. In the **Inspector** at the bottom of the components listed, click the **Add Component** button and type `Light` from the drop-down list.

   The `player_bullet` prefab will now have a **Light** component attached to it. We just need to change three property values to make the light suit the game object more.

3. Change the following property values in the `player_bullet` file's **Light** component:

   - **Range**: 50
   - **Color**: **R**: 0, **G**: 190, **B**: 255, **A**: 255
   - **Intensity**: 20

   The following screenshot shows the **Light** component after the values have been updated:

   Before moving onto the next section, because we have taken an existing prefab and added a material and a light component, we need to click the **Apply** button to confirm the new changes.

4. The following screenshot shows the **Apply** button in the top-right corner of the **Inspector** window for our `player_bullet` prefab:

5. Finally, delete the `player_bullet` from the **Hierarchy**.

In the next section, we will continue to update our three prefabs by applying Unity's own physics system, the **Rigidbody** component, to help detect collisions.

Adding Rigidbody components and fixing game objects

Because this game involves collisions with game objects, we need to apply collision detection to the player, the player's bullets, and the enemy. Unity offers a range of different shapes to wrap around a game object that functions as an invisible shield; we can set our code to react to contact being made with the shield.

Before we add colliders to the player and enemy game objects (the **Sphere** game object automatically comes with a collider), we need to add a Unity component called a **Rigidbody**. If a game object is going to collide with another at least one other game object, it requires a **Rigidbody** component; **Rigidbody** components can affect a game object's mass, gravity, drag, constraints, and more. If you would like to know more about **Rigidbody** components, check out the documentation at `https://docs.unity3d.com/Manual/class-Rigidbody.html`.

Unity has other physics types apart from the collider. **Joints** also require the **Rigidbody** system, and **Joints** come in different forms, such as **Hinge**, **Spring**, and others.

These **Joints** will simulate at a fixed point; for example, the **Hinge Joint** would be good at making a door swing back and forth around a door hinge's pivot point.

If you would like to know more about joints, check the documentation at `https://docs.unity3d.com/Manual/Joints.html`.

Let's add the **RigidBody** component to the `player_ship` and `player_bullet` prefabs:

1. In the **Project** window, navigate to the **Resources | Prefab | Player**.
2. Hold *Ctrl* (*command* on Mac) and click on the `player_ship` and `player_bullet` files.
3. In the **Inspector** window, click the **Add Component** button.
4. From the drop-down menu, type `Rigidbody`.
5. Select **Rigidbody** (not **Rigidbody 2D**).
6. The **Rigidbody** component has now been assigned to our two game objects.
7. With the two game objects still selected in the **Inspector** window, under **Rigidbody**, make sure the **Gravity** checkbox isn't ticked. If it were, our game objects would begin to sink into the scene while the game is being played.

Now we can add colliders to our `player_ship` and `enemy_wave` game objects (our `player_bullet` already has a **SphereCollider**). We will be adding a **SphereCollider** to our game objects because it's the cheapest collider to use relative to performance costs:

1. Click and drag the `player_ship` prefab from the **Project** window location of `Assets/Resources/Prefab/Player` into the **Hierarchy** window.
2. With the `player_ship` still selected in the **Hierarchy** window, click the **Add Component** button in the **Inspector** window and type `Sphere Collider` into the drop-down menu.
3. As soon as you see **SphereCollider** in the list, click it to add it to the `player_ship` game object.

   You will notice a green wireframe around the `player_ship` in the **Scene** window (with the `player_ship` still selected in the **Hierarchy** window, hover your mouse in the **Scene** window and press *F* on the keyboard to zoom in on the ship if you can't see it). This is the `player_ship` collider that will be used to detect hits. It may be too big for the purpose of a hitbox, so let's reduce its size.

4. With the `player_ship` prefab still selected in the **Hierarchy** window, alter the **Radius** of the **SphereCollider** component to `0.3` in the **Inspector** window, as shown in the following screenshot:

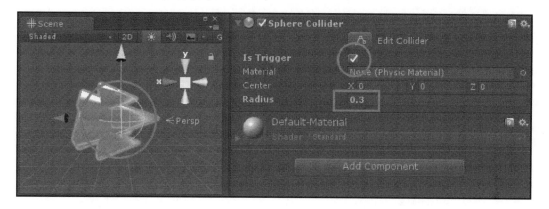

5. Also, while we still have the `player_ship` prefab selected, check the **Is Trigger** box as shown in the previous screenshot. This will make it so the `player_ship` prefab looks for another collider without causing any form of potential physics collision.

6. Click **Apply** in the top-right corner of the **Inspector** window to update the modifications we've made to our prefab with its **Rigidbody** and **SphereCollider** component.

7. We can now select the `player_ship` prefab in the **Hierarchy** window and press *Delete* on our keyboard as we no longer need it in our **Scene**.

We now need to apply the same methodology to our `player_bullet` **SphereCollider** component:

1. In the **Project** window, click and drag the `player_bullet` prefab from `Assets/Prefab/Player` into the **Hierarchy** window.

2. Check the **Is Trigger** box and adjust the **Radius** in the **SphereCollider** component in the **Inspector** window.

3. Click **Apply** in the top-right corner of the **Inspector** window to confirm the `player_bullet` changes and delete the `player_bullet` prefab from the **Hierarchy** window.

The last game object we need to update is the `enemy_wave` prefab. We have already covered the steps with the `player_ship` and `player_bullet` prefabs so it's not ideal to repeat the instructions in full; however, we need to do the following:

1. As a short brief, I want you to drag and drop the `enemy_wave` prefab from its location at `Assets/Resources/Prefab/Enemies` in the **Project** window.
2. Add a **SphereCollider** component to the `enemy_wave` prefab in the **Inspector** window.
3. Adjust the **SphereCollider** component so **Is Trigger** is checked and the **Radius** fits around the `enemy_wave` prefab with correct proportions, as we did with `player_ship`.
4. The `enemy_wave` prefab doesn't require a **Rigidbody** component, as it will be colliding with relevant game objects that hold one themselves.
5. Finally, **Apply** the prefab changes and remove the `enemy_wave` prefab from the **Hierarchy** window.

Use the following screenshot as a reference for the preceding mini brief and if you get stuck, use the previous steps that we discussed in this section:

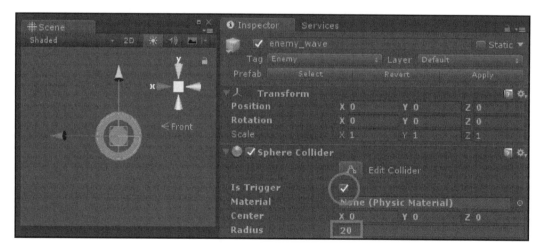

Hopefully, that went well for you. If you get stuck at any point, refer to the `Packt/Chapter2/Complete` folder containing all the completed files to check them out and compare.

Before moving on, note that if a game object is pink, like our `enemy_wave` object in the previous screenshot, it simply means that it doesn't have a material attached. In other cases, it can also mean there is something wrong with the shader attached to the material.

We can fix this pink issue by doing the following:

1. In the **Project** window, navigate to `Assets/Resources/Prefab/Enemies/enemy_wave`.

2. Expand the `enemy_wave` game object to show the two game objects attached.

3. Select the first game object titled `enemy_wave_core`.

4. In the **Inspector** window, select the small **remote** circle next to the **Element 0** parameter in the **Mesh Renderer** component (denoted by **1** in the following screenshot), then select **Default-Material** (denoted by **2**) from the drop-down list, as shown in the following screenshot:

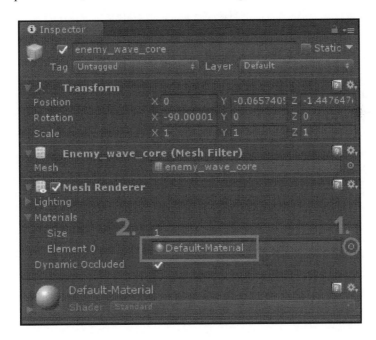

5. Follow the same steps for its sibling game object, `enemy_wave_ring`.

The `enemy_wave` object will now have a default material applied.

> If a game object requires a component such as `Rigidbody`, we can place, above the class name, what is effectively a reminder to the script that the game object needs:
>
> `[RequireComponent(typeof(Rigidbody))]`
>
> If the game object doesn't have the component, the script will create one, and if we try to remove the `Rigidbody` component, we will receive a message in the Unity editor that it is a required component.
>
> If you would like to know more about the `RequireComponent` attribute, check the documentation at `https://docs.unity3d.com/ScriptReference/RequireComponent.html`.

So, now we have our colliders and **Rigidbody** components applied to our game objects. This gives us the ability to create a reaction when colliders come into contact with each other.

Because we are starting to build up our project, let's quickly discuss saving our scenes, projects, and more.

Saving and publishing our work

It's easy to get stuck into our project, but as a brief reminder, save and publish your work with Unity Collaborate as often as possible. That way, if anything bad happens, you can always revert back.

Because we have created and saved our `testLevel` scene from the previous chapter, we can also add this scene to the **Build Settings** window. The reason for this is so that Unity is aware of what scenes we want to include in our project. It is also a requirement when it comes to packaging up our game as a build for deployment.

To add our scene to **Build Settings**, do the following:

1. At the top of the Unity editor, click **File | Build Settings**. The **Build Settings** window will appear.
2. Click the **Add Open Scenes** button to add the testLevel scene.
3. The following screenshot shows the **Add Open Scenes** button circled, as well as an arrow pointing to the number index of our testLevel scene. When we add more scenes later, each scene will be numbered:

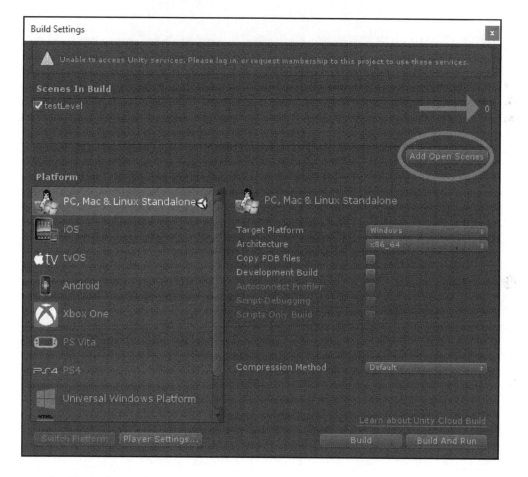

4. Close the **Build Settings** window. We will come back to this when we have more scenes to add in the next chapter.
5. It's a good habit to save the project by clicking **File | Save Project**.

Also, if you are a keen user of **Collaborate**, this is also a good time to publish (push) your work to the cloud. The following screenshot shows the top **Collab** button being clicked, followed by **Publish now!** to push the work into the cloud:

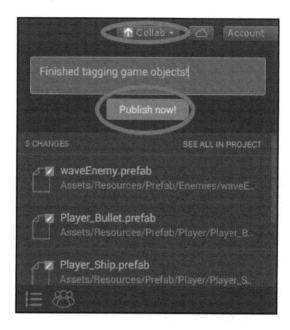

The end of each section, in this chapter and others, is a good time to save and publish your work. I won't remind you too often, but it's good to get into the habit.

Let's now continue with setting up our scene camera in the Unity editor.

Setting up our camera

For our side-scrolling shooter game *Killer Wave*, we need control over a camera to display the aspect ratio and visible depth of the scene, and to make sure we show the correct amount of our game's environment.

Let's get started and decide on the screen ratio of our game. We'll create our own resolution, which will be fairly common across most platforms.

To change the **Game** window's screen ratio to a custom aspect, do the following:

1. Click the current aspect ratio under the **Game** window tab and select the **+** symbol.
2. Enter the custom aspect ratio values shown in the following screenshot.
3. Click **OK** once done, and select the 1080 resolution we have just made:

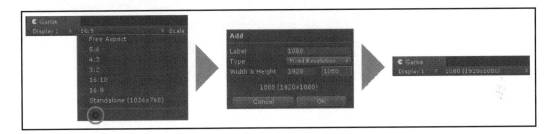

It is good to be aware of the need to make our game's artwork support (or to give it the scope to extend to) as many screen ratios as possible, especially if we ever wanted to make a game for portable devices such as tablets or mobile phones. This is because nearly every major brand of phone and tablet comes in different ratio sizes, and we don't want to start squashing and squeezing our content as it won't look right. It's also possible that our small mobile games will become successful and could later be ported to a console or PC. If that's the case, we need to make it so the game screen supports these ratios too. The main point to take from all of this is that we are targeting our game to cover all possible common screen ratios. The more platforms (consoles, portable devices, and so on) we can cover with flexible screen ratios, the easier it will be to extend our game out to those devices without requiring extra work. We explain more about screen size ratios in Chapter 8, *Adding Custom Fonts and UI,* and Chapter 9, *Creating a 2D Shop Interface and In-Game HUD,* where we discuss UI display settings. Additionally, in Chapter 13, *Effects, Testing, Performance, and Alt Controls,* we explain how to display our game screen on a raw image component.

Before we continue any further with our project, it's probably a good time to confirm our understanding of Unity's own UI layout. The following screenshot shows the Unity editor, where I have outlined and labeled the relevant windows:

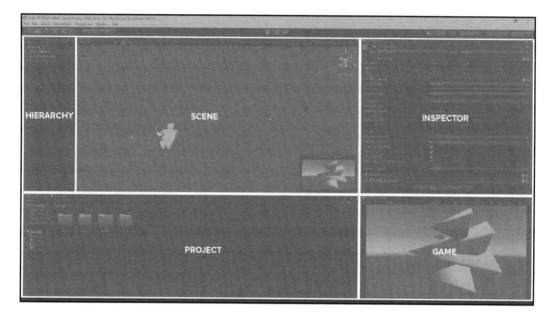

Typically, the Unity editor window is made up of five main windows:

- **Scene**: This is our two-/three-dimensional workspace.
- **Game**: This window is what the end user will see. By default, the **Game** tab shares the same space as the **Scene** window.
- **Hierarchy**: All game objects in our scene will be listed here.
- **Inspector**: When an object is selected, information about it will be displayed here.
- **Project**: This is our Unity project folder. Consider it a structure of files and folders that we can use in our game.

To drag each window around individually, left-click and drag the name of the tab and it will then snap into different locations.

My **Game** window is set to **1080** and because I don't have the luxury of a second screen, I've clicked its name tab (**Game**) and pulled it down in the bottom-right corner. The window is small, but as you can see at the top of the **Game** window, the scale is set to 1x, which means I have a full picture; nothing is hidden or cut out of view.

To check we have the main camera's **Transform** properties reset to its default settings, make sure its **Position**, **Rotation**, and **Scale** are all set to 0. We can also reset the **Transform** option as follows:

1. With the main camera selected in the **Hierarchy** window, click the silver cog in the top-right corner of the **Transform** panel in the **Inspector** window, as shown in the following screenshot:

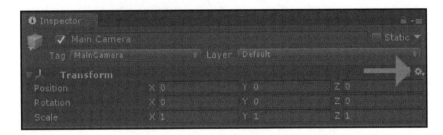

2. When the dropdown appears, click **Reset**.

Continuing on with setting up our main camera, let's get rid of the landscape background in our **Scene/Game** window by changing its **Background** setting:

1. Click the **Main Camera** in the **Hierarchy** window.
2. In the **Inspector** window, we have the **Camera** component with a property called **Clear Flags**. Click the **Skybox** value.
3. A dropdown will appear. Click **Solid Color,** as shown in the following screenshot:

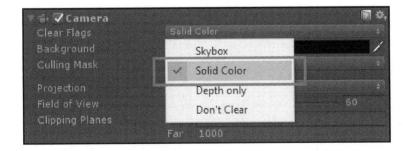

4. We will now be presented with a blue background, which is less distracting.

5. If you don't like blue, you can change it to any color in the **Background** property. I'm going to make mine black by changing the **Red, Green, Blue, and Alpha (RGBA)** values to **R:** 0, **G:** 0, **B:** 0, and **A:** 255, as shown in the following screenshot:

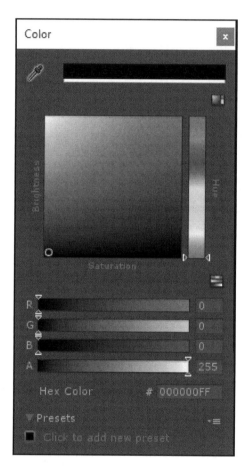

Great, now let's move on to coding these properties for our main camera.

Updating our camera properties via a script

We now have our main camera's behavior set in our **Scene**. Next, we need to code this into a script so that whenever a scene is loaded, Unity will read the script and understand how the main camera should be set up.

Observing our framework again, let's see where the camera script should be placed:

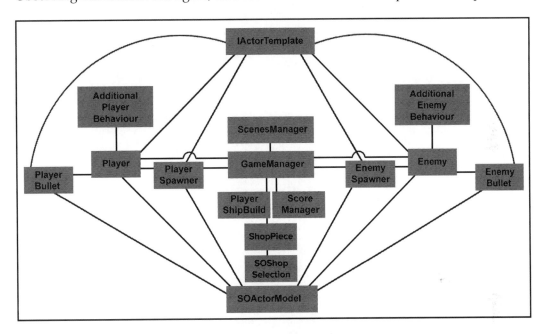

As you can see in the diagram, there is no reference to the camera, so should we make a script to support this? Arguably the only reason to make a script based on the camera would be if the camera had a complex purpose filled with multiple properties and functions. The camera in our game, however, is put in place when the game starts. Later on, on the third level, the camera will move from left to right with a simple component script, but it doesn't hold any other complexity. It would, therefore, be more ideal to use the GameManager, as it only takes up a small role. If the game became bigger and the camera took on more of a role, then this might justify the camera having a class of its own. Others might disagree based on personal preference, but this is the approach we'll take.

Let's make the `GameManager` script as follows:

1. Create a script in the same way that we created a folder. Right-click the open space area in the **Project** window, and a dropdown will appear. Click **Create | C# Script**, as follows:

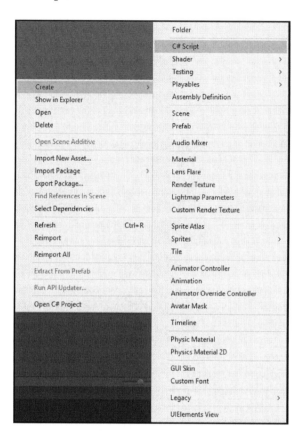

2. The script appears with the title `NewBehaviourScript`. We don't want to call it that, so type (in camel case) `GameManager`.

What's camel casing?
Camel casing is a way to avoid spacing between words. This is fairly common with programming as spaces are typically not welcomed for various reasons. Each new word starts with a capital letter, so in this case, the M in `GameManager` is the hump of the camel. However, variables typically start with lowercase, as you will see shortly.

We now have our `GameManager` script. Notice how Unity is trying to be helpful by changing the icon to a silver cog because what we are doing is a recognized method with Unity:

As we did with placing our three-dimensional models into the **Model** folder, move the `GameManager` into the `Script` folder.

Good. Now, before we open our script to code in it, we need to attach it to a game object in our scene so that when the scene runs, the script attached to the game object also runs.

To create our `GameManager` game object, we need to do the following:

1. Right-click in an open space in the **Hierarchy** window.
2. From the drop-down menu, select **Create Empty**.
3. Right-click the newly created game object and select **Rename** from the drop-down menu.
4. Rename this game object to `GameManager`.
5. Finally, with the `GameManager` game object still selected, click the **Add Component** button in the far-right **Inspector** window.
6. Type `GameManager` from the drop-down menu until you see the `GameManager` script, and select it.

Whenever we make an empty game object, we must be sure that all of its **Transform** property values are reset to their default values unless we are specifically changing them.

To reset a game object's **Transform** value, make sure the game object we are resetting is selected. Click the metal cog in the top-right corner of the **Inspector** window, then select **Reset**.

Double-click the GameManager script to open it up in your IDE (Visual Studio or whatever IDE you use), then proceed as follows:

1. Inside the GameManager script, we will be faced with the UnityEngine library being imported into our script to add extra functionality to Unity's own components:

   ```
   using UnityEngine;

   public class GameManager : MonoBehaviour
   {
   ```

   Also in the preceding code, we have the name of our script along with MonoBehaviour being inherited yet again to add more functionality to our script. MonoBehaviour is also required if the game object that attaches to this script needs to be used in the Unity editor.

   Let's start adding some of our own code into our GameManager script.

2. Create an empty method, CameraSetup, and then run this method in the Start function:

   ```
   void Start()
   {
       CameraSetup();
   }
   void CameraSetup()
   {

   }
   ```

3. Inside the CameraSetup method, add a reference to the camera and set the position and angle of the camera to zero apart from its z axis. We'll set z to −300, which will move the camera back and ensure all game objects are in the shot:

   ```
   GameObject gameCamera =
       GameObject.FindGameObjectWithTag("MainCamera");

   //Camera Transform
   gameCamera.transform.position = new Vector3(0,0,-300);
   gameCamera.transform.eulerAngles = new Vector3(0,0,0);
   ```

4. Next, we will change the properties of the camera within our `CameraSetup` method:

```
//Camera Properties
gameCamera.GetComponent<Camera>().clearFlags =
    CameraClearFlags.SolidColor;
gameCamera.GetComponent<Camera>().backgroundColor =
    new Color32(0,0,0,255);
}
```

This does the following:

- Removes the sky background and replaces it with a solid color
- Changes the solid color from the default blue to black

5. Finally, save the script.

Now you should have something like this:

```
using UnityEngine;

11 references
public class GameManager : MonoBehaviour
{

    0 references
    void Start()
    {
        CameraSetup();
    }

    2 references
    void CameraSetup()
    {
        GameObject gameCamera = GameObject.FindGameObjectWithTag("MainCamera");

        //Camera Transform
        gameCamera.transform.position = new Vector3(0,0,-300);
        gameCamera.transform.eulerAngles = new Vector3(0,0,0);

        //Camera Properties
        gameCamera.GetComponent<Camera>().clearFlags = CameraClearFlags.SolidColor;
        gameCamera.GetComponent<Camera>().backgroundColor = new Color32(0,0,0,255);
    }
}
```

If you would like to change other settings relating to the camera, you can find out about them at https://docs.unity3d.com/ScriptReference/Camera.html.

Press the **Play** button in the upper middle of the editor window, or by using the shortcut *Ctrl + P (command + P* on the Mac). The following screenshot shows where the **Play** button is located:

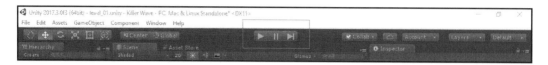

With the scene in play mode, we can now check out the **Main Camera** game object's properties by doing the following:

1. In the **Hierarchy** window, select **Main Camera**.

   Observe the **Inspector** window in the next screenshot to see the following changes our script has made.

2. In the **Transform** component of the **Inspector** window, we can see the **Position** and **Rotation** properties are set to the same values set in our script (denoted by **1** in the following screenshot).

3. In the **Camera** component of the **Inspector** window, we can see the **Clear Flags** and **Background** values are also set to the same values set in our script (denoted by **2i** and **2ii**).

   The following screenshot shows the **Main Camera** component properties being updated in Play mode:

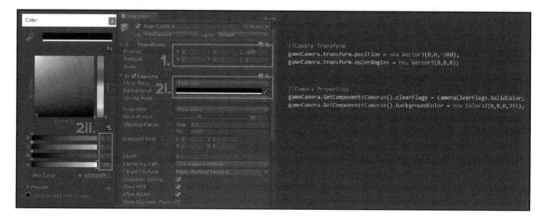

Now, hopefully, our properties should be the same as what we have scripted (with no errors). If not, you will likely have an error message in the **Console** window. If there is an error, it will likely tell you what line the error is on. You can also double-click the error, and it will take you to the line the error is on.

To double-check everything has worked, change the **Position** and **Rotation** of the camera in the editor and then press the **Play** button. The properties for the camera should now be set to our script's **Position** and **Rotation** properties.

At this point, while the editor is still playing, we could also make a prefab of the camera:

1. Click and drag the **Camera** from the **Hierarchy** window down into the **Project** window, and we will generate a blue cube with the camera's name or an empty icon. Depending on the scale of our icons, the size of the icon can be altered by moving the slider shown in the following screenshot:

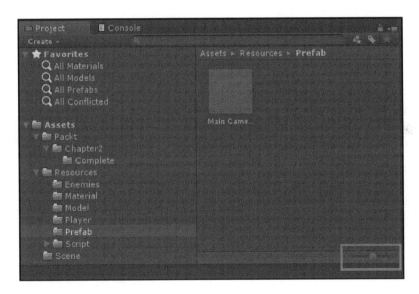

2. Move this camera prefab into the `Prefab` folder.

You might be thinking, *why didn't we just make a prefab of the camera in the first place instead of fiddling with its property settings in code?* However, two key things are important here: firstly, we are studying for an exam that is likely to cover such properties; and secondly, you now know how to change these settings dynamically through code.

Another benefit to scripting Unity's components is that we can sometimes be offered more functionality than what is displayed in the Editor. For example, the `Camera` component has a `layerCullDistances` property that is only accessible via scripting. This can offer functionality such as skipping the rendering of smaller game objects in the far distance to increase a game's performance.

To read up more on `layerCullDistances`, check the documentation at `https://docs.unity3d.com/ScriptReference/Camera-layerCullDistances.html`.

This brings this section to a close. So far, we have covered the following:

- Setting up a ratio for our game camera
- Setting up our Unity editor with individual windows
- Changing the properties of our **Camera** component in the Unity editor
- Repeating the changes we made to our camera in the `GameManager` script
- Adding our `GameManager` script to our scene as a game object

As a programmer, the importance of being able to understand and change the settings in the Unity editor (but to also be able to do the same in code) can be expanded to other components that are in the editor. This is what we will do next, with a focus on directional light.

Setting up our light

As a default setup, each scene comes with a directional light, and currently, this is all we need to get going; ideally, we want the scene to be well lit.

With the directional light already present in the scene as the default light, select it in the **Hierarchy** window. In the **Inspector** window, set the **Directional Light**'s **Transform Rotation** values to the following:

X: 50, **Y**:−30, **Z**:0

When we put our player ship into the scene, this will light it up well, as shown in the following screenshot:

 Unity provides three different types of real-time lights. As well as the **directional** light we mentioned, it also provides a **point** light, which is like a 360° glow that we will cover in Chapter 4, *Applying Art, Animation, and Particles*. The third type of light is a spotlight or as Unity refers to it, a **spot**. The **spot** can also have masks applied so it can project images known as cookies.

For more information about the three types of lights, check out https://docs.unity3d.com/Manual/Lighting.html.

We can now make sure these settings stay in place by adding them to the GameManager script. We can also alter the light's color.

Updating our light properties via a script

In the GameManager, we will set the **Transform Rotation** values and change the color tint from a light yellow to a cold blue:

1. Open the GameManager script and enter the following method:

```
void LightSetup()
  {
      GameObject dirLight = GameObject.Find("Directional
Light");
      dirLight.transform.eulerAngles = new Vector3(50,-30,0);
      dirLight.GetComponent<Light>().color =
        new Color32(152,204,255,255);
  }
```

2. Add LightSetup(); in the scope of the Start function.
3. Save the script.

The `LightSetup` method does three things:

- It grabs the light from the scene and stores it as a reference.
- It sets the rotation of the light with `EulerAngles`.
- Finally, it changes the light's color.

 `eulerAngles` allows us to give `Vector3` coordinates instead of `Quaternion` values. `eulerAngles` makes it so rotations are less complicated to work with. More information about `eulerAngles` can be found at `https://docs.unity3d.com/ScriptReference/Transform-eulerAngles.html`.

That's all we need to do with our light. As with the camera, we can access the light and change its properties via a script.

We have become familiar with our light by changing its settings in the Unity editor and the `GameManager` script. Next, we will set up our interface for the majority of our game objects.

Introducing our interface – IActorTemplate

The `IActorTemplate` interface is what we are using to prompt damage control, death, and scriptable object assets. The reason for using an interface such as this is that it ties general uses together between classes that inherit it.

A total of six classes will be using the `IActorTemplate` interface, which is as follows:

- `Player`
- `PlayerBullet`
- `PlayerSpawner`
- `Enemy`
- `EnemyBullet`
- `EnemySpawner`

The following diagram shows the `IActorTemplate` interface with a partial overview of our game framework:

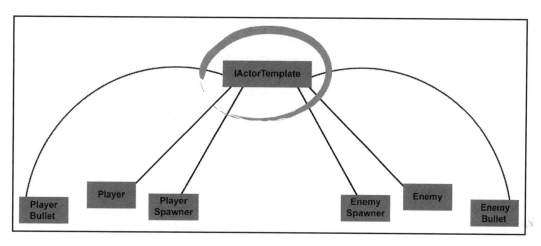

Let's create our interface and explain its content along the way:

1. Create a script in the `Assets/Resources/Scripts` folder with the filename `IActorTemplate`.

2. Open the script and enter the following code:

```
public interface IActorTemplate
{
int SendDamage();
void TakeDamage(int incomingDamage);
void Die();
void ActorStats(SOActorModel actorModel);
}
```

3. Make sure to save the script.

The code we just entered looks like we have declared a class, but it acts fundamentally differently. Instead of using the `class` keyword, we enter `interface` followed by the name of the interface, `IActorTemplate`. It's not a requirement to start any interface name with an `I` but it makes the script easily identifiable.

Within the interface, we make a list of methods that act like contracts to whichever class inherits the interface. For example, the Player script that we'll create later on in the chapter inherits the IActorTemplate interface. The Player script must declare the function names from IActorTemplate or the Player script will throw an error.

Inside the scope of the interface, we declare methods without accessors (it doesn't require private or public at the beginning of each method). Methods also don't require any content in them (that is, they are empty bodies).

For more information about interfaces, check out https://learn.unity.com/tutorial/interfaces.

The last method in our interface is ActorStats, which takes a type of SOActorModel. SOActorModel is a scriptable object that we are going to explain and create in the next section.

Introducing our ScriptableObject – SOActorModel

In this section, we are going to cover scriptable objects and their benefits. Similar to our interface, scriptable objects cover the same six classes. The reason for this is because our interface uses the SOActorModel and therefore creates an attachment with the other variables.

It is also good to remind ourselves of the **Game Design Brief** and how it is incorporated into the overview of the creation of our game.

Our game has three series of game objects that will hold similar properties: EnemyWave, EnemyFlee, and Player. These properties will include health, speed, score value, and more. The difference between each of these as described in the game design brief is the way they act and also how they are instantiated in our game.

Player will be instantiated at every level, EnemyWave will be spawned from EnemySpawner, and EnemyFlee will be placed in particular areas of the third level.

All of the mentioned game objects mentioned will relate to the `SOActorModel` object.

The following diagram is also a partial view of our game framework showing the scriptable object and the six classes that inherit it:

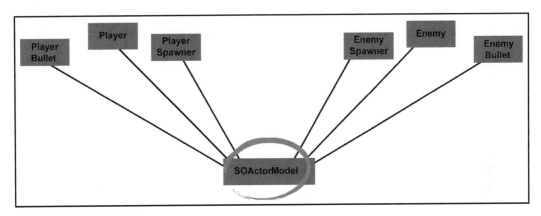

Similar to what was mentioned with the `interface` script is that the name of the scriptable object name starts with `SO`, which isn't a standard way of naming the script, but it's easier to identify as a `ScriptableObject`.

The purpose of this scriptable object is to hold general values for each of the game objects it's being given to. For example, all game objects have a name, so within our `SOActorModel` is a `string` named `actorName`. This `actorName` will be used to name the type of enemy, spawner, or bullet it is.

Let's create a scriptable object:

1. In the **Project** window in the Unity editor, create a script in the `Assets/Resources/Scripts` folder with the filename `SOActorModel`.
2. Open the script and enter the following code:

```
using UnityEngine;
[CreateAssetMenu(fileName = "Create Actor", menuName =
    "Create  Actor")]
public class SOActorModel : ScriptableObject

{
        public string actorName;
        public AttackType attackType;

        public enum AttackType
```

```
        {
            wave, player, flee, bullet
        }
    public string description;
    public int health;
    public int speed;
    public int hitPower;
    public GameObject actor;
    public GameObject actorsBullets;
}
```

3. Save the script.

Inside the SOActorModel we will be naming most, if not, all of these variables in the Player script. Similar to how an interface signs a contract with a class, the SOActorModel does the same because it's being inherited, but isn't as strict as an interface by throwing an error if the content from the scriptable object isn't applied.

The following is an overview of the SOActorModel code we just entered.

We named our scriptable object SOActorModel as a generic term to try and cover as many game objects as will likely use the scriptable object. This way of working also supports the SOLID principles we covered in the first chapter by encouraging us to try and keep our code concise and efficient.

The main categories we'll cover for this script are as follows:

- **Importing libraries**: As you can see, the only library we have imported in the SOActorModel script is the using UnityEngine; no other libraries are required.
- **Creating an asset**: The CreateAssetMenu attribute creates an extra selection from the drop-down list in the **Project** window in the Unity editor when we right-click and select **Create**, as shown in the following screenshot:

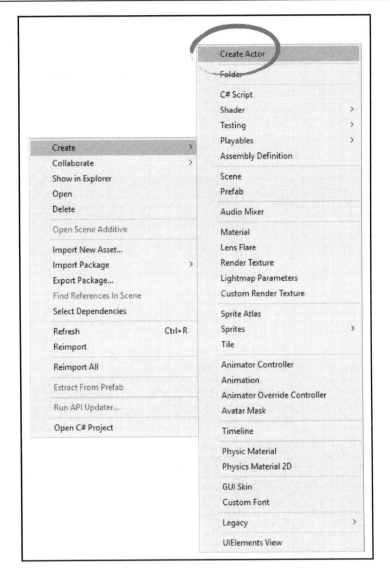

- **Inheritance**: We aren't inheriting `MonoBehaviour`, but instead inheriting `ScriptableObject` as it's a requirement when it comes to creating an asset.
- **Variables**: Finally, these are the variables that will be sent to our selected classes.

In the following sections, we are going to create assets from the scriptable object script to give our scripts different values.

Creating a PlayerSpawner ScriptableObject asset

With our `SOActorModel ScriptableObject` made, we can now create an asset that will act as a template that can be used not just by programmers, but also by designers who want to tweak game properties/settings without needing to know how to code.

To create an `Actor Model` asset, do the following:

1. Back in the Unity editor, in the **Project** window, right-click and choose **Create | Create Actor**.
2. Rename the newly created asset file in the **Project** window `Player_Default` and store the file in the `Assets/Resources/Scripts/ScriptableObject` folder.
3. Click on the new asset and, in the **Inspector** window, you'll see the content of the asset.

   The following screenshot shows the `Actor Model` asset's fields where I have entered in my own values:

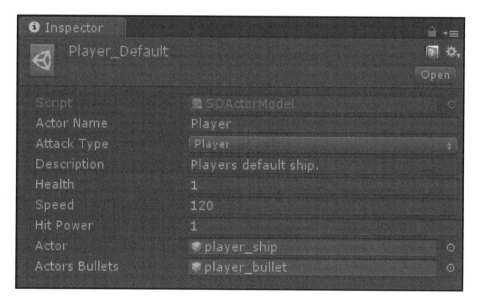

Let's break down each of the values that have been added to our newly created asset:

- **Actor Name**: The name of the actor (in our case, this is `Player`).
- **Attack Type**: Choose to pick which category this game object belongs to.
- **Description**: Designer/internal notes that don't affect the game but can be helpful.
- **Health**: How many times can the player get hit before dying.
- **Speed**: Movement speed of the player.
- **Hit Power**: Determines how much damage the player will cause if it collides with the enemy.
- **Actor**: Place the `player_ship` prefab here (`Assets/Resources/Prefab/Player/player_ship`).
- **Actors Bullets**: Place the `player_bullet` prefab here (`Assets/Resources/Prefab/Player/player_bullet`).

We will add this asset to our `PlayerSpawner` script once it's built later on in the chapter. Let's move on to the next scriptable object asset.

Creating an EnemySpawner ScriptableObject asset

In this section, we are going to make our enemy asset to attach to `EnemySpawner` for later on in the chapter. For the sake of keeping our work fresh and together, let's continue with that before moving onto the `EnemySpawner` script.

To make an enemy asset, follow these instructions:

1. Back in the editor, in the **Project** window, right-click and choose **Create | Create Actor**.
2. Rename the new file to refer to what it's being attached to (`BasicWave Enemy`) and store the file in the `Assets/Resources/Scripts/ScriptableObject` location.
3. Click on the new script and our **Inspector** window will show the content of our script.

The following screenshot shows what the `BasicWave Enemy` asset is going to look like once we've finished:

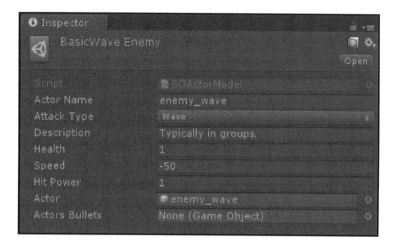

Lets briefly go through each of the values for our enemy:

- **Actor Name**: `enemy_wave`
- **Attack Type**: Here, this is `Wave`. This explains what type of enemy it is and how it attacks the player.
- **Description:** Here, this reads `Typically in groups`. As mentioned before, it's more of a guideline than a rule to comment anything.
- **Health**: `1`, which means it takes 1 hit to die.
- **Speed**: `-30`– because our enemy is moving from right to left, so we give it a minus figure.
- **Hit Power**: `1`– which means that if this enemy collides with the player, it will cause 1 hit point of damage.
- **Actor**: Place the `enemy_wave` prefab here (`Assets/Resources/Prefab/Enemies/enemy_wave`).
- **Actor Bullets**: This enemy doesn't fire bullets.

Hopefully, you can see how useful scriptable objects are. Imagine continuing to develop this game with `50` enemies, where all we need to do is create an asset and customize it.

We are going to move on to the final scriptable object asset for this chapter in the next section.

Creating a PlayerBullet ScriptableObject Asset

In this section, we are going to create an asset for the player's bullet for when they fire. Like the last two sections, create an asset, name it `PlayerBullet`, and store it in the same folder as the other assets.

The following screenshot shows the final results for the `PlayerBullet` asset:

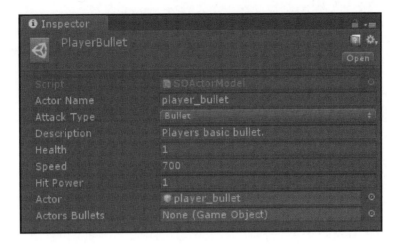

Let's briefly go through each variable's values:

- **Actor Name**: `player_bullet`.
- **Attack Type**: Bullet.
- **Description**: It is optional to enter any details about the asset here.
- **Health**: Our bullet has a health value of 1.
- **Speed**: `700`.
- **Hit Power**: 1 sends a hit point of 1.
- **Actor**: Place the `player_bullet` prefab here (`Assets/Resources/Prefab/Player/player_bullet`).
- **Actor Bullets**: **None (Game Object)**.

In a later chapter, when we build a shop for our game, we will be able to buy power-ups for our player's ship. One of the power-ups will be similar to the one that we just made but the **Actor Name** will be different and the **Hit Power** will have a higher number.

Now we can move on to the next section and create the player's scripts and attach these assets to them.

Setting up our Player, PlayerSpawner, and PlayerBullet scripts

In the following series of sections, we are going to create three of the scripts that will cover the following: spawning the player, the player's controls, and the player's bullet.

The scripts we will be creating and including are as follows:

- `PlayerSpawner`: Creates and calibrates the player.
- `Player`: Player controls and general functionality.
- `PlayerBullet`: Movement and general functionality.
- `IActorTemplate`: A template of the expected rules assigned to a given object (already made).
- `SOActorModel`: A set of values that can be altered by non-programmers (already made).

We will cover all of these scripts thoroughly and break down each of their purposes, as well as how they depend on and communicate with one another. We will start with the `PlayerSpawner`, which will create the player's ship and issue its values.

Setting up our PlayerSpawner script

The purpose of the `PlayerSpawner` script is to be attached to a game object, resulting in the player appearing at its position in the game. The `PlayerSpawner` script will also set the player's values when it is created. For example, if our player had a particular speed value, or if it had received an upgrade from the shop; the `PlayerSpawner` script would grab these values and apply them to the `Player` script.

The following diagram shows a partial view of the `PlayerSpawner` class in the game's framework and its relation with the other classes around it:

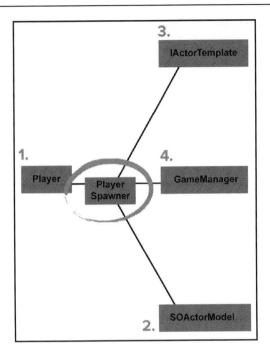

As we can see, the PlayerSpawner script is connected to four other scripts:

1. Player: PlayerSpawner is connected to Player because it creates the player.
2. SOActorModel - This is a ScriptableObject that gives the PlayerSpawner its values, which are then passed on to the Player.
3. IActorTemplate - This is the interface that generalizes the script with other common functions.
4. GameManager - This will send and receive general game information from and to the PlayerSpawner script.

Before we create our PlayerSpawner script, it would be good housekeeping to create an empty game object to store anything to do with our player, their bullets, and whatever else the player might create in our testLevel scene.

Make and name the game object by doing the following:

1. Right-click the **Hierarchy** window in its open space.
2. A drop-down list will appear. From the list, select **Create Empty**.
3. Name the game object _Player.

That's all that we need to do. Now, let's make a start with the `PlayerSpawner` script:

1. In the **Project** window, create a script in the `Assets/Resources/Scripts` folder with the filename `PlayerSpawner`.

2. Open the script and make sure we have the following library entered at the top of our script:

   ```
   using UnityEngine;
   ```

   We only require `using UnityEngine` as it covers all of the objects we need in the script.

3. Continue by making sure our class is labeled as follows :

   ```
   public class PlayerSpawner : MonoBehaviour
   {
   ```

   It is common in Unity to inherit `MonoBehaviour` to give the script more functionality.

4. Continue by entering the script's global variables:

   ```
   SOActorModel actorModel;
   GameObject playerShip;
   ```

   Inside the `PlayerSpawner` class, we add two global variables: the first variable is the `actorModel`, which holds a scriptable object asset that will contain values for the player ship, and the second variable will hold our player ship once it's created from our `CreatePlayer` method.

5. Continue by entering the script's `Start` function:

   ```
   void Start()
   {
     CreatePlayer();
   }
   ```

   After the global variables, we add a `Start` function that will run automatically as soon as the game object holding the `PlayerSpawner` script is active at runtime.

   Inside the scope of the `Start` function is a method that we are going to create called `CreatePlayer`.

6. Continue by entering the `CreatePlayer` method:

```
void CreatePlayer()
  {
    //CREATE PLAYER
    actorModel = Object.Instantiate(Resources.Load
        ("Script/ScriptableObject/Player_Default"))
            as SOActorModel;
    playerShip = GameObject.Instantiate(actorModel.actor)
        as GameObject;
    playerShip.GetComponent<Player>().ActorStats(actorModel);

  //SET PLAYER UP

  }
}
```

I have split the `CreatePlayer` method into two commented-out parts (`//CREATE PLAYER` and `//SET PLAYER UP`) due to its size.

This first part of the `CreatePlayer` method will `instantiate` the player ship `ScriptableObject` asset and store it in the `actorModel` variable. We then `instantiate` a game object that refers to our `ScriptableObject` that holds the game object called `actor` in our game object variable named `playerShip`. Finally, we apply our `ScriptableObject` asset to the `playerShip` method called `ActorStats` that exists in the `Player` component script (which we will create later on in this chapter).

7. Continue on inside the `CreatePlayer` method to add the second half:

```
//SET PLAYER UP
playerShip.transform.rotation = Quaternion.Euler(0,180,0);
playerShip.transform.localScale = new Vector3(60,60,60);
playerShip.name = "Player";
playerShip.transform.SetParent(this.transform);
playerShip.transform.position = Vector3.zero;
```

In the second half of the `CreatePlayer` method, we add more code at the same point where we have commented `//SET PLAYER UP`.

The code from `//SET PLAYER UP` onward is dedicated to setting up the player's ship in the correct position at the start of the level.

The code does the following:

- Sets the rotation of the player's ship to face the right way
- Sets the scale of the player ship to 60 on all axes

When we `instantiate` any game object, Unity will add `(Clone)` to the end of the game object's name. We can rename it to `Player`.

- We make the `playerShip` game object a child of the `_Player` game object in the **Hierarchy** window so that we can easily find it.
- Finally, we reset the player ship's position.

That is our `PlayerSpawner` script coded. Now, in the next section, we need to create and attach this script to a game object and name it. Make sure to save the script before moving on.

Creating the PlayerSpawner game object

In this section, we will create a game object that will hold our newly created `PlayerSpawner` script, and then we will position the `PlayerSpawner` game object in the `testLevel` scene.

To create and set up our `PlayerSpawner` game object, we need to do the following:

1. In the **Hierarchy** window, create an empty game object and name it `PlayerSpawner`.
2. Drag and drop the `PlayerSpawner` game object onto the `_Player` (remember `_Player` is the empty game object in our scene) game object to make the `PlayerSpawner` its child.

   Because our `PlayerSpawner` game object doesn't have anything visually applied to it, we can give it an icon.

3. With the `PlayerSpawner` game object still selected in the **Inspector** window, click the multi-colored box to the left of its name. A selection of colors will be offered, as shown in the following screenshot:

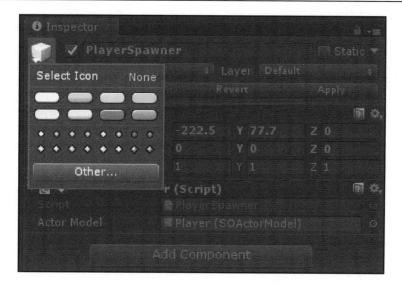

4. Pick a color. Now the `PlayerSpawner` game object will be given a label to show us where it is in the scene. This will now appear in the **Scene** window.

 If you still can't see the icon in the **Scene** window, make sure **3D icons** are turned off. You can check by clicking the **Gizmos** button in the top right of the **Scene** window and unchecking the **3D Icons** box.

With the `PlayerSpawner` game object sitting inside the `_Player` game object in the **Hierarchy** window, we now need to give it the following transform property values, which will help two things. The first thing it will help to set the boundaries of our ship within the games screen ratio (we explain more about this in the next chapter), the second is for later on in the book, where we make it so the player ship will animate into the screen view. For now, we just need to give our `PlayerSpawner` game object the following values.

5. With the `PlayerSpawner` game object still selected, in the **Inspector** window, give it the following **Transform** values:

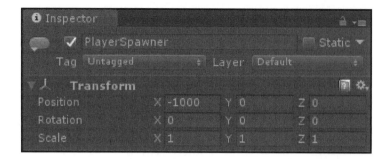

6. While still in the **Inspector** window, click **Add Component** and type `PlayerSpawner` until you see the script appear in the drop-down list.

7. Click the `PlayerSpawner` script to add this to the `PlayerSpawner` game object.

We can't move the ship yet, nor can we fire because we haven't coded this in yet. In the following section, we will go through the player's controls, then we will move on to coding our player and its bullet to travel across the screen.

Setting up our Input Manager

Remember that this is a side-scrolling shooter game, so the controls will be two-dimensional even though our visuals are three-dimensional. Our focus now is to get the `Players` controls set up. To do this, we need to access the **Input Manager**:

1. Select **Edit**, followed by **Project Settings**, then **Input**, as shown in the following screenshot:

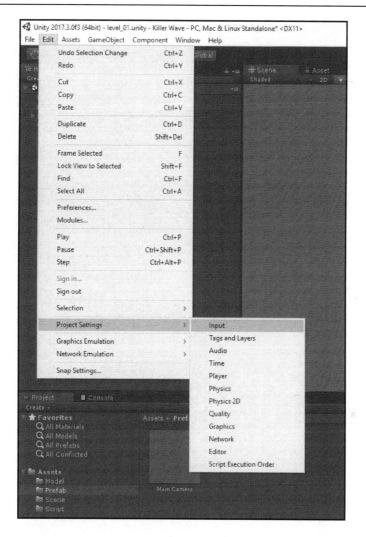

2. The **Inspector** window will change to the **Input** window.

The **Input Manager** will offer a list of all available controls for our game. We will first check what the controls are set to by default. There are a lot of options here, but as mentioned, we only need to browse through the properties that matter to us, namely:

- **Horizontal**: Moves the player's ship along its x-axis
- **Vertical**: Moves the player's ship along its y-axis
- **Fire1**: Makes our player shoot

To check these three properties, we need to do the following:

- Expand the **Axes** dropdown by clicking the arrow next to it.
- Expand **Horizontal**, as shown in the following screenshot:

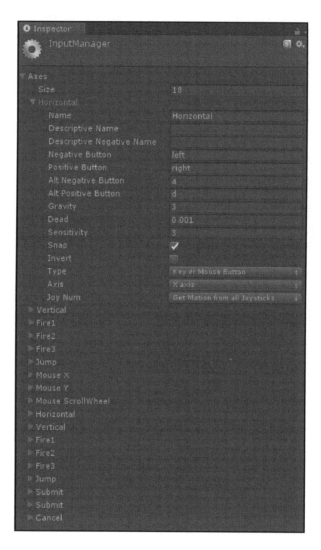

- **Horizontal**: The left button configures horizontal negatively (−1), and the right button configures it positively (+1). Alternative keypresses to this effect are *A* for left and *D* for right.

If we had analog controls such as a joystick or a steering wheel, we would likely need to be concerned about the influence of gravity when the player releases the controls and it returns to its center. Dead refers to the center of the analog controls. Sometimes controllers can be unbalanced and naturally lean to one side, so by increasing the dead zone, we can eliminate false feedback from the player that could be detected as a movement.

- **Vertical**: This is the same as **Horizontal**, apart from the fact the negative button is down (−1), and the positive button is up (+1). Alternative buttons are *S* for down and *W* for up.
- **Fire1**: This has a similar layout to **Vertical**, but with *Ctrl* as **Fire** (*command* on the Mac) (that is, the positive button), with its the alternative (positive) button being mouse 0 (that is, the left mouse button). For now, remove mouse 0 from the alternative button.

To find out more about the **InputManager** window, click the little blue book in the top right corner of the **Input Manager** panel.

Our controls are now set in the **InputManager** window, so let's move on to coding the Player script to take advantage of these controls.

Setting up our Player script

The Player script will be attached to the player ship game object, from which the player will be able to move and shoot, as well as inflict and receive damage. We will also make it so that the player ship won't go outside of the screenplay area. Before we continue, let's remind ourselves where the Player script lies in our game framework:

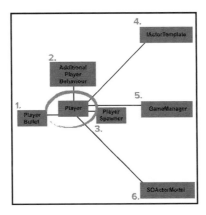

The `Player` script will be in contact with the following scripts:

1. `PlayerBullet`: The `Player` script will create bullets to fire.
2. `AdditionalPlayerBehaviour`: If the player ship has any extra information attached to it, as well as additional abilities, the `AdditionalPlayerBehaviour` will cover this.
3. `PlayerSpawner`: The `Player` script is created from the `PlayerSpawner`.
4. `IActorTemplate`: Contains damage control and the properties for `Player`.
5. `GameManager`: Extra information such as the number of lives, the score, the level, and whatever upgrades the player ship has accumulated will be stored in `GameManager`.
6. `SOActorModel`: Holds `ScriptableObject` properties for `Player`.

Now that we are familiar with the `Player` script's relation to the other scripts, we can start coding it:

1. In the **Project** window of the Unity editor, create a script in the `Assets/Resources/Scripts` folder with the filename `Player`.
2. Open the script and add the `IActorTemplate` interface to the existing default code:

   ```
   using UnityEngine;

   public class Player : MonoBehaviour, IActorTemplate
   {
   ```

   The script will by default create a `UnityEngine` library (including some others), the name of the class, and `MonoBehaviour`. All of these are essential to make the script work in the Unity editor.

3. Continuing with the `Player` script, enter the following global variables:

   ```
   int travelSpeed;
   int health;
   int hitPower;
   GameObject actor;
   GameObject fire;

   public int Health
   {
       get {return health;}
       set {health = value;}
   }
   ```

```
public GameObject Fire
{
    get {return fire;}
    set {fire = value;}
}

GameObject _Player;
float width;
float height;
```

We have entered a mixture of integers, floats, and game objects in our global variables; starting from the top, the first six variables will be updated from the player's SOActorModel script. travelSpeed is the speed of the player's ship, health is how many hits the player can take before dying, hitPower is the damage the ship would cause when colliding into something that could receive damage (the enemy), actor is the three-dimensional model used to represent the player, and finally, the fire variable is the three-dimensional model of which the player fires. If that seemed a little rushed, check the *Introducing our ScriptableObject – SOActorModel* section, where we go into more detail about these variables.

The two public properties of Health and Fire are there to give access to our two private health and fire variables from other classes that require access.

The _Player variable will be used as a reference to the _Player game object in the scene.

The last two variables of width and height will be used to store the measured results of the world space dimensions of the screen the game is played in. We will discuss these two more in the next block of code.

While we are on the approach to the Start function code block next, some may question why we would pick Start over Awake when it comes to running a function's code content. Both functions run once at runtime; the only noticeable difference is that Awake runs before Start with regards to Unity's execution order, as can be seen in the documentation at https://docs.unity3d.com/Manual/ExecutionOrder.html.

For simplicity in our Unity project, we will vary between which of the two functions to use. This is so we avoid conflicts between several `Awake` functions running at the same time. As an example, one script may try to update its Text UI, but the variable updating the text may still be null at runtime because the script with the variable is still waiting for its content to be updated.

There is a way around to avoid conflicts between several `Awake` functions being called by several scripts at runtime by going to Unity's **Script Execution Order** in **Edit | Project Settings | Script Execution Order**.

If you would like to know more about the **Script Execution Order**, check the documentation at `https://docs.unity3d.com/Manual/class-MonoManager.html`.

4. Continuing on with entering code into the `Player` script, next up, we will type out the `Start` function along with its content:

```
void Start()
{
  height = 1/(Camera.main.WorldToViewportPoint (new
     Vector3(1,1,0)).y - .5f);
  width = 1/(Camera.main.WorldToViewportPoint(new
Vector3(1,1,0))
     .x - .5f);
  _Player = GameObject.Find("_Player");
}
```

As previously mentioned, the `height` and `width` variables will store our world space measurements. These are required so that we can clamp the player's ship inside the screen. Both the height and width lines of code use similar methods, the only difference is with the axis we are reading.

The `Camera.main` component refers to the camera in our scene and the function it uses, `WorldToViewportPoint`, is to take the results from the game's three-dimensional world space and convert the results into viewport space. If you aren't sure what viewport space is, it's similar to what we know as a screen resolution, except its measurements, are in points and not pixels, and these points are measured from 0 to 1. The following diagram shows the comparison between screen and viewport measurements:

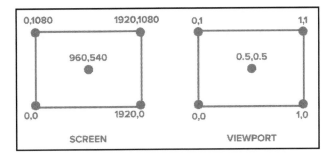

So, with viewports, no matter what the screens resolution is, the full height and width are 1 and everything between that is a fraction. So, for the height, we feed `Vector3` to `WorldToViewportPoint,` where `Vector3` represents a world space value followed by $-0.5f$, which sets its offset back to 0. Then we divide 1 (which is our full-screen size) by the result of our formula. This will give us our current world space height of the screen. We then apply the same principles for the width and use x instead of y and store the result.

Finally, the last line of code takes the reference of the `_Player` game object in the scene and stores it into our variable.

5. Continuing on with the `Player` script, we have our `Update` function that is called on every frame. Enter the function along with the following two methods:

```
void Update ()
{
    Movement();
    Attack();
}
```

The `Update` function runs the `Movement` method and `Attack` method every frame. We will go into depth about these two methods later on in the chapter.

The next method we are going to put into our `Player` script is the `ActorStats` method. This method is a requirement as we declare it in the interface we are inheriting.

6. Just after the scope of our `Update` function, enter the following piece of code:

```
public void ActorStats(SOActorModel actorModel)
{
```

```
            health = actorModel.health;
            travelSpeed = actorModel.speed;
            hitPower = actorModel.hitPower;
            fire = actorModel.actorsBullets;
        }
```

The code we have just entered assigns values from the player's `SOActorModel ScriptableObject` asset we made earlier on in the chapter.

This method doesn't get run in our script but gets accessed by other classes, the reason being these variables hold values regarding our player and don't need to be anywhere else.

7. Save the `Player` script.

   Before we test what we have so far we need to attach our `Player` script to our `player_ship` in the **Project** window.

8. In the **Project** window, navigate to `Assets/Resources/Prefab` and select the `player_ship` prefab.

9. Select the **Add Component** button in the **Inspector** window. Type `Player` until the script appears and then select it.

With our **Hierarchy** window containing the `_Player`, `PlayerSpawner` and the `GameManager` game objects. We can see the player ship get created in our **Game** window by pressing **Play** in the Editor.

The following screenshot shows our game in **Play** mode; note the **Hierarchy** window on the left with the `PlayerSpawner` game object as the parent of the `Player` game object; also note the **Game** window with its black background, and in the center, the player's ship is facing right and is located in the center of the screen. Finally, the far-right image showing our **Scene** window with our `PlayerSpawner` icon:

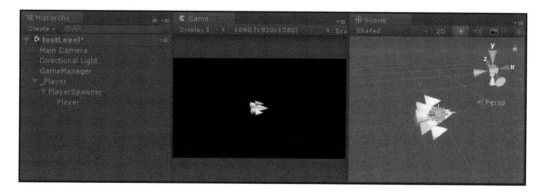

Before moving on to the next section, keep a back up of
the `PlayerSpawner` game object by dragging and dropping it into
the **Project** window to `Assets/Resources/Player`. That way, if
you lose the scene for whatever reason along with
its **Hierarchy** content, you can drag and drop your prefab back in.
This should be a rule with any common active game object.

Let's move on to the next section where we'll continue to work on the `Player` script,
but this time we will look at what happens when our player's game object comes in to
contact with an enemy.

Colliding with an enemy – OnTriggerEnter

In this section, we are going to add a function to our `Player` script that will check to
see what has collided with our player's game object during runtime. Currently, the
only thing that can collide with our player is an enemy, but we can still demonstrate
the use of Unity's own `OnTriggerEnter` function, which handles most of the work
for us:

1. Continuing on after the scope of our last method (`ActorStats`) in
    the `Player` script, we are going to add the following code that detects our
    enemy colliding with the player's ship:

    ```
    void OnTriggerEnter(Collider other)
    {
      if (other.tag == "Enemy")
      {
        if (health >= 1)
        {
         if (transform.Find("energy +1(Clone)"))
          {
           Destroy(transform.Find("energy
    +1(Clone)").gameObject);
            health -= other.GetComponent<IActorTemplate>
              ().SendDamage();
          }
          else
          {
              health -= 1;
          }
        }
        if (health <= 0)
        {
          Die();
    ```

```
            }
        }
    }
```

Let's explain some of the code we have just entered into the Player script.

OnTriggerEnter(Collider other) is a function that Unity recognizes to check what has entered into the player's trigger collider.

We use an if statement to check whether the tag to the collider is called Enemy. Note when we create our enemy, we will give them an Enemy tag so they are easily identified. If the tag does equal to Enemy, we drop into that if statement.

The next if statement checks to see whether our player's health is equal to or more than 1. If it is, that means the player can take a hit and continue without dying and also means we can go into its if statement.

We approach the third if statement that checks to see whether the collider has a game object named energy +1(Clone). The name of this object is the name of the shield the player can purchase in the game shop which we will add in Chapter 6, *Purchasing In-Game Items and Advertisements*. If the player has this energy +1(Clone) object, we can Destroy it with Unity's premade function. We also deduct the player's extra health from the enemies' SendDamage function. We will discuss SendDamage later on in the chapter.

Following after the third if statement is an else condition where, in the event that the player doesn't have an energy +1(Clone) game object, the player gets their health deducted.

Finally, if the player's health is at a value of zero or under, we run the Die method, which we will cover later in the chapter.

Don't forget to keep saving your work as we continue to add more code to the project.

Let's continue on with our Player script and add the functionality so the player can receive and send damage from and to the enemy.

In the next method, we are going to add two methods. The first method (`TakeDamage`) will take an integer called `incomingDamage` and use whatever the value is to deduct from our player's `health` value.

The second method (`SendDamage`) will `return` an integer of our `hitPower` value.

2. Just below and outside of the scope of our `ActorStats` method, now add the following code:

```
public void TakeDamage(int incomingDamage)
 {
    health -= incomingDamage;
 }

public int SendDamage()
 {
    return hitPower;
 }
```

Let's continue with another method for the `Player` script and make it possible so the player can control the player ship around the **Game** window.

The Movement method

In this section, we will code the `Movement` method, which will take input from the player's joypad/keyboard and also make use of the `height` and `width` floats to keep the player's ship within the screen.

1. Still in the `Player` script, make a start with the following method using the following content to check for the player's input:

```
void Movement()
{
  if (Input.GetAxisRaw("Horizontal") > 0)
  {
     if (transform.localPosition.x < width + width/0.9f)
     {
       transform.localPosition += new Vector3
          (Input.GetAxisRaw("Horizontal")
             *Time.deltaTime*travelSpeed,0,0);
     }
  }
```

The `Movement` method will consist of detecting movement in four directions being made from the player; we'll start with when the player presses right on the controller/keyboard. We run an `if` statement that checks whether the Input Manager has detected any movement from the `Horizontal` property. If the `GetAxisRaw` detects a value higher than zero, we fall into the `if` statement's condition. Note that `GetAxisRaw` has no smoothing so the player's ship will instantly move unless extra code is added.

Next, we have another `if` statement, this checks whether the player has exceeded past the `width` (that is, of the screen's world space that we calculated earlier on in the chapter). We've also added an extra partial `width` to avoid the geometry of the player's ship leaving the screen. If the player's position is still under the `width` (and its buffer) value, we run the content inside the `if` statement.

The player's position is updated with a `Vector3` struct, which holds the value of the `Horizontal` direction, multiplied by time per frame, multiplied by the `travelSpeed` we set from our `ScriptableObject`.

2. Let's continue in the `Movement` method and add a similar `if` statement for moving the player ship to the left:

```
if (Input.GetAxisRaw("Horizontal") < 0)
    {
      if (transform.localPosition.x > width + width/6)
      {
       transform.localPosition += new Vector3
         (Input.GetAxisRaw("Horizontal")
           *Time.deltaTime*travelSpeed,0,0);
      }
    }
```

As we can see, the code is close to the previous block; the only difference is that our first `if` statement checks whether we are moving left; the second `if` statement checks if the player's position is greater than the width and a slightly different buffer.

Apart from that, the `if` statement and its content serves the same position, just in the opposite direction.

3. Let's continue with our `Movement` method and add the `if` statement code for moving the player's ship down:

```
if (Input.GetAxisRaw("Vertical") < 0)
```

```
{
    if (transform.localPosition.y > -height/3f)
    {
     transform.localPosition += new Vector3
(0,Input.GetAxisRaw("Vertical")*Time.deltaTime*travelSpeed,0);
    }
}
```

Yet again, we follow the same rule from the previous two `if` statements, but this time, instead of `Horizontal`, we add the `Vertical string` property. In the second `if` statement, we check whether the player's y-axis is higher than a negative `height/3`. The reason why we divide by this value is that later on in the book (`Chapter` 9, *Creating a 2D Shop Interface and In-Game HUD*) we will be adding graphics at the bottom of the screen that will restrict the players view.

4. Let's move on to the last `if` statement in the `Movement` method, up:

```
if (Input.GetAxisRaw("Vertical") > 0)
    {
     if (transform.localPosition.y < height/2.5f)
    {
     transform.localPosition += new Vector3
(0,Input.GetAxisRaw("Vertical")*Time.deltaTime*travelSpeed,0);
    }
    }
}
```

As before, this `if` statement carries a similar role, but this time it's checking whether the player's position is under the `height/2.5f` value. A buffer is applied to stop the three-dimensional geometry from leaving the top of the screen.

> When making a game, sometimes it occurs that when the player moves diagonally, their speed increases. This is because the player is effectively pressing two directions at the same time instead of just one.
>
>
>
> To make it so a direction has just the magnitude of 1, we can use Unity's pre-made `Normalize` function.
>
> To find out more about this function, check the documentation at `https://docs.unity3d.com/ScriptReference/Vector3.` `Normalize.html`.

5. Don't forget to save the script.

We will continue on with the `Player` script by adding the `Die` method.

The Die method

Adding the `Die` method to the `Player` script will make it so our player can be destroyed. Currently, inside the `Die` method is a Unity function called `Destroy`; this function will delete whatever game object is within its parameter.

Enter the following method in the `Player` script to destroy the player:

```
public void Die()
  {
      Destroy(this.gameObject);
  }
```

Let's move on to the last method in the `Player` script, which is to attack.

The Attack method

In this section, we will add the content to the `Attack` method in the `Player` script.

The purpose of this `Attack` method is to receive input from the player, create a bullet, point the bullet in the correct direction, and make the bullet a child of the `Player` game object to keep our **Hierarchy** window tidy.

Enter the following `Attack` method into the `Player` script to allow the player to fire bullets:

```
public void Attack()
  {
   if (Input.GetButtonDown("Fire1"))
     {
        GameObject bullet = GameObject.Instantiate
           (fire,transform.position,Quaternion.Euler
             (new Vector3(0, 0, 0))) as GameObject;
        bullet.transform.SetParent(_Player.transform);
        bullet.transform.localScale = new Vector3(7,7,7);
     }
  }
}
```

Inside the `Attack` method, we call an `if` statement that checks whether the player has pressed the `Fire1` button (*Left Ctrl* on Windows; *command* if you are using a Mac). If the player has pressed the `Fire1` button, we will drop into the `if` statement's scope.

When a developer refers to the scope of a function, `if` statement, class, and so on, they are referring to what is happening between the opening and closing of the curly braces. For example, if the following code has a higher value in its `money` variable, the following `if` statement will run:

```
if (money > costOfPizza)
{
//Whatever happens between the top and bottom of the
two curly braces is within the if statements scope.
}
```

Within the `if` statement, we make another `if` statement to make sure that when clicking the mouse, we are clicking on the screen and not anything UI related. This will become more relevant when we look at adding a Pause button in `Chapter 10`, *Pausing the Game, Altering Sound, and a Mock Test*. If we do click something UI related we call `return`, which means we exit the `if` statement so that we don't fire a shot.

Next, we `Instantiate` our `PlayerBullet` game object from its instance name `fire`. We also face the `fire` game object to the right, relative to the screen, and move it toward oncoming enemies. We store the results of creating and orienting our game object in a variable named `bullet`.

We then set the size of the bullet to be seven times larger than its original size, which makes it look bigger.

Finally, within the `if` statement, we make our `bullet` game object sit within a single game object with the variable name `_Player`.

That is all of the code required for the `Player` script! Make sure to save the script before moving on.

In the next section, we are going to move on to a different player script that controls what happens when the player fires their bullet.

Setting up our PlayerBullet script

In this section, we will be creating a bullet that will travel across the screen from the player's ship.

You will notice how similar the `PlayerBullet` script is to the `Player` script because it carries the `IActorTemplate` and `SOActorModel` scripts, which are already coded into the `Player` script.

Let's create our `PlayerBullet` script:

1. In the **Project** window of the Unity editor, create a script in the `Assets/Resources/Scripts` folder with the filename `PlayerBullet`.

2. Open the script and check/enter the following code at the top of the script:

   ```
   using UnityEngine;
   ```

   By default, we require the `UnityEngine` library to give the script functionality.

3. Let's continue by checking the correct class name and entering the following inheritance:

   ```
   public class PlayerBullet : MonoBehaviour, IActorTemplate {
   ```

   We declare the `public` class and by default inherit `MonoBehaviour`. We also inherit the `IActorTemplate` interface to give our game object-related methods from the other game object scripts, such as `SendDamage`, and `TakeDamage`.

4. Enter the following global variables into the `PlayerBullet` script:

   ```
   GameObject actor;
   int hitPower;
   int health;
   int travelSpeed;

   [SerializeField]
   SOActorModel bulletModel;
   ```

All the variables we add are `private`. The last variable has a
`SerializeField` attribute added. `SerializeField` makes it possible for
this variable to be visible in the **Inspector** window, so even though it's
`private`, we can still drag and drop assets into its field (which we will do
shortly). More information on the `SerializeField` attributes can be found
at https://docs.unity3d.com/ScriptReference/SerializeField.html.

5. Next, we'll move on and enter the `Awake` function along with its content:

```
void Awake()
{
    ActorStats(bulletModel);
}
```

In our `Awake` function is the `ActorStats` method, which is a requirement
because we are inheriting an `interface` that declares it.

6. Continue by entering the `SendDamage` and `TakeDamage` methods:

```
public int SendDamage()
{
  return hitPower;
}

public void TakeDamage(int incomingDamage)
{
  health -= incomingDamage;
}
```

As mentioned already in this chapter, we require these methods to send and
receive damage.

7. Moving on, we enter the `Die` method along with its content:

```
public void Die()
{
    Destroy(this.gameObject);
}
```

Another method to include from our `interface` is the `Die` method.

8. Next, enter the `ActorStats` method:

```
public void ActorStats(SOActorModel actorModel)
{
  hitPower = actorModel.hitPower;
  health = actorModel.health;
  travelSpeed = actorModel.speed;
  actor = actorModel.actor;
}
```

The last method that we inherit from our `interface` is
the `ActorStats` method, which will hold our `ScriptableObject` asset.
This asset will then be assigned to our `PlayerBullet` script's global
variables.

9. The next function is the `OnTriggerEnter` along with its `if` statement
condition checks, as follows:

```
void OnTriggerEnter(Collider other)
{
if (other.tag == "Enemy")
{
    if(other.GetComponent<IActorTemplate>() != null)
    {
        if (health >= 1)
        {
            health -= other.GetComponent<IActorTemplate>
              ().SendDamage();
        }
        if (health <= 0)
        {
            Die();
        }
    }
  }
}
```

In the previous block of code, we run a check to see if our bullet has collided
with an `"Enemy"` tagged collider. If the collider is tagged as `"Enemy"` to the
player, we then check to see whether the collider holds an
`IActorTemplate` interface. If it doesn't then it's likely the `"Enemy"` collider
could be an obstacle. Otherwise, we deduct `health` from the Enemy game
object and check to see if it's dead.

10. Now, let's enter Unity's `Update` function for the bullet's movement:

```
void Update ()
  {
    transform.position += new
      Vector3(travelSpeed,0,0)*Time.deltaTime;
  }
```

The `Update` function adds to its x-axis each frame based on its `travelSpeed` value multiplied by `Time.deltaTime` (`Time.deltaTime` is the time in seconds from the last frame).

 If you would like to know more about `Time.deltaTime`, check the documentation at `https://docs.unity3d.com/ScriptReference/ Time-deltaTime.html`.

11. Next, enter Unity's `OnBecameInvisible` function:

```
void OnBecameInvisible()
{
  Destroy(gameObject);
}
}
```

This last function will remove any unnecessary bullets that have left the screen. This will help the performance of our game and keep it tidy. Make sure to have saved the script before continuing.

Next, we need to apply the `PlayerBullet` script to our `Player_Bullet` prefab:

1. Navigate to `Assets/Resources/Prefab/Player` and select `Player_Bullet`.
2. With `Player_Bullet` selected, click the **Add Component** button in the **Inspector** window and type `PlayerBullet` until you see the `PlayerBullet` script.
3. Select the script and add the `PlayerBullet` asset to it from the **Bullet Model** field (drag the asset into the field or click the remote button to the right of its field).

The following screenshot shows our `Player_Bullet` with its script and asset:

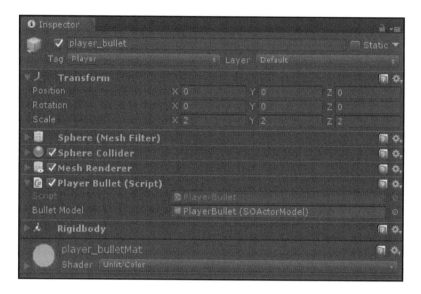

We can now move on to the next section about making enemies for the player to attack!

Planning and creating our enemy

We have a player that moves, shoots, and takes damage; we can now start looking into creating an enemy that shares these attributes.

To remind ourselves of the genre we are making, our game carries the same traits as classic arcade shooters such as Konami's *Gradius*, Capcom's *UN Squadron*, and Irem's *R-Type* (`https://raw.githubusercontent.com/retrophil/Unity-Certified-Programmer-Exam-Guide/master/Reference/shootEmUps.png`). Typically, with these types of games, the player is swarmed by enemies coming from the right of the screen and exiting to the left.

In this section, we will be repeating similar aspects of the `PlayerSpawner` and `Player` scripts. The `EnemySpawner` script needs to be tweaked so that it will instantiate a given number of enemy ships at a certain rate.

The Enemy game objects will be moving on their own, so there needs to be some extra code applied to their behavior. Before we go into creating our first enemy script, let's look at a part of our game framework and note the layout is basically the same as the player's side of the game framework:

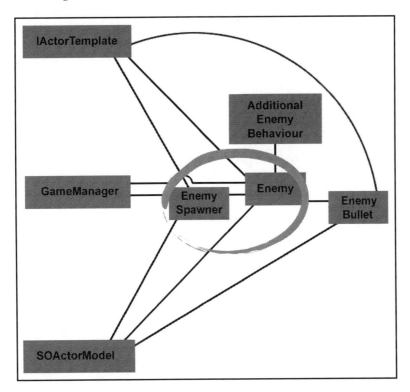

Before we jump into the EnemySpawner script, let's do the same housekeeping we did for our player game objects, namely creating an empty game object and storing all game objects relating to it in that one game object. The reason we did this is to remove the clutter in the **Hierarchy** window, so let's do the same for our enemies:

1. Right-click in the **Hierarchy** window's open space.
2. A drop-down list will appear, select **Create Empty**.
3. Name the game object _Enemies.

Let's move on to our enemy scripts.

Setting up our EnemySpawner and Enemy scripts

In this section, we are going to make a start on our EnemySpawner script and game object. The purpose of the EnemySpawner script is to have a game object spawn an enemy game object a series of times at a set rate. As soon as our testLevel scene begins, our enemy spawners will start releasing enemies. It will then be up to the enemies to move to the left of the screen. This is fairly simple, and as mentioned briefly in the previous section, the EnemySpawner uses the same interface and scriptable object as the PlayerSpawner to instantiate enemies. Let's start by creating our EnemySpawner script:

1. In the **Project** window in the Unity editor, create a script in the Assets/Resources/Scripts folder with the filename EnemySpawner.

2. Open the script and enter the following code:

   ```
   using System.Collections;
   using UnityEngine;
   ```

   As usual, we are using the default UnityEngine library to gain access to more functionality.

   We are also going to be using another library, called System.Collections. This is required when we come to using Coroutines, which will be explained later in this section.

3. Next, we will check/enter the class name and its inheritance:

   ```
   public class EnemySpawner : MonoBehaviour
   {
   ```

   Make sure the class is named EnemySpawner and that it also inherits MonoBehaviour by default.

4. Following on, add four global variables to the EnemySpawner script:

   ```
   [SerializeField]
   SOActorModel actorModel;
   [SerializeField]
   float spawnRate;
   [SerializeField]
   [Range(0,10)]
   ```

```
int quantity;
GameObject enemies;
```

All variables entered in the previous code have an accessibility level of `private`, and all of the variables apart from the `enemies` variable have a `SerializeField` and a `Range` attribute of between 0 to 10 applied. The reason for this is so that we or other designers can easily change the spawn rate and quantity of enemies from our `EnemySpawner` in the **Inspector** window, as shown in the following screenshot:

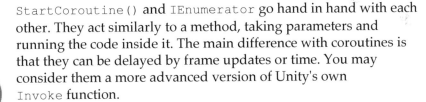

5. Now, let's enter Unity's `Awake` function along with some content:

```
void Awake()
{
    enemies = GameObject.Find("_Enemies");
    StartCoroutine(FireEnemy(quantity, spawnRate));
}
```

Inside the `Awake` function, we make an instance from the empty `_Enemies` game object divider and store it in the `enemies` variable.

The second line of code inside our `Awake` function is a `StartCoroutine`.

`StartCoroutine()` and `IEnumerator` go hand in hand with each other. They act similarly to a method, taking parameters and running the code inside it. The main difference with coroutines is that they can be delayed by frame updates or time. You may consider them a more advanced version of Unity's own `Invoke` function.

To find out more about coroutines and how to implement them in `IEnumerator` instances, check Unity's documentation at `https://docs.unity3d.com/ScriptReference/MonoBehaviour.StartCoroutine.html`.

This will be used to run our method of creating an enemy, but as you may also notice, it takes two parameters. The first is the `quantity` of enemies it holds and the second is the `spawnRate`, which delays each spawned enemy.

Next, in our `EnemySpawner` script, we have the `FireEnemy`, which will be used to run a cycle of creating and positioning each enemy, before waiting to repeat the process again.

6. Next, below and outside of the `Awake` function, we can add our `IEnumerator`:

```
IEnumerator FireEnemy(int qty, float spwnRte)
 {
  for (int i = 0; i < qty; i++)
  {
   GameObject enemyUnit = CreateEnemy();
   enemyUnit.gameObject.transform.SetParent(this.transform);
   enemyUnit.transform.position = transform.position;
   yield return new WaitForSeconds(spwnRte);
  }
   yield return null;
 }
```

Inside the `FireEnemy IEnumerator`, we start a `for` loop that will iterate over its `qty` value.

Within the `for` loop, the following is added:

- A method that we haven't covered yet, called `CreateEnemy`. The result of `CreateEnemy` will be returned into a game object instance called `enemyUnit`.
- The `enemyUnit` is the enemy flying out of the `EnemySpawner` game object.
- Our `EnemySpawner` position is issued to our `enemyUnit`.
- We then wait however many seconds the `spwnRte` value is set to.
- Finally, the process is repeated up until the `for` loop has reached its total.

7. Finally, below and outside of the `FireEnemy IEnumerator`, add the following method:

```
GameObject CreateEnemy()
 {
   GameObject enemy = GameObject.Instantiate(actorModel.actor)
     as GameObject;
   enemy.GetComponent<IActorTemplate>().ActorStats(actorModel);
   enemy.name = actorModel.actorName.ToString();
```

```
        return enemy;
    }
}
```

As we mentioned, there is a method called `CreateEnemy`. Apart from the obvious, this method will do the following:

- `Instantiate` the `enemy` game object from its `ScriptableObject` asset.
- Apply values to our enemy from its `ScriptableObject` asset.
- Name the enemy game object from its `ScriptableObject` asset.

Don't forget to save the script.

We can now move on to the next section where we will create and prepare the `EnemySpawner` with its game object.

Adding our script to the EnemySpawner game object

Finally, we need to attach our `EnemySpawner` script to an empty game object so that we can use it in our `testLevel` scene. To set up the `EnemySpawner` game object, do the following:

1. Create an empty game object and name it `EnemySpawner`.
2. Like what we did with the `_Player` and `PlayerSpawner`, we need to move the `EnemySpawner` game object inside the `_Enemies` game object in the **Hierarchy** Window.
3. After moving the `EnemySpawner` game object into the `_Enemies` game object, we now need to update the `EnemySpawner` game object **Transform** property values in the **Inspector** window:

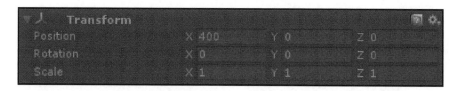

4. Still, in the **Inspector** window, click **Add Component** and type `EnemySpawner` until you see it in the list, then click it.

Also, for a visual aid in the **Scene** window, it is also recommended to add an **Inspector** icon to the `EnemySpawner` game object as we did with our `PlayerSpawner` game object in the *Creating the PlayerSpawner game object* section.

The following screenshot shows the icon I gave to my `EnemySpawner`:

We can now add an enemy to our **Enemy Spawner** along with **Spawn Rate** and **Quantity** values specified in the **Inspector** window. The following screenshot shows an example of a filled-in `EnemySpawner` game object with its script in the **Inspector** window:

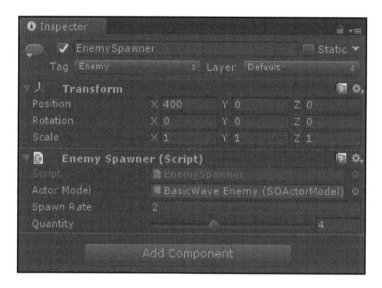

We can now move on to creating our enemy script in the next section.

Setting up our enemy script

Like our player ship being created from the `PlayerSpawner`, our first enemy will be created from its `EnemySpawner`. The enemy script will hold similar variables and functions but it will also have its own movement, similar to the `PlayerBullet` moving along its *x* axis.

Let's make a start and create our enemy script:

1. In the **Project** window of the Unity editor, create a script in the `Assets/Resources/Scripts` folder with the filename `EnemyWave`.

2. Open the script and check/enter the following required library code at the top of the script:

```
using UnityEngine;
```

Like the majority of our classes, we require the `UnityEngine` library for functionality.

3. Check and enter the class name and its inheritance:

```
public class EnemyWave : MonoBehaviour, IActorTemplate
{
```

We have a `public class` named `EnemyWave` that inherits `MonoBehaviour` by default but also adds our `IActorTemplate` interface.

4. Within the `EnemyWave` class, enter the following global variables:

```
int health;
int travelSpeed;
int fireSpeed;
int hitPower;

//wave enemy
[SerializeField]
float verticalSpeed = 2;
[SerializeField]
float verticalAmplitude = 1;
Vector3 sineVer;
float time;
```

The global variables for the `EnemyWave` class are the top four variables updated with values from its ScriptableObject asset. The other variables are specific to the enemy, and we have given two of these variables `SerializeField` attributes for debugging purposes in the **Inspector** window.

5. Add Unity's `Update` function along with its content:

```
void Update ()
{
```

```
        Attack();
    }
```

After the global variables, we add an `Update` function containing an `Attack` method.

6. Add our `ScriptableObject` method `ActorStats` and its content:

```
public void ActorStats(SOActorModel actorModel)
{
    health = actorModel.health;
    travelSpeed = actorModel.speed;
    hitPower = actorModel.hitPower;
}
```

We have our `ActorStats` method that takes in a `ScriptableObject` `SOActorModel`. This `ScriptableObject` then applies the variable values it holds and applies them to the `EnemyWave` script's variables.

7. Still in the `EnemyWave` script, add the `Die` method along with its content:

```
public void Die()
{
    Destroy(this.gameObject);
}
```

Another familiar method if you have been following along is the `Die` method, which is called when the enemy has been destroyed by the player.

8. Add Unity's `OnTriggerEnter` function to the `EnemyWave` script:

```
void OnTriggerEnter(Collider other)
{
    // if the player or their bullet hits you.
    if (other.tag == "Player")
    {
        if (health >= 1)
        {
            health -= other.GetComponent<IActorTemplate>
                ().SendDamage();
        }
        if (health <= 0)
        {
            Die();
        }
```

```
        }
    }
```

Unity's own `OnTriggerEnter` function will check to see whether they have collided with the player and if so, will send damage and the enemy will destroy themselves with the `Die` method.

9. Continue on and enter the `TakeDamage` and `SendDamage` methods:

```
public void TakeDamage(int incomingDamage)
    {
      health -= incomingDamage;
    }
public int SendDamage()
    {
      return hitPower;
    }
```

Another common set of methods from the `IActorTemplate` interface is to send and receive damage from the `EnemyWave` script.

Next is the `Attack` method, which controls the movement/attack of the enemy. This method is called in the `Update` function on every frame.

With this attack, we will have it so the enemy moves from right to left in a wavy animation (like a snake) instead of just going straight right to left. The following image shows our enemies moving from right to left in a wavy line:

10. Enter the following `Attack` method code into the `EnemyWave` script:

```
public void Attack()
    {
      time += Time.deltaTime;
      sineVer.y = Mathf.Sin(time * verticalSpeed) *
verticalAmplitude;
      transform.position = new Vector3(transform.position.x
         + travelSpeed * Time.deltaTime,
      transform.position.y + sineVer.y,
      transform.position.z);
    }
```

The `Attack` method starts with `Time.deltaTime` being collected into a `float` variable labeled `time`.

We then use a premade function from Unity that returns sine (`https://docs. unity3d.com/ScriptReference/Mathf.Sin.html`) using our `time` variable, multiplied by a set speed from the `verticalSpeed` variable, followed by the result being multiplied by `verticalAmplitude`.

The end result is stored in the `Vector3` *y* axis. What this basically does is make our enemy ship move up and down. The `verticalSpeed` parameter sets its speed and `verticalAmplitude` alters how far it goes up and down.

Then we do a similar task as we did with the `PlayerBullet` to make the enemy ship move along the *x* axis, and we also add a sine calculation to its `Y` position for it to move up and down.

Make sure to save the script before we wind down this chapter.

Before we summarize, click **Play** in the Editor and hopefully, if all is well, you will have a player ship that you will be able to fly around within the boundaries of the **Game** window's aspect ratio; enemies will come floating into the screen and move from right to left; you will be able to destroy these enemies with your bullets. These enemies will also be able to destroy you if they make contact with you. Finally, our **Hierarchy** window is all neat and well structured both before and after playing our game. The following screenshot shows what I have just explained:

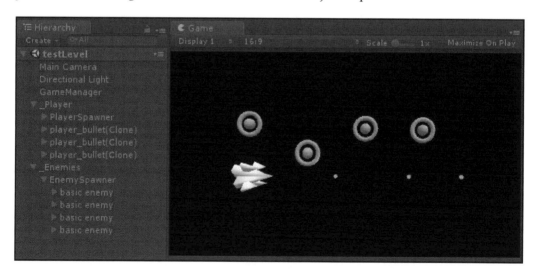

You have done so much already! The good news is you've just conquered one of the biggest chapters in the book – quite sneaky of me, I know. But we already have the backbone of our game and most importantly, we've covered a good chunk of the Unity Programmer exam.

Understandably you may have come across some possible issues on the way, and you may feel stuck. Don't worry if this is the case – check the `Complete` folder for this chapter to load up the Unity project and compare the code in that folder with your own to double-check. Make sure you have the right game objects in your scene, check that the right game objects are tagged, check the radius size of your **Sphere** colliders, and if you have any errors or warnings appear in the **Console** window double-click them and it will take you to the code that's causing an issue.

Let's wrap up this chapter and talk about our game so far.

Summary

We have reached the end of this chapter, and we have conquered the majority of our game framework, as we can see in the following diagram:

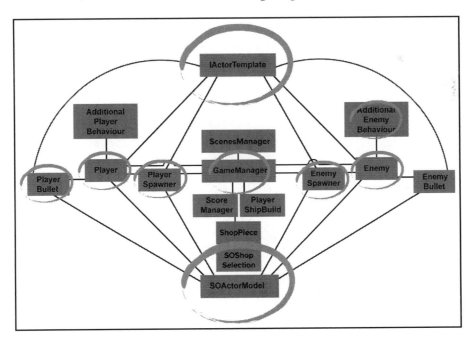

We have created a game framework that would need only a few changes if we added 1 or 1,000 more enemies to our game. Some of the benefits of this use of reusable code and `ScriptableObject` is that it will benefit non-programmers, save time, and prevent collaborators from being bogged down in the code.

We have also made it so that if and when we want to add more `EnemySpawner` points, we can drag and drop more prefabs into our scene and update its `ScriptableObject` to change the enemy without coding in exact `Vector3` locations.

We've covered other common Unity features including instantiating game objects such as enemies and player bullets.

In the next chapter, we will be covering the following scripts:

- `ScoreManager`: When an enemy is destroyed, the player will receive a score.
- `ScenesManager`: If the player dies, one life will be deducted; if the player loses all of their lives, the level will reset.
- `Sounds`: Our ships and bullets will also have added sounds.

Finally, we will be updating the overall structure of our code.

3
Managing Scripts and Taking a Mock Test

In this chapter, we are going to continue structuring our game by applying a **Singleton** design pattern to our `GameManager` script. This will allow our game to move on to another scene while keeping the script managers functioning and preventing them from being wiped (thereby preserving our data). We will then make a start with other details of our script and observe how information (such as the player's lives) travels through the game's frameworks. If and when the player dies, a life is deducted. If and when the player loses all of their lives, the game over scene will be triggered.

We will be extending our original code and introducing enemy points so that when we hit our enemies with bullets, the enemy will disappear as usual but will also generate points. This scoring mechanism will be handled by a new score manager that we will be creating.

We'll also be adding sound to the player's bullets, which is a simple, straightforward task. This will introduce us to extending and tweaking our audio sources, which we'll proceed with in a later chapter.

Finally, we will be quizzing ourselves with a couple of questions that suit the theme of this book, preparing you for the exam. The questions will cover what we have already learned, and if you have been following along with this book, you'll have a strong chance of passing.

By the end of this chapter, we will have extended our game's framework, added more features to our game, and tested our knowledge with some Unity exam questions.

In this chapter, we will be covering the following topics:

- Adding a **Singleton** design pattern
- Setting up our `ScenesManager` script

- Creating lives for the player
- Scoring enemy hits
- Creating sounds for the player's bullets
- Mock test

The next section will introduce the core exam skills that are covered in this chapter.

The core exam skills covered in this chapter

Programming core interactions:

- *Implementing and configuring game object behavior and physics*

Programming for scene and environment design:

- *Determining scripts for implementing audio assets*
- *Identifying methods for implementing game object instantiation, destruction, and management*

Working in professional software development teams:

- *Recognizing techniques for structuring scripts for modularity, readability, and reusability*

Technical requirements

The project content for this chapter can be found at `https://github.com/PacktPublishing/Unity-Certified-Programmer-Exam-Guide/tree/master/Chapter03`.

You can download the entirety of each chapter's project files at `https://github.com/PacktPublishing/Unity-Certified-Programmer-Exam-Guide/archive/master.zip`.

All content for this chapter is held in the chapter's `unitypackage` file, including a `Complete` folder that holds all of the work we'll carry out in the chapter.

Check out the following video to see the Code in Action: `https://bit.ly/2VgL1W5`.

Adding a Singleton design pattern

As you will recall, back in Chapter 1, *Setting Up and Structuring Our Project*, we spoke about design patterns and how useful they are to help maintain our code. One of the design patterns we briefly covered was the **Singleton** pattern. Without repeating ourselves, the **Singleton** pattern gives us global access to code that can then be obtained nearly at a point in our game. So, where can we see the benefits of using the **Singleton** design pattern? Well, we could use it so that Unity always keeps certain scripts accessible, no matter what scene we are in. We have already added a lot of structuring to our game framework and we still have a couple of manager scripts to add, such as ScoreManager and ScenesManager.

Now is a good time to make it so that all of the manager scripts have global access to all other scripts in the game. Managers give a general overview of what is going on and steer which way the game needs to go without getting caught up in the details of the other scripts that are running during gameplay.

In our current setup, when we run the testLevel scene, our GameManager object is in the **Hierarchy** window. We also have—and will be adding—more manager scripts to this game object. Currently, when we change scenes, our GameManager script, which sets up our scene's camera and lights, is no longer present.

To stop our GameManager game object and script from being wiped, we are going to add a **Singleton** design pattern so that our GameManager script will always be in the scene. This design pattern will also make it so that there is only one GameManager script (which is where this design pattern gets its name from).

In the following instructions, we will extend our original GameManager code to work as a **Singleton** script. Double-click on the GameManager script and let's make a start:

1. At the beginning of the class, we need to add a static variable and a public static property, both referring to our GameManager script:

   ```
   static GameManager instance;
   public static GameManager Instance
   {
     get { return instance; }
   }
   ```

   The reason we do this is that static means there is only one type of game manager. This is what we want; we don't want to have multiple versions of the same manager.

2. Next, we need to check and assign our `instance` variable with the `GameManager` class when the script begins with the `Awake` function.

3. The `Awake` function ends with a Unity function called `DontDestroyOnLoad`. This will make sure the game object holding our `GameManager` class will not be destroyed if the scene changes.

 If the player dies and loses all their lives, we can move from the level scene we are on to the `gameOver` scene, but we won't wipe the `GameManager` game object out from the scene as this holds the main core methods to run the game.

4. Add an `else` loop to avoid any possible duplicate `GameManager` game objects. We can see these two steps in the following code block:

```
void Awake()
{
  if(instance == null)
  {
    instance = this;
  }
  else
  {
    Destroy(this.gameObject);
  }
  DontDestroyOnLoad(this);
}
```

5. To make our code easier to identify, wrap the code we just typed out in the `Awake` function and put it in a method called `CheckGameManagerIsInTheScene`.

6. Call the method from the `Awake` function.

 A similar method to `DontDestroyOnLoad` is `MoveGameObjectToScene`, which can be used to carry a single game object over to another scene. This could be useful for moving a player from one scene to another:

https://docs.unity3d.com/ScriptReference/SceneManagement. SceneManager.MoveGameObjectToScene.html

That's it, our **Singleton** design pattern is done! The following screenshot shows a snippet of what our `GameManager` script should look like:

```csharp
using UnityEngine;

17 references
public class GameManager : MonoBehaviour
{
    static GameManager instance;

    public static GameManager Instance
    {
        get { return instance; }
    }
    void Awake()
    {
        CheckGameManagerIsInTheScene();
    }

    1 reference
    void CheckGameManagerIsInTheScene()
    {
        if(instance == null)
        {
            instance = this;
        }
        else
        {
            Destroy(this.gameObject);
        }
        DontDestroyOnLoad(this);
    }
}
```

7. Finally, save the `GameManager` script.

We have created a **Singleton** design pattern that will not be wiped away when we alternate through the scenes in our game, giving us global control of our game no matter which scene we are in.

Now, we can jump into adding the `ScenesManager` script and attaching it to the same game object as `GameManager` (in its **Inspector** window).

Setting up our ScenesManager script

We will take some responsibility away from the GameManager script by making another manager script to be more consistent with the data and methods it holds. ScenesManager will take and send information to and from GameManager. The following diagram shows how close to GameManager our ScenesManager script exists within the framework when only communicating with GameManager:

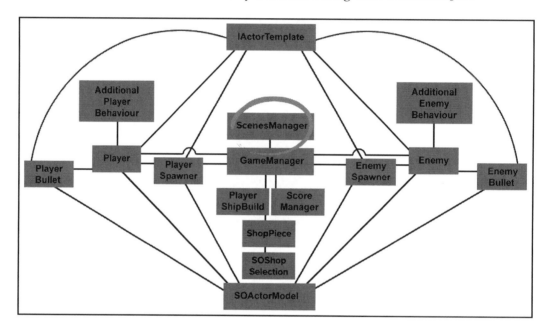

The purpose of ScenesManager, apart from taking the workload off GameManager, is to hold the role of dealing with anything related to creating or changing a scene. This doesn't mean we focus on only adding and removing game levels; a scene can also consist of a start-up logo, a title screen, a menu, and a game over screen, all of which are part of the ScenesManager script's responsibility.

In this section, we will be setting up a scene template and two methods. The first method will be responsible for resetting the level if the player dies (ResetScene()); the second will be the game over screen (GameOver()).

Let's make a start by creating a new script in the same way that we did in Chapter 2, *Adding and Manipulating Objects*. Follow these steps:

1. Name the script ScenesManager.

2. Add the script to the GameManager game object. If you need further details on adding a script to a game object, check out the *Adding our script to a game object* section of the previous chapter.

3. With our GameManager game object selected from the **Hierarchy** window, go to the **Inspector** window. We should now have the GameManager and ScenesManager scripts attached, as in the following screenshot:

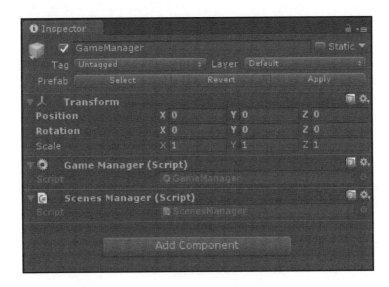

Let's open the ScenesManager script and start coding:

1. Because we are obviously going to be closing and loading scenes, we are going to need to import an extra library into our ScenesManager script that supports these operations:

   ```
   using UnityEngine.SceneManagement;
   using UnityEngine;
   ```

2. We will have a public class in our script name, followed by the usual MonoBehaviour being inherited:

   ```
   public class ScenesManager : MonoBehaviour
   {
   ```

Now, we need to create a list of references for our scenes, as mentioned earlier. I currently have the following scenes labeled:

- bootUp: Credits to game
- title: Name of the game with an instruction to start
- shop: Buy upgrades before starting the game
- level1: First level
- level2: Second level
- level3: Final level
- gameOver: Game over—delays until going back to the title scene

We will be labeling these scenes as enumerations (which is recognized as enum in the C# language). These values stay consistent.

 If you would like to know more about enumeration, check out https://docs.microsoft.com/en-us/dotnet/csharp/language-reference/keywords/enum.

3. Enter the following code into the ScenesManager script:

```
Scenes scenes;
public enum Scenes
{
    bootUp,
    title,
    shop,
    level1,
    level2,
    level3,
    gameOver
}
```

We will be making and adding these scenes in their respective order in the Unity editor. Before we do so, let's add two methods, starting with the ResetScene() method, which is typically used when the player dies and the current level is reloaded. The other method, GameOver(), is typically called when the player loses all of their lives or when the game has completed.

Adding the ResetScene() method

The ResetScene() method will be called when the player loses a life but still has another remaining. In this short method, we will set its accessibility to public and it returns nothing (void).

Within this method, we will refer to Unity's SceneManager script (not to be confused with our ScenesManager class), followed by Unity's LoadScene method. We now need to provide a parameter to tell LoadScene which scene we are going to load.

We use Unity's SceneManager script again, but this time we use GetActiveScene().buildIndex, which basically means getting the value number of the scene. We send this scene number to SceneManager to load the scene again (LoadScene):

```
public void ResetScene()
{
    SceneManager.LoadScene(SceneManager.GetActiveScene().buildIndex);
}
```

A small but effective method, this can be called whenever we need the scene to reset. Let's now move on to the GameOver() method.

Adding the GameOver() method

This method, as you can expect, is called when the player has lost all of their lives and the game ends, which means we need to move the player on to another scene.

In this method, we continue adding to the ScenesManager script:

```
public void GameOver()
{
    SceneManager.LoadScene("gameOver");
}
}
```

Similar to the previous method, we refer to this method as public with void return. Within the method, we call the same Unity function, SceneManager.LoadScene, but this time, we call the SceneManager Unity function, followed by the name of the scene we want to load by name (in this case, gameOver).

SceneManager.LoadScene also offers a LoadSceneMode function, which gives us the option of using one of two properties. By default, the first property is Single, which closes all the scenes and loads the scene we want. The second property is Additive, which adds the next scene alongside the current one. This could be useful when swapping out scenes, such as a loading screen, or keeping the previous scene's settings. For more information about LoadScene, check out https://docs.unity3d.com/ScriptReference/SceneManagement.LoadSceneMode.html.

That's our GameOver() method made, and when used in the same way as our ResetScene() method, it can be called globally. GameOver() can be called not only when the player loses all their lives but also when the user completes the game. It can also be used if, somehow, the game crashes, and as a default reset, we proceed to the gameOver scene.

The next method to bring into our ScenesManager script is BeginGame(). This method is called when we need to start playing our game.

Adding the BeginGame() method

In this short section, we will add the BeginGame() method to our ScenesManager script as this will be called to start playing our game after visiting the shop scene, which we will cover in Chapter 5, *Creating a Shop Scene for Our Game*.

With the ScenesManager script still open from the previous section, add the following method:

```
public void BeginGame()
{
  SceneManager.LoadScene("testLevel");
}
```

The preceding code that we have just entered makes a direct call to run the testLevel scene, which we play our game in already. However, as our game begins to grow, we will use more than one scene.

The next thing to do is to create our scenes and add them to the Unity build menu, so let's do that next. Remember to save the ScenesManager script before returning back to the Unity editor.

Adding scenes to our Build Settings window

Our game will consist of multiple scenes through which the player will need to navigate before they can fly their spaceship through the levels. This will result in them either dying or completing each level and the game, then being taken back to the `title` scene. This is also known as a game loop. Let's start by going back to Unity and in the **Project** window, creating and adding our new scenes. Follow theses steps:

1. Go to the `Assets/Scene` folder that we created at the beginning of the previous chapter.

2. Inside the **Scene** folder, in the open space, right-click so that the dropdown appears, then click **Create**, followed by **Scene**, as in the following screenshot:

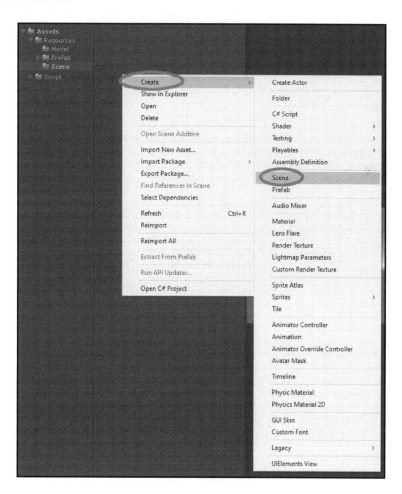

3. A scene file will appear. Rename it `bootUp`.
4. Repeat this process for the `shop`, `level1`, `level2`, `level3`, `gameOver`, and `title` scene files.

Once we have made all of our scenes, we need to let Unity know that we want these scenes to be recognized and applied to the project build order. This is a similar process to what we did in the last chapter when adding `testLevel` to the **Build Settings** window. To apply the other scenes to the list, do the following:

1. From the top of the Unity editor, click on **File | Build Settings**.
2. The **Build Settings** window will open and you should have `testLevel` in the list already. If you don't, fear not as we will be adding all our scenes to the **Scenes In Build** list.
3. From the **Project** window, click and drag each scene into the **Build Settings | Scenes in Build** open space.

Once we have added all the scenes, order them as follows:

- `bootUp`
- `title`
- `shop`
- `testLevel`
- `level1`
- `level2`
- `level3`
- `gameOver`

 Note that each scene automatically has a camera and a light by default in its **Hierarchy** window. This is fine and we will customize them later on in this book.

The **Build Settings** window should now look as follows:

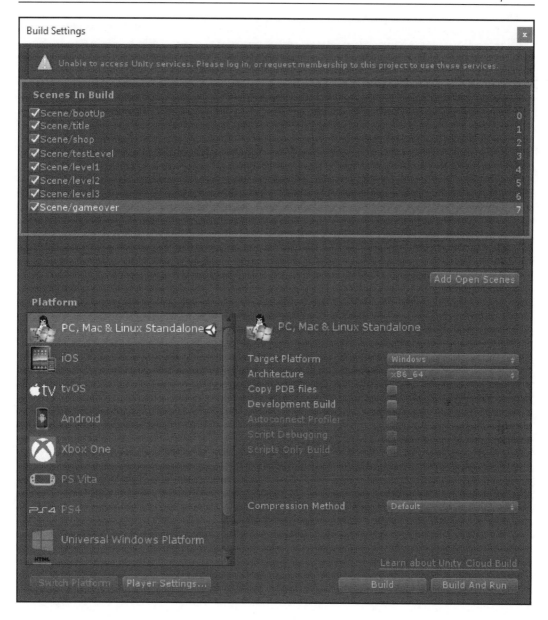

The reason why we are putting our scenes in this order is so that there is a logical progression in the levels. As you can see at the far right of each scene in the previous screenshot, the scenes are counted in increments.

Now that we have added multiple scenes to our game, we can consider the fact that we may not want our camera and light setup methods in our GameManager method to run in every scene of our game. Let's briefly return to our GameManager script and update our LightSetup and CameraSetup methods, as well as a few other things.

Updating our GameManager script

In this section, we are going to return to the GameManager script and make it so that the CameraSetup and LightSetup methods are called when we are controlling our spaceship only.

To update our GameManager script to support various scenes for our lights and camera, we need to do the following:

1. In the Unity editor, navigate to Assets/Resources/Script/GameManager from the **Project** window.

2. In the GameManager script, scroll down to the Start function and remove the LightSetup(); and CameraSetup(); methods.

3. Next, we will enter two static global variables at the top of the GameManager script with the rest of the global variables:

```
public static int currentScene = 0;
public static int gameLevelScene = 3;

bool died = false;
public bool Died
{
 get {return died;}
 set {died = value;}
}
```

currentScene is an integer that will keep the number of the current scene we are on, which we will use in the following method. The second variable, gameLevelScene, will hold the first level we play, which we will use later on in this chapter.

4. Still in the GameManager script, create an Awake function and enter the following code:

```
void Awake()
{
    CheckGameManagerIsInTheScene();
    currentScene = UnityEngine.SceneManagement.SceneManager.
```

```
                   GetActiveScene().buildIndex;
             LightandCameraSetup(currentScene);
      }
```

In the code we just entered, we store the `buildIndex` number (the numbers we have to the right of each scene in our **Build Settings** window from the previous section) in the `currentScene` variable. We then send the `currentScene` value to our new `LightandCameraSetup` method.

5. The last piece of code to add to our `GameManager` script is the `LightandCameraSetup` method, which takes an integer parameter:

```
      void LightandCameraSetup(int sceneNumber)
      {
        switch (sceneNumber)
        {
          //testLevel, Level1, Level2, Level3
          case 3 : case 4 :case 5: case 6:
          {
            LightSetup();
            CameraSetup();
            break;
          }
        }
      }
```

In the code we just wrote, we ran a `switch` statement to check the value of the `sceneNumber` variable, and if it falls into the 3, 4, 5, or 6 values, we run `LightSetup` and `CameraSetup`.

6. Save the `GameManager` script.

To reflect on this section, we have created a structure of empty scenes that will each serve a purpose in our game. We have also created a `ScenesManager` script that will either reset a scene when the player wins or dies and/or move to the game over scene.

Now that we have our scenes in place and the start of the `ScenesManager` script has been built, we can focus on the player's life system.

Creating lives for the player

In this section, we are going to make it so that the player has a set number of lives. If and when the player collides with an enemy, the player will die, the scene will reset back to the start, and a life will be deducted from the player. When all the lives are gone, we will introduce the game over scene.

We will be working with the following scripts in this section:

- GameManager
- SceneManager
- Player

Let's start by revisiting the GameManager script and setting up the capability of giving and taking the player's lives away:

1. Open the GameManager script and enter the following code:

    ```
    public static int playerLives = 3;
    ```

    At the top of the script, just after entering the class and inheritance, enter a static (meaning only one) integer type labeled playerLives, along with the value 3.

    Next, we need to create a new method for our GameManager script that will ensure the player loses a life. After we make this new method, the Player script will call it when it makes contact with an enemy.

    Let's continue with our GameManager script.

2. To create the LifeLost method, enter the following code in our GameManager class:

    ```
    public void LifeLost()
    {
    ```

    We need this to be a public method so that it can be accessed from outside of the script. It's set to void, meaning nothing is returned from the method, and it's followed by the name of the method with empty brackets as it isn't taking any arguments.

3. So, within the `LifeLost()` method, we will check the player's lives with an `if` statement with the following code:

```
//lose life
if (playerLives >= 1)
{
    playerLives--;
    Debug.Log("Lives left: "+playerLives);
    GetComponent<ScenesManager>().ResetScene();
}
```

After reviewing the `if` statement code we have entered, we will make a start by adding a comment to let ourselves or other developers know what this condition is doing (`//lose life`). We will then add the `if` statement condition checking whether the player has more than or equal to one life left. If the player does have one or more lives left, we will deduct the player's lives by 1 with the `--` operator, which is just a quicker way of saying `playerLives = playerLives - 1;`

The line of code following on from the deduction of the player's lives isn't required, but it will notify us, in the Unity editor **Console** window, with an information box telling us how many lives the player has left (for debugging purposes), as in the following screenshot:

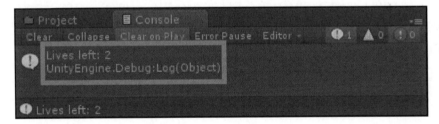

Following on from displaying how many lives the player has left in the **Console** window, we will refer to the `ScenesManager` script, which is attached to the `GameManager` game object. We can use `GetComponent` to access the `ScenesManager` script's `ResetScene` method, which will reset our scene back to the start.

4. We will now enter the `else` condition, which indicates that the player has died:

```
else
{
    playerLives = 3;
```

```
        GetComponent<ScenesManager>().GameOver();
    }
}
```

If our player doesn't have any more lives left, that means the `if` statement condition isn't met, so we can then offer an `else` condition. Within the scope of our `else` statement, we reset our player's lives back to 3.

We then access the `GameOver()` method from the `ScenesManager` class, which will take us from the scene we are on over to the `gameOver` scene.

Lastly, all that we need to do now is to make our `Player` script call the `LifeLost` method when the player has collided with the enemy or the enemy's bullets:

1. Save the `GameManager` script.
2. From the **Project** window, navigate to the `Player` script (`Assets/Resources/Script`).
3. Scroll down to its `Die` method.
4. Starting from above the destroy line (`Destroy(this.gameObject);`), enter the following code:

   GameManager.Instance.LifeLost();

   Note that we can call the `GameManager` script directly without finding the game object in the scene by using code such as `GetComponent` to acquire a script. This is the power of using the **Singleton** design pattern, calling directly to the `LifeLost` method.

5. Save the `Player` script.
6. Press **Play** in the Unity editor and collide with an enemy.

   The level should reset with a message in the **Console** window showing that we have a particular number of lives left. Repeat this three more times. On the third life lost, our scene should have changed from `testLevel` to `gameOver`.

   The following screenshot shows the **Console** window tab selected and logging the lives that are lost; also above the **Console** section is the **Hierarchy** window, showing that our game has gone from `testLevel` to the `gameOver` scene:

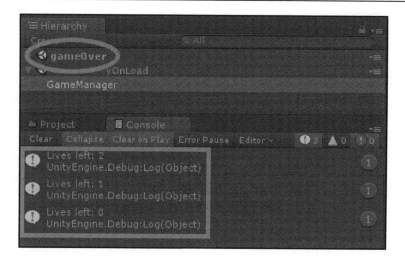

With minimal code, we have now made it so that our player has a number of lives. We have introduced a `ScenesManager` script into our game framework that talks directly to `GameManager`, regardless of restarting and changing scenes.

As a side note, you might have noticed that when we changed to the `gameOver` scene, our `GameManager` game object was carried over into the `gameOver` scene. If you recall back to the *Adding a Singleton Design Pattern* section, we set up the `CheckGameManagerIsInTheScene` method, which is called in the `Awake` function. This means that just because we are in a different scene, doesn't mean the `Awake` function is called again.

 Remember, the `Awake` function will only run when the script is active and will only run once—even if the script is attached to a game object and is carried through scenes.

This is because our `gameOver` scene only carried the `GameManager` game object over to the `gameOver` scene. It wasn't activated, which means the `Awake` function wasn't called.

We have our basic lives and scene structure and have also used the **Console** window to help us acknowledge the changes.

Before we move on, you may notice that when the player dies, the lights get darker in the scene. The following screenshot shows what I mean:

As you can see in the previous screenshot, on the left is the scene we start with and on the right is the scene that is reset when the player has died. To fix this, we just need to make it so that we generate our lighting manually instead of it being auto-generated by Unity.

To prevent our lighting from going dark between scenes, we need to do the following:

1. At the top of the Unity editor, click on **Window** | **Lighting** | **Settings**.

2. The **Lighting Settings** window will appear. At the bottom of the window, un-check **Auto Generate** and click on the button next to it, **Generate Lighting**. Use the following screenshot for reference:

3. This will take a minute as Unity will be setting up the new light settings. Once this is done, save the Unity project and that should fix it.

Note that we will likely need to set the lighting manually for other scenes, such as the other levels and the shop scene, later on in this book.

Let's now turn our focus to the enemy and add some functionality so that when it is destroyed by the player, we can add a score to ScoreManager, which is a new script that we will be making next.

Scoring enemy hits

As with most games, we need a scoring system to show how well the player has done at the end of the game. Typically, with side-scrolling shooter games, the player is rewarded for each kill they make. If we turn to our game framework diagram, we can see that ScoreManager is hooked up to GameManager like ScenesManager was:

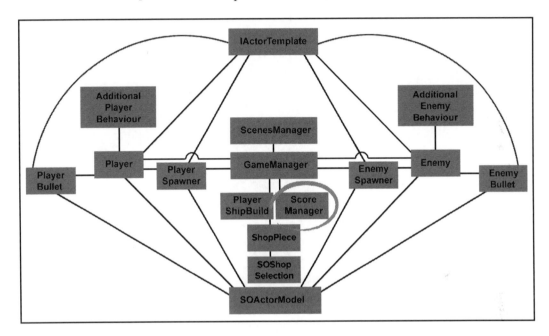

Our code for adding a scoring system will once again be minimal. We also want flexibility so that different enemies are worth different points. We also want it so that when we add another enemy to our game with a different scoring point, we can avoid altering our code each time.

We will be working with the following scripts in this section:

- EnemyWave
- ScoreManager
- ScenesManager
- SOActorModel

Seeing as the scoring system is an integral factor in our game, it would make sense to add a simple integer to `SOActorModel` that injects common values into our game objects. This trend will then follow on to other scripts. Let's start adding some code to our already-made scripts before we introduce `ScoreManager`.

Preparing the code for the ScoreManager script

If you recall back to `Chapter 1`, *Setting Up and Structuring Our Project*, we spoke about the SOLID principles and how important it is to add to our code rather than change it, else we risk errors and our code may start mutating toward being unfit for purpose. In order to prepare, we will add code to the scripts that we have already made to fit our `ScoreManager` script into place. Let's start with the `SOActorModel` first. Follow these steps:

1. Open the `SOActorModel` script from the **Project** window.
2. Anywhere within our list of variables' `SOActorModel` script, add the following code, which will be used to contain the enemy's score:

   ```
   public int score;
   ```

3. Save the `SOActorModel` script.

   Before we add more code to the other scripts to fit `ScoreManager` into our game, we need to acknowledge that we have made a change to our `ScriptableObject` template.

Let's check our `BasicWave Enemy` scriptable object in the Unity editor. Follow these steps:

1. From the **Project** window, navigate to the `Assets/Script/ScriptableObject` folder.
2. Click once on **BasicWave Enemy** and you will see that the **Inspector** window has a **Score** input field.
3. Give the **Score** field of `BasicWave Enemy` a value of your choice. I'm giving it a value of `200`. It really doesn't matter what value you give it as long as it's more than `0`. The following screenshot shows the **BasicWave Enemy** section with its updated **Score** value:

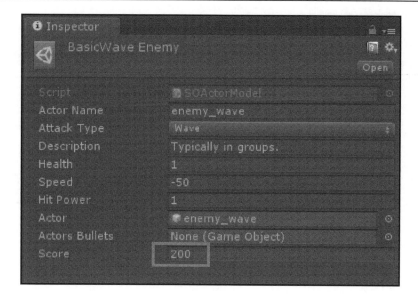

We have updated the `BasicWave Enemy` scriptable object. We now need to focus on the `EnemyWave` script to create and receive this new variable.

Open the `EnemyWave` script and enter the following code.

4. At the top of the script where we have our `health`, `travelSpeed`, and so on global variables, add an extra variable to the list:

```
int score;
```

We now need to update the `score` variable from the `ScriptableObject` value.

5. In the `EnemyWave` script, scroll down until you find the `ActorStats` method, then add the following extra line of code:

```
score = actorModel.score;
```

The `EnemyWave` script now has a `score` variable that is set from the value given to it by `SOActorModel`. The last thing we need to do is send the score value to `ScoreManager` when the enemy dies due to the actions of the player. Before we do that, let's create and code our `ScoreManager` script.

Setting up our ScoreManager script

The purpose of the `ScoreManager` script is to total up the score of the player during their game, concluding when they arrive at the `gameOver` scene. We could also give the `ScoreManager` script other score-related functionality, such as the ability to store our score data on the device that we are playing the game on or to send the score data to a server for an online scoreboard. For now, we will keep things simple and just collect the player's score.

We can create and add our `ScoreManager` script to the game framework, as follows:

1. Create and attach a script called `ScoreManager` to the `GameManager` game object, similar to how we did with `ScenesManager`.

   If you can't remember how to do this, then check the *Setting up our ScenesManager script* section of this chapter. The following screenshot shows `ScoreManager` attached to the `GameManager` game object in the **Inspector** window:

2. Next, we are going to open the `ScoreManager` script and add code that will hold and send score data. Open the `ScoreManager` script and enter the following code:

```
using UnityEngine;
```

Importing the usual `UnityEngine` library allows the majority of the functionality of Unity to work, such as `MonoBehaviour` being recognized in inheritance.

3. Continue on by checking and entering the name of the class:

```
public class ScoreManager : MonoBehaviour
{
```

This is a public class with `ScoreManager` inheriting `MonoBehaviour` to increase the functionality of the script.

4. Next, we add our variables and properties to our script. The only value we are concerned about is `playerScore`, which is private to the script (as we don't want other classes to have access). This variable is also set to `static`, meaning we don't need duplicate references for this variable.

Following on from this is our `public` property, which gives outside classes access to the `playerScore` variable. As you'll notice, the `PlayerScore` property returns an integer. Within this property, we use the `get` accessor to return our private `playerScore` integer. It is a good habit to keep our variables private, else you risk exposing your code to other classes, which can result in errors. The following code shows you how to complete this step:

```
static int playerScore;
public int PlayersScore
{
    get
    {
        return playerScore;
    }
}
```

To find out more about accessors, check out `https://docs.microsoft.com/en-us/dotnet/csharp/language-reference/keywords/get`.

5. We will now move on to the `SetScore` method; it is public and doesn't return a value (`void`), with the `SetScore` name taking in an integer parameter named `incomingScore`. Within this method, we use `incomingScore` to add to the `playerScore` script (as its total score):

```
public void SetScore(int incomingScore)
    {
        playerScore += incomingScore;
    }
}
```

6. The last method to add is the `ResetScore` method. Enter the following code:

```
public void ResetScore()
    {
        playerScore = 00000000;
    }
}
```

We can call this method at the beginning or end of a game to stop the score from carrying on into the next game.

7. Save the script.

As mentioned earlier, we can now return to the `EnemyWave` script to send the value of the enemy's score points to the `ScoreManagers` method, `SetScore`, thereby adding them to the player's total score:

1. Open the `EnemyWave` script from the **Project** window and scroll down to the `OnTriggerEnter` Unity function.
2. Within the scope of the `if` statement labeled `if (health <= 0)`, enter the following line of code at the top of its scope:

```
GameManager.Instance.GetComponent<ScoreManager>().SetScore(sco
re);
```

When this particular enemy dies as a result of the player, this line of code will send the enemy's `score` value directly to the `playerScore` variable and increment it toward its total until the player loses all of their lives.

3. Finally, to confirm the score has totaled correctly, let's do what we did before with the `playerLives` integer in the `LifeLost` method of the `GameManager` script and add a `Debug.Log` message to the **Console** window.

4. In the `ScenesManager` script under the `GameOver()` method, add the following line of code at the top within its scope:

```
Debug.Log("ENDSCORE: " +
    GameManager.Instance.GetComponent<ScoreManager>
        ().PlayersScore);
```

This code will tell us how much the player has scored because it directly accesses `ScoreManager` and grabs the `PlayerScore` property when the game is over. The following screenshot shows an example of a totaled score:

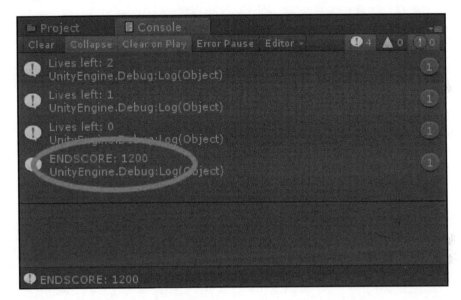

5. Finally, save all the scripts.

In this section, we introduced the `ScoreManager` script with its basic working structure of totaling up our end score and displaying the final count in the **Console** window. We have also added more code to a selection of scripts without deleting and changing any of their content. Next, we will be doing something different that doesn't involve any coding but gets us more familiar with Unity's sound components.

Creating sounds for the player's bullets

Up until now, our game has been silent, but sound is an important factor in any game. In this section, we will be introducing our first sound component. We will make a start by creating sound effects for when our player fires a bullet.

Feel free to add your own type of bullet sound if you wish. You can add sound to your player's standard bullets as follows:

1. In the Unity editor, navigate to the **Project** window and create a new folder inside the Resources folder. Name the new folder Sound.
2. Drag and drop the Player_Bullet prefab from the **Project** panel into the **Hierarchy** panel.
3. With Player_Bullet still selected, click on the **Add Component** button in the **Inspector** panel.
4. In its dropdown, start typing (and select) Audio Source.
5. Drag and drop the PlayerLaser.mp3 file into the **AudioClip** section of the **Audio Source** component. The following screenshot shows Player_Bullet selected. The audio file at the bottom left needs to be dragged into the **Audio Source** component at the right:

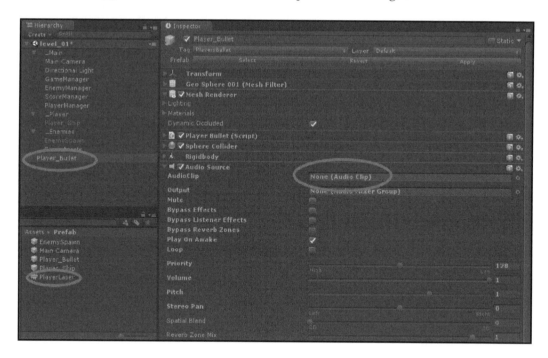

6. **Play on Awake** is automatically ticked. As you can imagine, as soon as Player_Bullet is instantiated, the sound will play.
7. If the volume is too high, simply lower it in the **Audio Source** component of the **Inspector** window.

As well as the **Volume** option in the **Audio Source** component, there is **Pitch** to change the sound of our bullet and **Stereo Pan** to make the sound more dominant on the left or right speaker. Finally, because this is a two-dimensional game, we don't want the sound to be affected by how close our camera is to the bullet. So, we slide the **Spatial Blend** toggle all the way to the left to make sure it is not affected by its distance.

8. Finally, click on **Apply** at the top-right corner to save and update the `Player_Bullet` prefab and remove the bullet from the **Hierarchy** window.
9. Play the scene and start firing. You will hear laser noises and in the scene view, you will see speaker symbols now attached to the player's bullets.

That brings us to the end of this short section on audio, but we will cover more on audio throughout this book. Don't forget that if you get stuck at any point, check the `Complete` folder for this chapter and compare the scenes and code to make sure nothing is missing.

Summary

In this chapter, we have extended our game framework structure by implementing and reinforcing the `GameManager` script by extending its code. This means that it will never be deleted, regardless of scene changes. We have also introduced the score and scenes managers, which were originally planned in our game framework. These two additional managers take responsibility away from the game manager and add additional features to your game. We ensured these scripts don't mutilate our original code (removing, overflowing, or compensating for our game manager). Your game now has a working scoring system, as well as multiple scenes that can be restarted and changed with very little code. We also introduced sound, which we'll implement in more detail in later chapters.

In the next chapter, we'll focus less on code-heavy content and instead concern ourselves with the art of the game. Even though we are programmers, we need to understand how to manipulate assets and how to animate with Unity's API. With just a little bit of coding, this will allow us to understand the connection between the editor and our script. We'll also touch on some particle effects.

Well done—you've done and covered a lot. Before we move on, have a go at the following questions. They resemble what you will encounter in your programmer exam.

Mock test

This is your first mini mock test. These tests represent sections of your final Unity exam. This first mini mock test consists of just five questions. Later on in this book, we'll introduce more mini mock tests with more questions.

Fortunately, you will only be tested on what we have covered so far:

1. You have been asked to develop a horror survival game where your player relies on a pocket torch. Here is what you've coded so far:

```
void Start()

{
    Light playersTorch = GetComponent<Light>();
    playersTorch.lightMapBakeType = LightMapBakeType.Mixed;
    playersTorch.type = LightType.Area;
    playersTorch.shadows = LightShadows.Soft;
    playersTorch.range = 5f;
}
```

You notice, however, that the player's torch isn't casting any light or shadows. What should you change for this code to work as desired?

A) Set `playersTorch.lightBakeType` to `LightmapBakeType.Realtime`.

B) Set `playersTorch.range` to `10`.

C) Set `playersTorch.shadows` to `LightShadows.Hard`.

D) Set `playersTorch.type` to `LightType.Point`.

2. You have started creating your first indie game, Super Moped Racer 64. You have coded your input controls to work with a joystick and started testing your moped around corners. You've noticed that after turning the moped around the first corner, the moped still turns even after you've let go of the joystick.

You've checked your code and the joystick and both seem to be working fine, suggesting the issue is with the input manager.

What change should you make within the input manager?

A) Increase the gravity.

B) Set `Snap` to `true`.

C) Increase `Deadzone`.

D) Decrease `Sensitivity`.

3. You have started to template a game framework with pen and paper. You have drawn up several manager scripts that will all lead to the creation of a single `GameManager` script. You only require one `GameManager` script, which will always be in your scene.

   Which design pattern suits having a `GameManager` script in a persistent instance role?

   A) **Prototype**

   B) **Abstract Factory**

   C) **Singleton**

   D) **Builder**

4. You have been requested to create a prototype for a side-scrolling game where your player throws rocks at their enemies. The game works well and the camera moves from left to right until the level is over. To throw a rock, your code instantiates a prefab of a rock, which is then given a force (`Rigidbody.AddForce`) to launch the rock to give the illusion of the rock being thrown.

   Your lead developer says that your method is costing too much in-memory performance and wants you to store a maximum of 10 rocks from within an array of rocks using a design pattern. Once a rock is used, instead of being destroyed, it should return to the array.

What design pattern is the developer referring to?

A) **Abstract Factory**

B) **Object Pool**

C) **Dependency Injection**

D) **Builder**

5. You and a few other developers have been using Unity's Collaborate service for a while with regular pushes. Everything is going well until you realize you have accidentally deleted a file from the project.

    What feature would you use to get this file back?

    A) **Collab History**

    B) **Profiler**

    C) **Services**

    D) **Inspector**

That's the end of your first mini mock test. To check your answers, refer to the *Appendix* section at the back of this book. How did you do? To review any incorrect answers, I suggest flicking back through the last couple of chapters to the relevant section and refreshing your memory where needed. Sadly, exams can be a bit of a memory game. Everyone's memory is different and the majority of people that pass these exams have failed on certain sections before passing.

Either way, the more you complete these tests, the stronger you will become at them. Just stay focused and you'll get through it!

4
Applying Art, Animation, and Particles

In this chapter, we'll apply several art effects to the player's ship and the scene that we previously created. We will use several maps that wrap around your player's ship to give it a sci-fi theme, including some pretty particle effects that we will add to our neon-blue jet. We will also introduce a space background, which will also be built from particle effects. Then, you will get your hands dirty by setting up your own Unity animator controller, which we can use to manipulate the particles we've created in our scene to give the impression that our player's ship is thundering through space at light speed, then slowing down before the enemies come to attack. Finally, we will apply some animation to the enemies in our script.

A lot of this chapter is about becoming familiar with what Unity can do as an editor and the majority of what we learn in the editor is also possible to achieve through code. This is why, as a programmer, it's important to know what we can manipulate in a project.

In short, we will be covering the following topics:

- Adding visuals to the player's ship
- Creating a particle effect
- Importing and animating scenery
- Animating three-dimensional enemies with a script

So, let's jump in and make a start on changing the appearance of the player's ship.

The core exam skills covered in this chapter

We will look at programming core interactions:

- *Implementing and configuring game object behavior and physics*

We will also look at working in the art pipeline:

- *Understanding materials, textures, and shaders, and writing scripts that interact with Unity's rendering API*
- *Understanding lighting and writing scripts that interact with Unity's lighting API*
- *Understanding two-dimensional and three-dimensional animation and writing scripts that interact with Unity's animation API*
- *Understanding particle systems and effects and writing scripts that interact with Unity's particle system API*

We will cover the programming for scene and environment design:

- *Identifying methods for implementing game object instantiation, destruction, and management*

Finally, we will cover working in professional software development teams:

- *Recognizing techniques for structuring scripts for modularity, readability, and reusability*

Technical requirements

The project content for this chapter can be found at `https://github.com/PacktPublishing/Unity-Certified-Programmer-Exam-Guide/tree/master/Chapter04`.

You can download the entirety of each chapter's project files at `https://github.com/PacktPublishing/Unity-Certified-Programmer-Exam-Guide/archive/master.zip`.

All the content for this chapter is held in the chapter's `unitypackage` file, including a `Complete` folder that holds all of the work we'll carry out in this chapter.

Check out the following video to see the Code in Action: `https://bit.ly/2VxvAsL`.

Adding visuals to the player's ship prefab

In this section, we will focus on the player's ship. We'll create a series of different art visual techniques to make our ship look futuristic without physically changing its geometry. We will create and apply a type of material to our ship that is used as housing to hold and display several maps. These maps are responsible for targeting specific channels on our player's ship. Because this book is specifically for programmers, I have created several of these maps that you can drag and drop into the material component that sits within the **Inspector** window.

Normally, if a three-dimensional model, such as the player's ship, has a texture applied to the model, the model needs to undergo a method called **unwrapping**. Unwrapping is like peeling off the faces of the model and laying them down flat so that they can have textures applied to them. Then, the unpeeled faces are wrapped back around the three-dimensional model. If the model isn't unwrapped before we apply the texture, the texture of the ship will be scrambled as it doesn't know where it should display the textures correctly. We don't need to go any further into the details of unwrapping as it's beyond the scope of this book, but just remember that the player's ship model has to be unwrapped.

The following screenshot shows the three-dimensional model of our player's ship on the left and its unwrapped version, which is textured, on the right:

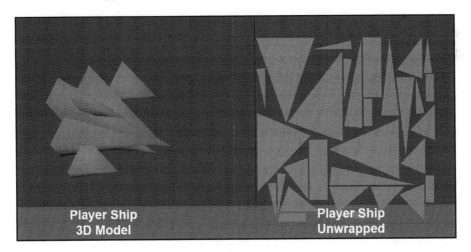

We will also be shining a colored light onto the ship, but only allowing certain parts of it to emit and ensuring the light doesn't shine on any other game object with Unity's layer system. The other major part of Unity that we will cover is the particle system; we will create our own particle jet that will animate from the rear of the ship.

The following screenshot shows what our player's ship looks like currently on the left. By the end of this section, we will have a sci-fi-looking ship with an animating jet, shown on the right side of the screenshot:

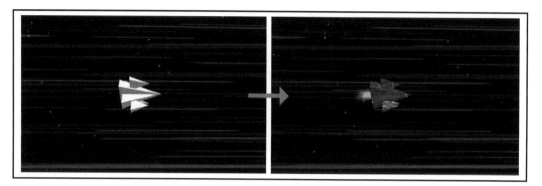

Let's now move on to creating a material that can be used to store the maps found in our chapter's `download` folder.

Creating a material for our player's ship prefab

Currently, our player's ship has a default material applied to it, which we can't edit in the Unity editor. To be able to change the ship's color and apply several maps, we first need to create a material and then apply it to the player's ship. To do this, follow these steps:

1. In the **Project** window, navigate to `Assets/Resources/Material/Player` and right-click in an open space.
2. Left-click on **Create** at the top.
3. Then, left-click on **Material**.
4. A material icon will appear, highlighted in blue.
5. Rename this material `PlayerShip`.

To rename a material when it isn't selected, left-click on the text below the icon twice to bring the blue highlight back up. Then, enter a name—in our case, `PlayerShip`.

The following screenshot shows how the material is created:

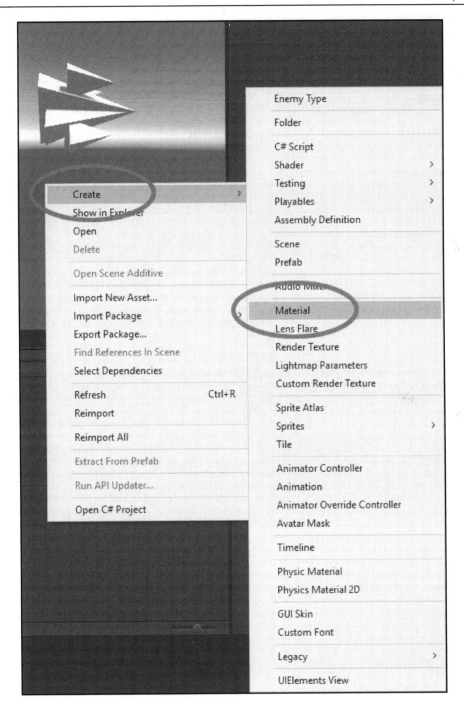

There are two ways to apply a material to the ship. The first and easiest way is to drag and drop the material to the `PlayerShip` model in the **Scene** view.

A material can be created and updated in the script through the `Renderer.material` **property**. Check out `https://docs.unity3d.com/ScriptReference/Renderer-material.html` to find out more.

The second—and probably the better—way, as it's a more controlled method in updating a material, is to select `PlayerShip` in the **Scene** window or select `PlayerShip` from its prefab folder. Then, in the **Inspector** window, do the following:

1. Next to the **Mesh Renderer** component is the **Materials** drop-down arrow. Click on the arrow so that it points downward.
2. The two main points to look for within the component are the following:

   - **Size**: How many materials are attached to this model. This should be set to `1`.
   - **Element 0**: This is the material that is currently attached, `Default-Material`.

3. Either click on the small button to the far right of `Default-Material` (or whatever the material is called), as in the following screenshot, or drag and drop the `PlayerShip` material we just made into the same location as `Default-Material`.

   The following screenshot shows the location of the **Mesh Renderer** component situated within the **Inspector** window:

Once that's done, **Element 0** will be updated to PlayerShip, **Size** will remain as 1, and Default-Material at the bottom of the **Inspector** window will now be editable and named PlayerShip (or whatever you named the material).

Default-Material cannot be edited as it is typically shared with new **Mesh Renderer** game objects.

Now, we need to update the ship's prefab (prefabs were explained in Chapter 1, *Setting Up and Structuring Our Project*). If the PlayerShip model is still selected, go to the **Inspector** window and click on the **Apply** button in the top-right corner. If you made changes directly to PlayerShip from the Prefab folder, this will not be necessary as we have updated the prefab directly. In the next section, we will break down the various maps we can now apply to the material.

Applying maps to our PlayerShip material

Our newly created material for our PlayerShip prefab is now able to hold various maps. Our material will have empty slots for each map; these maps will add details to the player's ship, ranging from the color to fake details, such as cuts, dents, and grooves, that aren't physically modeled into the player's ship. We can also emphasize where the light will be absorbed onto the player's ship.

Here is a selection of maps that we will apply to the PlayerShip prefab:

- **Albedo map** (playerShip_diff): The albedo map contains the color of the image, which is similar to a diffuse map but without light and shadow. The following screenshot shows our albedo map:

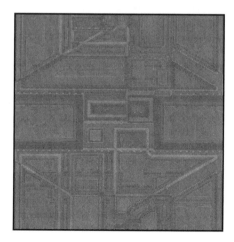

- **Metallic map** (`playerShip_met`): The metallic map focuses on the reflectivity and light of the surface. The following screenshot shows our metallic map:

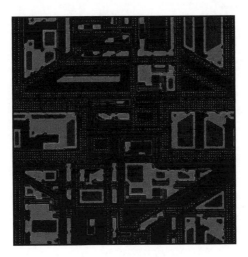

- **Emissive map** (`playerShip_em`): The emissive map receives no light, so any pixels are shown at full intensity, which is ideal for a glow-in-the-dark effect. The following screenshot shows our emissive map:

- **Normal map** (`playerShip_nrm`): The normal map stores the direction of each pixel. The general use for this map is holding high-resolution details that give the illusion of more polygons in a mesh. The following screenshot shows our normal map:

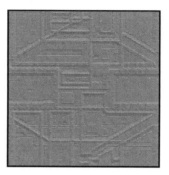

- **Occlusion map** (`playerShip_oc`): The occlusion map provides information on which areas of the model receive light. The following screenshot shows our occlusion map:

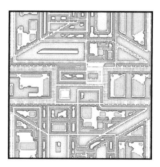

Now, we will apply these maps to the `PlayerShip` model by taking the following steps:

1. Select the `player_ship` game object, which can be selected in either the **Scene** or in the **Project** window (under the `Assets/Resources/Prefab/Player` file path location).

2. To make things easier when applying our maps to the `player_ship` material slots, lock the **Inspector** window while we still have `player_ship` selected at the top of the **Inspector** window, as in the following screenshot. (Make sure you unlock the **Inspector** window once you've finished dragging and dropping files over):

3. In the **Project** window, drag and drop each map file from the newly imported `Textures` folder into the `PlayerShip` material component slots. Check the following screenshot for reference:

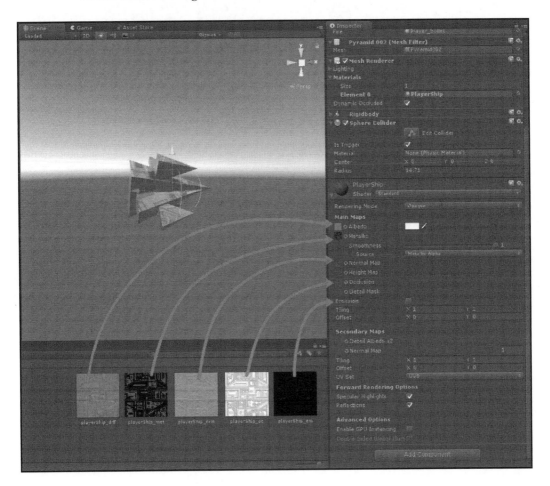

When it comes to applying a normal map, there are some extra procedures to cover. The first is that Unity may not recognize **Normal Map** as a normal map file. When we drag and drop the normal map file into its slot in the **Material** component, as in the previous screenshot, an information box appears in the **Inspector** window under the **Normal Map** slot. This contains a message (**This texture is not marked as a normal map**) with a **Fix Now** button. Click on this button so that the normal map is configured correctly. The following screenshot shows what the information box looks like:

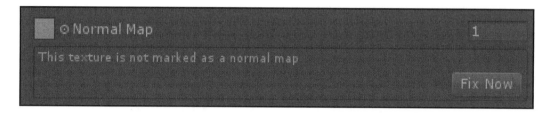

Another way of fixing this issue with the normal map is by doing the following:

1. Select the normal map file in the **Project** window.
2. Then, in the **Inspector** window, we have a panel showing the normal map's **Import Settings** option.
3. At the top of the options area, click on the dropdown next to **Texture Type** and make sure it is selected as a normal map.
4. Finally, click on **Apply** at the lower-right corner of the **Inspector** window.

The following screenshot shows a normal map file selected from the **Texture Type** dropdown and the **Normal map** selection in the dropdown:

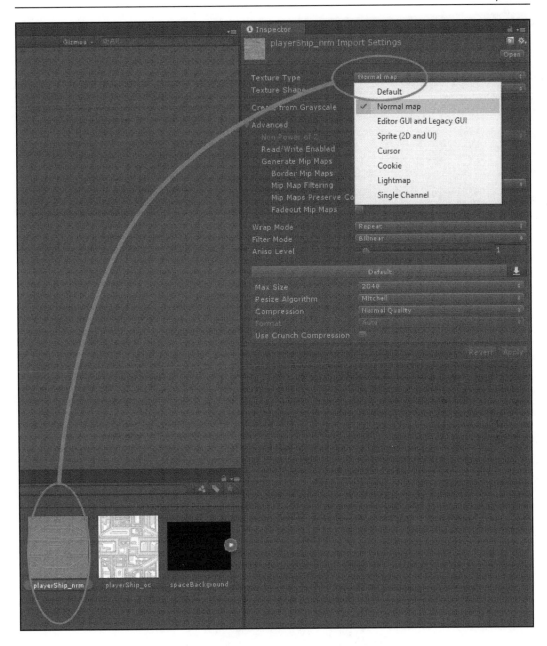

Another potential issue when dragging and dropping maps into the **Material** component is that you need to check the box next to the **Emission** slot before it can accept a map. The following screenshot highlights the **Emission** slot and shows you the box that needs to be checked:

 The material properties, such as the emission color, can be made and altered via script with the use of the `SetColor` property. For more information on changing a material's color or emission color, check out `https://docs.unity3d.com/ScriptReference/Material.SetColor.html`.

Once we have dragged and dropped all the maps into their designated slots, our `player_ship` model should look different as it now has a metallic complexion. However, we aren't finished yet. We need to add some neon lights to the ship next.

Adding neon lights to our PlayerShip prefab

Our ship currently looks like metal, slightly dull with some sci-fi-style patterns on it. As this isn't an art exam, our preliminary mission isn't to make this ship look fantastic, but rather to understand the maps and effects that we're adding to it. As mentioned briefly in the previous section, we can add some light to the ship that will also react to the ship's maps. The following screenshot shows what our ship currently looks like with all the maps applied; yours may be shiny, but that doesn't matter:

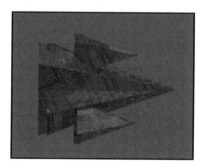

Next, we are going to make parts of the ship light up in a sci-fi neon-blue color, combining a **Point** light with the emissive map.

To add a light to our ship, we need to do the following:

1. From the **Project** window, navigate to `Assets/Resources/Prefab/Player`.
2. Select `player_ship` and drag it to the **Hierarchy** window.
3. Click on the **Add Component** button in the **Inspector** window and type `Light` into the dropdown.
4. When you see the **Light** component in the drop-down list, select it.

If the **Scene** window is too far away from the ship, select `player_ship` from the **Hierarchy** window, hover your mouse in the **Scene** window, and press *F* on your keyboard to zoom in.

This **Point** light will act as a glow around the ship that will affect only the player's ship and the emissive map with Unity's layer system. But first, we will focus on the **Light** component settings in the **Inspector** window:

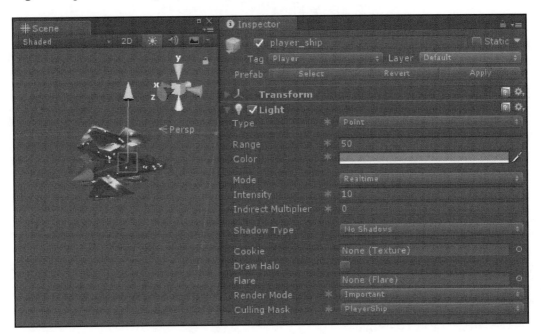

With the **Point** light selected from the **Hierarchy** window, we can alter our new light settings in the **Inspector** window:

- **Type (Point)**: At this stage, we can change the type of light without having to delete the light and add a new type. For this instance, we want a **Point** light. The player_ship will also have a yellow gizmo wrapped around it to represent the size of the light as shown in the following image:

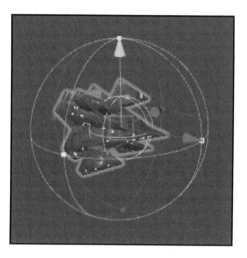

 A gizmo is an indicator that shows up in the **Scene** window, which you will not see in the **Game** window. A gizmo is displayed as guidance to show the location and/or the scale of something.

- **Range** (50): The range will increase/decrease the size of the yellow sphere, pushing the light out more. I have set mine to 50 as I feel this covers the ship well enough.
- **Color** (blue): I have gone for a light-blue color, but you can pick whatever color you wish to. If you want to use the same color as mine, do the following:

    1. Click on the current **Color** bar and the **Color** window will appear.
    2. At the bottom of the settings window, change the **Hex Color** value to 0080FFFF. (This will set the red, green, blue, and alpha settings).

- **Intensity** (10): The strength of the light.
- **Indirect Multiplier** (0): The light bouncing onto other objects. Real-time indirect bounce shadowing is not supported for the **Point** light.
- **Render Mode (Important)**: Makes sure the light remains on at all times and doesn't turn off with performance drops.
- **Culling Mask** (PlayerShip): We will talk about this next. We are using a blue light (in my case) to give the maps on the ship a neon light effect. We ideally don't want the light to spread onto other assets if they come near the player's ship.

 Play around with the **Light** component; don't feel like it has to have the exact color or intensity as mine.

Once these settings (apart from the culling mask) for our light have been updated in the **Inspector** window, our ship should have neon lights lit across it in various areas. In the following screenshot, I have placed eight spheres behind the player's ship model. Notice now how our new neon light clashes against the spheres. I'll explain how we can fix the issue of the light clashing with other objects in our game next:

A culling mask will fix this issue as we can make the blue light only display on the player's ship with a specific layer mask.

To make a new layer, we need to go to the **Tags & Layers** section, which can be accessed in two ways:

1. The first way is by clicking on the **Layers** tab at the top-right of the screen in the toolbar section. A dropdown will appear with the available layers. Click on the bottom option, **Edit Layers...**.

2. The second way is by selecting any game object in the **Hierarchy** window and clicking on the tab next to **Layer**. Then, click on the bottom option, **Add Layer...**:

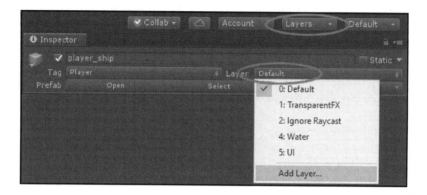

The **Tags & Layers** panel will appear within the **Inspector** window with grayed-out layers that cannot be edited as they are built-in. Also, it is recommended that you don't use layer 31 as it has an internal use for the editor.

3. Layers 8 to 30 are okay to use. I'm going to enter PlayerShip into the **User Layer 8** field, as in the following screenshot:

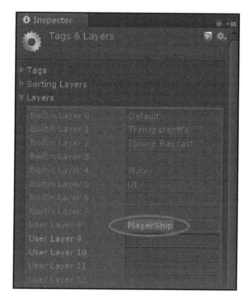

4. Now, click on the `player_ship` model in the scene or within the `Prefab` folder and change its point light **Culling Mask** option from **Everything** to **PlayerShip**:

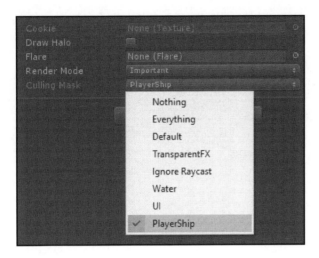

5. Then, select the `player_ship` model from **Hierarchy**.

6. In the `player_ship` **Inspector** window, change its layer to our newly created layer, `PlayerShip`. Because we added a **Point** light to our player's ship, we are given a warning asking us whether we want to change the children within the `player_ship` model.

7. Click **Yes, change children**, as in the following screenshot. This will change the **Point** light layer to **PlayerShip**:

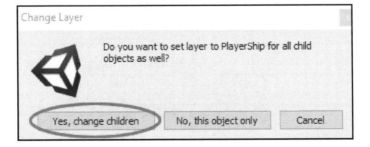

Once you have brought something into the **Hierarchy** window that typically doesn't remain in the scene, don't forget to remove it once you're done. As an example, the `player_ship` prefab will always be instantiated by `PlayerSpawner`.

The end result gives us a cool, neon shiny-blue ship that doesn't affect any of the surrounding game objects, as in the following screenshot (yours may differ from this):

So, let's now move on to the particles for the player's ship.

Adding particles to our PlayerShip prefab

In this section, we will create a particle effect that will give the ship's thrusters the illusion of movement. The particle system itself is split into different component categories that will affect the behavior of how a particle acts. We will focus on placement, direction, and the life cycle of a particle effect, which is a skill that can be transferred to other effects, such as fire, smoke, water leakage, and more. The following screenshot shows our player's ship with an animated particle effect, which we are going to create now:

So, let's make an empty game object to hold the particle system:

1. Right-click in an open space of the **Hierarchy** window.
2. From the drop-down menu that appears, select **Create Empty.**
3. Name the empty game object something such as `playerJet`.

4. We want this to follow the player's ship, so drag and drop the `player_ship` object back into the **Hierarchy** window and then drag and drop `playerJet` onto the `player_ship` game object.

5. Finally, we need to move `playerJet` to the rear of our `player_ship` object to the point where the particles start firing. I'm moving mine onto its **X** position by `0.5`.

The following screenshot indicates where the particles will start and the `playerJet` transform settings:

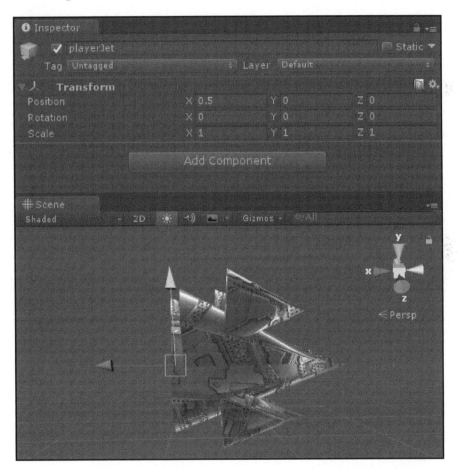

That's our empty game made and in place behind the player's ship model. Now, we can add our particle effect to the empty game object in the next section.

Creating a particle effect

In this section, we will start creating our particle effect within the empty game object from the previous section; similar to what we did a couple of sections back, we need to make all particle systems a child to the `playerJet` game object:

1. In the **Hierarchy** window, right-click on `playerJet`.
2. From the dropdown, select **Effects**, then **Particle System**.
3. Rename the **Particle System** game object `thruster`.

We should now see a particle system that gives out its default particle spray pointing directly at us, as in the following screenshot:

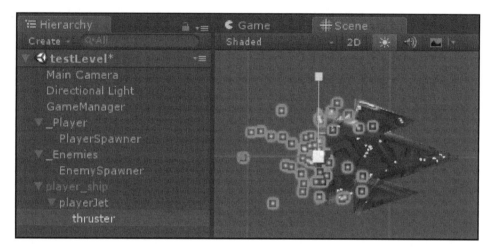

Next, we need to scale and rotate the particle system to the correct size and make sure it's spraying in the correct direction.

With our `thruster` object still selected, in the **Inspector** window, change its **Transform** component settings to the following:

- **Position**: **X**: 0, **Y**: 0, and **Z**: 0
- **Rotation**: **X**: 0, **Y**: 90, and **Z**: 0
- **Scale**: **X**: 0.3, **Y**: 0.3, and **Z**: 0.3

Sometimes, our **Particle System** object might not update or it might disappear in the **Scene** window when we alter or undo its settings.

To attempt to restart **Particle System** to active or animating in the **Scene** window, select **Particle System** in the **Hierarchy** window. You will notice a **Particle Effect** popup at the bottom-right corner of the **Scene** view. Then, take the following steps:

1. Click **Stop** to stop the **Particle System** object from emitting.
2. Click **Restart**.

   The following screenshot shows the **Particle Effect** menu found at the bottom-right corner of the **Scene** window:

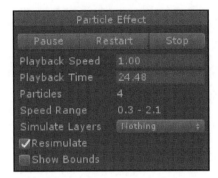

Hopefully, if the particle system wasn't active, it is now. If it still isn't, try selecting a different game object in the **Hierarchy** window, then go back to the particle system and repeat the stop/restart method again.

With our thruster particle system still selected in the **Hierarchy** window, click the drop-down button in the **Inspector** window, as in the following screenshot:

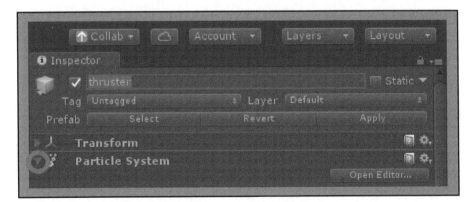

We are now presented with a list of options in the **Inspector** window that might seem overwhelming, but we will only be changing a few options to give our particle system the effect we are after. Most of the Unity properties have their own **ToolTips** options. If you don't know what any of these are, with the Unity editor top bar selected, hover your mouse over one of the particle system properties. After a few seconds, a description telling you about the properties will appear.

The options we need to change for our particle system are the following:

- **Duration**: The length of time the particle system emits particles. If the system is looping, this indicates the length of one cycle. This option should be changed to 0.00:

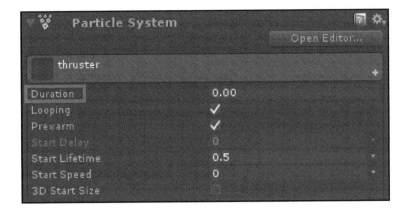

- **Prewarm**: When played, a pre-warmed system will be in a state as if it had emitted one loop cycle. It can only be used if the system is looping. This option should be ticked.
- **Start Lifetime**: This option is in seconds. The particle will die when its lifetime reaches 0. This option should be set to 0.5.
- **Start Speed**: This is the start speed of particles applied in the starting direction. This option should be set to 0.
- **3D Start Size**: This is the start size of particles.

Start Size should be set to 1, 2. To get the option of more fields, do the following:

1. Click on the down arrow to the right of the option.
2. From the dropdown, click on **Random Between Two Constants**, as in the following screenshot:

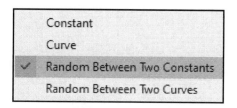

The least expensive curve is **Constant** as it only requires one value.

- **3D Start Rotation**: If enabled, we can control the rotation separately for each axis. This option should be ticked. To get the option of more fields, do the following:

1. Click on the down arrow to the right of the option.
2. From the drop-down menu, click on **Random Between Two Constants** and enter the following vector rotations:

X: 60	Y: 20	Z: 90
X: 30	Y: 10	Z:-90

- **Start Color**: This is the start color of particles. The **Hex Color** option should be set to 00FFD5B7.
- **Simulation Speed**: This scales the playback speed of the particle system. This should be set to 4.

The following screenshot provides a reference for the settings that should be set:

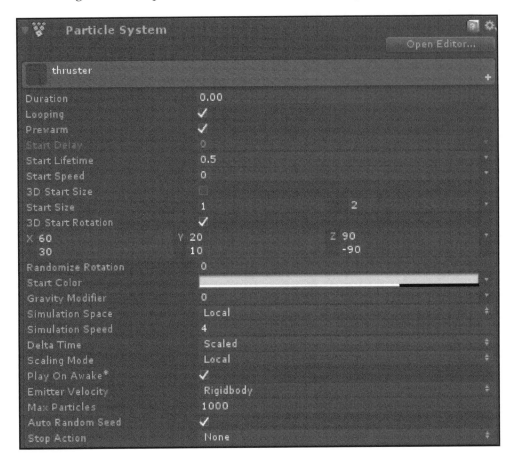

We've changed a lot of settings here. To summarize, we've created a cluster of particles that appear and soon get destroyed. If they last too long, our `thruster` object will travel across the screen (which you may or may not want). We have eliminated its direction because we will later change this to a force that will push the particles in a rough direction, making a less predictable pattern.

Remember that the more particles we have on the screen at once, the more demanding the scene will become. To keep things as smooth as possible, we make it so that our particles last as long as they need to (that is, they have a short lifetime) and we keep each particle size as small as possible, rather than big.

The following screenshot shows our flickering particle system as it is now:

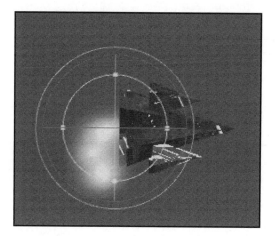

Let's now continue going through the **Particle System** settings within the **Inspector** window.

Setting up the Emission section of our particle system

In this section, we will control the rate of the particles in our particle system; under each heading, I will display an information box showing the tooltip description for this section. You can view tooltips by moving your mouse over the name of the section. This also works within the **Inspector** window for some values. An example of a tooltip is shown in the following screenshot:

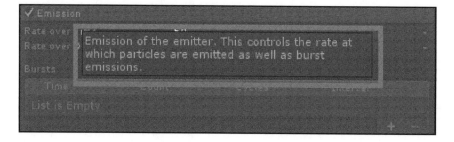

The next subsetting for the `thruster` particle system is **Emission**. It contains two properties (**Rate over Time** and **Rate over Distance**) but we're only going to change one of them. We will change **Rate of Time** (the number of particles emitted per second) to 50.

As mentioned before, if in doubt, crank the settings all the way up or down to see whether there are any instant visual answers to what the property does. You can always undo the setting. As an extra precaution, you can always save your work before changing any settings:

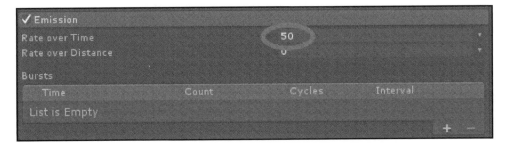

We're not doing anything drastic here, just lowering the number of particles a little. Later on in this chapter, it may be a good idea, for performance sake, to lower the variable even further, depending on what platform this game is being ported to.

In the next section, we will set up how the particles enter the scene.

Setting up the Shape section of our particle system

In the next part of our setup of the particle system, we can alter the **Shape** setting and its properties.

The **Shape** tooltip description is **Shape of the emitter volume, which controls where particles are emitted and their initial direction.**

In the **Shape** section, we will tighten the spawn point that the particles come from. The settings that we will change are as follows:

- **Shape**: Defines the shape of the volume from which particles can be emitted and the direction of the start velocity. Set this option to **Sphere**.
- **Radius**: The radius of the shape. Set this to 0.02.

All we need to focus on is the point that the particles have come from. Here's a screenshot of the settings that need to be set:

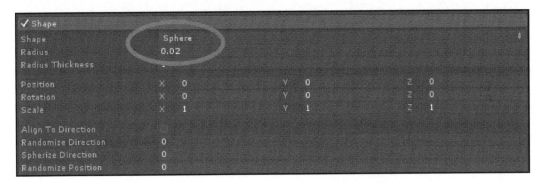

Our player's ship's thrusters display more of a concentrated glow now:

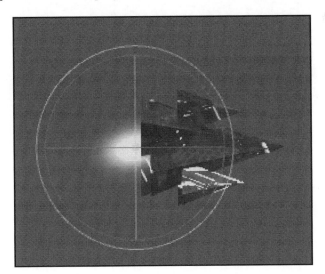

As already mentioned, we stopped the direction of our particle system in the very first section, and in the next section, we will use **Force over Lifetime** to roughly direct where the particles will go.

Setting up the Force over Lifetime section of our particle system

In this short section, we'll alter the force of where we want our particles to go. Referring back to the previous screenshot, we can see that our ship has a glow that now just needs to be pushed back slightly to give the illusion of travel.

 The **Force over Lifetime** tooltip description is **Controls the force of each particle during its lifetime**.

Unlike other properties, this one needs to be turned on by selecting the tick box to the left of its name.

Once activated, the only setting we need to adjust is setting **Z** to 10, as in the following screenshot:

 As mentioned before, be adventurous with the settings. Accidents and pushing limits can create new effects that might be useful for other parts of this game and future projects.

So, now our particle looks stretched out and resembles a thruster, as in the following screenshot:

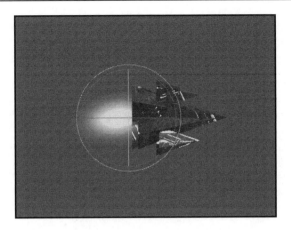

Let's now move on to changing the texture to see whether we can add some more detail to the particles.

Setting up the Renderer section of our particle system

The **Renderer** section controls the visuals of each particle. This is where we can apply our own material. Within the material is a custom texture.

 The **Renderer** tooltip description is **Specifies how the particles are rendered**.

We are going to update the **Particle System** material so that it displays a sprite sheet, which we will use for animations in the next section.

 What's a sprite sheet? It is a series of images, typically in a grid formation, that is used for animation.

Drag and drop the `thruster` material file within the **Project** window located in the `Assets/Resources/Materials` file path location to the **Material** field within the **Renderer** section, as in the following screenshot.

The player_ship object now has the new thruster particle system material assigned, which looks dotty. In the following screenshot, the thumbnail of the thruster material is dragged and dropped into the **Material** field of the **Renderer** part:

With our material and texture applied, we now have lots of dots where the glow from the rear of the ship was. We have done everything correctly, but because this texture behaves like animation, we need to update its **Texture Sheet Animation** settings.

Setting up the Texture Sheet Animation section of our particle system

The final step to creating this particle effect is to let Unity animate a sprite sheet correctly. Before we set this up, let's take a look at the texture we are feeding into the particle system.

 The **Texture Sheet Animation** tooltip description is **Particle UV animation. This allows us to specify a texture sheet (a texture with multiple tiles/subframes) and animation or randomize over it per particle**.

The following screenshot is from our `thruster` material:

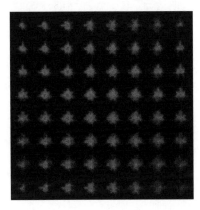

The previous screenshot contains 64 images in an 8 x 8 grid. No extra settings are needed for this texture. If there were an uneven number of multiple images, then we would have to approach this differently by using Unity's sprite editor to cut out each image individually, which can get tedious.

 More information about the sprite editor can be found at `https://docs.unity3d.com/Manual/SpriteEditor.html`.

Thankfully, we don't need to worry about doing that. Let's take a closer look at the material.

In the following screenshot, we can see that the **Shader** option (at the top of the screenshot) is set to the **Particles/Additive** category, which is one of the most common shaders used for a particle system.

In the **Project** window, under the Assets/Resources/Materials file location, we have our thruster material file. Clicking on the file displays its properties in the **Inspector** window:

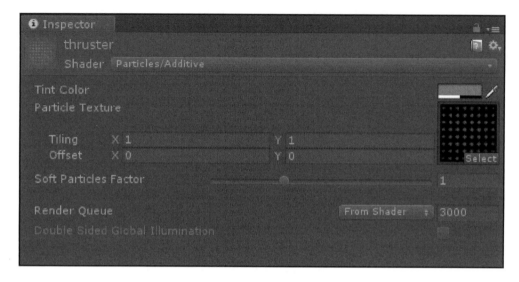

We can change the strength of the particle by changing its **Tint Color** brightness value, as in the previous screenshot. Feel free to make your own changes. I'm going to leave mine the way it is.

Coming back to the **Texture Sheet Animation** section, as explained, we have an 8 x 8 texture grid. This means we have to change the tiles to **X**: 8 and **Y**: 8.

As you will recall, in the previous section, our particles looked dotty. That's because we were displaying all 64 images from your texture sheet into one particle. With the texture animation sheet, we have divided those 64 images into single images that will animate onto each particle.

The following screenshot shows the continuation of our particle system with the **Texture Sheet Animation** settings:

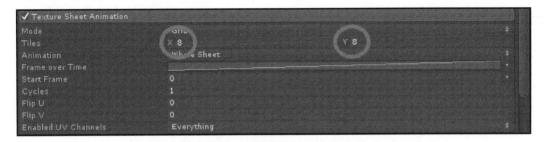

This is our end result:

If you're happy with the final result, we need to make one final step before saving our player_ship prefab. Because we changed the scale of player_ship in the PlayerSpawner script, we need to do the same for our thruster game object.

To change the localScale setting of the thruster game object, we need to do the following:

1. In the **Project** window, navigate to Assets/Resources/Script.
2. Double-click on the PlayerSpawner script and scroll down to the line of code that reads as follows:

```
playerShip.transform.localScale = new Vector3(60,60,60);
```

3. Just below the previous line of code, add the following code to size the `thruster` game object:

```
playerShip.GetComponentInChildren<ParticleSystem>
    ().transform.localScale = new Vector3(25,25,25);
```

The previous code accesses the player's ship's `ParticleSystem` component and changes its scale to `25` on all axes.

4. Save the `PlayerSpawner` script.

5. Back in the Unity editor, with the `player_ship` object selected in the **Hierarchy** window, click on the **Apply** button in the **Inspector** window.

As mentioned, be brave with the particle system; use the tooltips if you aren't familiar with them and play around with the settings—you'll soon get used to it. You could copy and paste the `thruster` game object and alter its color, emissions, force, scale, and more. Mix things up to create different types of thrusters.

Here's one I made earlier with six particle systems:

Particle systems can also be manipulated via scripting, which is why as a Unity programmer, we are familiar with the properties but not so much with mastering the techniques. It is also likely you will be asked, in the Unity programmer exam, about the properties of a particle system and what a particle system is good for when it comes to creating effects. Even though we didn't cover all of the properties in this section, it's good practice to have a general understanding of what each property does—for example, knowing that the **Size over LifeTime** property simply shrinks the particle over time.

One of the particle system properties we made use of was **Texture Sheet Animation**, where we provided a pre-made texture sheet to divide up our individual images to create an animation.

When a particle system is made, it generates a predictable pattern. This is known as **Procedural Mode**; the benefits to this is that Unity knows where the particle is in the past and the future. It also helps performance when, for example, the camera is looking away from the particle system; then, it can be culled. However, if the particle system is modified by a property such as changing its simulation space to **World Space**, the particle system will become unpredictable and non-procedural, which will disable its ability to improve performance.

For more information about **Procedural Mode**, check out the following link:

```
https://blogs.unity3d.com/2016/12/20/unitytips-
particlesystem-performance-culling/
```

In the next section, we will use particle systems again, but this time for the background to create stars that appear to whizz past us. We will also animate the stars at different speeds using Unity's animator controller.

Importing and animating the background

In this section, we are going to get familiar with Unity's animator controller. We will make our player's ship travel at light speed (well, give the impression that it is, anyway) by creating a fast-moving background of stars and particles (yes, that's right, more particles) at the start of the level, then we'll slow everything down when there are enemies up ahead.

Before we start animating at "light speed," we need to prepare the **Hierarchy** window:

1. In the **Hierarchy** window, right-click on an open-space area.
2. Select **Create Empty** from the dropdown.
3. Click on the new game object and rename it GameSpeed.
4. Do this again and name the second game object _SceneAssets.
5. Drag GameSpeed onto the _SceneAssets game object.
6. Make sure both game objects' **Transform** property values are set to **Reset**.
7. Finally, drag the _SceneAssets game object from the **Hierarchy** window into the Assets/Prefab **Project** window.

Remember, as well as regularly saving our scene and project, we also need to make sure we make prefabs that will be situated in the scene and used on a regular basis to store the game object and its components, settings.

That's the **Hierarchy** window set up and ready for some extra game objects to be added to our scene. Looking at how we create an active animating scene for our game, we can tackle this with one of two approaches for a side-scrolling shooter. One way is to have a large, static background and move the player and camera through the level, tackling enemies. The other way is to keep the camera still and make the background move or animate past the camera while we trigger enemies into the scene at set times. Why would we use the second way? Because when we make a game, as a programmer, we need to focus on what is important to us—in this case, the player is most important. Also, the player is clamped within the screen ratio. Arguably, it would be more awkward for us to develop and bug-test a moving clamped camera, forcing our player across a world scene with other game objects coming into play. We can also consider physics as a factor with debris and even more game objects colliding into each other, which can cause potential issues. As a programmer, I find it is always best to look for the simplest option.

With that said, let's move on to making our background:

1. Right-click on `GameSpeed` in the **Hierarchy** window.
2. Select **Create Empty** from the dropdown.
3. Click on the new game object and rename it `spaceBackground`.

The `spaceBackground` game object is going to house the stars particle system. The particle system that we will bring into our scene is pre-made; I didn't think it would be necessary to continue making more particles as we have already made one for our player's ship.

From the `Assets/Resources/Particles` **Project** window, drag the `warpStars_pe` prefab on to the `GameSpeed` game object in the **Hierarchy** window to make it a child.

With the changes we have made in this section, the **Hierarchy** window content should resemble the following screenshot:

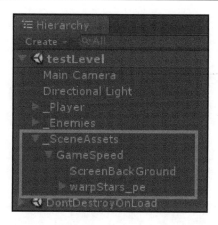

We have updated our **Hierarchy** window again with the second particle system for this chapter. This has improved the structure and increased clarity as our game starts branching out into more functionality. Let's now continue focusing on the particle system with its placement in the world scene:

1. In the **Hierarchy** window, select warpStars_pe if it isn't selected already.
2. Moving our attention over to the **Inspector** window, set its **Transform** settings to the following:

Position	X	0	Y	0	Z	0
Rotation	X	0	Y	90	Z	0
Scale	X	50	Y	50	Z	50

With our particle system set up in the correct place, we can now focus on adding another layer to the background of our game, which will be a spaceBackground texture on a large quad polygon.

Let's continue adding more functionality to the spaceBackground game object:

1. In the **Hierarchy** window, select spaceBackground.
2. In the **Inspector** window, click on the **Add Component** button.
3. From the dropdown that appears, start typing Mesh Filter until it is available to click on from the list.

The following screenshot shows the **Inspector** window for `spaceBackground`, equipped with a three-dimensional **Quad** polygon mesh:

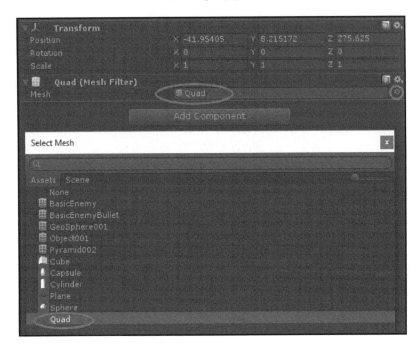

With the **Quad** mesh created, we need to make it visible in our **Scene** and **Game** windows with the **Mesh Renderer** component:

1. Select the `spaceBackground` game object in the **Hierarchy** window and in the **Inspector** window, click on the **Add Component** button.
2. In the dropdown, start typing `Mesh Renderer` until you see it in the list, then click on it.

Similar to what we did for our `player_ship` prefab and our previous particle system, we need to create and apply a material to our `spaceBackground` object:

1. Right-click in the open space of the **Project** window in the `Assets/Resources/Materials` file location.
2. Click on **Create** from the dropdown.
3. Then, click on **Material**.
4. With the new material selected, rename it `backGround_Wallpaper`.

Because our `spaceBackground` game object now has a `MeshRenderer` object and we have created a material for it, we now need to apply it:

1. In the **Hierarchy** window, select `spaceBackground`.
    - Drag and drop the `backGround_Wallpaper` material from the **Project** window to the **Mesh Renderer** section, into the **Element 0** slot of the **Materials** subsection, as in the following screenshot:

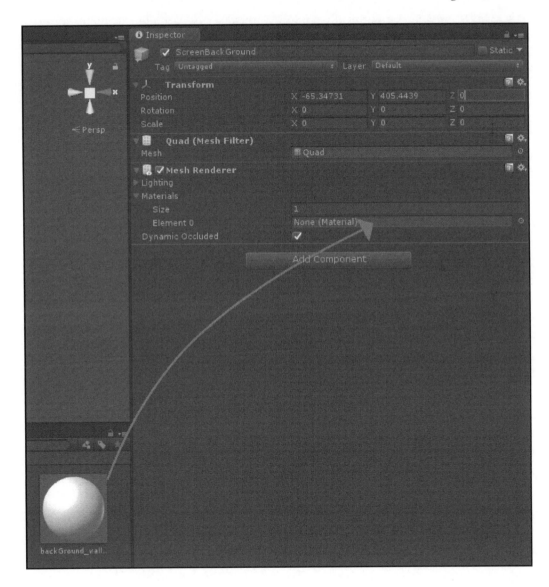

Let's rewind and confirm what we have done so far in this section. We have our game objects in their correct positions in the **Hierarchy** window and we have our second particle system set up, positioned, rotated, and scaled. We've just created our material, named it, and placed it into backGround_wallpaper.

Now, we'll set the material up to be something quite basic. It doesn't require a lot of fancy shaders, so just a simple low-resource mobile shader will be fine.

 Shaders are typically a mathematical script that tells our material how its graphics and light behave.

Make sure spaceBackground is still selected in the **Hierarchy** window.

In the **Inspector** window, scroll down to the **Material** component:

1. If the **Material** component isn't expanded, click on the arrow next to the white sphere.
2. With the **Material** component expanded, we can see a lot of maps that we won't need, so let's change the shader to a more basic one.
3. Click on **Standard** (highlighted in the following screenshot).
4. From the dropdown, click on **Mobile**.
5. Then, click on **Diffuse**.

   The following screenshot shows this procedure:

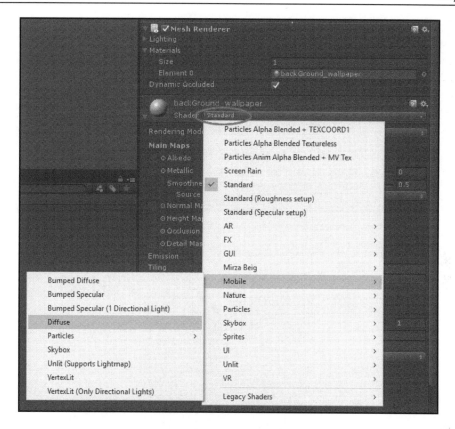

This has chopped our **Material** properties down to the minimum requirement, as in the following screenshot:

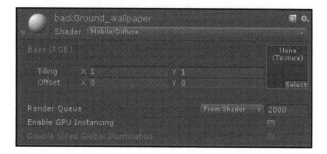

The two things we really care about in this **Material** component is the **Texture** we are going to supply to it and its **Offset** value.

What's an offset? **Offset** is the position where our texture is applied to on our UV map. For example, if we increase the **Offset** property's **X** position, the texture applied to the material will overlap and appear on the other side of our quad.

We will now continue working with our background **Material** component by adding our spaceBackground texture:

1. With the **Material** component still in the **Inspector** window, there is a large square at the top right called **None (Texture)**. Click on **Select** (use the previous screenshot as a reference).
2. A dropdown appears. Start typing spaceBackground until the option comes up, then click on it.

    We should have a quad named spaceBackground that is black with white dots on it, as in the following screenshot:

Before we start animating this texture, we need to do the same as what we did for our particle system and update its **Transform** properties: **Position**, **Rotation**, and **Scale**. We need spaceBackground to cover the camera's frustum angle and our image to show up after the **Transform** update:

1. In the **Hierarchy** window, select the spaceBackground game object.
2. In the **Inspector** window, update its **Transform** component with the following settings:

Position	X	−65	Y	405	Z	690
Rotation	X	0	Y	0	Z	0
Scale	X	3260	Y	3260	Z	3260

The following screenshot shows our current scene view:

- We have a very large quad with a space texture.
- We have a white grid-like camera view.
- Our player's ship is in between the camera and the quad.
- The bottom right shows us what the user sees as an end result:

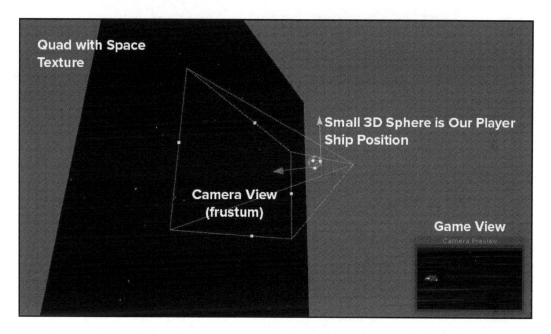

We have updated our **Hierarchy** window to hold two background layers. The first layer show passing stars with the second particle system we added from this chapter's downloads file. The second is a game object that holds a quad polygon with a texture. Let's now move on to creating the animator controller for our background and space warp particle.

Adding an animator controller

Using the animator controller is a way of controlling animation states. We will have our player's ship traveling at light speed for a couple of seconds, then we'll slow things down just before the enemies come to attack our player.

The left-hand-side depiction of our ship in the following screenshot shows more streaking particles than the ship on the right. The starry background also moves faster on the left than on the right (which you can't really see in these still screenshots):

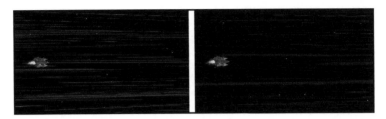

So, let's create and attach the animator to the parent of the spaceBackground object and the particle system.

 With the animator controller, if you are animating multiple game objects at once, make sure your animator controller is the parent to these game objects. You can't have a child animating its parent (**parent** refers to the game objects above the object in the **Hierarchy** window).

Looking at the **Hierarchy** window, we have made all the background effects in this chapter within the GameSpeed game object. As mentioned in the information box, the animator controller animates all the children, but it can't animate parents. With that said, let's add the animator controller:

1. In the **Hierarchy** window, select the GameSpeed game object.
2. In the **Inspector** window, click on the **Add Component** button.
3. In the dropdown, start typing Animator until it appears and then click on it.

   The following screenshot shows the **Animator** component (which houses the animator controller) selected for the GameSpeed game object:

We now have the **Animator** component attached to our `GameSpeed` game object. The next thing to do is create and attach the animator controller to the **Controller** field. The following screenshot shows the **Animator** component settings:

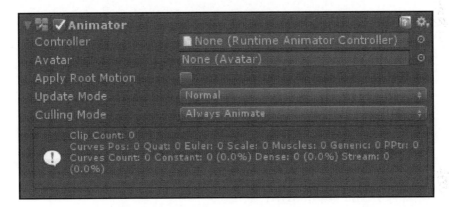

Before we do that, we need to create an `Animator` folder. In the **Project** window, navigate to `Assets/Resources` and create an empty folder. Name it `Animator`.

Go inside the `Animator` folder and continue making the animator controller:

1. Right-click in the **Project** window open space.
2. Click on **Create**.
3. Click on the animator controller (see the left side of the following screenshot for reference).
4. Rename the new animator controller `GameSpeed_Controller`.
5. Finally, drag and drop this animator controller to the `GameSpeed` animator controller in its **Inspector** window (refer to the right-hand side of the following screenshot for reference).

The following screenshot shows the creation of an animator controller and how to apply it to the **Animator** component:

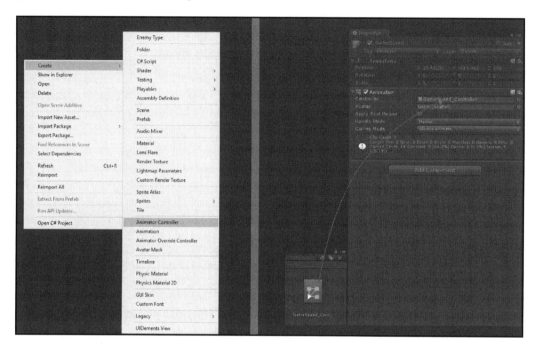

In this section, we created and applied our **Animator** component and **Animator Controller** to our GameSpeed game object. In the next section, we will look at animation states within the animator controller.

Creating states in the animator controller

In this section, we will use the animator controller to create a state for animating the background scene and particles at high speed; followed by the second state, which will slow the background and particles down to represent the player's ship going at a slower speed (which also helps make our game less distracting). Let's make the first state:

To create a state, follow these instructions:

1. Double-click on the GameSpeed_Controller object that we placed in the GameSpeed **Animator** component.

2. The **Animator** window will open with some default states: **Entry, Any State,** and **Exit**.

3. Right-click in an open space within the **Animator** window.

4. A dropdown will appear. Click on **Create State**.

5. Then, click on **Empty**:

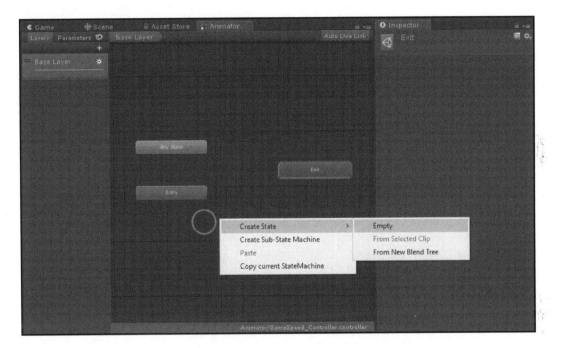

As you can guess, we've just created an empty state.

6. Repeat this process to create a second state.

Unity's animator controller also offers layering with our animation. So, for example, we can animate a player who can run, jump, and shoot. It's likely that we will want a couple of these animations playing at the same time, and we can do so with **Layers** (see the top-left corner of the previous screenshot). We can change the influence over each animation, or **weight**, as it's referred to in Unity, and we can use the **Override** (information from other layers will be ignored) or **Additive** (added on top of another animation) settings to the blend between animations.

If you would like to find out more about animation layers, go to https://docs.unity3d.com/Manual/AnimationLayers.html.

Once we have created our second state, let's do a bit of housekeeping:

7. Click and drag **Exit** and **Any State** out of the way. We won't be using these. **Entry** will automatically attach itself to the first state we make.

Let's now rename our states:

1. Click on the orange state called **New State**.
2. In the **Inspector** window, click in the top-right corner where it says **New State**.
3. Delete this and rename it `BackGround_Intro_Speed`.
4. Press *Enter* on your keyboard to make sure it saves the name. If you click away, it sometimes doesn't save the change.
5. Now, rename the other state we made, currently titled `New State 0`. Rename this second state to `BackGround_InGame_Speed`.

You can zoom in and out and pan around the **Animator** window with your mouse wheel.

To zoom in, scroll the wheel up.
To zoom out, scroll the wheel down.
To pan, hold the middle mouse button down.

Don't worry about the exact placement of the states; that's more of a cosmetic issue. We just need to have an **Entry** state connecting to a `BackGround_Intro_Speed` state, with a `BackGround_InGame_Speed` state near to it.

The following screenshot shows the three states we should be focusing on:

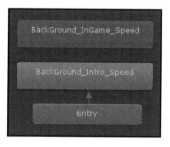

These three animation states will eventually have lines attached to each of them; these lines allow a condition to be made (such as an `if` statement; see `https://docs.microsoft.com/en-us/dotnet/csharp/language-reference/keywords/if-else` for more information) so that one state can move to another.

Before we look at this, we also need to be aware that each state can run at different speeds. We will alter the speed of the states to go inline with the speed of the animations they house. To change the animation speeds of our state, do the following:

1. In the **Animator** window, click on the `BackGround_InGame_Speed` state.
2. In its **Inspector** window, change its **Speed** value from 1 to `0.1`.

The other state will remain the same.

As the scene starts, the first state is `BackGround_Intro_Speed`, then once that animation is connected to it (which we currently haven't done yet), `BackGround_InGame_Speed` is played next. We need to connect the last state so that it can be played after.

To connect a state, do the following:

1. In the **Animator** window, right-click on the `BackGround_Intro_Speed` state.
2. From the dropdown, click on **Make Transition**.
3. Then, click on `BackGround_InGame_Speed`.

We should now have one state connected to another.

In this section, we delved deeper into the animator controller, creating our intro and in-game animation states. We set the speed of the state and, finally, connected up the transition lines so that we know the flow of our animation states. All this structuring of extra game objects, the animator controller, and the states means we are now at the stage where we can start animating our scenery.

Animation

Finally, we are actually going to animate something. We will only cover a basic animation but will give us an understanding of the animation setup, which will support us in the exam and future projects.

So, let's just jump in and animate the background and our background particles:

1. In the **Project** window, go to the `Assets/Resources/Animator` folder location.
2. Right-click in the open space and click on **Create** from the dropdown.

3. Then, click on **Animation**.

4. Name the new animation `BackGround_InGame_Speed`.

5. Repeat the process and name the new animation `BackGround_Intro_Speed`.

The following screenshot shows the creation of an **Animation** file:

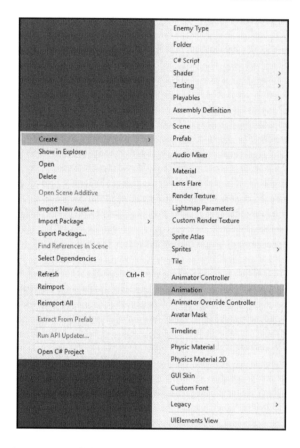

The introduction animation will be played once because it will be a surge of stars, then the second animation will loop, playing continuously to give the illusion of never-ending stars and particle stars moving past the **Game** window.

With that said, in the **Project** window, click on the `BackGround_InGame_Speed` animation file, and in the **Inspector** window, tick the box next to **Loop Time**.

We now need to apply our two **Animation** files to their animation states in the **Animator** window.

To hook these new **Animation** files up, do the following:

1. In the **Hierarchy** window, select the GameSpeed game object.
2. Double-click on GameSpeed_Controller.
3. The **Animator** window opens up. Select one of the two animation states we created in the animator controller.
4. Drag and drop the **Animation** file we just made to the **Motion** field of the **Inspector** tab (refer to the following screenshot).
5. Select the other state that we created and repeat the drag and drop process with the other matching **Animation** file.

We now have the two animator controller states with an empty animation clip applied.

The following screenshot shows our BackGround_Intro_Speed animation file dragged and dropped into the **Animation State** | **Motion** field:

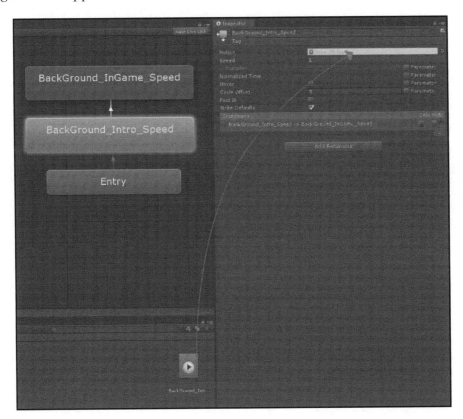

You can also create a blend tree in the animator controller. A blend tree is specifically built to blend a series of animations as one form. Within the blend tree, there are different types: **1D**, a series of **2D**, and **Direct**.

Blend trees can be useful to change an animation from walking to running (**1D**) or for more complex animations, such as facial expressions (**Direct**).

To learn more about blend trees, check out `https://docs.unity3d.com/Manual/class-BlendTree.html`.

Let's stay focused on our **Animation** file and start animating the scene.

First, we need to open the **Animation** window:

1. At the top of the Unity editor window, click on **Window**.
2. Then, click on **Animation**, or you can use the *Ctrl (or command* on macOS) + 6 shortcut.
3. Next, back in our **Project** window, we need to click on the `BackGround_Intro_Speed` animation file (this should be located in the `Assets/Resources/Animator/Animation` folder structure). This will update the **Animation** name within the window (use the following screenshot as a reference):

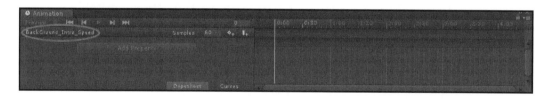

Like most windows within Unity, we can lock the window so that it doesn't update to another game object or, in this case, animation.

To lock the window, click on the padlock symbol in the top-right corner of the **Animator** window.

Locking the animation is probably a good idea, at this point, as we will be clicking on different game objects within the **Hierarchy** and **Inspector** windows. We will animate the spaceBackground texture first:

1. Keep the GameSpeed game object selected in the **Hierarchy**. If we select something else, we will lose the animation functionality in the **Animation** window.
2. In the **Animation** window, click on the round red record button (above the **Animation** filename). Notice how the **Animation** window turns partially red, telling us we are in record mode.
3. Then, in the **Hierarchy** window, click on spaceBackground.
4. Now, in the **Inspector** window, we need to focus on changing backGround_Wallpaper material settings.
5. Also, make sure our **Animation** white indicator line is all the way to the left, as in the following screenshot.
6. Next, change the **X** value of **Offset** from 0 to -10. Notice how the fields turn red as this is noted in the **Animation** window.

7. Now, click and hold the white line in the **Animation** window and move it across to the right so that it isn't sitting on top of the animation it has just made:

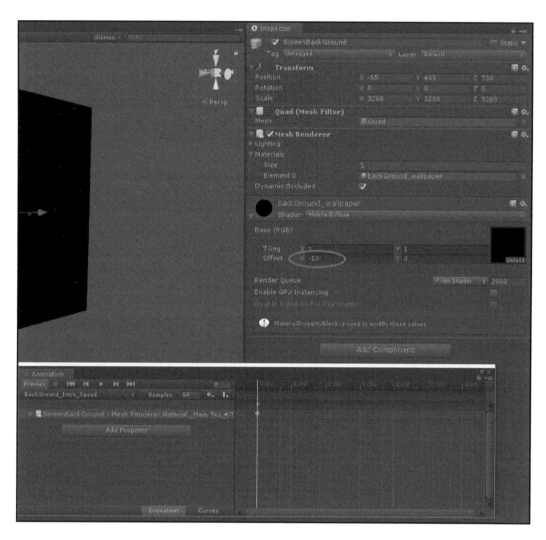

8. Change the **X** value of **Offset**, this time from −10 to 1. Notice, in the following screenshot, how the white lines in the **Animation** window have moved to roughly 300 (5 minutes):

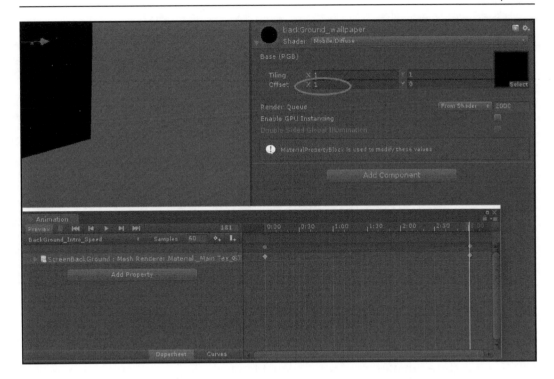

9. Try moving the white lines backward and forward (**scrub** is the term used for this by animators) between our two animation points. Notice how the stars on the quad are moving.

Let's now do something similar with the `warpStars_pe` particle system:

1. Check that the **Animation** window is still locked and recording.
2. Move the animation indicator line all the way back to the left to the start of the other animation keyframe.
3. From the **Hierarchy** window, select `warpStars_pe`.

In the **Transform** section of the **Inspector** tab, make the following changes:

Position	X	−1364	Y	0	Z	−400
Rotation	X	0	Y	90	Z	0
Scale	X	50	Y	50	Z	50

Then, scrub (move) the white lines to the exact same spot as the starry background keyframe.

We can click the **Next Frame** button in the **Animation** window to jump to the next keyframe (the button to the right of the **Play** button, not the editor play button).

With the **Animation** window still in record and the warpStars_pe game object still selected, update its **Transform** settings in the **Inspector** window with the following values:

Position	X	−85	Y	0	Z	0
Rotation	X	0	Y	90	Z	0
Scale	X	50	Y	50	Z	50

1. Try scrubbing backward and forward in the **Animation** window to see how it looks in the **Scene** view. You should see the particles moving from right to left.
2. In the **Animation** window, turn off the record-setting.

That's one animation down and one to go. The next process is similar to what we've already done but a little quicker.

While still in the **Animator** window, do the following:

1. Click and drag to select all keyframes with your mouse, as in the following screenshot:

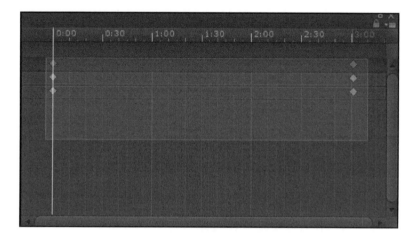

2. Let go of the mouse and press *Ctrl* (or *command* on macOS) + *C* to copy the keyframes.

3. Let's now switch over to the `BackGround_InGame_Speed` animation by clicking on the name of our current animation and selecting the other, as in the following screenshot:

4. Notice how the name has changed to reflect the animation we are in.
5. Now, click in the graph area and use the *Ctrl* (or *command* on macOS) + *V* keyboard commands.
6. We should now have pasted the previous animation into this one. We can manipulate the results within the window, as in the following screenshot:

 If you can't see all keyframes in the **Animation** window, select an open area within the window and press *F* on the keyboard. This will auto-fit all keyframes in.

Finally, we can manipulate the keyframes:

1. Click on the **Animation** window to start recording.
2. From the **Hierarchy** window, select `spaceBackground`.
3. From the **Inspector** window, change the `backGround_Wallpaper` **Offset** settings, setting **X** from −10 to 1.

4. Click on the **Next Frame** button (the button to the right of **Play** in the **Animation** window) to go to the last frame and change the **X** value of **Offset** from 1 to 2.

5. Next, we alter the warpStars_pe animation within the **Animation** window.

6. Click on the first warpStars_pe keyframe at the far left and press *Delete* on the keyboard. Now, move the last keyframe from the end to the beginning.

Before we stop recording, we need to stop the animation from easing out (slowing down near the end of the animation).

To make it so that our backGround_Wallpaper setting is on a fixed animation speed, we need to do the following:

1. In the **Animation** window, click and drag to select all the keys.
2. Right-click, and from the dropdown, select **Both Tangents | Linear**.
3. Stop recording.

Let's recap what we have done so far. We have taken the **X** value of **Offset** from the last animation and pasted it to the start of this animation. Then, we incremented the **X** value of **Offset** by 1 so that it comes back to the start of its **X** value of **Offset**.

We moved the particles from left to right in the first animation; we kept the particles on right in the second animation to stop the scene from being too cluttered and to show that we aren't going as fast.

We are now at the final steps of the animation; the rest of the work is done within the animator controller. From the animator controller, we can state what needs looping and how our animations relate to each other.

For the last time in this chapter, let's visit the animation controller and start splicing our states from one to another:

1. From the **Hierarchy** window, select the GameSpeed game object.
2. Then, in the **Inspector** animator component, double-click on GameSpeed_Controller.
3. Now, click on the transition line between BackGround_Intro_Speed and BackGround_InGame_Speed (circled in the following reference screenshot).

With regard to the transition between one animation to another, the following screenshot sets the example of these states via the two blue bars. Select the following settings:

- **Has Exit Time**: Ticked
- The **Has Exit Time** tooltip reads **Transition has a fixed exit time**.
- **Exit Time**: 0.1
- The **Exit Time** tooltip reads **Exit time is the normalized time from the current state**.
- **Fixed Duration**: Ticked
- The **Fixed Duration** tooltip reads **Transition duration is independent of state length**.
- **Transition Duration (s)**: 2.5
- The **Transition Duration (s)** tooltip reads **Transition duration in seconds**.
- **Transition Offset**: 0.1
- The **Transition Offset** tooltip reads **Normalized start time in the next state**.
- **Interruption Source**: **None**
- The **Interruption Source** tooltip reads **Can be interrupted by transitions from:**

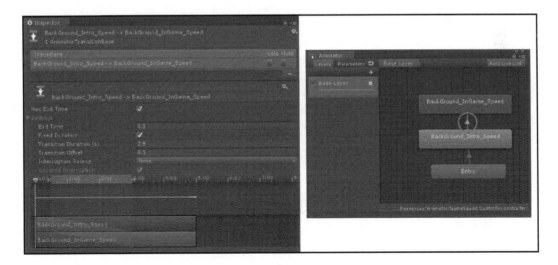

The figures are rough for this transition. It's also quite unnatural to enter perfect figures for an animation. I recommend removing any enemies from the scene. Press the **Play** button and alter the selection bar above the graph. Each time this selection changes, the animation will play again. Keep an eye on the animator controller; you will see a progress bar start and end. This will help the timings of when the animation will splice over.

Animation transitions can help blend one animation into another. For example, if we want an animation to move into another in an exact time frame, we would focus on the **Fixed Duration** and the **Transition Duration** parameters (shown in the previous screenshot).

For more information on animation transitions, check out the `https://docs.unity3d.com/Manual/class-Transition.html`.

The results I have are very smooth and work well, but I recommend forgetting the figures. Put the editor in **Play** mode and drag the selection bar back and forth until you get the splice that is right for you.

That is the end of the animator controller settings. It's one of those things that takes a long time to explain but is very quick to do once you know how.

You might be eager to get back to coding as we have mainly been working in Unity's editor tools. So, let's return to the IDE and start looking at animating next.

Animating our three-dimensional enemies

Here's a really easy, quick animation with the script for your enemies. Currently, the enemies just move up and down in a wave pattern. However, the units themselves remain static.

Let's give our enemies a bit of extra life with some code:

1. In the **Project** window, go to `Assets/Resources/Prefab/Enemies`.
2. Expand the content of the `enemy_wave` prefab and select the `enemy_wave_ring` child game object.
3. In the **Inspector** window, click on the **Add Component** button.

4. Click on **New Script** at the bottom of the dropdown.

5. Name the new C# script `BasicEnemyRotate`.

6. Then, enter this code:

```
using System.Collections;
using System.Collections.Generic;
using UnityEngine;
public class BasicEnemyRotate : MonoBehaviour
{
 [SerializeField]
 float speed = 0;

void Update ()
  {
    transform.Rotate(Vector3.left*Time.deltaTime*speed)
  }
}
```

This is a tiny script that animates the part of our enemy. There are two things to look closely at:

- The variable is a private float named `speed` with a `SerializeField` attribute so that it can be seen in the **Inspector** window. More about this attribute can be found at `https://docs.unity3d.com/ScriptReference/SerializeField.html`.

- In our `Update` function, we are rotating the game object over time based on the speed we are setting it at. I have set my enemy rotation speed to `200`.

Before we press **Play** to test these results, update the enemy's materials by doing the following:

1. Navigate to the **Project** window and select the `enemy_wave` prefab in `Assets/Resources/Prefab/Enemies`.

2. Drag `enemy_wave` to the **Hierarchy** window.

3. Expand the `enemy_wave` game object in the **Hierarchy** window and select `enemy_wave_core`.

4. Select the small, round remote button to the right of the **Element 0** parameter in the **Mesh Renderer** component under the **Inspector** window.

5. Select the `basicEnemyShip_Inner` material.

6. Select `enemy_wave_ring` from the **Hierarchy** window.
7. From the **Inspector** window, click on the small, round remote button in the **Mesh Renderer** component, and from the dropdown, select `basicEnemyShip_Outer`.
8. Click **Apply** in the top-right corner of the **Inspector** window to confirm our prefab changes.
9. Remove the `enemy_wave` object from the **Hierarchy** window.
10. Click **Play** at the top of the editor and we should now see our enemies rotating and in color:

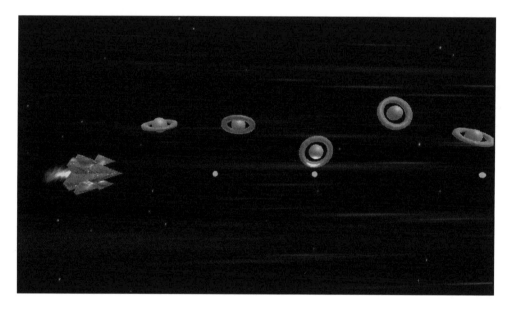

Lastly, move all new scripts into the `Script` folder.

Later on, we could speed up the enemies' rotation, depending on the player's skill level, to make them look more aggressive.

This was a long chapter, but we covered particles and animation, which are important to know for the exam. With more practice and understanding, the benefits of what we've learned will really start to show. Now is a good time to get used to these two skills as they are commonly overlooked. It's these skills that will make you stand out from the rest.

Summary

In this chapter, we jumped into the art world. We brought our player's ship to life, giving it a series of maps and a light. Then, we moved on to Unity's particle system and created a `thruster` object with an option to expand it. Then, we moved into animation and got our hands dirty, adding and animating the scene background and animating particle warp stars. We covered states and transitions, then calmed things down with some animation code for our enemies.

That was a lot! If you ever revisit this chapter, you will go through it much quicker as you'll see, if you haven't already, that you can copy and paste animation keyframes, copy and paste particle systems, and tweak them. Apply maps in a regular return. The pace does pick up.

In the next chapter, we will look at a new scene where we upgrade the player's ship with the introduction of a shop before a level starts. We will also introduce the popular concept of **free to play**, which is typically found in mobile games where the game is free to download and the user is given the option of earning in-game credits by watching an advert.

Well done! What you have learned will all contribute toward your exam and future projects.

5

Creating a Shop Scene for Our Game

In this chapter, we will incorporate and extend the scriptable objects that heavily helped make our player and the enemy ships in the previous chapter. We will customize a new shop scene, where we will add new upgrades for the player's ship with the use of scriptable objects.

We will also look at the common uses of raycasts; if you aren't familiar with them, they're best described as an invisible laser that shoots from one point to another:

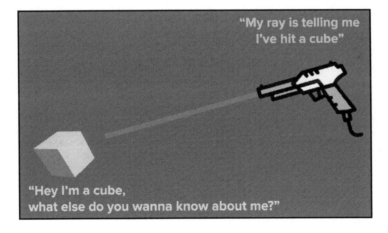

When the ray hits a game object with a collider, it can retrieve information about the object, and then we can go a little further and manipulate the object we've hit. For example, we can cast a ray to a game object cube and the ray will confirm to us that it's a cube. Because we have the cube's reference, we could change its color, scale, or position or destroy it—we could pretty much do whatever we want with it. Here, we will use this raycast system to shoot a point from the camera's position to the button in three-dimensional space when we click or touch the screen.

In this chapter, we will cover the following topics:

- Introducing our shop scripts
- Customizing our shop selection
- Selecting game objects with raycasts
- Adding information to our description panel

The core exam skills covered in this chapter

We will cover programming core interactions:

- *Implementing and configuring game object behavior and physics*
- *Implementing and configuring inputs and controls*

We will also cover working in the art pipeline:

- *Understanding materials, textures, and shaders, and writing scripts that interact with Unity's rendering API*

This chapter also covers developing application systems:

- *Interpreting scripts for application interface flow, such as menu systems, UI navigation, and application settings*
- *Interpreting scripts for user-controlled customization, such as character creators, inventories, storefronts, and in-app purchases*
- *Analyzing scripts for user progression features, such as scoring, leveling, and in-game economies, utilizing technologies, such as Unity Analytics and PlayerPrefs*
- *Analyzing scripts for two-dimensional overlays, such as **Heads-Up Displays (HUDs)**, minimaps, and advertisements*

We will also cover programming scene and environment design:

- **Identifying methods for implementing game object instantiation, destruction, and management**

Finally, we will cover working in a professional software development team:

- *Recognizing techniques for structuring scripts for modularity, readability, and reusability*

Technical requirements

The project content for this chapter can be found at https://github.com/ PacktPublishing/Unity-Certified-Programmer-Exam-Guide/tree/master/ Chapter05.

You can download the entirety of each chapter's project files at https://github.com/ PacktPublishing/Unity-Certified-Programmer-Exam-Guide/archive/master.zip.

All the content for this chapter is held in the chapter's unitypackage file, including a Complete folder, which holds all of the work we'll carry out in this chapter.

Check out the following video to see the Code in Action: https://bit.ly/3dqH5bq.

Introducing our shop scripts

In this section, we will make some new scriptable objects, as we did when we created our player's ship settings (health, speed, firepower, and so on). You can refer to *Introducing our scriptable object (*SOActorModel*)* section of Chapter 2, *Adding and Manipulating Objects*, for a reminder of how this is done. Instead of changing our enemy's or player's ships, we will be manipulating the shop's selection of powerups (with a selection grid) to add our own ship upgrades that the player will be able to choose from. These upgrades will then be transferred to the player's ship, which will be visually recognized, and two of the three upgrades will carry alterations to the gameplay.

Before we go into further detail, let's refresh our memory on where the shop scripts are within the game framework that we introduced in Chapter 1, *Setting Up and Structuring Our Project*.

The following diagram shows the location of the shop scripts:

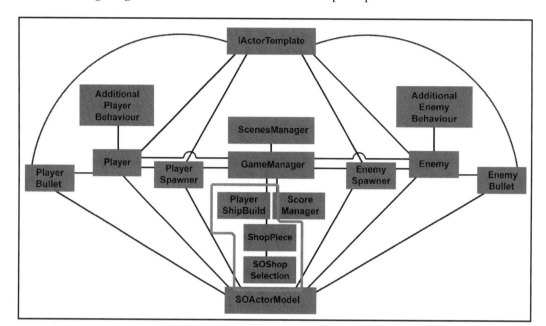

Our three shop scripts (`PlayerShipBuild`, `ShopPiece`, and `SOShopSelection`) connect to each other from where the `PlayerShipBuild` connects to the main, center `GameManager` script. In short, each script's responsibility in the shop scene is as follows:

- `PlayerShipBuild` is the overall function of the shop, including adverts and in-game credit control. This script can be broken down into more scripts, but for the sake of trying to keep our framework to a minimum, as it is is OK for a demo.
- `ShopPiece` handles the content of the player ship's upgrade selections.
- `SOShopSelection` this scriptable object holds the data types that will be used in each selection grid in our shop scene.

Let's take a look at the scene we will be creating and applying shop scripts to:

1. From the **Project** window, navigate to the `Scene` folder.
2. Double-click on the `shop` scene.

3. Drag and drop the `ShopManager` prefab from the **Project** window location (`Assets/Resources/Prefabs`).

4. Select **Camera** from the **Hierarchy** window and set its **Transform Position** settings to **X**: 0, **Y**: 0, and **Z**: 0.

5. If you want a different-colored background, with **Camera** still selected in the **Hierarchy** window, change the **Clear Flags** property from **Skybox** to **Solid Color** and then the **Color** parameter just below it in the **Camera Component** section of the **Inspector** window.

 Make sure the camera remains in the same screen ratio we set in *Chapter 2, Adding and Manipulating Objects* (that is, 1920 x 1080). Use the following screenshot for reference.

The following scene is broken into four sections:

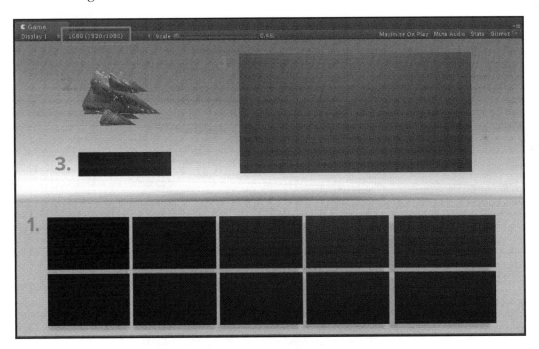

Looking at the previous image, let's go through each of the numbered points:

- Starting with **1**, the bottom 10 boxes will hold 3 ship upgrades, an option to watch an advert to gain credits, and a start button to move on to the next scene, which will be our `testLevel` scene (the scene we have been working on in the previous four chapters).
- At the top left (**2**), we have a visual representation of the player's ship. We can see what it looks like on our player's ship if they buy an upgrade.
- Below the player's ship (**3**) is a small rectangle that will display the in-game credit balance.
- At the top right (**4**), a larger rectangle will hold information about our selected upgrade. It will also contain a button that, if the player has enough credits and/or hasn't purchased the item already, will give them the option to buy an upgrade.

We can make a start with the selection grid (the shop's row of buttons). To save time, I have provided some template art for this scene because we will be replacing it in the next chapter when we create our own UI.

To make a start with the first button in our shop's selection grid, we need to go to the **Hierarchy** window in the Unity editor and do the following:

1. At the top-right corner of the **Hierarchy** window, we have a search bar with a magnifying glass and **All** written in its field. Click on the field and type in `upgrade`, as in the following screenshot:

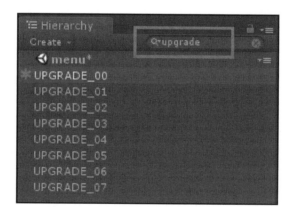

2. Now, select the top game object titled `UPGRADE_00`.

Notice the content of the **Scene** window is grayed out, apart from the selected game object in the **Hierarchy** window in the Unity editor. This is to help us locate the game object we are searching for.

3. Click on the round **X** symbol to the right of the search bar. This will bring our **Hierarchy** content back and expand the parent game objects for us, as in the following screenshot:

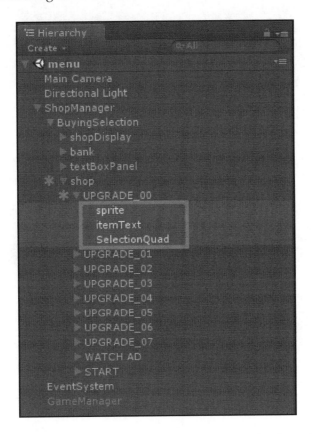

4. Hold down *Ctrl* (or *command* on macOS) on your keyboard and select the three game objects:

   - sprite
   - itemText
   - SelectionQuad

With these three objects selected, select the top-left tick box in the **Inspector** window to make these objects active. The location of the box is shown in the following screenshot:

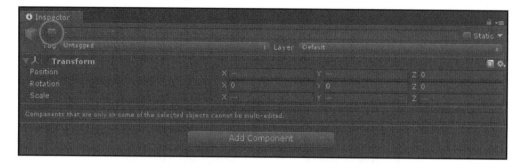

Our grid should now show its first selection, as in the following screenshot:

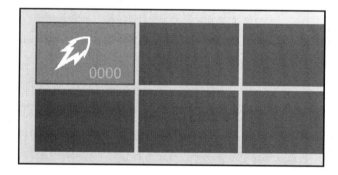

Our shop has started to take form. With the first selection set up, we can now go further by customizing these selections with code in the next section.

Importing and calibrating our sprite game object

The game object that I have labeled sprite will receive and display a ship upgrade image that will be displayed in the selection grid. To understand how this sprite can be displayed correctly, we can view its properties when its game object is selected in the **Hierarchy** window.

The **Inspector** window in the following screenshot shows that our sprite game object has a **Sprite Renderer** component attached to it:

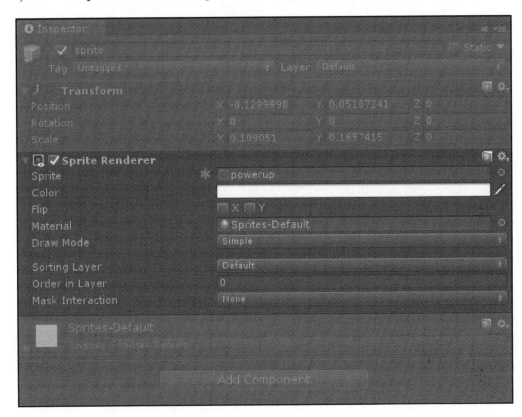

I have grayed out the **Transform** and **Material** options in the **Inspector** window, but left the **Sprite Renderer** component clear in the previous screenshot. The main focus of this sprite game object property is what object type we are going to be supplying the **Sprite Renderer** component with. The previous screenshot shows the sprite powerup property, which gives us a fire-like icon in the **Scene** window.

Let's check the powerup property so that we are certain of its data type and how it's recognized in the Unity editor.

To view the sprite's data type, do the following:

1. With the `sprite` game object still selected in our **Hierarchy** window, click once on the `powerup` property in the **Inspector** window of the **Sprite Renderer** section.

2. The `powerup` sprite location will appear in the **Project** window with a yellow border around it. The following screenshot shows the `powerup` sprite location pinging when selected from the **Sprite Renderer** component:

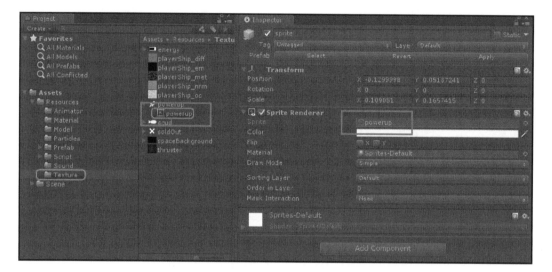

3. Next, click on the parent of the `powerup` property in the **Project** window. The **Inspector** window will change to the `powerup` sprite's import settings.

4. The majority of the information doesn't require altering, but the main point of focus is making sure the **Texture Type** setting is recognized as **Sprite** to make the file compatible with the **Sprite Renderer** component.

The following screenshot shows our `powerup` file recognized as a sprite, with an image preview at the bottom of the window:

It is possible that when a sprite, such as a powerup texture in the previous screenshot, is imported into Unity, it may not be recognized as a sprite and will be given the Default name. This is because Default is the most common selection for textures, especially with three-dimensional models. Default also offers more options with regard to texture properties.

If you would like to know more about the texture types, check out `https://docs.unity3d.com/Manual/TextureTypes.html`.

With regard to our `powerup` texture, we do not need to change it to `Default`. When we add another selection, the same principles of checking the image type should be carried out. Let's now move on to the second game object of the UPGRADE_00 game object—`itemText`.

Displaying credit on our itemText game object

The second child game object from UPGRADE_00 is `itemText`. This game object has a **Text Mesh** component that holds the responsibility of displaying text. We will use this component to receive and display the selection upgrade's credit value and also to notify the player when the item has been purchased by displaying SOLD in the text.

I grayed out the majority of the following screenshot to expose the connection between the **Text Mesh** component and the text in the **Scene** window:

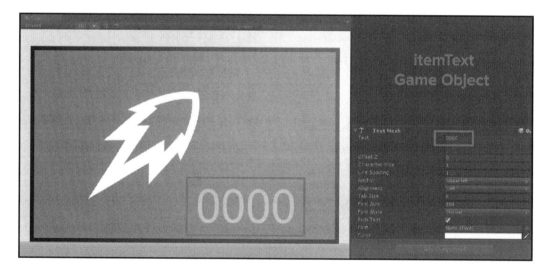

Let's now move on to the final child game object of the UPGRADE_00 hierarchy, which is `SelectionQuad`.

Project files diagnosis when making SelectionQuad

In this section, I am going to briefly explain how the shop's selection grid is prepared.

SelectionQuad is the third child game object of the UPGRADE_00 game object, as shown in the following screenshot:

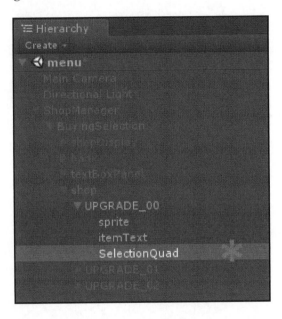

This game object simply serves to show the player that they have made a selection. It consists of a quad mesh, which is a standard primitive that can be made in Unity (by right-clicking in the **Hierarchy** window and selecting **3D Object | Quad**).

Once the Quad object is moved into position, change its **Material** properties from an **Opaque** rendering mode to **Transparent (1)**

Then, click on the **Albedo** thumbnail color (**2**) and change its color settings (**3**) to **R**: 64, **G**: 152, **B**: 255, and **A**: 140). The following screenshot shows the color property changes made to the `SelectionQuad` material:

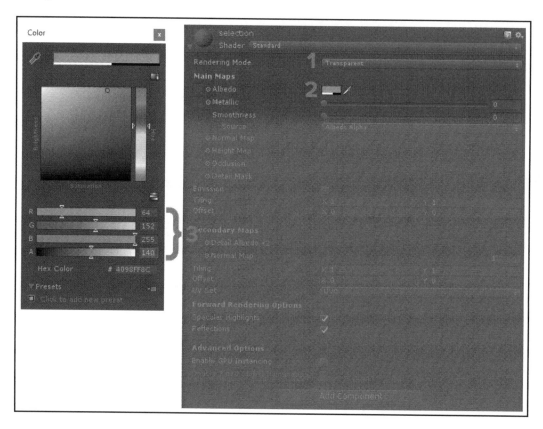

That is the entirety of our UPGRADE_00 selection. Then, copy and paste each game object on to two more black rectangles and rename them UPGRADE_01 and UPGRADE_02.

The following screenshot shows the three game objects:

For the purpose of this chapter, having three selections demonstrates how we can manipulate and carry information from one scene to another. Before we start making scripts for these selections, I want to show you some text that will be added to the two slightly larger buttons at the far right of the grid:

1. Scroll down in the **Hierarchy** window until you get to two game objects titled WATCH AD and START. These two game objects will hold the following responsibilities:

   - WATCH AD is used when the player selects this button, an advert will play. Once the advert is finished, the player is rewarded with credits. These credits are used to buy more upgrades.
   - START is used when the player is finished with the shop. They can move on by pressing the **START** button.

2. Expand WATCH AD and START by clicking on each arrow to the left of them.
3. Click on each game object and make them active in the **Inspector** window, as we did earlier in the *Introducing our shop scripts* section.

In each expanded game object, we have a label game object; this holds a **Text Mesh** component, which we have been introduced to already in this section, that displays our button text.

The following screenshot shows the expanded WATCH AD and START objects in the **Hierarchy** window:

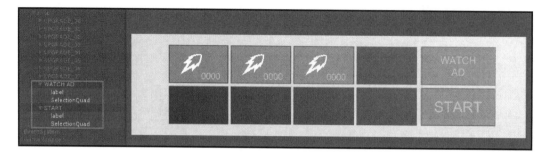

So far, we understand that we have a shop scene that will contain scriptable objects for our ship's upgrades; we are also aware of how the option to watch adverts to gain credits is a popular mechanism with free-to-play games.

That is all that we need for the selection grid. We can now start considering how to turn the buttons on and off, change each upgrade art, and more in the next section.

Customizing our shop selection

In this section, we are going to use scriptable objects to customize each selection. We have already used scriptable objects in Chapter 2, *Adding and Manipulating Objects*. This time, we will use a similar method but for our selection grid; hopefully, this will make you appreciate how scriptable objects can be expanded and used across the game.

As mentioned in Chapter 2, *Adding and Manipulating Objects*, I make a habit of initialing scriptable objects with an SO tag so that they're easy to identify. Let's create an SOShopSelection script:

1. In the Unity editor, go to the **Project** window and navigate to Assets/Resources/Script.
2. Create a script (using the same method as in Chapter 2, *Adding and Manipulating Objects*) and name it SOShopSelection.

This SOShopSelection script will create a template of data types for our asset files (the same as with our player and enemy ships). These asset files will be attached to each of the player ship upgrades.

An individual selection from the grid will take four property types, as follows:

- `icon`: A picture of the selection
- `iconName`: Identifies what the selection is
- `description`: Used to describe what the upgrade is in the large selection box at the top right of the scene
- `cost`: Calculates how many credits it is worth so that it can be displayed in the credit values of the selection.

Let's open the `SOShopSelection` script and begin to code:

1. At the top of the script, make sure we have entered the following library:

   ```
   using UnityEngine;
   ```

   As with most scripts in Unity, we need the `UnityEngine` library so that we can use the `ScriptableObject` functionality.

2. To make it so that we can create assets from the scriptable object, we enter the following attribute above our class name:

   ```
   [CreateAssetMenu(fileName = "Create Shop Piece", menuName =
       "Create Shop Piece")]
   ```

3. Enter the following code to inherit `ScriptableObject` to the `SOShopSelection` script. This will give us the functionality for creating template asset files:

   ```
   public class SOShopSelection : ScriptableObject
   {
   ```

4. Enter the following code to hold the specific variables:

   ```
   public Sprite icon;
   public string iconName;
   public string description;
   public string cost;
   }
   ```

5. Save the script.

We have made the script to hold our data for each potential selection in the grid. As mentioned, we have already made these types of scripts before—we are just using them here to customize buttons, rather than space ships.

We can now customize our three UPGRADE game objects in the Unity editor—let's do that next.

Creating selection templates

In the last section, we made a scriptable object that allowed us to create an asset file that holds custom parameters and values. These assets and their properties can be created by users who don't hold programming knowledge, which is ideal for designers and programmers.

We have three selections to add to our selection grid:

- **Weapon upgrade**: Gives the player's ship a stronger weapon
- **Health upgrade**: Allows the player's ship to get hit twice by an enemy object
- **Atom bomb**: Wipes all the visible enemies out

So, let's go back to the Unity editor and make some asset templates for our selection grid:

1. From the **Project** window, navigate to
   `Assets/Resources/Script/ScriptableObject`.
2. Right-click in an open space of the **Project** window and, from the dropdown that appears, select **Create** and then **Create Shop Piece**, as in the following screenshot:

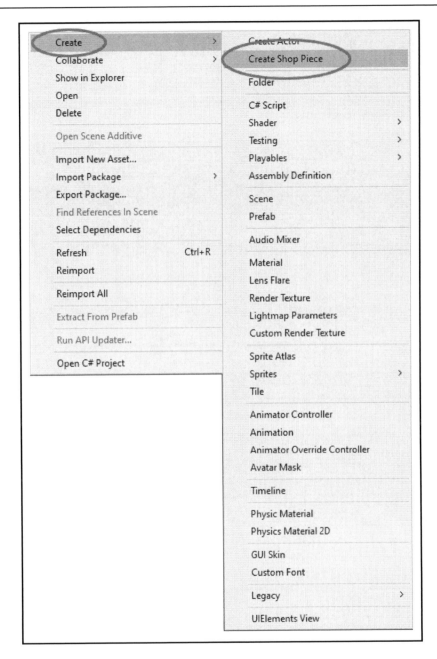

3. Rename the new Create Shop Piece file Shot_PowerUp.

4. With Shot_PowerUp still selected, take your attention to the **Inspector** window, where we have the data types that we can enter.

The following screenshot shows the Shot_PowerUp properties that we are going to change next:

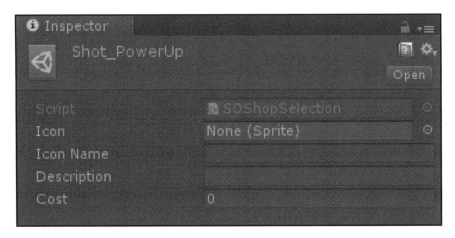

5. We will apply our powerup sprite icon to the **Icon** data type by clicking on the small circle to the right of its field.

6. Scroll down in the **Select Sprite** window until you see the powerup sprite and double-click it, as in the following screenshot:

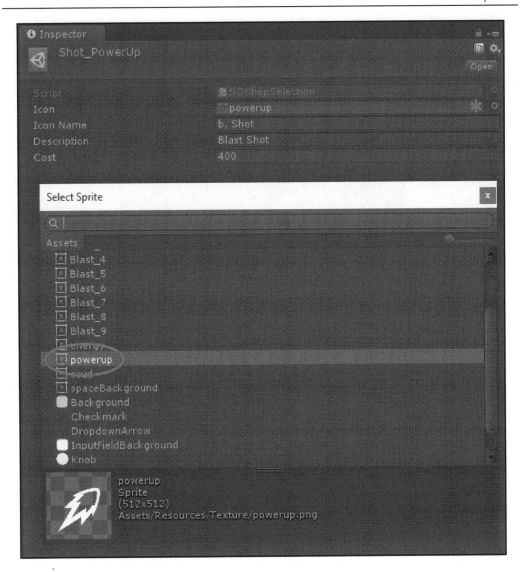

7. Now, enter the following property names and the values we are going to give them:

- **Icon Name**: b. Shot
- **Description**: Blast Shot
- **Cost**: 400

8. Create another `ShopPiece` asset as we did before.

9. This time, change the asset name from `Create Shop Piece` to `Health_Level1` and give it the details shown in the following screenshot:

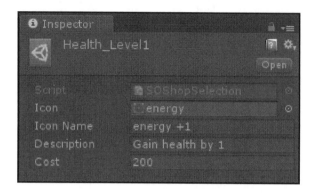

10. Let's now make the third asset file, using the exact same process as the last two assets, but this time name it `Bomb_Cluster` and give it the following details:

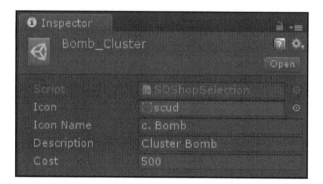

We have made the scriptable objects and configured them for our ship's upgrades. Let's now make the second main script for the shop, `ShopPiece`. This script will hold each of the asset files we have just made and will display their content around the shop's grid scene.

Customizing our player ship's upgrade selection

The purpose of this script is to send information to each of the selection buttons in our shop scene. For each of the three UPGRADE game objects, we will create and attach a script that takes reference from the SOShopSelection scriptable object (the three asset files we made in the previous section) and assign them to each player ship's upgrade button.

To create the ShopPiece script, do the following:

1. Let's start by navigating to Assets/Resources/Script from the **Project** window.
2. Create the script the same way as we did at the start of the *Customizing our shop selection* section and name the script ShopPiece.
3. Open the script and begin to code, starting with the script contains the UnityEngine library at the top of the script:

   ```
   using UnityEngine;
   ```

   Because we are using elements of Unity and attaching the ShopPiece script with the Unity editor, this script will require the UnityEngine library.

4. Check and enter the next following code to declare the class name and inheritance:

   ```
   public class ShopPiece : MonoBehaviour
   {
   ```

   By default, our script should be automatically named, along with its default inherited MonoBehaviour, as this is a requirement of the Unity editor and other functionalities.

5. Enter the following code to allow the shopSelection instance to be updated:

   ```
   [SerializeField]
     SOShopSelection shopSelection;
     public SOShopSelection ShopSelection
     {
       get {return shopSelection; }
       set {shopSelection = value; }
     }
   ```

We added a reference to the SOShopSelection script that we made in the last section. This reference is private (because it isn't labeled as public) but we expose it to the Unity editor with a [SerializeField] function above it. This means we can drag and drop each scriptable asset file to its field in the Unity editor. If another script requires access to the private shopSelection variable, we can refer to the ShopSelection property that will receive and send its data (get and set).

6. Enter the following code to update the shopSelection sprite:

```
void Awake()
  {
   //icon slot
   if (GetComponentInChildren<SpriteRenderer>() != null)
   {
    GetComponentInChildren<SpriteRenderer>().sprite =
      shopSelection.icon;
   }
```

When this script is active and runs for the first time, it runs its Awake function. Inside the function are two if statements; the first checks whether there is a SpriteRenderer component in any of its child game objects. If there is, then it grabs reference from its shopSelection asset file and applies its icon sprite to display on the button.

7. Enter the following code to update the cost value:

```
   //selection value
    if(transform.Find("itemText"))
    {
       GetComponentInChildren<TextMesh>().text =
  shopSelection.cost;
    }
  }
}
```

The alternative if statement checks whether any of the child game objects of this class have a game object titled itemText.

If there is a game object titled itemText, we update its TextMesh component's text value with the shopSelection cost value.

8. Save the script.

Back in the Unity editor, we can attach the ShopPiece script, along with each asset script we made in the last section.

To attach each ShopPiece script to each UPGRADE game object file, do the following:

1. From the **Hierarchy** window, locate and select the UPGRADE_00 game object.
2. Either drag and drop the ShopPiece script from the **Project** window (Assets/Resources/Scripts) or click on **Add Component** in the **Inspector** window and type the script's name into the dropdown search.
3. UPGRADE_00 will be our weapon power-up button, so for the **Shop Selection** parameter, either locate the file we made earlier in the **Project** window (Assets/Resources/Script/ScriptableObject) or click on the small circle to the right of the **Shop Selection** field and type in the asset file that we named Shot_PowerUp. Use the following screenshot as a reference to how your **Inspector** window should look:

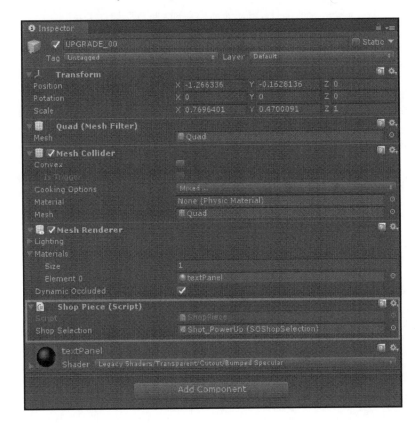

4. Now, repeat this process for UPGRADE_01 by giving the game object the ShopPiece script with the Health_Level1 asset in its **Shop Selection** field. The following screenshot shows the ShopPiece component for UPGRADE_01:

5. Finally, complete the same procedure for UPGRADE_02, adding the ShopPiece script and applying Bomb_Cluster to the Shop_Selection field. The following screenshot shows the ShopPiece script with the Bomb_Cluster asset applied:

6. To test whether the three selection pieces work in the selection grid, save the scene so far and click the **Play** button in the Unity editor.

Our selection grid should go from the top three buttons with the same image and same value (not in play mode) to each image and value different (in play mode):

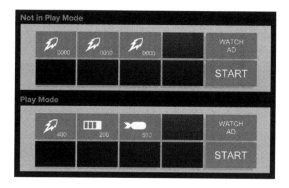

If you recall, our asset files have a name and description data; we can use this for the large rectangle in the shop scene when it comes to supplying information about the item. Also, we need to update the player ship's visuals to show what a purchase looks like on the ship, as well as a few other things. In the next section, we are going to create a script that allows the user to press a button from the selection grid.

Selecting game objects with raycasts

In this section, we are going to create the final shop script, `PlayerShipBuild`. This script holds properties such as selecting any button from the selection grid, running adverts, communicating with our existing game framework scripts, launching our game to play, and a few other things that we will cover.

One of the subjects you will likely come across in your Unity programmer exam and when developing games/applications in Unity is shooting invisible lasers that are used for things such as shooting a gun, making a selection in three-dimensional space, and more. In this section, we are going to make it so that when the player presses a button on the selection grid, the button lights up blue to let the player know that it has been selected. We already have each of our buttons set up with blue rectangles that are permanently on. So, all that we need to do now is turn them all off when the scene becomes active and make it so that any of the buttons turn on when a ray (invisible laser) comes into contact with it.

The following screenshot shows an example of how the player sees the selection screen (**SELECTION 2D**) and the same scene at an angle so that we can see the main camera's clipping planes (**SELECTION 3D**). When the player presses a button on the selection grid, an invisible line (ray) will travel across it. If the line comes into contact with a game object that has a collider attached to it, we can get information from that game object:

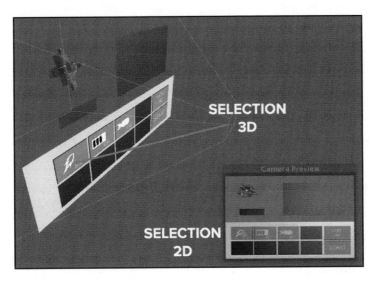

So, what we are going to do for this selection is start by creating a `PlayerShipBuild` script and giving it the functionality to shoot rays, which will then change the color of the button.

Let's start by creating a script in the usual **Project** window location (`Assets/Resources/Script`) and naming it `PlayerShipBuild`. You should know how to make a script now as we did so in the previous section (*Customizing our player ship's upgrade selection*).

To create a raycast selection, open the `PlayerShipBuild` script, and follow these steps:

1. Enter the following code to use Unity's functionality and apply this script to a game object in the editor:

   ```
   using UnityEngine;
   ```

2. Enter the following code to declare our class:

   ```
   public class PlayerShipBuild : MonoBehaviour
   {
   ```

   Our script has a `public` access modifier and is named the same as the `PlayerShipBuild` file.

   This script inherits `MonoBehaviour`, so it is recognized when attached to a game object in the editor.

3. Enter the following code to hold each of the `shopButtons`:

   ```
   [SerializeField]
   GameObject[] shopButtons;
   ```

   We have a `private` variable that is exposed in the Editor with `[SerializeField]` (so we can see and edit it) that will hold an array of all 10 game object buttons on the selection grid.

4. Enter the following code to hold two game objects for raycasting:

   ```
   GameObject target;
   GameObject tmpSelection;
   ```

   The `tmpSelection` variable is used to store the raycast selection so that we can check to see what we have made contact with. The target variable will be used later on in the script.

`tmpSelection` will be used at the end of the selection process when it comes to turning the game object on.

5. Enter the following code within the `Start` function to run our method:

```
void Start()
{
    TurnOffSelectionHighlights();
}
```

Unity's `Start` function will be the first thing called when this script becomes active.

6. Next, we will enter the following code to create the `TurnOffSelectionHighlights` method:

```
void TurnOffSelectionHighlights()
{
    for (int i = 0; i < shopButtons.Length; i++)
    {
        shopButtons[i].SetActive(false);
    }
}
```

Within the `TurnOffSelectionHighlights` method, we run a `for` loop that makes sure all of the buttons have their blue rectangles turned off.

7. Enter the following code into the `Update` function that is called at every frame:

```
void Update()
{
    AttemptSelection();
}
```

The `AttemptSelection` method is responsible for receiving the player's input for a button selection. The content of this method will be covered in detail when we come to it.

8. Enter the following code to create our `ReturnClickedObject` method:

```
GameObject ReturnClickedObject (out RaycastHit hit)
{
    GameObject target = null;
    Ray ray = Camera.main.ScreenPointToRay
(Input.mousePosition);
    if (Physics.Raycast (ray.origin, ray.direction * 100, out
hit))
    {
        target = hit.collider.gameObject;
    }
    return target;
}
```

The `ReturnClickedObject` method also takes an argument of an `out` raycast hit, which will contain information of what collider the ray has made contact with.

Within this method, we reset the `target` game object to remove any previous data. We then take reference from the camera to find where the player tapped or clicked their mouse on the screen and store the result in the form of a ray.

More information about `ScreenPointToRay` can be found in Unity's scripting reference at `https://docs.unity3d.com/ScriptReference/Camera.ScreenPointToRay.html`.

We then check whether the origin and the direction of the camera from where we have shot the ray have made contact with a collider (within 100 world space meters).

If we have made contact with a collider, the `if` statement is acknowledged as `true`; we then take the reference of the game object it has hit and store it in the `target` game object.

Finally, we send out (`return`) the `target` game object that the ray has come into contact with.

If you recall, we referred to an `AttemptSelection` method earlier in the `Update` function. The `AttemptSelection` method will check when a condition is made when the player has made contact by tapping the screen or clicking a mouse button in our shop scene.

9. Enter the following code to write out the `AttemptSelection` method:

```
void AttemptSelection()
{
    if (Input.GetMouseButtonDown (0))
    {
      RaycastHit hitInfo;
      target = ReturnClickedObject (out hitInfo);

      if (target != null)
      {
        if (target.transform.Find("itemText"))
        {
          TurnOffSelectionHighlights();
          Select();
        }
      }
    }
}
```

If the player has pressed the mouse button or tapped the touch screen, we will fire the ray and send all `RaycastHit` objects into the `ReturnClickedObject` method that we mentioned in the previous section of code. The results from the `ReturnClickedObject` method are returned to the `target` game object that we made at the start of the script.

We then check whether this `target` game object has anything inside it or whether it is just empty. If there is something inside it, we then run another check to see whether this `target` game object is holding a game object named `itemText`. If it does have a game object with this name, we refresh the selection grid by turning all the blue quads off, followed by a method called `Select`, which is what we are going to talk about next.

We have finally dug down into the last bit of our script where we have to acknowledge that we have located and named the game object. We now just need to turn `SelectionQuad` of that game object on.

10. Enter the following method into our code; this will make the player's button selection active:

```
void Select()
{
  tmpSelection =  target.transform.Find
      ("SelectionQuad").gameObject;
```

```
            tmpSelection.SetActive(true);
        }
```

The `Select` method doesn't need to check any conditions with `if` statements as this has mostly been done for us with the previous code. We carry out a search for `SelectionQuad` and store its reference as `tmpSelection`.

Finally, we set the `tmpSelection` game objects activity to `true` so that it is seen in our `shop` **Scene** window.

11. Save the script and return to the Unity editor.

We can now attach our `PlayerShipBuild` script to our shop game object (using the same attaching method we used earlier in this chapter for `ShopPiece`), which is the parent to all of the buttons in the selection grid, as in the following screenshot:

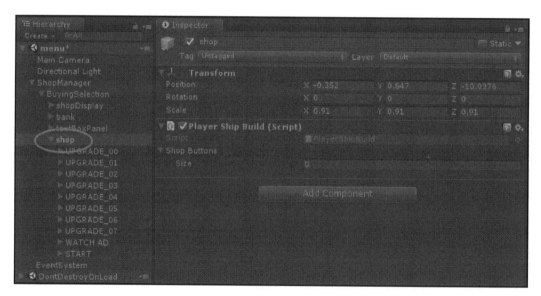

Also, if you recall at the start of the `PlayerShipBuild` script, we added a game object variable that would take an array of `shopButtons`. We could have a `for` loop to add each `UPGRADE` game object automatically at the start of the script, but if, in the future, we wanted to consider using a joypad or keyboard to guide us through the selection grid, we would have more control in knowing which button is assigned to each array number. Also, this is just another way of programming without relying on code as Unity is a component-based engine. Other controller inputs and interactions are something we are going to cover in Chapter 13, *Effects, Testing, Performance, and Alt Controls*, where we will start thinking about other platforms to port our game to.

With the potential of updating our controls in a later lesson, here is how you should attach the game objects to the `shopButtons` array in the Unity editor:

1. With the shop game object still selected in the **Hierarchy** window, it's probably best to lock the **Inspector** window at this point (as we did in Chapter 4, *Applying Art, Animation, and Particles*) as we are going to be selecting and dragging different game objects.

2. Change the shop button's size from 0 to 10 in the **Inspector** window.

   We will now get a burst of empty game object fields in the **Inspector** window, which will allow us to drag and drop each `SelectionQuad` game object to each field.

3. Next, to make things even easier, click on the arrow to the left of each game object under the shop game object to expand each of the child game objects. This will uncover the `SelectionQuad` game objects we need to drag across.

The following screenshot shows the **Inspector** window with a list of empty game objects and the **Hierarchy** window game objects expanded out:

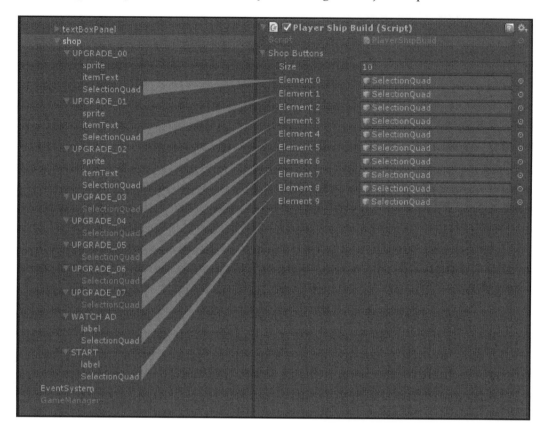

I have also added arrow stripes to the previous screenshot to show which SelectionQuad objects need to go to which game object field in the **Inspector** window.

4. Save the scene. If you did lock your **Inspector** window, don't forget to unlock it.

5. Press the **Play** button in the editor.

Now, when the scene starts, all the blue selection quads disappear, but if you click on either one, it will light up, depending on which button is pressed.

The following screenshot shows the atom bomb button selected when the mouse clicks on it in the game window. This will also work with touchscreen devices:

That covers using raycasts, which is a transferable skill and can be used for anything that involves shooting to grab information from another game object, providing it has a collider attached to it.

Let's now move on to updating the description panel so that when a selection is made from the grid, we get the text on the large, dark rectangle with information we stored from the same scriptable objects that give information to each player upgrade button.

Adding information to our description panel

When a selection is made in the shop scene, we can take the information from the selection's scriptable object asset file and display its details within its `textBoxPanel` game object.

Let's take a look at the `textBoxPanel` object in the **Hierarchy** window:

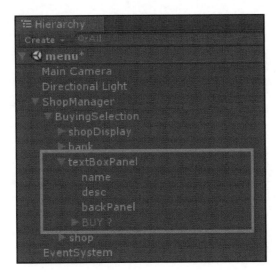

The `textBoxPanel` game object holds a black quad that is used for its background. It also holds four other game objects, as follows:

- `name`: This game object contains a **TextMesh** component that receives data from the selection that was made that contains the `iconName` scriptable object variable.
- `desc`: This game object also holds a **TextMesh** component that receives data from the selection's `description` scriptable object variable.
- `backPanel`: This game object serves as a background for the selection grid.
- `BUY?`: This game object will be covered later on when we want to confirm that we want to purchase the item we have selected.

The following screenshot identifies the two scriptable object data types from the `Health_Level1` asset file we made earlier on in this chapter. The information on this large rectangle will change depending on which button is selected:

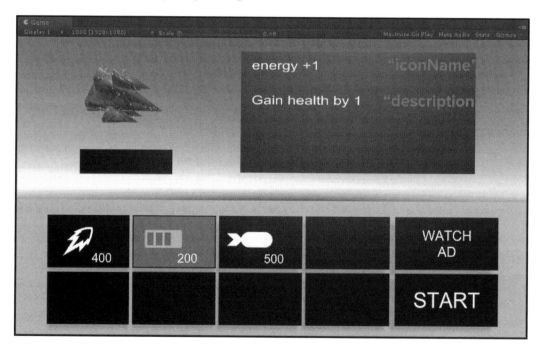

Let's now go back to the `PlayerShipBuild` script and add some more code to update the description panel (the `textBoxPanel` game object):

1. Reopen the `PlayerShipBuild` script and add the following variable to the top of the script with the other global variables:

   GameObject textBoxPanel;

   This game object variable will hold a reference to the `textBoxPanel` game object in our scene. Next, we need to grab and refer this game object from our **Hierarchy** window.

2. Scroll down to the `Start` function and enter the following line of code to store the `textBoxPanel` game object as a reference:

   ```
   textBoxPanel = GameObject.Find("textBoxPanel");
   ```

   Now, scroll down to the content of `AttemptSelection`.

3. Scroll down until we get to the following `if` statement and add `UpdateDescriptionBox();` into the content of that statement:

   ```
   if (target.transform.Find("itemText"))
   {
     TurnOffSelectionHighlights();
     Select();
     UpdateDescriptionBox();
   }
   ```

   The `UpdateDescriptionBox` method will grab the selected button's asset file variable content, `iconName` and `description`, and apply it to the `TextMesh` text component of `textboxPanel`.

4. Let's now enter the content of this method with the following code:

   ```
   void UpdateDescriptionBox()
   {
   textBoxPanel.transform.Find("name").gameObject.GetComponent
      <TextMesh>().text = tmpSelection.GetComponentInParent
         <ShopPiece>().ShopSelection.iconName;
   textBoxPanel.transform.Find("desc").gameObject.GetComponent
      <TextMesh>().text = tmpSelection.GetComponentInParent
         <ShopPiece>().ShopSelection.description;
    }
   ```

The `UpdateDescriptionBox` method will get the reference name and description from the shop button that's selected and will apply the string values to the shop's black noticeboard (`textBoxPanel`).

5. Save the script.

Test the results by pressing **Play** in the Unity editor.

The following screenshot shows the first selection grid being selected with the description panel details displayed:

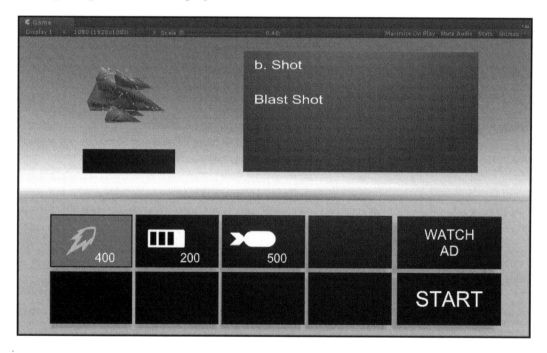

With a small amount of code, the description panel lights up and displays information from any of the items that are selected. This is useful as if we ever want to extend the selection grid with more items we wouldn't need to bloat our code to compensate for each selection.

We now have a shop scene that shows what is available to buy and descriptions of what each item is. Let's summarize what we have learned in this chapter.

Summary

In this chapter, we started creating a shop scene that holds various buttons and panels created from three-dimensional polygons. We then created our own script to fill the scene with images, values, names, and descriptions of assets that could potentially be purchased with virtual credits.

We also made use of scriptable objects to create a template for our code so that it can be topped up with various in-game powerups without inflating our game's framework. We also made it interchangeable, so if a weapon needs changing, replacing, or removing, we can simply remove the template without affecting the rest of the code in our game framework.

The other lesson we learned in this chapter is being aware that we can create games that are free to download, but also knowing how to create a form of income with a monetization game design to create revenue.

In the next chapter, we will continue with our shop scene and focus more on the content of each button and the overall functionality of our shop in adding content to our player's ship. We will also look at game advertisements as a form of currency for the player to upgrade their space ship.

6
Purchasing In-Game Items and Advertisements

In this chapter, we will continue with building our shop scene by adding functionality such as introducing the player's in-game currency and looking at how to deduct and increase it. We will make great use of the Unity Monetization package, which is free to download from the Asset store.

Monetization is when a game is free to download (typically titled **free-to-play**) and the developer encourages or offers the player to buy items, such as the latest weapon, extra art modification visuals, and more, with the player's real money (with a bank/debit card). Another way of creating profit from a free-to-play game is by offering adverts that are incorporated into the game. For example, if the player wants a new ship or an extra life, they can watch a 30-second advert at no real monetary cost to them, but as the developer, we can receive revenue when an advert is watched. Of course, a balance must be considered when a game is made and some companies will use all sorts of addictive psychology to encourage the player to buy upgrades or watch as many adverts as possible. This could lead a single player to sometimes pay well into the thousands of their real money. It is up to you how you want to plan and make your own game outside of this book; but for this chapter, we will create our own shop that offers players the chance to watch an advert to gain extra in-game credits.

- Buying upgrades for our player's ship
- Buying items, watching adverts, and preparing to start a game
- Extending the `PlayerSpawner` script

Let's get started!

The core exam skills covered in this chapter

We will cover programming core interactions in this chapter:

- *Implementing and configuring game object behavior and physics*
- *Implementing and configuring inputs and controls*

We will also cover developing application systems:

- *Interpreting scripts for application interface flow, such as menu systems, UI navigation, and application settings*
- *Interpreting scripts for user-controlled customization, such as character creators, inventories, storefronts, and in-app purchases*
- *Analyzing scripts for user progression features, such as scoring, leveling, and in-game economies, utilizing technologies such as Unity Analytics and PlayerPrefs*
- *Analyzing scripts for two-dimensional overlays, such as **Heads-Up Displays (HUDs)**, minimaps, and advertisements*
- *Identifying scripts for saving and retrieving application and user data*

We will also cover programming for scene and environment design:

- *Identifying methods for implementing game object instantiation, destruction, and management*

Finally, we will cover working in professional software development teams:

- *Recognizing techniques for structuring scripts for modularity, readability, and reusability*

Technical requirements

The project content for this chapter can be found at `https://github.com/PacktPublishing/Unity-Certified-Programmer-Exam-Guide/tree/master/Chapter06`.

You can download the entirety of each chapter's project files at `https://github.com/PacktPublishing/Unity-Certified-Programmer-Exam-Guide/archive/master.zip`.

All of the content for this chapter is held in the chapter's `unitypackage` file. There is no `Complete` folder for this chapter.

Check out the following video to see the Code in Action: `https://bit.ly/2NuTgJQ`.

Buying upgrades for our player's ship

In this section, we will cover the process of buying upgrades for our player's ship. This includes the following:

- Credit balance
- Option to buy
- Letting the player know the item has been sold

The following screenshot shows our shop scene with its selection grid and two purchased items marked as **SOLD**. Above the selection grid, to the left, is the user's current in-game bank balance and an image showing what the player's ship currently looks like with the two upgrades applied. Lastly, to the right is the option to buy the currently selected item, which is `C. Bomb`:

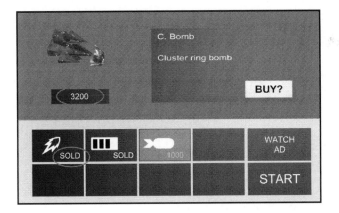

In this section, we will return to the script that is responsible for purchasing upgrades and applying them to the player's ship. In the `PlayerShipBuild` script, we will add global variables that will hold the player's weapon upgrades in an array, as well as game object buttons and the player's in-bank balance.

We will then hook up each of these new variables to the text and game object buttons in our scene and from there, we will add our own methods to turn buttons on or off and to know whether the player has enough in-game credits to make purchases.

Let's start by entering these new variables to our shop scene by going to the
Project window and opening the `PlayerShipBuild` script in
the `Assets/Resources/Script` folder:

1. Enter the following global variables to our `PlayerShipBuild` script:

```
[SerializeField]
GameObject[] visualWeapons;
[SerializeField]
SOActorModel defaultPlayerShip;
GameObject playerShip;
GameObject buyButton;
GameObject bankObj;
int bank = 600;
bool purchaseMade = false;
```

   We have mainly added game objects that hold the visualization of our shop
   scene, but we have also added a scriptable object that's used to give the
   player's ship its own property values, such as speed, health, what type of
   bullets are used, and more. We will make use of some of these variables in
   the next code block.

2. Next, we will update the `PlayerShipBuild` script by adding code to
   the `Start` function by getting a reference to the bank game object and the
   BUY? button in our shop scene:

```
purchaseMade = false;
bankObj = GameObject.Find("bank");
bankObj.GetComponentInChildren<TextMesh>().text =
bank.ToString();
buyButton = textBoxPanel.transform.Find("BUY ?").gameObject;

TurnOffPlayerShipVisuals();
PreparePlayerShipForUpgrade();
```

   This code resets or assigns the variables to game objects in
   the **Hierarchy** window of the Unity editor. I will explain these variables
   briefly here and go into more detail when we use them:

     - `purchaseMade` is a Boolean variable that will only accept a
       `true` or `false` value. We are setting it to `false` here as a
       form of reset.

- `bankObj`: In the **Hierarchy** window, we have a game object called `bank`. We are assigning that game object of this variable for later.
- We then take the `bank` integer that currently contains a value of `600` and we cast (assign) it as a `string` value so that it displays the value in our shop scene under the three-dimensional model of the player's ship.
- The last variable is then assigned the `BUY ?` game object so that we can activate and deactivate the buy functionality whenever required in the **Scene** or **Game** window.
- `TurnOffPlayerShipVisuals`: This method will reset the visuals of the player's ship.
- `PreparePlayerShipForUpgrade`: This method creates a player's ship so that when it has all the upgrades applied, it can be sent into the game to be played.

3. Now that we have our variables made and assigned, we can move on to the conditions of the code. Scroll down in the script until you get to the following line:

```
if (target.transform.Find("itemText"))
```

4. Within the `if` statement, we are going check whether the item we are attempting to buy has not already sold out in the shop (the only reason for an item to be sold out is because we have already bought it) and that we can afford it:

```
if (target.transform.Find("itemText"))
{
    TurnOffSelectionHighlights();
    Select();
    UpdateDescriptionBox();

//NOT ALREADY SOLD
if
(target.transform.Find("itemText").GetComponent<TextMesh>().
    text != "SOLD")
{
    //can afford
    Affordable();

    //can not afford
    LackOfCredits();
```

```
    }
    else if (target.transform.Find("itemText").GetComponent
       <TextMesh>().text == "SOLD")
    {
       SoldOut();
    }
}
```

We start by entering a comment to notify ourselves or any other programmer that at this point in the code, we are going to check whether the item we are attempting to buy is not already sold out. From here, we add an `if` statement condition that checks the `target` variable (the item we raycasted, as mentioned in the *Selecting game objects with raycasts* section of the previous chapter) to see whether it contains a `TextMesh` component holding a `string` (text) value that doesn't already hold the `"SOLD"` value. If it does, then we run the `SoldOut` method.

If the item hasn't already sold out, then we run two methods—the first is `Affordable`, which means we're going to check whether we can buy the item with the current amount of credit we have. If we don't have enough credit, the `LackOfCredits` method is run.

We have created three new methods called `Affordable`, `LackOfCredits`, and `SoldOut`; so, let's now go through each one, starting with `Affordable`.

5. Outside of the `AttemptSelection` method, add the following code:

```
void Affordable()
{
   if (bank >=  System.Int32.Parse(target.transform.
      GetComponent<ShopPiece>().ShopSelection.cost))
   {
      Debug.Log("CAN BUY");
      buyButton.SetActive(true);
   }
}
```

The `Affordable` method checks whether the `bank` integer (which currently contains the value `600`) is equal or greater than the value of the button that we have selected (`target`).

Next is an `if` statement that checks whether the `bank` integer value is greater than or equal to the `string cost` value of the selected item. Because we can't compare the value of a `string` variable to an `int` variable, we need to convert the `string` variable to an `int` variable. To do this, we use `System.Int32.Parse()` and enter the `ShopeSelection.cost` string value in the parse brackets.

If we can buy the item, then we set `buyButton` to active, which is a button the player can press to buy the item. Above `buyButton.SetActive(true)` is a log to Unity's **Console** window to confirm that a purchase is being made for bug-checking purposes.

6. The second method we wrote earlier was the `LackOfCredits` method, which checks in a similar way by casting the `TextMesh` component value if it's less than the `bank` integer value. If it is, we send a `"CAN'T BUY"` message to Unity's **Console** window:

```
void LackOfCredits()
{
  if (bank < System.Int32.Parse(target.transform.Find
    ("itemText").GetComponent<TextMesh>().text))
  {
    Debug.Log("CAN'T BUY");
  }
}
```

There are multiple ways to get a reference from a game object and we use them throughout this book.

In the previous code, `.Find` is much slower compared to something like `.GetComponent` used on its own. `.Find` has to go through each game object until it finds the matching string—if it even exists.

 We could also compare performance versus flexibility as well—for example, `transform.GetChild` (`https://docs.unity3d.com/ScriptReference/Transform.GetChild.html`) will get the child that is specific to the number given to it in its parameter, which is also faster than using `.Find`. However, if the game object's hierarchy has changed during development this would cause an error as it is no longer able to find the game object. The same could be said for `.GetComponent`, which can cause errors if it doesn't exist in the code.

7. The third is the `SoldOut` method, which is currently set to log out to the Unity editor **Console** window saying `SOLD OUT`, but yet again, we could add other functionality to this at a later date, such as applying a sound effect or playing an animation:

```
void SoldOut()
{
  Debug.Log("SOLD OUT");
}
```

8. Make two empty methods. We will fill their content in later on in the chapter:

```
void TurnOffPlayerShipVisuals()
{

}

void PreparePlayerShipForUpgrade()
{

}
```

9. Save the script and return to the Unity editor.

Reflecting on this section, we have coded in our variables and assigned them when the script begins with the `Start` function. We have also coded in a few methods that check the balance credit compared to the selected value.

We can now move on to updating our player ship's visuals in the shop scene and we can also see what the player's ship looks like in the game.

Updating visual representations of our player's ship

In this section, we are going to code in capability so that the player's ship visuals update when a purchase is made and create and update another ship behind the scenes so that it can be sent on to the next scene to play.

In the *Selecting game objects with raycasts* section, we dragged and dropped our `SelectionQuad` game objects from the **Hierarchy** window into the **Inspector** window.

The following screenshot shows the majority of the shop game objects grayed out on the **Inspector** window so that we can focus on the new variable entries under **Visual Weapons**:

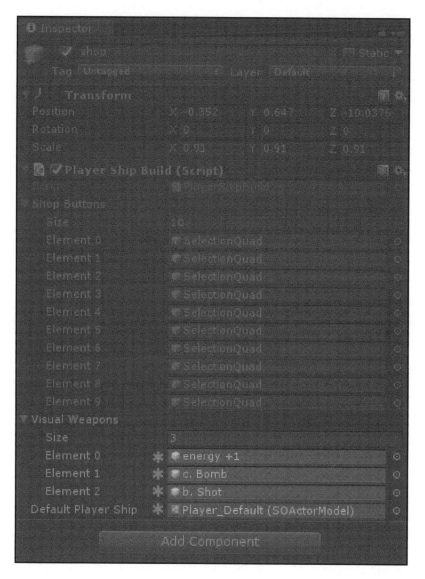

To update the housing of the potential player ship upgrades, we need to apply the following to the `Visual Weapons` game object array using the previous screenshot as reference:

1. Change the **Size** value to 3.
2. For the three empty game object fields, click on the first far-right side circle, and from the dropdown, begin typing `energy +1` into the search bar.
3. As soon as you see **energy + 1**, double-click it.
4. Repeat this process for `c. Bomb`.
5. Repeat this process for `b. Shot`.
6. Lastly, update the **Default Player Ship** scriptable object field with the `Player_Default` asset file via the small remote circle to the right of it. We will go into more detail about this when we put it into practice in code.
7. Save the scene and return to the `PlayerShipBuild` script.
8. We can now enter the content for our `TurnOffPlayerShipVisuals` method. This method is implemented in the `Start` function to simply reset the scene so that the only visual representation is the three-dimensional model of the player's ship:

```
void TurnOffPlayerShipVisuals()
{
   for (int i = 0; i < visualWeapons.Length; i++)
{
   visualWeapons[i].gameObject.SetActive(false);
 }
}
```

The code runs a `for` loop that goes through each of the game objects in the array of the `Visual Weapons` object that we dragged and dropped into the **Inspector** window.

We have updated our player's ship model so that when we buy an item, it will update in the **Scene/Game** window by simply manipulating the activity of our game objects.

We are now going to focus more on the player's ship code and the two other buttons on the selection grid—**BUY?** and **WATCH AD**.

Preparing our player's ship to be used in the game

This section is aimed at preparing our player's ship so that it can be sent to the next scene to play. We will create a standard ship first that the player will not be able to see, apart from a visual representation of it (there are two ships in the scene but the player can only see one).

So, if the player makes some purchases in our shop, we need to create a ship and add it's visual and physical upgrades so that we can see it in action in the next scene.

We need to return to the `PlayerShipBuild` script and add in the content to our empty `PreparePlayerShipForUpgrade` method to help support making a player's ship with its new upgrades:

```
void PreparePlayerShipForUpgrade()
{
  playerShip = GameObject.Instantiate(Resources.Load
    ("Prefab/Player/Player_Ship")) as GameObject;
  playerShip.GetComponent<Player>().enabled = false;
  playerShip.transform.position = new Vector3(0,10000,0);
  playerShip.GetComponent<IActorTemplate>
    ().ActorStats(defaultPlayerShip);
}
```

The method creates (`instantiates`) a `Player_Ship` game object from the `Resources` folder. We then turn off (`enabled = false`) its own script attachment; otherwise, we would be able to move and shoot with it in the shop scene.

We then move the `Player_Ship` object completely out of the **Scene/Game** window view.

Finally, we assign it the `defaultPlayerShip` asset file that we dragged and dropped into the scriptable object field in the **Inspector** window in the previous section.

In this section, we revisited the `PlayerShipBuild` script and added more global variables and functionality to support the shop scene. Our game now has an in-game credit score and works out whether the player can afford a game item or not; the rest of the code in this section was for hiding game objects and preparing our player's ship to be carried over into the game scene.

In the next section, we will carry on with the `PlayerShipBuild` script and look into actually starting a game to play with the player's ship. We will also look at how the player can buy in-game credits by watching adverts with the use of the Unity dashboard and Unity Monetization from the Asset store.

Buying items, watching adverts, and preparing to start a game

In this section, we will look at adding three more buttons to our shop scene. The first is `BUY?` for when we want to purchase an item. The second is `Watch Ad`—as soon as the player presses this button, an advert will load; once it's finished, the player is rewarded with `300` credits. Lastly, the `START` button, which will take the player to the `testLevel` scene with the upgrades they have purchased (if any).

We need to head back to the `PlayerShipBuild` script and scroll down to the `AttemptSelection` method, where we will add three `else if` statements to launch three different types of methods. The reason for this is that the three selections don't follow on from the scriptable object buttons; therefore, these items will never have outcomes such as `SOLD` or `itemText`.

The following screenshot shows the complete `AttemptSelection` method with the focus drawn to the other three non-scriptable object buttons:

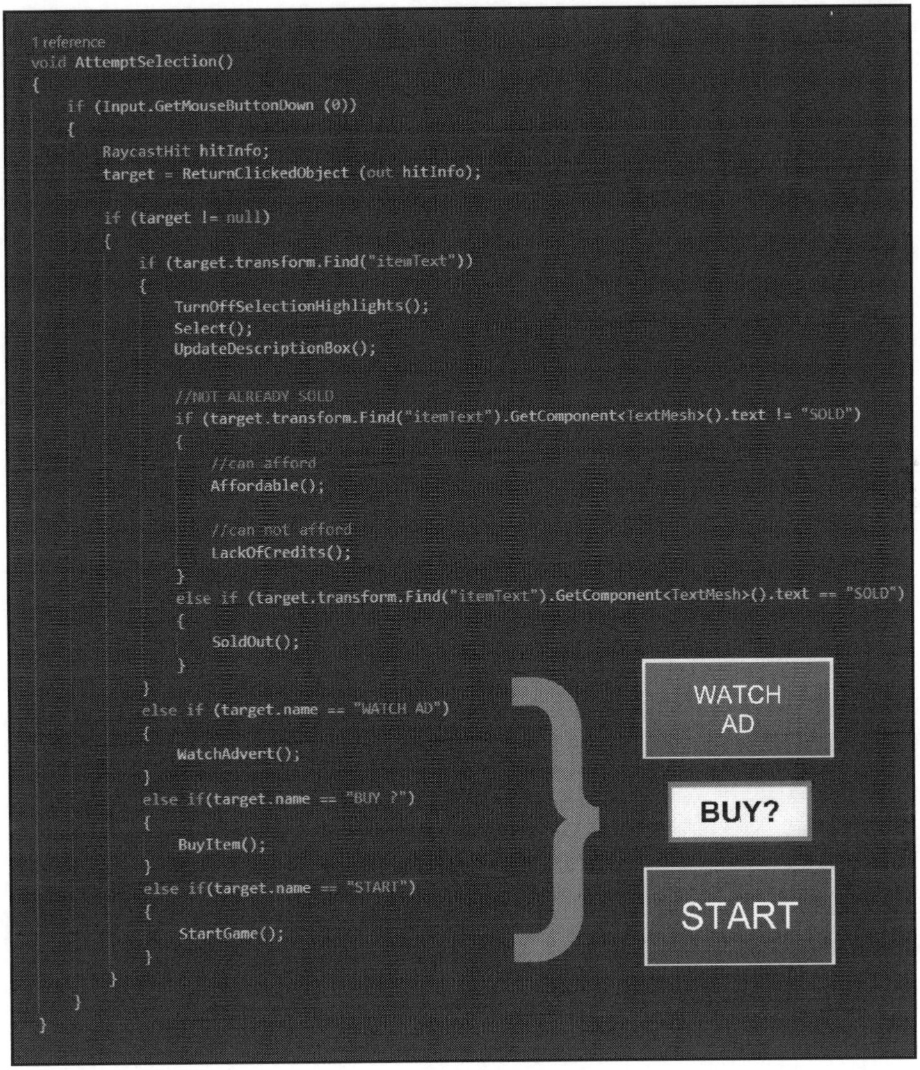

```
1 reference
void AttemptSelection()
{
    if (Input.GetMouseButtonDown (0))
    {
        RaycastHit hitInfo;
        target = ReturnClickedObject (out hitInfo);

        if (target != null)
        {
            if (target.transform.Find("itemText"))
            {
                TurnOffSelectionHighlights();
                Select();
                UpdateDescriptionBox();

                //NOT ALREADY SOLD
                if (target.transform.Find("itemText").GetComponent<TextMesh>().text != "SOLD")
                {
                    //can afford
                    Affordable();

                    //can not afford
                    LackOfCredits();
                }
                else if (target.transform.Find("itemText").GetComponent<TextMesh>().text == "SOLD")
                {
                    SoldOut();
                }
            }
            else if (target.name == "WATCH AD")
            {
                WatchAdvert();
            }
            else if(target.name == "BUY ?")
            {
                BuyItem();
            }
            else if(target.name == "START")
            {
                StartGame();
            }
        }
    }
}
```

}

WATCH AD

BUY?

START

We are going to look at the BUY? button first as it relates to what we are covering in this section.

Setting up the BUY? button

In this section, we will be hooking up the **BUY?** button so that it appears at the right time in the description panel. This button will only be displayed if the player hasn't already bought the item and if they have enough credits.

The following screenshot shows our shop scene with the **BUY?** button highlighted:

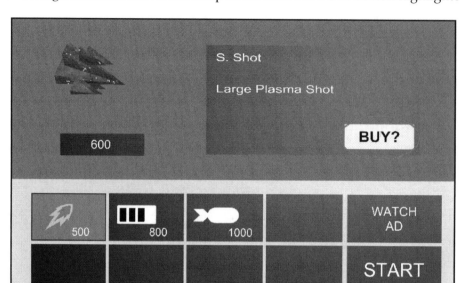

Let's make a start by coding the **BUY?** button to work in our `PlayerShipBuild` script:

1. Open the `PlayerShipBuild` script.

2. Scroll down to the `AttemptSelection` method to after the curly brace, as in the following:

   ```
   if (target.transform.Find("itemText"))
       {
           //CODE WE HAVE ENTERED...
           //CODE WE HAVE ENTERED...
           //CODE WE HAVE ENTERED...
       }
           <---- BEGIN CODING "ELSE IF" HERE
   ```

3. Add the following `else if` code, as indicated in the preceding code. We can also use the screenshot from the previous section as a reference:

   ```
   else if(target.name == "BUY ?")
   {
     BuyItem();
   }
   ```

4. So, if the player clicks on the **BUY?** button (`target.name` equals the name of **BUY?**) a `BuyItem` method is called. Inside this method, the following code is executed:

```
void BuyItem()
{
    Debug.Log("PURCHASED");
    purchaseMade = true;
    buyButton.SetActive(false);
    tmpSelection.SetActive(false);
```

We message the **Console** window in the editor with a note that a purchase has been made for the editor's debug purposes to make sure that this area of code is acknowledged. This doesn't affect our code in any other way. We then set `purchaseMade` to `true`. This Boolean value is used later when we leave the shop scene to start the game. If `purchaseMade` is `true`, a set of procedures follows. The next line turns off the `buyButton` function as we no longer need to display the results. Finally, we remove the selection from the grid at the bottom of the screen as a refresh.

Following on from the `BuyItem` method, we now turn our focus to the `visualWeapons` game object, which, if you remember from earlier in this chapter, covers the visual representation of what we have bought and what our player ship will look like when playing in a game.

5. Continuing on inside the `BuyItem` method, add the following code to name and make all cases of `visualWeapons` active:

```
for (int i = 0; i < visualWeapons.Length; i++)
{
    if (visualWeapons[i].name ==
        tmpSelection.transform.parent.gameObject.
            GetComponent<ShopPiece>().ShopSelection.iconName)
    {
        visualWeapons[i].SetActive(true);
    }
}
```

We run a `for` loop to count how many `visualWeapons` objects we have in the array. Within the `if` statement, we check each `visualWeapon` name from the array to see whether it matches with the selection made in the selection grid's name. If it does, then we turn that particular `visualWeapon` object on so that we can see it in the shop selection.

6. Continuing on in the `BuyItem` method, we add another method to send our upgrades to our player's ship, along with our `bank` credit, with the following code:

```
UpgradeToShip(tmpSelection.transform.parent.gameObject.GetComp
onent
    <ShopPiece>().ShopSelection.iconName);

  bank = bank -
System.Int32.Parse(tmpSelection.transform.parent.
    GetComponent<ShopPiece>().ShopSelection.cost);

bankObj.transform.Find("bankText").GetComponent<TextMesh>().te
xt
    = bank.ToString();
  tmpSelection.transform.parent.transform.Find("itemText").
    GetComponent<TextMesh>().text = "SOLD";
}
```

We run another method, called `UpgradeToShip`. This method will load the game object of the item purchased to the player ship we play in our game; we will go into further detail about this method shortly.

Next, we deduct from the `bank` value (using `System.Int32.Parse`, so it reads the `string` value as an `int` value) with the selection's `cost` scriptable object. We then represent the deduction by grabbing the reference from the bank's game object, called `bankText`, and update its `text` value in the `TextMesh` component.

Finally, we update the selection from the selection grid that the item has been sold. This is updated to the button's value text.

That brings us to the end of the `BuyItem` method. But, as mentioned, we run the `UpgradeToShip` method, which loads the game object of that particular ship part and attaches it to a ship that is away from the screen.

7. Still, in the `PlayerShipBuild` script, let's add the `UpgradeToShip` method:

```
void UpgradeToShip(string upgrade)
{
GameObject shipItem = GameObject.Instantiate(Resources.Load
    ("Prefab/Player/"+upgrade)) as GameObject;
shipItem.transform.SetParent(playerShip.transform);
```

```
shipItem.transform.localPosition = Vector3.zero;
}
```

The `UpgradeToShip` method takes a `string` parameter titled `upgrade`. Earlier, we sent it the following line of code:

```
tmpSelection.transform.parent.gameObject.GetComponent
    <ShopPiece>().ShopSelection.iconName
```

This line of code came from the selection's scriptable object item name. This item's name (`ShopSelection.iconName`) is sent to `UpgradeToShip` as a `string` name (`upgrade`).

Inside the `UpgradeToShip` method, we create (`instantiate`) a game object from the resources folder from the name of the shop's selection icon and store it in a game object variable, `shipItem`.

We then attach this `shipItem` game object to our `playerShip` object. This is the `playerShip` object that is not in the **Game** window view but will be sent to the next scene—the game-playing scene.

The `shipItem` game object's local position (its position compared to its parent game object, `playerShip`) is set to 0 (that is, its *x*, *y*, and *z* positions are set to 0):

1. Save the script and return to the Unity editor.
2. Click on the **Play** button to begin play mode, and in the **Game** window, select the first item in the selection grid.

We should now have the ability to buy this item. If we click on buy, the button will no longer say the value, but instead will display **SOLD**, and the **BUY?** button will disappear if we attempt to select the same item again.

We have two buttons left to hook up and then we will have a fully functioning shop. Let's continue with the **START** button.

Setting up the START button

START is the button the player presses when they want to leave the shop scene and move on to playing the game.

The following screenshot shows where the **START** button is located in the shop scene:

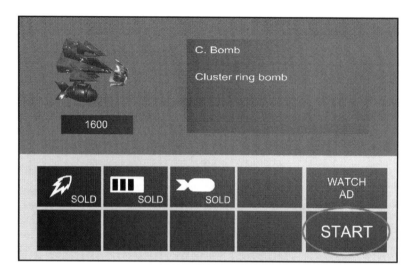

So, we can recall that in the previous section, we were coding in our AttemptSelection method, which runs when the player presses one of the buttons on the selection grid in the shop.

At the bottom of this method are three else if statements. We have already set up one of the three buttons, the **BUY?** button, in the previous section. We will now move on to the next else if statement, which is the **START** button. The following screenshot shows the reference to the AttemptSelection method:

```
else if (target.name == "WATCH AD")
{
    WatchAdvert();
}
else if(target.name == "BUY ?")
{
    BuyItem();
}
else if(target.name == "START")
{
    StartGame();
}
```

1. So, at the bottom of the `AttemptSelection` method in our `PlayerBuild` script, enter the following `if` statement:

```
else if(target.name == "START")
{
   StartGame();
}
```

When our `target` game object selection carries the `START` game object name, we fall into the `else if` statement and run the `StartGame` method. This method is small and the majority of its code depends on whether a purchase has been made.

2. Continuing on in our `PlayerShipBuild` script, add the `StartGame` method:

```
void StartGame()
{
    if (purchaseMade)
{
  playerShip.name = "UpgradedShip";
  if (playerShip.transform.Find("energy +1(Clone)"))
  {
      playerShip.GetComponent<Player>().Health = 2;
  }
  DontDestroyOnLoad(playerShip);
  }
UnityEngine.SceneManagement.SceneManager.LoadScene("testLevel"
);
  }
```

If `purchaseMade` is set to `true`, we fall into the `if` statement and name our `playerShip` game object `"UpgradedShip"`. We then check whether the `playerShip` object has a purchase made for more health (`"energy +1(Clone)"`). If the player has bought more health, we will set our `playerShip` object's `health` value to 2. This means that our player can get hit twice before dying.

The `DontDestroyOnLoad` function takes the argument of `playerShip`, which means when the next scene loads, the `playerShip` game object will be carried over to the next scene.

Finally, we start our `testLevel` scene.

3. Save the script.

So, after a purchase (or no purchase) is made, our shop scene will close and our `testLevel` will open with or without any purchases made.

Return to the Unity editor and run **Play** mode to check whether the player ship upgrade is carried over.

Let's now move on to the final `if else` statement—the **WATCH AD** button.

Setting up the WATCH AD button

The last button we will be covering in this chapter is the **WATCH AD** button. In a lot of mobile device (Android/iOS) free-to-play games (the game is free to play but makes money back with in-game purchases or adverts), the option for the player to enhance their experience with the game is to receive upgrades, modifications, gain in-game credits, and more if the player watches a 30-second advert. After watching the advert, the player is rewarded with credit. In this section, we are going to create this functionality with our code and Unity's online dashboard.

The following screenshot shows the location of the **WATCH AD** button in the selection grid:

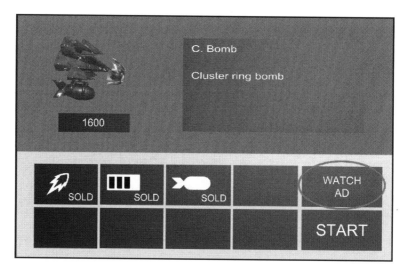

Before we begin coding, we need to import a free package from the Unity Asset store called **Unity Monetization**. This will give us an extra library to work with so that we can inherit ready-made classes and functions to help us run adverts and trigger when to reward the player's in-game credits.

To install **Unity Monetization**, click on the **Asset Store** tab at the top of the Unity editor. If it isn't there, it might have been closed, but we can load it up by clicking on **Window** at the top of the Unity editor, followed by **Asset Store**:

1. In the **Asset Store** window, click on the search bar at the top that says **Search for assets** and type in `Unity Monetization`.
2. If the search bar completes what we're typing, click on the link. If not, hit *Enter* on the keyboard and select the first option in the list.

   The following screenshot shows the Asset store with **Unity Monetization** ready to download:

3. Click on the **Download** button.
4. Once the download has finished, the **Download** button will change to **Import**.
5. Click on the **Import** button to import **Unity Monetization** into our project.

6. A list of ticked boxes will appear showing a list of the assets you may wish to import into the project. Leave them all ticked and click on the **Import** button in the bottom-right corner of the window.

We now have the capability to use monetization in our game.

Now, we need to turn on Unity's ad services in the Unity editor:

1. As before, if the **Services** tab isn't available, we can find it under the Unity editor **Window** tab, followed by **Services**, as in the following screenshot:

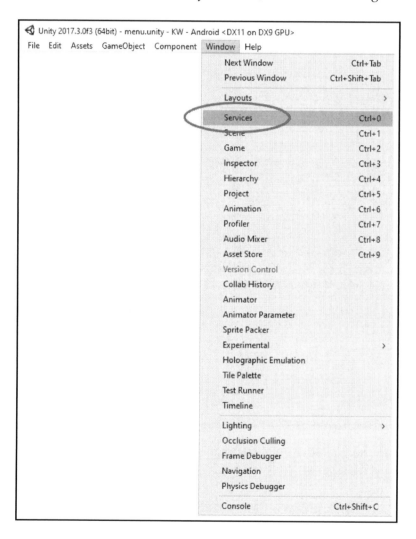

2. Click on the **Services** tab and select **Ads**, as in the following screenshot:

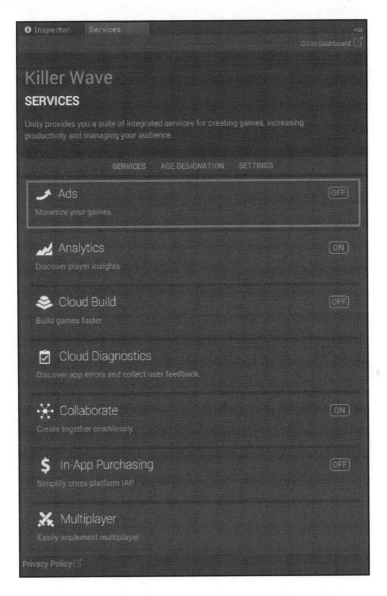

The **Services** tab will be updated with the **Ads** content. We will need to make the following changes:

- Turn **ADS** on.
- Turn off **Enable built-in Ads extension** as we will be using the Asset store's **Unity Monetization** app as it is recommended by Unity themselves in their Unity Ads installation process guide (`https://unityads.unity3d.com/help/unity/integration-guide-unity#basic-ads-implementation`):

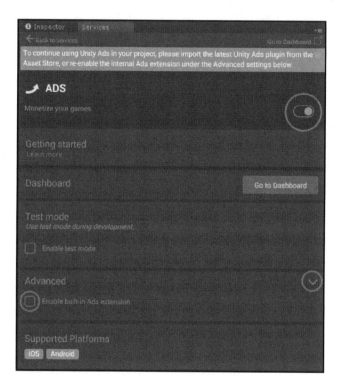

So, we have now installed our monetization library and we have enabled and configured our ad service in the Unity editor.

The next thing to do is to access the Unity dashboard to get our game IDs. These IDs are the reference for our game that the Google Play and Apple app stores will use to identify our game when it comes to sending adverts.

Each game ID will be different, so your game ID will be different from mine. When it comes to entering your game ID code, make sure you refer to yours, not mine.

Connecting Unity ads to our game

In this section, we will move to the Unity dashboard, where we can obtain details of our game's ID number to attach to our monetization setup in our game.

To access your game's ID number, start in the Unity editor and click on the **Account** button at the top of the editor, then click on **Go to account**, as in the following screenshot:

You will be presented with your account settings, which will contain information about your Unity account setup and projects:

1. Click on the **Unity Ads** link, as in the following screenshot:

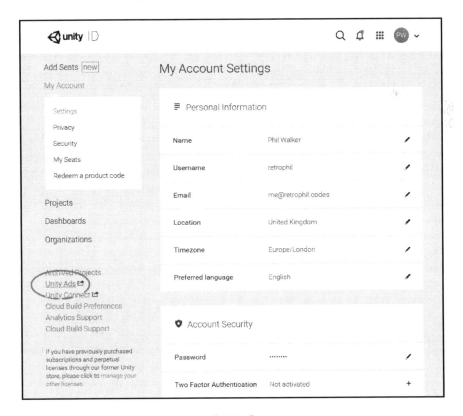

2. Click on the **Projects** tab to the left of the screen.

   You are now presented with all of the projects you have made in Unity. We are currently only interested in the project we are working on, which I named Killer Wave.

   The following screenshot shows that we are in the **Operate** tab at the top, with the **Projects** tab selected on the left, and the projects listed underneath.

3. Click on **Killer Wave** (or whatever you named your project):

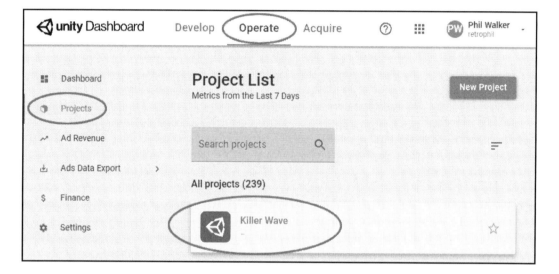

4. Click on the **Monetization** tab to the left of the screen, then **Placements**.
5. The following screenshot shows my game IDs. As mentioned earlier, my game IDs will be different from yours. Make a note of these game IDs as you will code them into your game shortly:

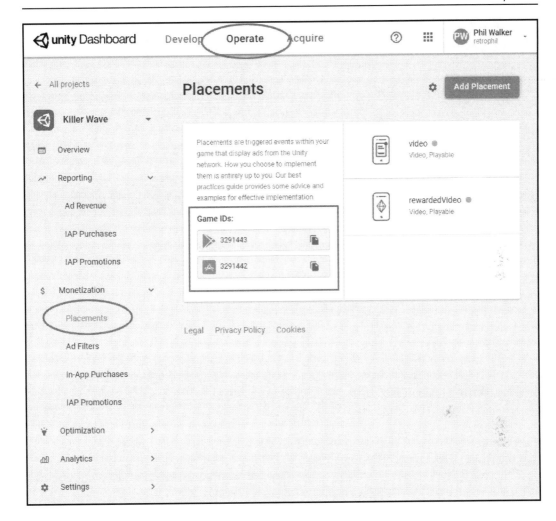

6. Close the browser.

We can now return to our `PlayerShipBuild` script and make a start with hooking up our **WATCH AD** button to display adverts.

Attaching Unity reward adverts to our script

In this section, we are going to take placement information and extra functionality from the **Monetization** library to create our reward adverts.

In the Unity editor, from the **Project** window, navigate to the `Assets/Resources/Script` folder, then take the following steps:

1. Open the `PlayerShipBuild` script and at the top of the code that we need, we will import two extra libraries alongside our `UnityEngine` library:

```
using System.Collections;
using UnityEngine;
using UnityEngine.Monetization;
```

`System.Collections` contain extra tools, such as `IEnumerator`, which is used for the `StartCoroutine` functions, which we will cover shortly.

The other line of code imports Unity's **Monetization** library, which we downloaded from the Asset store earlier and supports your advert needs.

2. Next, we need to add what type of advert we require and a placeholder for your game ID; enter two lines of code at the top of the script where we typically place the global variables:

```
string placementId_rewardedvideo = "rewardedVideo";
string gameId = "1234567";
```

`placementId_rewardedvideo` holds the `rewardedVideo` string. This string is used later to tell your Unity ads what type of video we want to display. The choices are as follows:

- `video`: The advert can be skipped by the player after a certain amount of time.
- `rewardedVideo`: The advert cannot be skipped by the player after a certain amount of time.

The `gameId` variable will hold the game ID that we got from the Unity dashboard that holds your project ID. As a default value, we will give the variable a `1234567` string.

3. Scrolling down the `PlayerShipBuild` script, we come to the `Start` function. In this function, we need to add the following method:

```
CheckPlatform();
```

4. Scroll past the `Start` function and add the method mentioned in the previous code block. This will set the `gameId` value to the one from the Unity dashboard:

```
void CheckPlatform()
{
  if (Application.platform == RuntimePlatform.IPhonePlayer)
  {
    gameId = "REPLACE-THIS-TEXT-FOR-YOUR-IPHONE-GAMEID";
  }
  else if (Application.platform == RuntimePlatform.Android)
  {
    gameId = "REPLACE-THIS-TEXT-FOR-YOUR-ANDROID-GAMEID";
  }
  Monetization.Initialize(gameId, false);
}
```

In the previous code, an `if` statement checks whether the player is running on an iPhone. If they are, we fill the `gameId` reference with the Apple app store ID we noted down from the Unity dashboard (your ID will be different to mine). If they aren't using an iPhone, we then use an `else if` statement to check whether they are playing the game with an Android phone. If they are using an Android phone, we update the `gameId` variable with the Google Play store ID from the Unity dashboard.

Finally, in this method, we put the `gameId` value into the monetization function, along with the `bool` value of `false`, which means we aren't running this advert as a test. If we were, we would receive fake adverts.

5. Still in the `PlayerShipBuild` script, scroll down to the `AttemptSelection` method, where we already have the two `else if` statements, and enter the final `else if` statement to trigger an advert when the player presses the **WATCH AD** button in our shop scene:

```
else if (target.name == "WATCH AD")
{
  WatchAdvert();
}
```

If this button is pressed, we run a method called `WatchAdvert`. We will talk about this method next.

6. Scroll to some space outside of all the other methods/functions and enter the following method to run a check for internet connection and then a method that will start to set up an advert for the player:

```
void WatchAdvert()
{
  if (Application.internetReachability !=
    NetworkReachability.NotReachable)
  {
    ShowRewardedAds();
  }
}
```

Going through the `WatchAdvert` method, our first check is made to see whether the internet is on and active. If the internet is active, we run the method inside the `if` statement titled `ShowRedwardedAds`.

7. Scroll to some space outside of all other methods/functions and enter the following method to wait until the advert is finished:

```
void ShowRewardedAds()
{
  StartCoroutine (WaitForAd());
}
```

The `ShowRewardedAds` method contains a `StartCoroutine` function, which is similar to a method but can be paused at any point.

8. Scroll to some space outside of all other methods/functions and enter the following `IEnumerator` variable, which will run the advert:

```
IEnumerator WaitForAd ()
{
    string placementId = placementId_rewardedvideo;
    while (!Monetization.IsReady (placementId))
    {
        yield return null;
    }

    ShowAdPlacementContent ad = null;
    ad = Monetization.GetPlacementContent (placementId)
        as ShowAdPlacementContent;

    if (ad != null)
```

```
        {
            ad.Show (AdFinished);
        }
    }
}
```

Within the `WaitForAd` function, we create a string titled `placementId`, which takes in the `string` variable we made earlier that contains the `rewardedVideo` string.

Next, we run a `while` loop that checks on every frame when the monetization is ready to show its advert. If it isn't ready, the `WaitForAd` function returns `null`.

We then create a `null` variable named `ad`, which is an object representing the monetization content (`ShowAdPlacementContent`).

`ad` is then assigned to the advert.

An `if` statement is then set to check whether the `ad` variable contains the advert. If it does, we then show the advert to the player (`ad.Show`), containing a method (`AdFinished`) that is run if the advert is fully run successfully.

9. Still within our `PlayerShipBuild` script, add the `AdFinished` method, which will reward the player when the advert has been watched:

```
void AdFinished (ShowResult result)
{
    if (result == ShowResult.Finished)
    {
        bank += 300;
        bankObj.GetComponentInChildren<TextMesh>().text =
bank.ToString();
        TurnOffSelectionHighlights();
    }
}
```

Inside the `AdFinished` method, we run an `if` statement that checks whether the advert has finished. If it has, then we reward the player with `300` extra credits to their virtual bank. We then update the credit balance visually by accessing the bank's game object and updating its `TextMesh` component. Finally, we turn off all selections made on the selection grid to reset the selection.

10. Save the `PlayerShipBuild` script and return to the Unity editor.

11. In the editor, click on the **Play** button.

In the **Game** window, click on the **WATCH AD** button. We should be presented with the following screen:

12. Click on the **Close** button at the top-right corner.

13. Hopefully, your on-screen credit should have gone from 600 to 900.

14. That is the end of adding the functionality for the **WATCH AD** button. Save the script.

Our shop scene is complete and fully functioning with the ability to watch an advert to gain credits so that the player can purchase items to use in their game. We now need to expand the `PlayerSpawner` script to support new items that can potentially be added to the player ship.

Extending the PlayerSpawner script

If an item is purchased from our shop scene, this will affect what happens to our game scene when our player's ship loads into the game. Our current `PlayerSpawner` script will not accommodate the `shop` scene ship, so we need to revisit this script to update its `CreatePlayer` method.

In the Unity editor **Project** window, locate and open
the `PlayerSpawner` script (`Assets/Resources/Script/PlayerSpawner`):

1. At the top of the `PlayerSpawner` script, with the other global variables,
    add a `bool` value:

    ```
    bool upgradedShip = false;
    ```

    The `upgradedShip` Boolean will switch to `true` if a modified player ship is
    found in the level.

2. Scroll down to the `Start` function in the `PlayerSpawner` script and add
    this as the last line with the `Start` function:

    ```
    GetComponentInChildren<Player>().enabled = true;
    ```

    Currently, our `PlayerShipBuild` script disables the `Player` script in
    the `shop` scene, to stop the player from shooting in the `shop`. When we
    start our `testLevel` we need to enable the `Player` script back on so they
    can move and shoot.

3. Replace the content of the `CreatePlayer` method with the following code
    to update detection of what ship is in our scene:

    ```
    //been shopping
    if(GameObject.Find("UpgradedShip"))
    {
        upgradedShip = true;
    }
    ```

    We first need to confirm that the `PlayerSpawner` script can see whether an
    upgrade has been purchased in the scene. If a purchase has been made, the
    modified player ship will carry over to the level scene. If this is the case, we
    set the `upgradededShip` variable to `true`.

4. Continuing on with the `PlayerSpawner` script, and still within the
    `CreatePlayer` method, we add an `if` statement, which instantiates the
    player:

    ```
    //not shopped or died
    //default ship build
    if (!upgradedShip || GameManager.Instance.Died)
    {
        GameManager.Instance.Died = false;
        actorModel = Object.Instantiate(Resources.Load
    ```

```
        ("Script/ScriptableObject/Player_Default"))
            as SOActorModel;
        playerShip = GameObject.Instantiate(actorModel.actor,
            this.transform.position,
Quaternion.Euler(270,180,0))
            as GameObject;

        playerShip.GetComponent<IActorTemplate>().
            ActorStats(actorModel);
    }
```

Continuing on inside the `CreatePlayer` method, we will now need to check whether there is a player ship in the scene or whether the player has died. If there hasn't been an upgrade or the player has died, we will create a default player ship with the following code.

Inside the `if` statement, we create our default player ship by doing the following:

1. Set the `Died` property to `false` to stop the `if` statement repeating if the player has died.
2. Instantiate the `Player_Default` scriptable object, which contains all the standard properties for our player's ship, and store it as in a variable named `actorModel`.
3. Next, we instantiate our player ship, position it, and rotate it in the correct direction.
4. Finally, in this `if` statement, we issue the `actorModel` variable containing all the properties that the player ship game object needs.

   However, if our player has been shopping and bought one or more upgrades, this will fall into the `else` condition, where we will find a game object called `UpgradedShip`. We will attach this game object to our global `playerShip` game object variable:

5. Enter the following code to set a store reference to `playerShip`:

   ```
   //apply the shop upgrades
   else
   {
       playerShip = GameObject.Find("UpgradedShip");
   }
   ```

With our `playerShip` game object stored as an instance, we can now set it up so that it's in the correct position and has the correct size, rotation, and so on..

6. Enter the following functions to set our `playerShip` object up for the start of a game:

```
playerShip.transform.rotation = Quaternion.Euler(0,180,0);
playerShip.transform.localScale = new Vector3(60,60,60);
playerShip.GetComponentInChildren<ParticleSystem>
    ().transform.localScale = new Vector3(25,25,25);
playerShip.name = "Player";
playerShip.transform.SetParent(this.transform);
playerShip.transform.position = Vector3.zero;
    }
}
```

We then move on to the last bit of code for the `PlayerSpawner` script where our player's ship is set up ready to start. Take note that even if the player purchases an upgrade, this won't create any complications with regard to getting the reference of the player ship.

7. Set the rotation so the player's ship faces the correct way.

8. Scale the player's ship correctly.

9. Turn the `Player` script off so the player can't control the ship while it carries out its intro animation.

10. Name the player's ship `Player`.

11. Finally, set the player's ship as a child to the `playerSpawner` game object as it belongs to the `playerSpawner` game object.

12. Save the script.

We have updated the player's ship so that it is created for a default ship or as a customized one from the shop scene. Also, we have made it aware of the `PlayerTransition` script so that when the player's ship is created it won't get stuck in the screen boundaries or the player won't be in a position where they aren't able to control the ship until it's introductory animation has finished.

Finally, we now need to create and add our b. `Shot` weapon asset to our game. The majority of the scripting has already been done; it just needs to be attached to the correct components.

To give our b. Shot prefab weapon its behavior, we need to do the following:

1. In the **Project** window, navigate to Assets/Resources/Prefab/Player and select b. Shot.

2. Now in the **Inspector** window, click the button **Add Component**. Type BShot Component until it appears in the drop-down list, and then select it.'.

   We now need to apply our b. Shot bullet to the script.

3. Click the small round remote circle next to the **B Shot Bullet** field and, from the drop-down list, select player_BshotBullet as shown in the following image:

Our b. Shot weapon will now fire. Next, we need to make the bullet travel, following a similar process as we did in Chapter 2, *Adding and Manipulating Objects*, where we made our first player bullet fire and travel across the screen. This means we can use the script we've already made and attach it to the player_BShotBullet prefab.

To attach and customize the player_BShotBullet prefab we need to do the following:

1. In the **Project** window, navigate to Assets/Resources/Prefab/Player and select player_BshotBullet

2. In the **Inspector** window, select the **Add Component** button. Type PlayerBullet until you see it in the drop-down list, and then select it.

3. Back in the **Project** window, navigate to Assets/Resources/Script/ScriptableObject

4. Right-click in the open space on the right side of the **Project** window and select **Create | Create Actor**.

5. Name the new file in the **Project** window bShotBullet and select it.

6. Give it the following values in the **Inspector** window as shown in the following image:

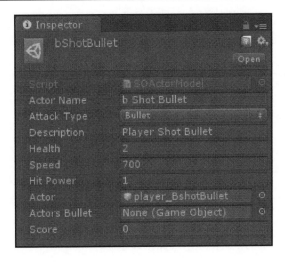

We are approaching the end of this chapter. Now is the time to check everything out to see how it all plays out for us:

1. Save all the open scripts.
2. Save the shop scene.
3. Click on **Play** mode in the Unity editor.
4. Try and buy all three ship upgrades (you will need to watch a couple of the Unity notification advert displays to get them all).

Click on the **START** button and you should see a screen such as the following one with our ship holding all three upgrades:

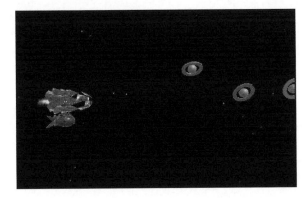

Our player is fully equipped! If the player gets hit, they will lose a shield and the front cover on the ship will disappear. If the ship fires with the firepower upgrade, it will wipe out all the enemies. The atom bomb currently isn't programmed to do anything.

If you have come across any issues with this final section, you can check the official Unity guide, which also contains other information about adverts and rewards, if you are interested (`https://unityads.unity3d.com/help/unity/integration-guide-unity`). Or, compare our script and scene with the `Complete` folder of `Chapter6` from the downloaded project files link at the beginning of this chapter.

Congratulations, you have reached the end of this chapter and also the end of the shop scene! Hopefully, you found this beneficial and can appreciate how Unity is keen to encourage developers to look at alternative ways of making money from a game with adverts instead of simply selling the games they develop. We have also left the Unity editor and made use of the Unity dashboard, which does a lot more than help you to monetize a game and can also be used for other things such as analytics, which we will cover later on in this book. For now, we will summarize what we covered in this chapter and look at how we will build our game even further.

Summary

In this chapter, we created a scene that we can interact with to modify our player with in-app purchases and that we can also use to gain more in-game credits by watching adverts on an iPhone or Android phone to buy more items to further upgrade the player. We will look at building the game on mobile in the *Appendix* section of this book, as well as how to hide the **AD** button on PC/macOS platforms.

Finally, we carried all the items we bought over into the game because of which the player's gameplay has been altered thanks to the modifications.

As mentioned a few times in this chapter, the scene had already been made for us in terms of the art. The reason for this was to allow you to experience raycasting objects and to understand that this is an alternative way of interacting in a scene. But what if the platform we are playing this game on is an iPad? An iPad is more of a square shape, compared to the letterbox shape of an iPhone or Android phone. If this is the case, our game camera would clip parts of our shop scene out.

You could also think of a more efficient way of using things such as `.Find` in your coding. If this is a concern of yours, don't worry—we address these issues in `Chapter 9`, *Creating a Two-Dimensional Shop Interface and In-Game HUD*, where we implement Unity's own event system. For now, however, let's look at what we will cover in the next chapter.

In the next chapter, we are going to link up all of our scenes to create what we refer to as a game loop. This will help us understand the actual game layout as a whole.

7
Creating a Game Loop and Mock Test

In the previous chapter, we moved from the `testLevel` scene (where we controlled the player ship) to a `shop` scene (buying and calibrating the player's ship). In this chapter, we will be following a similar trend of stretching out to the rest of the other game scenes in our `Scenes` folder (found in the **Project** window in the `Assets` folder).

As part of scene management, all games we play have something called a "Game Loop" – if you're not familiar with the term, it basically means our game will have alternative routes to take. Each route will load a particular scene. We will need to cater for either outcome at each stage of the game.

Eventually, all game loops will loop back to somewhere near the beginning. The following image shows what our game loop will look like by the end of this chapter:

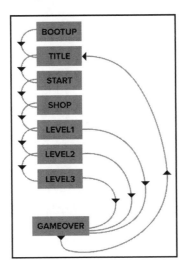

Referring to the game loop image still, each name in its rectangular box represents a scene in Unity that we have in our `Scenes` folder inside the **Project** window. The flow of each scene goes in one overall direction, starting at the top with **BOOTUP**. This is when the game is launched for the first time. The flow will fall through each scene until the player beats all three levels or dies. Either way, they will eventually reach the **GAMEOVER** scene, which will then loop back up to the **TITLE** scene to create a loop.

By the end of this chapter, we will be in the position to run our game from the `bootUp` scene, where it will automatically move onto the `title` scene. From there, the player will press the fire button or tap the screen to then load up the `shop` scene, which is where purchases can be made.

Once the player presses the **START** button in the `shop` scene, the first level (`level1`) will start. If the player dies, the level will restart, whereas if the player completes the level, they will move onto the next level.

The final outcome from all of this will be that if the player dies three times, they will be taken back to the `title` scene, whereas if the player completes the `level3` scene, then the game will be over and the player will be taken to the `gameOver` scene.

Finally, we will cover a few mock test questions related to what we have covered so far.

In this chapter, we will cover the following topics:

- Transitioning our player ship
- Expanding our `ScenesManager` script
- Preparing to loop our game
- Mock test

Core exam skills covered in this chapter

The following are the core exam skills that will be covered in this chapter:

- *Programming core interactions:*
    - *Implement and configure game object behavior and physics*
    - *Implement and configure camera views and movement*

- *Working in the art pipeline:*
  - *Understand materials, textures, and shaders, and write scripts that interact with Unity's rendering API*
  - *Understand 2D and 3D animation, and write scripts that interact with Unity's animation API*
- *Programming for scene and environment design:*
  - *Identify methods for implementing Game Object instantiation, destruction, and management*
  - *Recognize techniques for structuring scripts for modularity, readability, and reusability*

Technical requirements

The project content for this chapter can be found at `https://github.com/PacktPublishing/Unity-Certified-Programmer-Exam-Guide/tree/master/Chapter07`.

You can download the entirety of each chapter's project files at `https://github.com/PacktPublishing/Unity-Certified-Programmer-Exam-Guide/archive/master.zip`.

All the content for this chapter is held in this chapter's `unitypackage` file, including a `Complete` folder that holds all of the work we'll carry out in this chapter.

Check out the following video to see the Code in Action: `https://bit.ly/2BD2dOm`.

Transitioning our player ship

Currently, our levels can only be completed when the player dies, causing the level to restart, or when the player loses all three lives. Only then are we taken to the game over screen. We now need to start thinking of how a player starts and ends a level. Currently, the player just appears at the start of a level.

In this section, we are going to write some code that animates our player into the scene and, when the level completes, we will have the player ship exit the camera view.

So, let's make a script the same way we did all the other scripts (Chapter 2, *Adding and Manipulating Objects*, if you need a reference). Name the script PlayerTransition and make sure we have the file in our Scripts folder in the Unity Editor **Project** window.

We now need to attach the PlayerTransition script to our player_ship prefab:

1. Load up the testLevel scene from Assets/Scene in the **Project** window.
2. Then, navigate to the Assets/Resources/Prefab/Player folder, and select the player_ship prefab.
3. Finally, drag and drop the PlayerTransition script into an empty area of the player_ship **Inspector** window. Then make sure the PlayerTransition component in the **Inspector** window is turned off by unticking its box. If this box is left ticked, the PlayerTransition component will start animating player_ship in the shop scene.

Now that our script has been created and attached, we can go into it and start setting up the following code:

- Adding variables to our PlayerTransition script
- Adding methods/functions to our PlayerTransition script
- Adding if statement checks
- Adding content to PlayerMovement IEnumerator
- Moving the player ship out of the screen

Let's take a look.

Adding variables to our PlayerTransition script

In this section, we are going to make a start by setting up our PlayerTransition script. We'll do this by adding global variables so that these can be used to position the player ship.

To start adding our global variables, follow these steps:

1. Open our newly created `PlayerTransition` script.

2. At the top of the script, make sure we have the following library:

   ```
   using UnityEngine;
   using System.Collections;
   ```

   By default, our script should be automatically named along with its default inherit `MonoBehaviour` as it's a requirement regarding the Unity Editor and other functionalities. The `System.Collections` library will be used for our `StartCoroutine`. Without this library, we can't create coroutines; we will explain more about this when we come to coding it in.

3. Check/enter the following code for our `PlayerTransition` script, which holds the script's default name and `MonoBeaviour` inheritance for added functionality:

   ```
   public class PlayerTransition : MonoBehaviour
   {
   ```

4. Within the `PlayerTransition` class, enter the following global `Vector3` variables:

   ```
   Vector3 transitionToEnd = new Vector3(-100,0,0);
   Vector3 transitionToCompleteGame = new Vector3(7000,0,0);
   Vector3 readyPos = new Vector3(900,0,0);
   Vector3 startPos;
   ```

The `startPos` and `readyPos` variables are used to measure the distance from where our player ship is and where we want it to travel to.

At this point, be sure that the `_Player` game object's **Transform Position** property values are set to zero on its X, Y, and Z axes in the **Inspector** window. Otherwise, the player ship may animate into the wrong position when entering the level.

The `transitionToEnd` variables will be used as the coordinates where we want our player game object ship to travel to at the start of the level, as well as when the player's ship is about to leave a level. `transitionToCompleteGame` is only used when the player completes the third and final level and is used to alter the player's ending animation.

5. Continue entering the following `float` global variables in our `PlayerTransition` script:

```
float distCovered;
float journeyLength;
```

`distCovered` will hold time data that will be used later to measure between two `Vector3` points (we will talk about this in more detail when we make `PlayerMovement IEnumerator`).

`journeyLength` will hold the distance between the two `Vector3` points mentioned previously (`startPos` and `readyPos`).

6. The final set of global variables are the bools to be added to our `PlayerTransition` script:

```
bool levelStarted = true;
bool speedOff = false;
bool levelEnds = false;
bool gameCompleted = false;

public bool LevelEnds
{
    get {return levelEnds;}
    set {levelEnds = value;}
}
public bool GameCompleted
{
    get {return gameCompleted;}
    set {gameCompleted = value;}
}
```

`levelStarted` is the only `bool` set to `true` as it confirms that the level has started and will only be set to `false` after the transition of the player's animation has finished. `speedOff` will be set to `true` when we want the player's ship to leave the level.

`levelEnds` is set to `true` when the level has come to the end and the player ship will then move to its exit position. The last `bool` is for when the whole game has been completed. This is used to change the ending animation. The two properties are used for accessing the `levelEnds` and `gameCompleted` variables from outside of the script.

That's our global variables added to our script. Now, let's continue to the `PlayerTransition` methods and functions.

Adding methods/functions to our PlayerTransition script

As we continue through our `PlayerTransition` script, we will add Unity's `Start` function and create our own `Distance` method to position the player's ship in the correct location:

1. Starting with the `Start` function, continue entering the following code for our `PlayerTransition` script:

```
void Start()
{
    this.transform.localPosition = Vector3.zero;
    startPos = transform.position;
    Distance();
}
```

The `Start` function gets called as soon as this script is enabled. In this function, we will reset the position of the player's ship to its parent game object, which is the `PlayerSpawner` game object.

We will then assign the player ship's beginning world space position to one of the vectors we created earlier in this section (`startPos`). We will use this in the `Distance` method, which we will talk about next.

2. Enter the `Distance` method and its content in the `PlayerTransition` class:

```
void Distance()
{
    journeyLength = Vector3.Distance(startPos, readyPos);
}
```

`Vector3.Distance` is a ready-made Unity function that will measure the distance between two vector points and gives the answer in the form of a `float` that we will be storing in `journeyLength`. The reason for this is that we will want to know the length between where our player ship is and where it needs to go (which we'll cover later in this chapter).

In the next section, we will move into Unity's `Update` function, where we will check for when the level has ended so that we can exit (move) our player ship out of the screen.

Adding if statement checks

In this section, we are going to make use of Unity's frame update function, `Update`, so that we can run checks to see what state our game is at within the level.

Within our `Update` function, we will have three `if` statements. `levelStarted` is from one of the `bool` variables that we introduced earlier on in this section, which is already set to `true`. So, this `if` statement is going to be called instantly. Let's take a look:

1. Let's start by entering the first `if` statement in the `PlayerTransition` script's `Update` function:

```
void Update()
{
    if (levelStarted)
    {
        StartCoroutine(PlayerMovement(transitionToEnd, 10));
    }
```

Within the first `if` statement is a `StartCoroutine` that runs an `IEnumerator` called `PlayerMovement`, which also takes two parameters. We already covered what `StartCoroutine` and `IEnumerator` are, but if you can't remember, refer to the *Setting up the "WATCH AD" button* section in Chapter 5, *Creating a Shop Scene for Our Game*. With regards to what the `PlayerMovement` `StartCoroutine` does, we will review its content after we have covered the entirety of the `Update` function.

Now, let's continue with the second `if` statement in the `Update` function.

This `if` statement checks to see if the `levelEnds` variable is `true`, which, as you may recall, we set to `false` by default. This `bool` is accessed outside of the `PlayerTransition` class, which we will cover later, but for now, all we need to know is that it becomes `true` at the end of a level.

Inside the `if` statement, there are several lines that prepare our player's ship to begin the end of the level, starting with disabling the `Player` script by setting its `enabled` bool setting to `false`. This will knock out the player's controls so that we can animate the player ship into position for the end of the level.

Next, we disable the player ship's `SphereCollider` so that if an enemy or one of its bullets comes into contact with the player's ship, it won't destroy the ship while it's preparing to end the level.

2. Enter the second following `if` statement inside the `PlayerTransition` `Update` function:

```
if (levelEnds)
  {
    GetComponent<Player>().enabled = false;
    GetComponent<SphereCollider>().enabled = false;
    Distance();
    StartCoroutine(PlayerMovement(transitionToEnd,200));
  }
```

Then, we measure the distance between where the player's ship was at the start of the level and where it needs to go with the `Distance` method.

Finally, within the `if` statement, we have the same `StartCoroutine` that we mentioned earlier, with the only difference being that the argument value is set to `200`. These values will be explained after the fourth `if` statement for this `Update` function.

While we're still within the `Update` function, we can enter the `if` statement that covers when the player completes the third and final level:

```
if (gameCompleted)
  {
    GetComponent<Player>().enabled = false;
    GetComponent<SphereCollider>().enabled = false;
StartCoroutine(PlayerMovement(transitionToCompleteGame,200));
  }
```

If the `gameCompleted` bool is `true`, we fall into the `if` statements condition. Inside, we turn off the `Player` script to disable the player's controls. The second line disables the player's collider to avoid any collisions with any enemy-related game objects, while the third line makes the player ship translate from its current position to the value of `transitionToCompleteGame`.

3. Enter the fourth `if` statement in our `PlayerTransition` `Update` function:

```
if (speedOff)
  {
      Invoke("SpeedOff",1f);
```

```
      }
   }
```

In the fourth `if` statement, we run a check to see if the `speedOff bool` holds the value of `true`. If it does, we run Unity's own `Invoke` function, which delays the execution of the `SpeedOff` method with a 1-second delay.

 More about `Invoke` can be found on the Unity Scripting reference site: `https://docs.unity3d.com/ScriptReference/MonoBehaviour.Invoke.html`.

In the next section, we will write some code so that the player is moved from where they are to where they need to be. The two cases where this will need to be achieved are as follows:

- When the player starts the game, we animate them into the scene.
- When the player has completed the level, they need to move into a position to leave the level.

We will be covering two new Unity functions (`Mathf.Round` and `Vector3.Lerp`).

Adding content to the PlayerMovement IEnumerator

In the previous section, during our `if` statements, we came across a `StartCoroutine` titled `PlayerMovement` twice, but didn't refer to its content as we were going through the `Update` function's content. In this section, we will go through `PlayerMovement` and focus on why we need to call it twice.

The `PlayerMovement IEnumerator` holds the responsibility of animating our player ship in the near center of the screen in order to begin and also exit the level. Let's go into more detail to fully understand this.

The following piece of code can be entered anywhere inside the `PlayerTransition` class and, obviously, outside of any function/method. Let's take a look:

1. Enter the start of our `IEnumerator`, along with its two parameters:

```
IEnumerator PlayerMovement(Vector3 point, float
transitionSpeed)
   {
```

As mentioned previously, our `PlayerMovement` takes two parameters: a `Vector3` with the reference name `point` and a `float` with the reference name `transitionSpeed`. As you can imagine, `transitionSpeed` is the speed of the player ship moving from one point to another.

If we trace back to what the value of `point` is, it's coming from a variable that we've already initialized, `transitionToStart`, with a `Vector3` at the beginning of this script with a value of (`-100,0,0`).

So, effectively, `transitionToStart` and `point` are the same – they're just different in terms of their names, for the sake of keeping their references separate. Anyway, coming back to `point`, this value is for our player's ship position. The following screenshot shows our player ship with **Transform Position** set to `-100,0,0`:

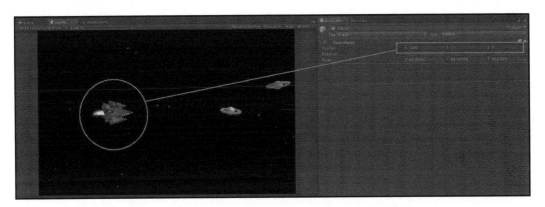

So, when a level begins, our player ship will be on the far left, outside of the screen, and animate into the position we have marked in the previous screenshot.

Carrying on with the `PlayerMovement` `IEnumerator`, we begin with an `if` statement that checks when a series of conditions are made.

2. Enter the following `if` statement, along with its four conditions:

```
if (Mathf.Round(transform.localPosition.x) >= readyPos.x -5 &&
    Mathf.Round(transform.localPosition.x) <= readyPos.x +5 &&
    Mathf.Round(transform.localPosition.y) >= -5f &&
    Mathf.Round(transform.localPosition.y) <= +5f)
{
```

In the previous code, we've run a check on four occasions to see if the player is in the correct position before executing the rest of the code. Each line of code checks the following:

- If the player ship's X position is more than or equal to the value that is stored in `readyPos` variable's X position, minus 5.
- If the player ship's X position is less than or equal to the value that is stored in `readyPos` variable's X position, plus 5.
- If the player ship's Y position is more than or equal to the value that is stored in `readyPos` variable's Y position, minus 5.
- If the player ship's Y position is less than or equal to the value that is stored in `readyPos` variable's Y position, plus 5.

3. Still within our `PlayerMovement IEnumerator`, enter the following `if` statements:

```
if (levelEnds)
{
   levelEnds = false;
   speedOff = true;
}

if (levelStarted)
   {
      levelStarted = false;
      distCovered = 0;
      GetComponent<Player>().enabled = true;
   }
   yield return null;
}
```

In the previous code block, we have two `if` statements (`levelEnds` and `levelStarted`) that check that each of the `bool` conditions are `true`. Let's go through both of their content:

- `levelEnds`: if `levelEnds` becomes `true`, we apply `false` to the `levelEnds` bool and apply `true` to the `speedOff` bool.

- `levelStarted`: if `levelStarted` is given the value `true`, we apply false to the `levelStarted bool`, set the `distCovered float` to 0, and we set the `Player` script to `true`.

After both of these two `if` statements, we `yield return null` (we wait a frame for instructions to be applied).

4. Lastly, in our `PlayerMovement IEnumarator`, enter the following `else` condition:

```
else
    {
        distCovered += Time.deltaTime * transitionSpeed;
        float fractionOfJourney = distCovered / journeyLength;
        transform.position = Vector3.Lerp(transform.position,
point,
        fractionOfJourney);
    }
}
```

Referring to the `else` condition code block, we add time and multiply it by `transitionSpeed`, which, as you may recall, is one of the two arguments this `IEnumerator` takes.

We then divide the `distCovered` variable by the `journeyLength` variable, which, as you may recall, is a measurement between two points. We store the division in a `float` variable called `fractionOfJourney`.

The last thing we do in this `else` condition is use one of Unity's pre-made functions called `Lerp`, which linearly interpolates our player's ship between two points. `Lerp` takes three arguments: point A, point B, and the time scale it's going to move between these two points. `transform.position` is our player's ship, the second is the `Vector3` point, which is the other variable we brought into `IEnumerator`, and the third is the active `float fractionOfJourney`.

It's also possible to `Lerp` colors over time with `Material.Lerp`.

For more information about changing one color into another, check out: `https://docs.unity3d.com/ScriptReference/Material.Lerp.html`.

We now need to add a single line of code in the `PlayerSpawner` script to turn the `PlayerTransition` script on after the player leaves the shop scene. As mentioned earlier in the chapter, if the `PlayerTransition` was left on in the shop scene, the `player_ship` would animate across the screen.

So, to turn on the `PlayerTransition` script at the start of the `level1` scene, we need to do the following:

1. In the **Project** window, navigate to `Assets/Resources/Script` and open the `PlayerSpawner` script.
2. Scroll down to the following line of code:

```
playerShip.transform.position = Vector3.zero;
```

3. Enter the following line of code just after it:

```
playerShip.GetComponent<PlayerTransition>().enabled = true;
```

This line of code will make our player ship animate into the `level1` scene.

The last change we need to make in the `PlayerSpawner` script is to remove the ability to enable the `Player` script in the `PlayerSpawner Start` function, as we enable this via the ScenesManager script:

1. In the `PlayerSpawner` script, remove the following line in the `Start` function:

```
GetComponentInChildren<Player>().enabled = true;
```

2. Save the `PlaywerSpawner` script.

Now, let's move onto the last bit of code, where we'll be moving our player ship out of the screen at the end of the level.

Moving the player ship out of the screen

The last method we need to cover in the PlayerTransition script is the SpeedOff method. This method simply makes our players ship jet off, out of the screen, when the level is completed. Let's take a look:

1. Enter the following code for our PlayerTransition script:

```
void SpeedOff()
{
transform.Translate(Vector3.left * Time.deltaTime*800);
}
```

This code block uses Unity's pre-made Translate function, which takes a Vector3.left multiplied by time, with 800 being used to make the player ship move a little faster.

2. Save the script.

That is the end of the PlayerTransition script. Now, our game has an introduction and an ending for our player ship. Originally, our player would just be present at the start of the level and when it was classed as being completed, the next level would load. e also technically covered three new functions, as follows:

- Vector3.Distance, which measures between two Vector3 points.
- Vector3.Lerp, which moves the player ship, smoothing between two Vector3 points.
- MathF.Round, which rounds off a number.

We combined these new skills to make our player ship move into position to start the level and, when completed, no matter where the player was on the screen, we moved them into position. Finally, our player zooms off the screen.

In the next section, we are going to revisit the ScenesManager script and apply some code so that there's a time limit, counting down to when the level is over.

Expanding our ScenesManager script

In this section, we are going to make our ScenesManager script recognize levels 2 and 3 from our scenes folder (Assets/Scenes). We will then add these levels to the game loop. Also, we will be adding a game timer for each level. When the timer reaches its limit, we can then trigger the player leaving the level with an animation that will play out. Lastly, we will add a few common methods to move the game onto the next level.

Let's start by opening the ScenesManager script (Assets/Resources/Script/Scenesmanager.cs) and adding some global variables to assist with what we were talking about. Follow these steps:

1. At the top of the ScenesManager script, add the following global variables:

    ```
    float gameTimer = 0;
    float[] endLevelTimer = {30,30,45};
    int currentSceneNumber = 0;
    bool gameEnding = false;
    ```

    The gameTimer variable timer will be used as our current counter to time how long the level has left until it is over. The following variable is an array that holds the time until each level ends. So, we have three levels in total, but the question is, how long do we want each level to last? We need to enter a value that represents the seconds until the level ends, so I've chosen 30 seconds for levels 1 and 2. Level 3, however, will last 45 seconds. This is because we will be building a special level in Chapter 12, *NavMesh, Timeline, and Mock Test*. We will go into more detail about this when we reach that chapter.

    As you can imagine, currentSceneNumber will hold the number that denotes which scene our player is currently on. Lastly, we have the gameEnding bool, which will be used to trigger the end of the level animation for the player's ship. We will cover these variables in more detail later in this section, let's start with currentSceneNumber.

    Following on from the global variables we just set, let's make sure that the ScenesManager script is always aware of what scene our player is on during the game. This will help our code know which scene the player is on and what scene they will be going to next.

2. Add the Update function, which will be called on every frame to check which scene we are at. Do this by entering the following code in the ScenesManager script:

```
void Update()
{
    if (currentSceneNumber !=
        SceneManager.GetActiveScene().buildIndex)
    {
        currentSceneNumber =
SceneManager.GetActiveScene().buildIndex;
        GetScene();
    }
    GameTimer();
}
```

Inside the Update function, we use an if condition to check if the currentSceneNumber variable is not equal to the buildIndex we are grabbing from the active scene we are in.

If it is not equal, we update currentSceneNumber with the current scene's buildIndex, followed by the GetScene method. The GetScene method is a small method that is worth covering now instead of later as it relates to everything we've just said.

Inside the GetScene method is a single line of code that updates the scene's variable. This is an instance from the Scenes enum that holds the names for each scene in our game. Also, the code in the GetScene method is casting currentSceneNumber to an enum, which is why the Scenes type is in brackets. More about casting can be found at https://docs.microsoft.com/en-us/dotnet/csharp/programming-guide/types/casting-and-type-conversions.

3. Enter the following code for our ScenesManager script:

```
void GetScene()
{
    scenes = (Scenes)currentSceneNumber;
}
```

We can put the GetScene method anywhere in the ScenesManager class, as long as it's not within another method.

Coming back to the `Update` function, after calling the `GetScene` method, we close the `if` conditions brackets. The last thing we do before closing the `Update` function is run the `GameTimer` method, which will keep track of our game's time and set up some basic methods that will start, reset, and end our game levels.

In the following sections, we will cover the following topics:

- Adding a timer to each game level. When the timer is up, that notifies the player has completed the level.
- Make it so that when a level is completed, the `ScenesManager` script knows what to do next; that is, load a level, which level, and so on.

Let's get started.

Adding a game level timer

In the `ScenesManager` script, we will set up a method that will be responsible for acknowledging the level has ended. The `GameTimer` method serves the purpose of adding time to a `gameTimer` variable and checking to see if it has reached its limit, depending on the `endLevelTimer` it's comparing to. Finally, if the game has been triggered to end the player ship's animation, it is set to start and the next level is loaded after 4 seconds.

With your `ScenesManager` script still open, add the following method to your code:

```
void GameTimer()
  {
    switch (scenes)
    {
      case Scenes.level1 : case Scenes.level2 : case Scenes.level3 :
      {
        if (gameTimer < endLevelTimer[currentSceneNumber-3])
        {
          //if level has not completed
          gameTimer += Time.deltaTime;
        }
        else
        {
        //if level is completed
        if (!gameEnding)
        {
          gameEnding = true;
          if (SceneManager.GetActiveScene().name != "level3")
        {
```

```
            GameObject.FindGameObjectWithTag("Player").GetComponent
                <PlayerTransition>().LevelEnds = true;
        }
        else
        {
            GameObject.FindGameObjectWithTag("Player").GetComponent
                <PlayerTransition> ().GameCompleted = true;
        }
            Invoke("NextLevel",4);
        }
    }
    break;
    }
  }
}
```

Inside the `GameTimer` method, we run a `switch` statement holding the `scenes` instance that will contain all of the `enum` names of each level. We run a check on three possible cases: `level1`, `level2`, and `level3`. If the `scenes` instance is set to either of the three possibilities, we will fall into an `if` condition that will then compare whether the `gameTimer` variable is less than what the `endLevelTimer` array has been set to.

We only need to know what build index number levels 1, 2, and 3 are on. So, to avoid the first three scenes, we must subtract by 3.

The following screenshot shows the **Build Settings** window (**File | Build Settings**), which contains the scenes and their build numbers in your project on the right-hand side:

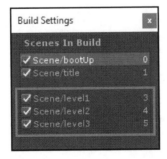

If `gameTimer` is less than `levelTimer`, we will continue to increment `gameTimer` with the `Time.deltaTime` fixed function that Unity has pre-made for us. More information about `Time.deltaTime` can be found here: https://docs.unity3d.com/ScriptReference/Time-deltaTime.html.

If gameTimer is equal to or more than levelTimer, we will move into the else condition, which checks the condition of the if statement of the gameEnding bool being false. If the condition is false, we fall into the content of the if statement, which first sets the gameEnding bool to true. This will stop the if statement from repeating in the Update function's frame cycle.

The last if statement checks which level our game is on. If we are not on "level3", we set the LevelEnds property in the PlayerTransition script to true. Otherwise, we must have completed the game. So, in the else condition, we set the GameComplete property to true in the PlayerTransition script.

In this section, we created a method in the ScenesManager script that made our game aware of how long each level will last before classing the level as completed.

We will now continue with the ScenesManager script by adding methods that will start, reset, and move our player onto the next level when triggered by the GameTimer method.

Beginning, resetting, and skipping levels

ScenesManager will have the responsibility of starting a level, resetting it when the player dies, and moving onto the next level when the current one has been completed. Thankfully, these require minimal work thanks to Unity's SceneManagement library.

Let's start by revisiting the ResetScene method we have already started, but now, we will simplify it even more:

1. Replace the content from our ResetScene method with the following code in our ScenesManager script:

```
public void ResetScene()
{
  gameTimer = 0;
  SceneManager.LoadScene(GameManager.currentScene);
}
```

Inside the ResetScene method, we reset the gameTimer variable to zero, followed by replacing its parameter from the current SceneManager.LoadScene buildIndex to GameManager.currentScene, which we coded back in Chapter 3, *Managing Scripts and Mock Test*. This is basically just holding the current build index as a static integer so that any script can access it.

With ResetScene updated, we can now move onto the next method, which is very similar to what we have just done, but it is separate to ResetScene in order to support the expansion of our code.

When a player completes a level, the NextLevel method runs, which will reset the gameTimer variable. The gameTimer bool will be set back to false and the same SceneManager.LoadScene command will be used to increment the GameManager currentScene integer by 1.

2. Enter the following method in the ScenesManager script:

```
void NextLevel()
{
  gameEnding = false;
  gameTimer = 0;
  SceneManager.LoadScene(GameManager.currentScene+1);
}
```

The last method we need to change in our ScenesManager script is our BeginGame method, which will be called when the player is in the shop scene and pressing the "START" button.

3. Enter the following code for our ScenesManager script:

```
public void BeginGame(int gameLevel)
{
  SceneManager.LoadScene(gameLevel);
}
}
```

The BeginGame method will take an integer parameter called gameLevel. Inside this method is the same SceneManager.LoadScene we have already used, but this time, it will load the gameLevel integer we are providing it.

4. Save the script.

Because we have changed the `BeginGame` method to now take a parameter, we must update our `PlayerShipBuild` script, which has a `StartGame` method that runs the `BeginGame` method with, currently, no parameter value. To update the `PlayerShipBuild StartGame` method, we need to do the following:

1. In the Unity Editor, navigate to the `Assets/Resources/Script/PlayerShipBuild` folder in the **Project** window.
2. Open the file.
3. Scroll down to the `StartGame` method and find this line of code:

```
UnityEngine.SceneManagement.SceneManager.LoadScene("testLevel"
);
```

Now, change the preceding line of code to this:

```
GameManager.Instance.GetComponent<ScenesManager>
    ().BeginGame(GameManager.gameLevelScene);
```

This code change will now call the `level1` scene directly.

With what, we have reached the end of this section. So far, we have covered the following:

- Our game is now aware of how long a level will take until it is classed as completed.
- The `ScenesManager` script can now call methods that will start, reset, and move the player onto the next level.

The majority of our code was created with the use of `switch` statements and an `enum` to call when the scenes need to be changed. To load the scenes themselves, we used Unity's own `SceneManager` class, which is fundamental to loading any scene in a Unity Project.

In the next section, we will prepare the rest of the scenes in our project that aren't game levels (the `bootUp` scene, the `title` scene, and the `gameOver` scene).

Preparing to loop our game

In this section, we are going to move away from the `testLevel` scene and introduce three other levels (`level1`, `level2`, and `level3`) to demonstrate the game loop.

By the end of this section, our game loop will be complete. We will be able to start our game from the `bootUp` scene. From there, we will be able to progress through each scene.

Let's start by removing the placeholder levels in the Unity Editor. Go to the **Project** window and the `Assets/Scene` location. Follow these steps:

1. Delete `level1`, `level2`, and `level3`.
2. Select `testLevel`, hold the *Left Ctrl (command* on the Mac*)* key on the keyboard, and press *D* twice. We should now have three `testLevel` instances.
3. Rename `testLevel` to `level1`.
4. Rename `testLevel 1` to `level2`.
5. Rename `testLevel 2` to `level3`.

   We now need to check the **Build Settings** window to check on the order of our scenes.

6. At the top of the Unity Editor, click **File | Build Settings.**

Our order should look like the one shown in the following screenshot. If it doesn't, select and move the scenes into the correct position by clicking and dragging them in the **Build Settings** window and by selecting and deleting any extra scenes in the list:

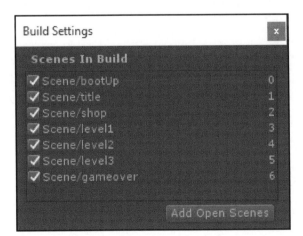

We have duplicated our first level twice to test that our levels can be completed and move forward. Next, we will go back to the first scene in our project list and set it up so that it's ready to act like a boot up scene.

Because we have removed our `testLevel` scene, we need to update our `GameManager` script with regards to the `LightandCameraSetup` method to keep its `Switch` statement in sync with the levels we need to light up, as well as set up our camera.

To make it so our camera and lights work correctly for each scene, we need to do the following:

1. In the **Project** window, navigate to the `Assets/Resources/Script` folder.
2. Double-click `GameManager`.
3. Scroll down to the `LightandCameraSetup` method's content and make it so that each case number follows this pattern:

   ```
   case 3 : case 4 : case 5:
   ```

   Each case represents the levels the player is going to play.

4. Save the script.

In the next few sections, we will be customizing a placeholder look for each nonlevel scene (basic but informative). These scenes are as follows:

* `bootUp`
* `title`
* `gameOver`

Each of these scenes will also require basic coding so that the player either presses a button to continue or a timer will be issued. This timer will count down until the next scene is loaded.

Setting up the BootUp scene

When we play a game, typically, the game doesn't start straight away – there's normally a splash screen to show who developed/published the game. Sometimes, it's used as a loading screen, but for us, it will be used to get our game started. In this section, we are going to take away the typical Unity sky background and replace it with a neutral grey color background with a text title that states what screen has loaded up.

Let's make a start and open the bootUp scene in the Unity Editor:

1. In the **Project** window, navigate to the bootUp scene by going to Assets/Scene.
2. Double-click the bootUp file.
3. Drag and drop the GameManager prefab from the **Project** window location, Assets/Resources/Prefab, to the **Hierarchy** window.
4. Create an empty game object in the **Hierarchy** window. If you have forgotten how to do this, refer to Chapter 2, *Setting up Our Player Spawner Script*.
5. Name the newly created game object BootUp Text.
6. Create another empty game object as before and name that BootUpComponent.

The following screenshot shows the components on the left-hand side of the **Hierarchy** window. These are as follows:

- **Main Camera**
- **Direction Light**
- **GameManager**

- **BootUpComponent**
- **BootUp Text:**

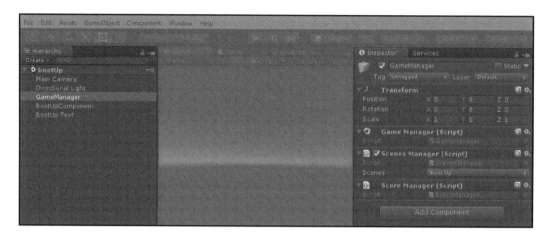

On the right-hand side of the preceding screenshot, we have our GameManager game object selected showing its three main component scripts:

- Game Manager
- Scenes Manager
- Score Manager

As you may recall, our GameManager script will always remain in a scene, even if the scene is replaced with another, so it's vital we have these components in our Game Manager prefab.

Next, we are going to change the background from sky to grey, as mentioned previously. To do this, select **Main Camera** from the **Hierarchy** window. Now, follow these steps:

1. In the **Inspector** window, click the **Clear Flags** selection and change it from **Skybox** to **Solid Color**.
2. Just below **Clear Flags**, click to change the **Background** selection and replace whatever the **Hex Color** value is with 32323200.
3. This will change the RGB values to 50,50,50 with an alpha setting of zero.

Use the following screenshot as a reference for the location for **Clear Flags**, **Background**, and **Hex Color**:

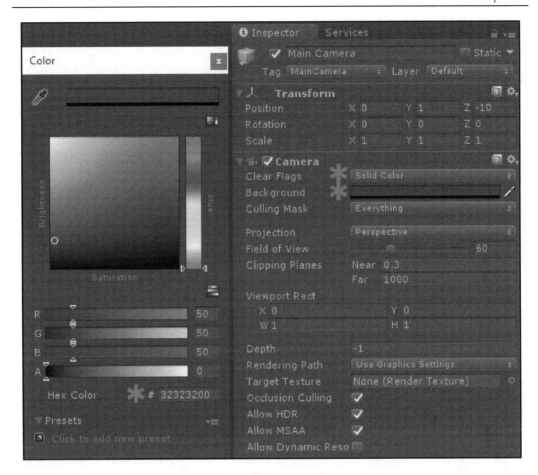

This will change the background in the **Game** window to gray.

Next, we will select `BootUp Text` and add a **Text Mesh** that will be at the bottom center of the screen. Follow these steps:

1. Select the `BootUp Text` game object in the **Hierarchy** window.
2. Then, in the **Inspector** window, click the **Add Component** button.
3. In the drop-down, type `Text Mesh` until you see it in the drop-down list.
4. Select **Text Mesh** from the drop-down.

With the `BootUp Text` game object still selected, change its **Transform** Position to the following:

X:	0	Y:	−2	Z:	3

Now that our text is in the correct position, we need to fill out the **Text Mesh** component in **Inspector**. Follow these steps:

1. In the **Text** section of **Text Mesh**, type `BootUp`.
2. Set **Anchor** to **Middle center**.
3. Set **Alignment** to **Center**.
4. Open the **Game** window (shortcut: *Ctrl (command* on Mac*) + 2*). Now, we should have a gray screen with white text so that we can easily identify the scene we are in. The following screenshot shows the "BootUp" text's settings, along with its **Inspector** properties for reference:

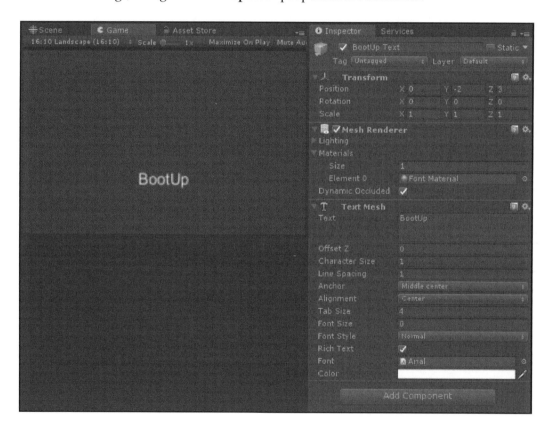

The last thing we need to do for this `bootUp` scene is to make it function like most `bootUp` screens.

When the `bootUp` screen appears, it stays there for a couple of seconds and then moves onto the next scene.

To make it so the `bootUp` screen loads onto the next screen after a few seconds, we will need to create a script and add it to the `BootUpComponent` game object.

5. When we make the script, we need to store it with our other scripts in the **Project** window (`Assets/Resources/Script`).

    If you have forgotten how to make a script, check out the *Updating our camera properties via script* section in `Chapter 2`, *Adding and Manipulating Objects*.

6. Name the script `LoadSceneComponent`.

    The following screenshot shows what the `BootUpComponent` game object should look like when it's selected in the **Hierarchy** window:

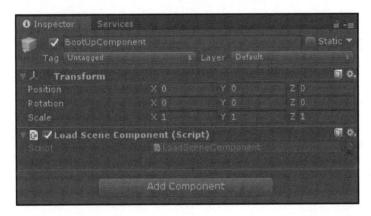

7. Double-click the grayed-out field of `LoadSceneComponent` in the **Inspector** window to open the file.

    The following code is similar to the code that we entered previously for loading a level, just in a shorter form. The basic principle is that we load in `UnityEngine.SceneManagement` to inherit Unity's `SceneManager` class.

    Our game's score gets reset at the start of the script to stop any previous scores being carried over.

    Then, we create a timer and increment the time in Unity's `Update` function. Once the timer goes over 3 seconds, `SceneManager` will load whatever we have put in the `loadThisScene` public variable, which in our case is `"title"`.

The following screenshot shows the `LoadSceneComponent` script in **Inspector** with a field where we can enter the scene we wish to load:

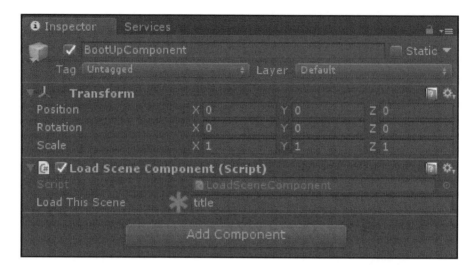

It's as simple as that – we don't need to worry about anything else as the `bootUp` scene isn't part of the game loop. The `bootUp` scene is only played once when the game starts.

8. Enter the following code into `LoadSceneComponent`:

```
using UnityEngine.SceneManagement;
using UnityEngine;

public class LoadSceneComponent : MonoBehaviour
{
 float timer = 0;
 public string loadThisScene;

 void Start()
 {
   GameManager.Instance.GetComponentInChildren
     <ScoreManager>().ResetScore();
 }

 void Update()
 {
     timer += Time.deltaTime;

     if (timer > 3)
     {
```

```
                    SceneManager.LoadScene(loadThisScene);
            }
        }
    }
```

9. Once you're done, save the script.
10. Go back into the Unity Editor and type `title` into the Load This Scene variable field in the Inspector window, as shown in the preceding screenshot.
11. Save the `bootUp` scene and press **Play** in the Unity Editor. The `bootUp` scene should load up and then, after 3 seconds, load up the `title` scene.

We can now repeat the majority of what we've done in the `bootUp` scene and duplicate this for the `title` and `gameOver` scenes. We will do this next.

Setting up the title and gameOver scenes

The way we set the `bootUp` scene in the previous section is similar to how we want the `title` and `gameOver` scenes to look and act before we add any new art and custom functionality.

Thankfully, with Unity, we don't have to repeat the entire process of making these two scenes from scratch. We can copy, paste, and rename the game objects we have already created in the `bootUp` scene's **Hierarchy** window and paste them into the `title` and `gameOver` scenes.

To copy the gray background and white **Text Mesh** text from the `bootUp` scene, do the following:

1. With the `bootUp` scene still active in the Unity Editor, select all of the 5 game objects from the **Hierarchy** window (click the top or the bottom of the list, hold *Shift*, then click either end of the list to select all).
2. Press *Left Ctrl (command on Mac)* + *C* to copy these 5 game objects.
3. Open the `title` scene from the **Project** window (`Assets/Scene/title`).
4. Select and delete all game objects in the **Hierarchy** window.
5. Click anywhere in the open space of the **Hierarchy** window and hold *Left Ctrl (command on Mac)* + *V* to paste the `bootUp` game objects.
6. Select `BootUp Text` in the **Hierarchy** window and rename it `Title Text`.
7. With the `Title Text` game object still selected, change the **Text** field in the **Text Mesh** component to `Title`.

8. Select `BootUp Component` in the **Hierarchy** window and rename it to `Title Component`.

9. With the `Title Component` game object still selected, click the cog in the **Inspector** window next to **BootUp Component (Script).**

10. A drop-down will appear; click **Remove Component** from it.

We now need to make a script for the `Title Component` game object so that when the player taps or clicks the mouse button, the `shop` scene will load up next.

11. Repeat the same process of making and attaching a script as we did with `BootUp Component`, but this time, name the script `TitleComponent` (also, as with the `TitleComponent` script, make sure it is moved into the correct folder in the **Project** window, `Assets/Resources/Script`) and paste in the following code:

```
using UnityEngine.SceneManagement;
using UnityEngine;

public class TitleComponent : MonoBehaviour
{
 void Update()
 {
    if (Input.GetButtonDown("Fire1"))
    {
        SceneManager.LoadScene("shop");
    }
 }
  void Start()
  {
    GameManager.playerLives = 3;
  }
}
```

The difference between this `TitleComponent` script and the previous `BootUpComponent` script is that `TitleComponent` will move onto the next scene (`shop` scene) when a mouse button (or finger touch on a touch screen) is pressed and released in **Play** mode. And as a temporary solution, it will make sure, as a failsafe, that the player starts with three lives. This is unlike `BootUpComponent`, which is dependent on a timer to increment the past 3 seconds to load the next scene, where its failsafe is to reset the game's score if the player completes the game.

12. Save the `TitleComponent` script and `title` scene.

The following screenshot shows what the `title` scene should look like in the Unity Editor:

We now need to repeat the exact same process for the `gameOver` scene.

Open the `gameOver` scene from the **Project** window (`Assets/Scene/gameOver`) and repeat the process of pasting and renaming the game objects. Do the following:

1. In the **Hierarchy** window, change the name of the `BootUp Component` game object to `GameOver`.

2. Still in the **Hierarchy** window, rename `BootUp Text` to `GameOver Text`.

3. Select the `GameOver` component in the **Hierarchy** window. Then, in the **Inspector** window, click the **Add Component** button and type `Load Scene Component` until we see it in the list. Then, select it.

The following screenshot shows the `GameOver` component with the same `LoadSceneComponent` script where I added `"title"` to the **Load This Scene** variable field:

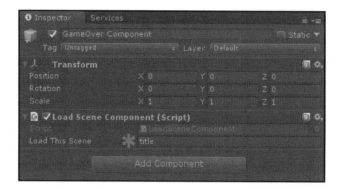

4. Save the `gameOver` scene.

Our Unity Project is now ready to run its full game loop. We will talk about the game loop in more detail in the next section.

Demonstrating that the game loop is complete

In this final section, we will confirm what we have achieved in this chapter. Our game now has a game loop, so if we load up the `bootUp` scene and press **Play** in the Unity Editor, the sequence will be as follows:

- `bootUp`: Scene runs for 3 seconds and then moves to the `title` scene.
- `title`: If the player presses the mouse button, the `shop` scene will load.
- `shop`: The player presses the **START** button to load `level1`.
- `level1`: The player completes the level after 30 seconds (45 seconds for level 3) or dies. If the player dies more than 3 times, they will be presented with the `gameOver` scene.
- `level2`: The same rules apply as the ones present for `level1`.
- `level3`: The same rules apply as the ones present for `level1`, but if the player completes the level, they will be presented with the `gameOver` scene.
- `gameOver`: The scene runs for 3 seconds and then moves to the `title` scene.

The following image shows the process of our game loop moving through each scene, then going back to the `title` scene:

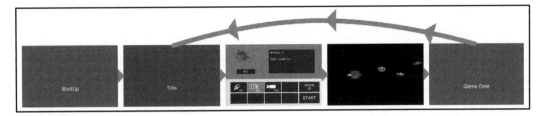

> Remember that if any of our scenes look darker than usual, we will need to bake it lights manually, as we did back in `Chapter 3`, *Managing Scripts and Mock Test*.

With this, we have created a series of scenes that carry their own individual responsibilities. When a scene comes to its end, either by its own choice or prompted to by the player, the next scene in the sequence will load. Eventually, by the player either completing all three levels or losing all their lives, our game will reach the `gameOver` scene. From the `gameOver` scene, we send the player back to the `title` scene. This is our game loop, and this is what every game will have. Game loops are a fundamental requirement for game development, and it's also possible that this will be mentioned in the exam.

This concludes this section and this chapter, where we have created and managed our scenes in order to create a game loop.

Summary

In this chapter, we created a game loop; these are fundamental to game development, and sometimes application development. To create a game loop for our project, we needed multiple scenes that served their own purposes. We also needed to know when a scene started and when it should end. A scene ends when the player presses a button to continue, such as the 7 scene, or when the `bootUp` title automatically moves onto the next scene after so many seconds.

Apart from making our game loops, we also learned some new vector math components on the way, including `Mathf.round`, which is used to round off figures `Vector3.distance`, which is used to measure the distance between two `Vector3` points; and `Vector3.lerp`, which is used to interpolate between two `Vector3` points.

These are useful components in game development and will also likely be mentioned in the exam.

In the next chapter, we will be adding some polish to our placeholder scenes with custom fonts, creating our own images, and applying some UI animation in the Unity Editor.

Mock test

1. What would be the best way for a UI menu system to be worked on from a programmer's perspective, but at the same time doesn't interfere with an artist working on the same workflow?

   A) Make it so that each UI component has its own class so that any art changes won't affect either outcome.

   B) Give each UI component a separate material so that any changes in the code will be isolated.

   C) Use prefabs for each UI component so that any artist can modify them individually.

   D) Have a separate script that sweeps through all UI components to check any changes that are made so that they're known to everyone.

2. When using Unity's own Version Control Collaborate, which of the following can be excluded using the `.collabignore` file?

   A) Assets
   B) Editor
   C) MetaData from the `Library` folder
   D) Any file or folder made outside of the Unity Project

3. An **Image** component has a sprite in its **Source Image** parameter and its **Image Type** is set to **Filled**. What does **Filled** do?

    A) Fills open spaces in the sprite.

    B) It offers various ways to fill in the sprite.

    C) Makes it so no other sprite can override it.

    D) Inverts the color of the sprite.

4. What component does `CrossPlatformInputManager` replace?
    A) `anyKey`
    B) `Input`
    C) `mousePosition`
    D) `acceleration`

5. When testing a top-down shooter game you have just developed, you want the controls to have an "Arcade" feel. To make the controls snap into position when moving the player, which property would help create what is required?

    A) `GetAxisRaw`
    B) `GetJoystickNames`
    C) `InputString`
    D) `gyro`

6. When writing code such as variable names, which is the correct naming convention to use?

    A) Pascal case
    B) Lower case
    C) Cake case
    D) Camel case

7. You are working with a team to create a realistic simulation for the military that includes a series of explosions. You have been asked to take over from the previous developer who has, so far, created a framework that issues a series of explosions from a bank of prefabs. The prefabs are updated on a regular basis by one of the artists on the team. As impressive as this looks, the program has gotten quite big and the artist will need to have the option to update, swap out, replace, and delete prefabs from the framework.

What solution can you offer the team that keeps this framework from not going against SOLID principles and is accessible to the artist in the team?

A) Create a series of prefabs that hold a cluster of prefabs that randomize on each occasion when they're used in the Unity scene.

B) Create a single scriptable object that holds an array of prefabs that holds a reference to either script.

C) Create a non-procedural particle system that creates its own explosions.

D) Hold all the explosions in the scene at runtime but off-camera and then bring in which is required using a random selection script.

8. Which collider is the fastest for the Unity physics system to calculate?

A) Hinge
B) Sphere
C) Mesh
D) Box

9. Which is the cheapest MinMaxCurve to use?

A) Optimized Curve
B) Random between two constants
C) Random between two curves
D) Constant

10. Which property needs to be accessed through code to create a strobe effect for a night club scene?

A) `color.a`
B) `spotAngle`
C) `range`
D) `intensity`

Adding Custom Fonts and UI

8

In this chapter, we are going to take the scenes that we created from our game loop in the previous chapter and move our focus on to text, imagery, and animation through various customizations.

A requirement of the Unity Programmer Exam is to be confident with not only your C# programming skills, but it is also important to be familiar with what the Unity Editor offers in terms of its components and tools. Therefore, in this chapter, we will do no programming and, instead, focus on our **User Interface** (**UI**), which consists of **Image** and **Text** components. It's also worth mentioning that we will make our UI expand and contract with the screen's ratio size, which isn't possible with 3D assets alone (please refer to the previous chapter for more details). We will also import and apply our own custom font while we learn about our **Text** component. Finally, we will animate the UI with the **Animator** and make use of the **Animator Controller**, which involves creating our own states.

The following screenshot shows what our title screen should look like by the end of the chapter:

We will cover the following topics in this chapter:

- Introducing the Canvas and UI
- Applying text and images to our scenes

By the end of this chapter, you will feel more confident about combining **Text** and **Image** components together, along with animating the UI.

Core exam skills being covered in this chapter

Programming core interactions:

- *Implement and configure game object behavior and physics.*

Working in the art pipeline:

- *Understand materials, textures, and shaders, and write scripts that interact with Unity's rendering API.*
- *Understand 2D and 3D animation, and write scripts that interact with Unity's animation API.*

Developing application systems:

- *Interpret scripts for application interface flow such as menu systems, UI navigation, and application settings.*

Technical requirements

The project content for this chapter can be found at `https://github.com/PacktPublishing/Unity-Certified-Programmer-Exam-Guide/tree/master/Chapter08`.

You can download the entirety of each chapter's project files at `https://github.com/PacktPublishing/Unity-Certified-Programmer-Exam-Guide/archive/master.zip`.

All content for this chapter is held in the chapter's `unitypackage` file, including a `Complete` folder that contains all of the work that we'll carry out in this chapter.

Check out the following video to see the Code in Action: `https://bit.ly/2YyRVYO`.

Introducing the Canvas and UI

The Canvas holds images and text in a 2D world. Its primary purpose is to allow the user to interact with things, such as clicking on buttons, pushing volume sliders, and turning knobs, which is more commonly known as the UI.

Unity (quite confusingly) makes it such that the 2D Canvas also shares the same space as it's a 3D world. Therefore, in our scene, we will typically have a large canvas area with the UI; then, further down in the bottom-left of the screen, we will have our 3D world.

The following screenshot shows an example of a Unity scene with an implemented **Canvas** component, along with a cube and a UI button:

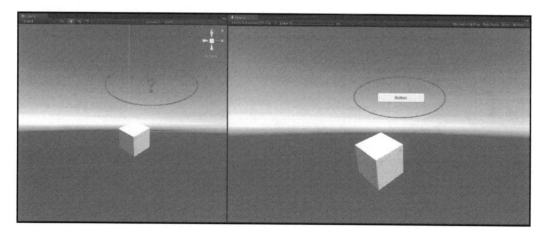

As you can see in the preceding screenshot, on the right-hand side, we have the **Game** view showing a 3D cube and UI **Button**. On the left-hand side, we have the **Scene** view showing the same cube but with the **Button** missing. This is because, in the **Scene** window, the Canvas that holds the UI button is located in its own 2D space. To resolve this issue, we need to zoom out of the **Scene** view, and we will see where the UI button is located. Additionally, we will see the outline of a large white rectangle that represents the screen ratio.

Note that because we have zoomed out so much, the 3D cube is really small. In the following screenshot, we can't even see the cube on the left-hand side marked with a circle outline. It's a little complicated to understand at first, but consider it like two projects sharing the same space:

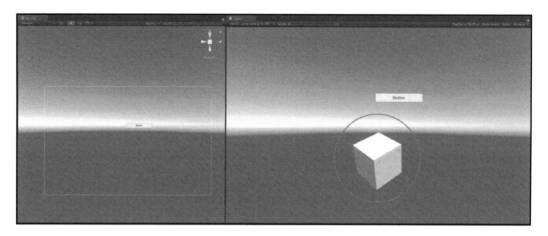

With that brief example of how the Canvas shares space with the 3D space, let's move on to the next section, where we'll start using the Canvas and add some text and images.

Applying text and images to our scenes

In this section, we are going to change the following scenes:

- The gray background
- The white **TextMesh** (3D text, which doesn't require the Canvas)

We'll replace those scenes with the following:

- A black background
- Custom red **Text** (2D text, which requires a Canvas)

As mentioned in the introduction, the benefit of doing this is that the text will remain the same size, no matter the ratio or resolution of the screen.

The following screenshot shows the current BootUp scene on the left and what it should look like after making the changes on the right:

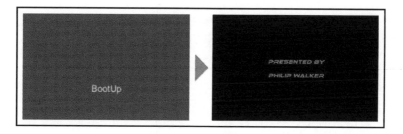

If you haven't already opened the scene in the Unity Editor, go to the **Project** window and open the `bootUp` scene from `Assets/Scene/bootUp`.

Let's start by changing the background color from gray to black. If you have forgotten how to do this, follow these steps:

1. Select the **Main Camera** in the **Hierarchy** window.
2. With the **Main Camera** selected, in the **Inspector** window, under the Camera component, click on the gray **Background** field and change its RGBA values to 0, 0, 0, 255, as shown in the following screenshot:

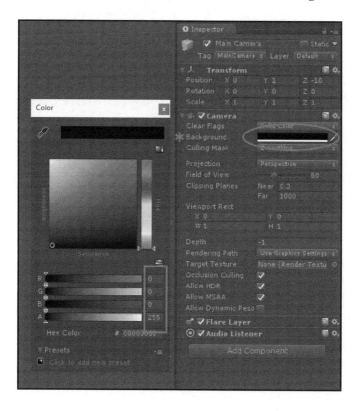

The **Game** window will now change from gray to black, and then we will remove the BootUp text and replace it with our new 2D text.

3. Select BootUp Text from the **Hierarchy** window and delete it.

We are now going to add the Canvas and 2D text to the scene.

4. In the open space of the **Hierarchy** window, right-click and select **UI** | **Text**, as shown in the following screenshot:

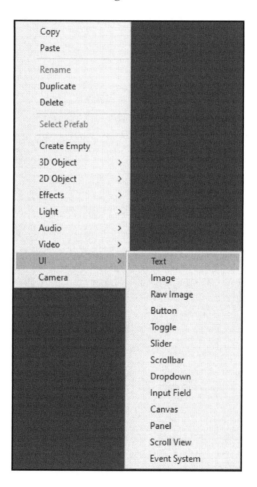

Because we have added the 2D text, Unity helps us out by automatically adding the Canvas to the scene. The following screenshot shows the bootUp **Hierarchy** window containing the Canvas game object along with its child, the Text game object:

5. Right-click on the `Text` game object and rename it to `presented`.

   With `presented` still selected in the **Hierarchy** window, pay attention to the **Inspector** window because we need to update its **Text** component.

6. In the **Text** field, change the default input from **New Text** to `presented by`.

   Let's continue modifying the `presented` game object's **Text** component settings.

7. We will change the font from the typical **Arial** style to something more fitting for our game. In this chapter's project files, there should be a font in the **Project** window, which is located in `Assets/Resources/Font/ethnocentric rg it`. We can select this font from our `presented` game object.

8. Click on the small circle that appears to the right of the **Font** field, and then select `ethnocentric rg it` from the drop-down list.

9. Change the **Font Size** field to `0`.

   At this point, our font will have disappeared from the **Scene** window. This is because the **Rect Tool** isn't big enough and we need to resize it. We will do this next.

What is a Rect Tool?

The **Rect Tool** is an area for the images or text to sit in. Consider it as a similar tool to the **Transform** component, where we enter the `Vector3` values for the **Position, Rotation,** and **Scale** of our game's objects, which we have been altering from `Chapter 2`, *Adding and Manipulating Objects* onward.

10. In the **Scene** window with our `presented` game object still selected, make sure that the **Rect Tool** is selected, as shown in the following screenshot:

11. Make sure we are in 2D mode, as we don't need to be concerned about the 3D space while adjusting the 2D text. Either press 2 on the keyboard, or click on the following button:

12. Additionally, check whether the **Game** window ratio is set to **1080 (1920x1080)** (this is the screen ratio that we set in `Chapter 2`, *Adding and Manipulating Objects*). You can do this using the drop-down list below the **Game** tab, as shown in the following screenshot:

13. Click and drag the outer edge of the **Rect Tool** to the far left until it clips to the outer edge, as indicated in the following screenshot:

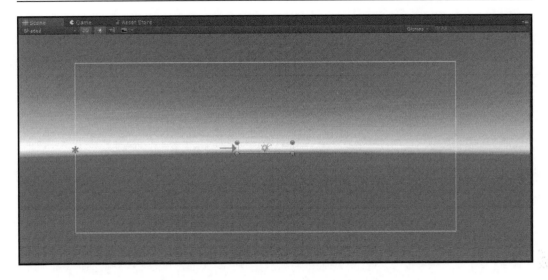

14. Once done, drag the right edge of the **Rect Tool** to the right side of the outer edge.

15. Now, widen the top and the bottom of the **Rect Tool** edges. This is so that the height is approximately a quarter of the white outer rectangle. We should now see our text reappear, and our **Rect Tool** proportions should be similar to those in the following screenshot:

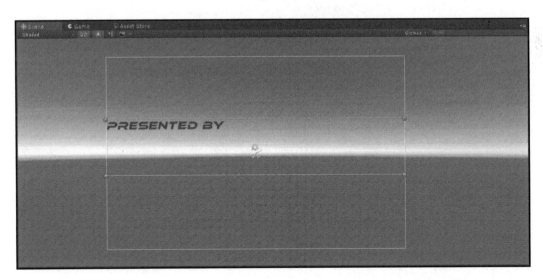

Now that we have the **Rect Tool** spacing set up, we need to set the **Anchors** so that the text remains the correct size no matter what the screen ratio or resolution is.

In the center of the Canvas screen, we should be able to see four arrows pointing toward each other (the left-hand side of the following screenshot has these four arrows circled in red).

To set the **Anchors** in the same location as the four blue circles, perform the following steps:

1. One at a time, click and drag each white arrow to where each blue circle is:

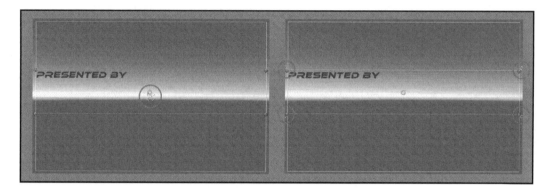

Now that our **Anchors** are roughly sitting on top of the **Rect Tool**, which is denoted by blue circles, we can make it so that the **Position** and **Anchors** are both aligned.

2. To set the **Rect Transform** into place, enter a value of zero in the **Left**, **Top**, **Pos Z**, **Right**, and **Bottom** positions. The following screenshot shows our highlighted values (on the left). It's likely that yours won't be the same since we positioned the **Rect Tool** manually earlier on:

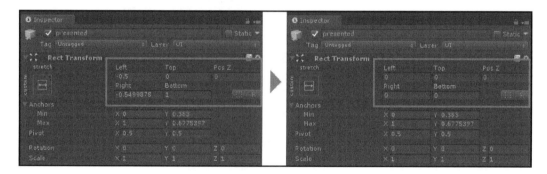

Now, we can continue with the **Text** component in the **Inspector** window in order to set the color and position of the text.

3. To center the `presented by` text in the **Text** component, select the two middle buttons in the **Alignment** section, as shown in the following screenshot:

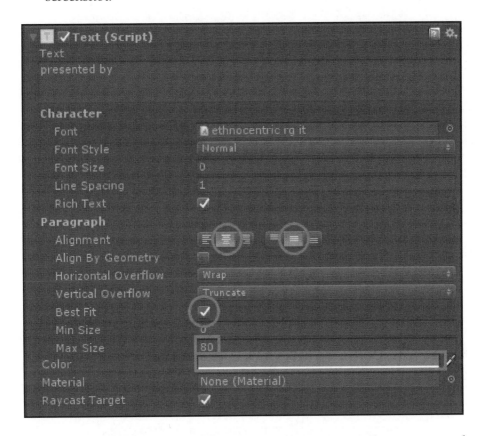

4. Tick the **Best Fit** box. This will ensure that our text scales to support the screen's ratio dynamically.

5. With the **Best Fit** box ticked, we will set **Min Size** to 0 and **Max Size** to 80.

6. Change the color by clicking on the **Color** field and choose red, as shown in the preceding screenshot.

We have now had a full run with the **Canvas** and **Text** components, and we have set our own custom 2D text up. Additionally, this text will be able to adjust to the screen ratios compared to the `bootUp` **TextMesh** that we had before.

The following screenshot shows our custom text, color, size, and alignment:

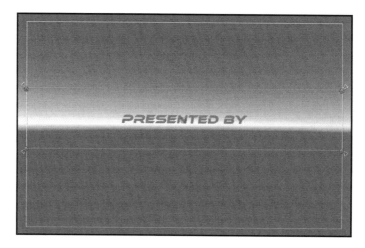

As you can imagine, we haven't quite finished yet because we need to have the name or company's name appear underneath the **PRESENTED BY** text. Thankfully, we only need to repeat about a quarter of the work we've just done. And, as you've probably guessed – yes – we can copy and paste this text.

To set our own name or company name underneath **PRESENTED BY**, perform the following steps:

1. Select the `presented` game object from the **Hierarchy** window.
2. Press *Ctrl (command* on the Mac*)* and *D* to duplicate the game object.
3. Press *T* to switch to the **Move Tool**:

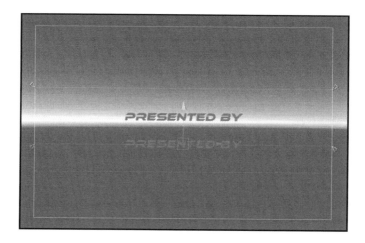

4. Now click and drag the green *y-axis* arrow downward (as shown in the preceding screenshot) to roughly sit on the white line where the original **PRESENTED BY** text's **Rect Tool** lies.

5. All we need to do next is to click and drag each of the four white arrow outlines of the **Anchors** downward to fit in our newly created game object, as shown in the following screenshot:

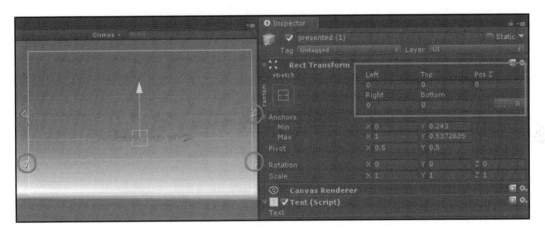

6. If you have moved the **Anchors** into their correct places, then our **Rect Transform** positions will be zero. If they are close to zero, click on each field and enter 0.

   So, our new text is in place. All we need to do now is to change what has been typed in.

7. We know how to do this: just scroll down to the **Text** component and enter your name, company name, pet name, or any name – it doesn't matter for the purpose of this tutorial.

8. Once you have entered your name, don't forget to name the presented(1) game object to something like yourName.

   Click on the **Game** tab window to see how it looks. This is what ours looks like:

9. Save the scene.

We have covered the fundamentals of a **Canvas** component and how to apply 2D text. Next, we will be repeating a similar procedure and using the **Image** component. This is equivalent to the **Sprite Renderer** that we used for our shop scene buttons in Chapter 5, *Creating a Shop Scene for Our Game*. However, here, the **Image** component is for a 2D space.

From this point to the end of the chapter, we will go through a series of subsections in order to polish and animate our scenes. We will cover the following:

- Starting with our title scene, we will improve its visuals by creating and applying **Text** and **Image** components.
- We will use a custom font because we can, and it'll make our game look better than the standard fonts that come with Unity. From there, we will be able to further customize the **Text** component to make our title scene look more suitable for our game.
- We will then take what we have applied to the title scene and copy and paste it into the other scenes. From there, we will change the content of the text and its position slightly.
- Finally, we will set up our **Animator** and **Animator Controller** states and animate our UI to introduce each game level.

Let's continue with polishing our title scene.

Improving our title scene

In this section, we will repeat the procedure that we already learned in the previous section without going into too much depth, as we already know how to create a Canvas, add custom text, and perform duplicating. In this section, we will also make use of Unity's **Image** component.

The following screenshot shows the transformation we will be undergoing, starting with our current title scene on the left and using the same techniques we applied in the previous section, along with adding **Image** components, to create the red stripe on the right:

As mentioned earlier, we won't be going into all of the details; however, if you do struggle at any point, then please refer back to the previous section to guide you through what you should already know. Let's get started:

1. Let's begin by loading up our `title` scene from the **Project** window, which is located in `Assets/Scenes/title`.
2. Change the **Camera** component's **Background** color from gray to black with the alpha value set to `255`.
3. Delete the `Title Text` game object from the **Hierarchy** window.
4. Create just a `Canvas` game object in the **Hierarchy** window. Use the following screenshot as a reference:

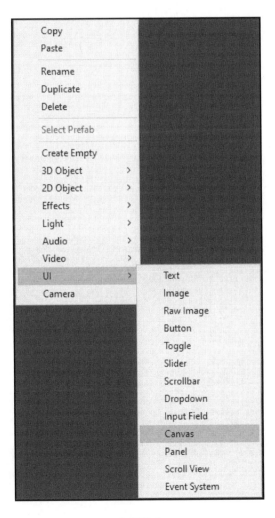

We are now going to create an empty game object. Inside this game object, we are going to store our **Text** and **Image** components:

1. Create an empty game object by right-clicking in the lower open space of the **Hierarchy** window, and then select **Create Empty** from the drop-down list.
2. The new empty game object will default to the name of GameObject.
3. Right-click on this game object and select **Rename** from the drop-down list. Rename the game object to Title.
4. Move the Title game object into the Canvas game object so that the former becomes a child.

Typically, when a new game object is created, it will automatically be given a **Transform** component that holds the game object's **Position**, **Rotation**, and **Scale** for a 3D space. In this section, our focus is on 2D space, so we need to change this game object from a **Transform** component into a **Rect Transform** component.

To change the Title game object from **Transform** to **Rect Transform**, perform these steps:

1. With the Title game object selected in the **Hierarchy** window, click on the **Add Component** button in the **Inspector** window.
2. A drop-down list will appear. Type rect transform into the drop-down list search bar until it is possible to select it from the list, as shown in the following screenshot:

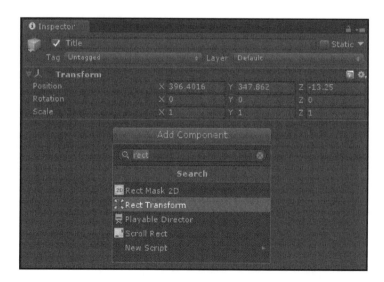

We are now going to set our `Title` game object's **Anchor** sizes. This is so any game objects that become a child to it will be restricted within the `Title` game object's **Anchors**.

I have set my `Title` game object's **Rect Transform** component to the following settings:

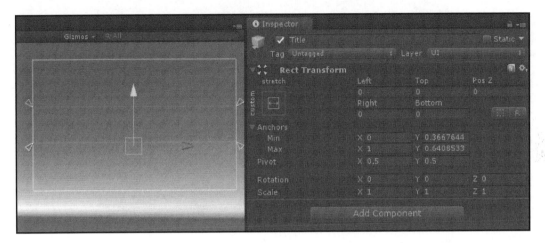

As you can see, in the previous screenshot, the **Anchors** for the `Title` game object are centered in the canvas's white box outline. Also, note that the **Rect Transform** component's **Left**, **Top**, **Pos Z**, **Right**, and **Bottom** positions are all set to the value of zero.

The next step will be to add a red transparent stripe within the `Title` game object. To add an **Image** component, follow these instructions:

1. Create a new game object in the **Hierarchy** window.
2. Name the game object `mainCol`.
3. Drag the `mainCol` game object on top of the `Title` game object to make `mainCol` a child of `Title`. Refer to the following screenshot for reference:

4. With our `mainCol` game object still selected, we want its **Anchors** to be at their maximum size, which, in this case, is the same size as the `Title` game object as it is the parent of our `mainCol` game object. The following screenshot is a reference to our `mainCol` **Rect Transform** properties:

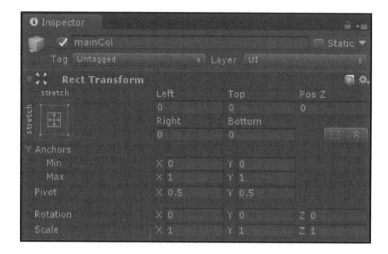

5. With the `mainCol` game object still selected, select the **Add Component** button in the **Inspector** window and begin to type `Image` into the drop-down list until it appears. When it does appear, select it. Use the following screenshot as a reference:

We have now added an **Image** component to our `mainCol` image.

6. Next, we will adjust the **Image** component's **R**, **G**, **B**, and **A** values. To do that, click on the **Image** component's **Color** field (denoted by **1**) and set its **RGBA** values (denoted by **2**) in accordance with the following screenshot. From there, you will see our `mainCol` image react to the color change (denoted by **3**):

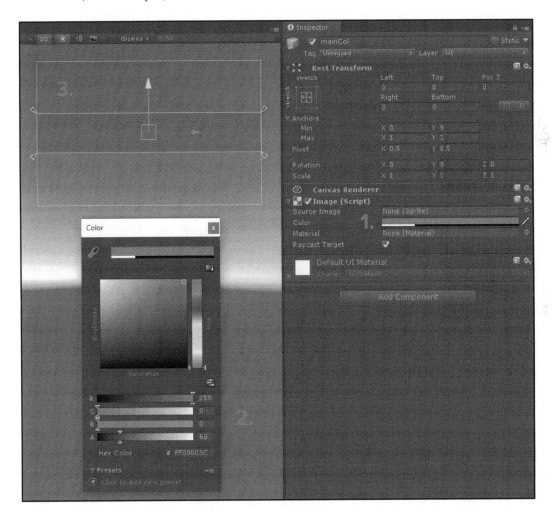

With the **Image** component, if we added a sprite to the parameter instead of just changing the color alone, we would also have the ability to alter its **Image Type**. One of the types that can be used is called **Filled**. This can give you the impression that the sprite is filling up, which would be useful for a loading bar or a time limit that is counting down.

If you would like to know more about the **Image** component and its other uses, view the documentation at `https://docs.unity3d.com/2017.3/Documentation/Manual/script-Image.html`.

Next, we will add a strip to the top of the image we've just made with another game object containing an **Image** component. To do that, we will repeat our earlier methodology but with a tighter, thinner strip. Follow these steps:

1. With `mainCol` still selected, press *Ctrl (command* on the Mac) and *D* on our keyboard to duplicate the game object.
2. Rename the new game object to `trim00`.
3. Change the `trim00` game object's **Rect Transform** to the following properties. The left-hand side of the screenshot shows the top of the main red strip with our `trim00` game object at the top:

For our trim set, we don't need to change the color as it duplicates from the `mainCol` game object. We now need to repeat this process for the bottom part of the `mainCol` image.

Here are the steps that we need to accomplish to copy another trim game object:

1. Duplicate the `trim00` game object and rename it to `trim01`.
2. Set the `trim01` game object's **Rect Transform** settings to the same settings shown in the following screenshot:

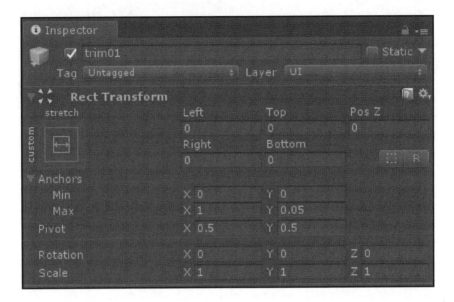

Now it's time to enter our main title text, KILLER WAVE, by following these instructions:

1. Create another empty game object in the **Hierarchy** window.
2. Give the new empty game object the name `TitleText`.
3. In the **Hierarchy** window, drag the `TitleText` game object inside the `Title` game object. This is so that `TitleText` becomes a child of `Title`.
4. With `TitleText` still selected, click on **Add Component** in the **Inspector** window and select **Rect Transform** from the drop-down list as before.

5. Set the `TitleText` **Rect Transform** settings to the following values:

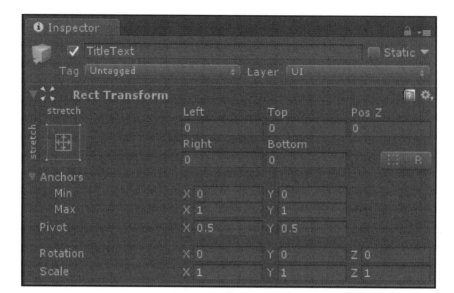

This will fill our `TitleText` **Rect Transform** settings to the same size as the parent game object (`Title`).

The final steps for our `TitleText` game object are to give it a **Text** component and set its values in the **Inspector** window:

1. With the `TitleText` game object still selected in the **Hierarchy** window, click on the **Add Component** button and select the **Text** component (type in `text` if it isn't there) from the drop-down list as before.
2. In the **Text** field of the **Text** component, enter `killer wave`.
3. Click on the small circle to the right of the **Font** field (the remote button), and select the font that we chose in our `bootUp` scene (`ethnocentric rg it`).
4. Set both **Alignment** buttons to center and middle.
5. Tick **Best Fit**. This will leave it up to Unity to try and fit the text depending on the ratio it is in.
6. Set **Max Size** to `140`. This will give us a fairly large title.
7. Select a bright red color in the **Color** field.

Our title is set. The last thing we need to do in this scene is to set a message at the bottom of the screen to prompt the player to start the game.

Similar to what we did in the bootUp scene, we can duplicate our TitleText game object. However, this time, we are going to move the duplicated game object outside of the **Rect Transform** restrictions of its parent. The final text we will display will be a message to prompt the player to tap on the screen or shoot to begin playing the game.

To enter the SHOOT TO START text, follow these instructions:

1. Select the TitleText game object in the **Hierarchy** window.
2. Press *Ctrl (Command* on the Mac) and *D* to duplicate it.
3. Rename the duplicated game object to shootToStart.
4. With shootToStart still selected, change its **Text** component's **Text** field from **Killer Wave** to SHOOT TO START in the **Inspector** window.
5. Set **Max Size** to 50.

As mentioned earlier, we are going to move the **Text** selection from its current area to outside its parent:

1. Hold *Ctrl (command* on the Mac) and click on any one of its white arrows. Then, pull the **Rect Tool** downward so that it is completely outside its parent **Rect Tool**, as highlighted in the following screenshot:

2. Zero out the **Left**, **Top**, **Pos Z**, **Right**, and **Bottom Rect Transform** properties. This will move our SHOOT TO START text down and into the location where the white arrows are. The following screenshot shows the placement of the text along with its **Rect Transform** property values:

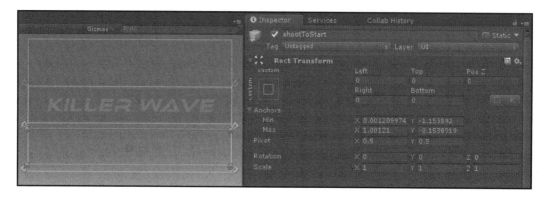

We don't need to change any of the functionality of the scene as we have already set this up.

3. Save the scene.

The following screenshot shows what our title scene now looks like:

So far, we have gone further with our text by duplicating it, altering it, and moving it outside of its parent **Rect Tool** game object. We have also introduced images and used them in a similar way to our 2D text.

We will now continue and work on the next scene: gameOver.

Duplicating our game objects

In this section, we will improve the gameOver scene from its gray background and blocky white text and replace it with the same images and text from the title scene. However, this time, we won't be repeating the same steps from the previous sections to recreate the same outcome.

We will copy, paste, and tweak the game objects to save time and effort rather than repeat what we have already achieved with the title scene.

As an overview, here is what our gameOver UI game objects will contain and do:

- Canvas: This parents all of the UI game objects.
- GameOverTitle: This holds all of the individual game objects relating to the **Text** and **Image** components.
- mainCol: The main red stripe in the center (holds the **Image** component).
- trim00: The red line at the top (holds the **Image** component).
- trim01: The red line at the bottom (holds the **Image** component).
- GameOverText: The main **GAME OVER** text(holds the **Text** component).

Thankfully, we don't really need to worry too much about what their roles are because we have already established this in the previous section. To duplicate our game objects and move them from the title scene to gameOver, perform these steps:

1. While still in our title scene, hold *Ctrl* (*command* on the Mac) on the keyboard and select **Main Camera** and **Canvas**.
2. Both our objects will be highlighted. Right-click on either one of them and select **Copy** from the drop-down list.
3. Open the gameOver scene.
4. In the **Hierarchy** window, select and delete **Main Camera** and GameOverText. We will replace these with our copied game objects.
5. Right-click in an open space of the **Hierarchy** window and select **Paste**.
6. Click on the arrow next to the Canvas game object in the **Hierarchy** window. Right-click on the Title game object and then click on **Rename** from the drop-down list.
7. Rename the game object to GameOverTitle.
8. Click on the arrow next to GameOverTitle and rename the TitleText game object to GameOverText.
9. Select the shootToStart game object and press *Delete* on your keyboard.

To confirm what we have done so far, the following screenshot shows the **Hierarchy** window for the `gameOver` scene:

10. With `GameOverText` still selected, change its **Text** field in the **Text** component of the **Inspector** window from `killer wave` to `game over`.

11. Save the scene.

This is what our `gameOver` scene should look like:

In this section, we discovered that we can simply copy and paste game objects from one scene to another as long as we work within the same Unity project. This saves time and effort and keeps our game looking uniform in accordance with the rest of the scenes.

In the next section, we will learn how to animate our UI game objects.

Preparing to animate UI game objects

In this section, we will use a number of techniques that we have already covered, so we won't be going into the same level of detail. Once we have duplicated and changed the game objects, we will also be adding animation elements to make our 2D visuals less static.

We will be using a similar methodology to the gameOver scene by copying our previous scene's Canvas with its child game objects (not the **Main Camera** game object). The most suitable scene for this would be the gameOver scene as it has the basic elements we need. This only requires a couple of amendments before moving on to the animation phase.

To set up the level1 scene, perform the following steps:

1. Make sure our gameOver scene is still open in the Unity Editor. This is because we are going to copy some game objects over into the level1 scene.
2. In the **Hierarchy** window, right-click on the Canvas game object and click on **Copy** from the drop-down list.
3. Open the level1 scene from the **Project** window.
4. Right-click in the **Hierarchy** window and select **Paste**. We should now have the game over Canvas in our level1 scene.
5. Next, we will rename two game objects to suit our level1 scene.
6. Expand the Canvas game object in the **Hierarchy** window and select the GameOverTitle game object. Right-click on it and select **Rename** from the drop-down list.
7. Rename the game object to LevelTitle.
8. Expand the LevelTitle game object in the **Hierarchy** window.
9. Select GameOverText in the **Hierarchy** window and rename it to Level.

That's all that we need to do to our Canvas game object in the **Hierarchy** window. We can now move on to changing the main text itself from **GAME OVER** to LEVEL 1.

With the `Level` game object still selected, remove **Game Over** from the **Text** component's **Text** field and replace it with `LEVEL 1`, as shown in the following screenshot:

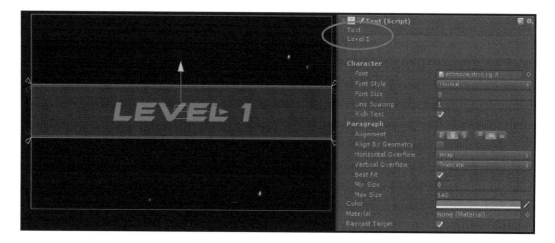

We are now ready to start animating the UI 2D text and its image. All the game objects that we will be animating sit within the `LevelTitle` game object.

To set up our animation, we need to do the following:

1. While you are still in the `level1` scene, select `LevelTitle` under the **Canvas** game object in the **Hierarchy** window.
2. In the **Inspector** window of `LevelTitle`, click on the **Add Component** button at the bottom.
3. Type in `Animator` until you see the word **Animator** appear, and then select it.

Our `LevelTitle` game object now has an **Animator** component. We now need to give it an **Animator Controller** to manage when to animate the contents of the `LevelTitle` game object. To do that, follow these steps:

1. In the **Project** window, navigate to `Assets/Resources/Animator`.
2. Right-click in an open space of the **Project** window and select **Create** from the drop-down list, followed by **Animator Controller**.
3. Change the name of the new **Animator Controller** from **New Animator Controller** to `LevelTitle`.

We now need to attach the new `LevelTitle` **Animator Controller** to our **Animator** component.

4. Back in the **Hierarchy** window, reselect the `LevelTitle` game object, and click on the small round circle (which is referred to as remotes, denoted by an arrow in the following screenshot) next to the **Animator** component's **Controller** field. Select the newly created `LevelTitle` game object from the drop-down list.

The following screenshot shows the `LevelTitle` game object with the `LevelTitle` controller selected:

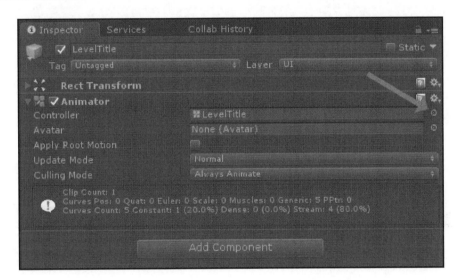

Next, we need to create an animation so that we can add it to the **Animator Controller**:

1. In the **Project** window, in the `Assets/Resources/Animator` location, right-click in an open space. Select **Create | Animation**.
2. Rename the **New Animation** game object clip to `levelTitle_A`.

    Let's now open the **Animator Controller** and add the `levelTitle_A` clip to it.

3. At the top of the Unity Editor, click on **Window** followed by **Animator**.

    This will open the **Animator** window.

4. Select the `LevelTitle` game object in the **Hierarchy** window. The content for the **Animator** will appear with its three states (**Any State**, **Entry**, and **Exit**).

The following screenshot shows the **Animator** window with its three default states and also a reference to the location of the **Animator Controller** that is selected:

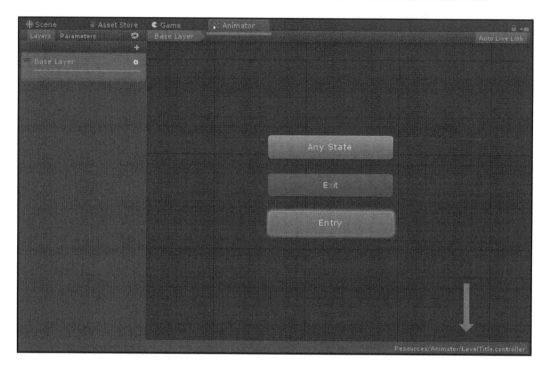

Before we drop the animation clip in, it will benefit us to have a small time delay before the clip is played; otherwise, the animation might play too soon. In order to fix this, we can make an empty state that has a time limit. We can set this **idle** state to play at any speed or point we want before we play the intended animation clip (`levelTitle_A`).

To create an **idle** state and hook it up to the intended animation clip, follow these steps:

1. Right-click in an empty part of the **Animator** window and select **Create State | Empty**. The following screenshot shows the drop-down list we should expect:

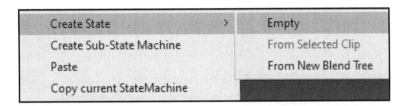

2. Select the **New State** and, in the **Inspector** window, change the **New State** name to **Idle**. Then, press *Enter* on your keyboard.
3. Now we can drag `levelTitle_A` from the **Project** window to the **Animator** window.
4. We now need to join the transition from our `Idle` game state to the `levelTitle_A` state.
5. Right-click on the **Idle** state and select **Make Transition** from the drop-down list.
6. Select **levelTitle_A** to make a connection between the two states.

The following screenshot indicates what our states should look like now:

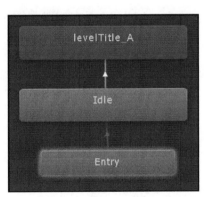

It will not be necessary to use the **Animator** window after the animation is complete, and we may need to tweak the delay. However, for this, we will need to use the **Animation** window, so it's ideal to have this at the bottom of the screen. To do that, perform these steps:

1. In the **Project** window, click on the **Add Tab** button from the drop-down list.
2. Click on **Animation**.

   The following screenshot is in accordance with the preceding numbered bullets:

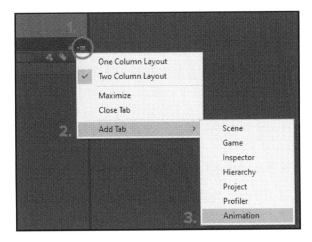

In this section, we have brought in the **GAME OVER** UI art and altered it to represent the level we are on. We then prepared the game objects to be animated with the **Animator Controller** and its states, followed by creating a blank **Animation** clip.

We can now start animating the entrance and exit for our **LEVEL 1** UI art in the next section.

Animating our UI level title

We are going to animate two game objects: the level title and the main strip bar in the `level1` scene. In the previous section, we set up the **Animation** window at the bottom of the Unity Editor. The following screenshot shows our current setup for the placement of the windows, which may be helpful for reference purposes:

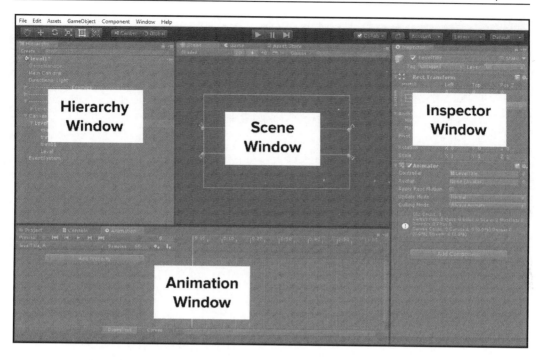

With regard to the animation itself, we will be animating the following:

- The level text that moves on to the screen.
- The main center strip will glow red.
- The text that will exit the screen.

The following screenshot shows the steps that were mentioned:

So, the four main elements to animate are the Level game object, which contains the 2D **Text** component. The other three to be animated will be the mainCol, trim00, and trim01 game objects that contain the **Image** component's color values. Let's start by animating the Level game object first.

Animating the 2D text component

In this section, we are going to animate the text from the left to the center. It will pause so the player has a chance to read it. Then, it will move out of the screen:

1. In the **Hierarchy** window, click on the arrow next to the Canvas game object to expand its content if it isn't expanded already.
2. Click on the arrow next to the LevelTitle to do the same.
3. Select the Level game object.
4. In the **Animation** window, click on the record button, as shown in the following screenshot:

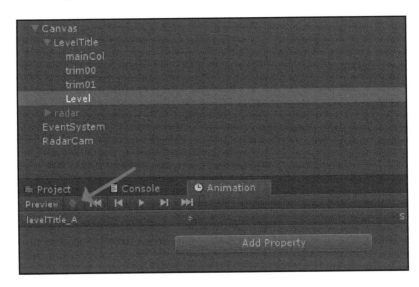

With our animation track line scrubbed (note that scrub is an animation term for dragging our timeline indicator) all the way back to **0:00**, which is its default, let's move our Level game object from the center of the Canvas to the left in the **Scene** view by doing the following:

1. With the Level game object still selected in the **Hierarchy** window, type the following values into the **Inspector** window's **Rect Transform** (**Left:** −2000 and **Right:** 2000) property fields to move our 2D LEVEL 1 text out of the **Canvas** view, as shown in the following screenshot:

Now that our LEVEL 1 2D text is pushed out of the way, we can scrub the animation line forward.

2. Click and drag within the timeline digits, as shown in the following screenshot:

3. In the **Animation** window, drag the white vertical line from **0:00** to **0:34**.
4. In the **Inspector** window, change the Level game object's **Rect Transform Left** and **Right** properties to zero.

   The fields will turn red to show the change has been recorded. The animation timeline in the **Animation** window will gain keyframes from the movement of the 2D text.

The following screenshot shows the changes made to the timeline:

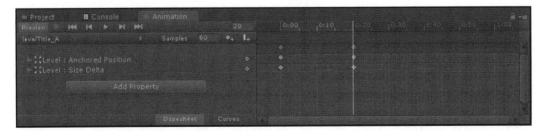

We obviously want the LEVEL 1 text to stay where it is for a few seconds before it leaves the screen again. To make the text pause in the center before moving, follow these steps:

1. In the **Animation** window, move the white line from **0:34** to **1:25**.
2. Click on the **Add keyframe** button.

   The following screenshot shows the timeline is at **1:25**, with new keyframes added while the record button is clicked on:

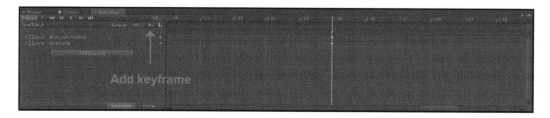

3. For our next keyframe point, drag the white line to **1:50**.

Now we have come to the stage where we want to move the UI text from its center position to out of view of the camera:

1. Select the Level game object.
2. In the **Inspector** window, change the **Rect Transform** properties to the following:
     - **Left**: 2000
     - **Right**: -2000

   This will push the LEVEL 1 text out of the camera view, as shown in the following screenshot:

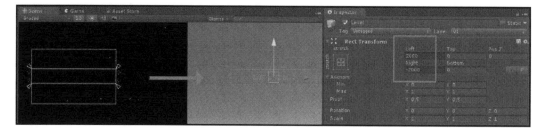

3. Move your mouse cursor down to the timeline **Animation** window. Then, click and press *F* on your keyboard. This will show all of the keyframes for the total animation we have just done.

4. Click on the **record** button in the **Animation** window timeline to stop recording, and scrub backward and forward to see our 2D text animating in, pause, and then move out of the screen.

We have made a start by animating the `Level 1` text within the `Canvas` with Unity's **Animation** system.

Our UI text starts on the far left (out of view of the camera), animates into the center, pauses, and then animates out of view.

Now we can continue to animate the UI and move our focus from positioning to changing our UI's color (R, G, B, A) to a glowing red in the next section. This will show that our animation doesn't happen with just one component, but is shared through a series of components. We will animate the **Image** component next.

Animating the Image component's center strip

The second part of the animation phase is to have the center strip for the level title to glow red and then disappear. To do this, all animation for the `mainCol`, `trim00`, and `trim01` game objects will be manipulated in the **Inspector** window through their **Image** component's **Color** settings.

Let's start animating the **Image** components for all three game objects:

1. In the **Hierarchy** window, hold *Ctrl* (*command* on the Mac) on the keyboard and select `mainCol`, `trim00`, and `trim01`. These are the game objects we will be animating.

2. In the **Animation** window, move the line bar all the way back to **0:00**.

3. Click on the **record** button in the **Animation** window.

4. With all three game objects still selected, click on the **Color** field and set the **R**, **G**, **B**, and **A** values to **R**: 255, **G**: 0, **B**: 0, and **A**: 0. Refer to the following screenshot:

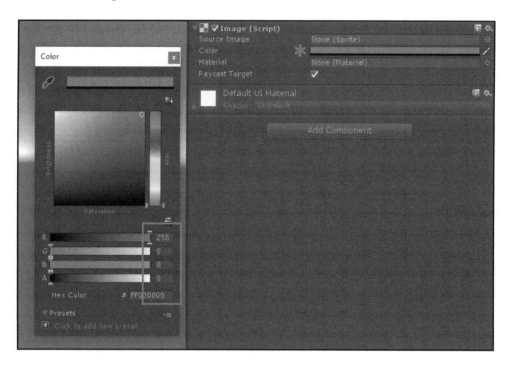

Our **Animation** window will update to indicate that the three changes have been made. In the following screenshot, we can see the properties have been changed for the `mainCol`, `trim00`, and `trim01` **Image** component's alpha color properties (note that alpha is the **A** from **R**, **G**, **B**, and **A**). The **Alpha** setting will alter the transparency of the image:

In basic terms, the three game objects are invisible at the start of the animation in the **Scene** window. Next, we need to make the images come out of the transparency phase and glow red. To do that, we now need to move our timeline indicator over to **0:55** and perform the following steps:

1. With the three game objects still selected, change the **Color** values on their **Image** components to **R**: 255, **G**:0, **B**:0, and **A**: 120, as shown in the following screenshot:

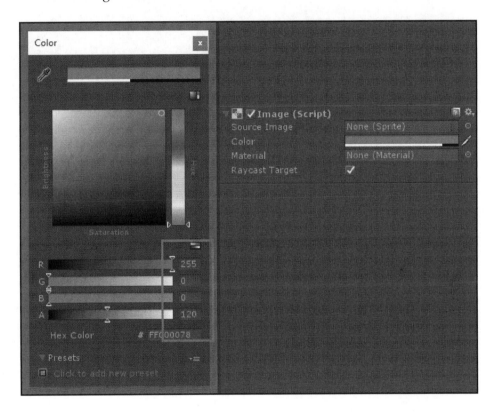

Our three game objects have now become visible again in the **Scene** view. The final part of the animation is to make the three game objects turn invisible again. Instead of going back into the **Color** value settings, we can simply copy and paste the keys we created in timeline **0:00**. To copy our keyframes, do the following:

2. With our three game objects and the record button still selected in the **Animation** window, move the timeline indicator back to **0:00**.

3. Select all three `Image.Color.a` changes in the **Animation** window, as shown in the following screenshot:

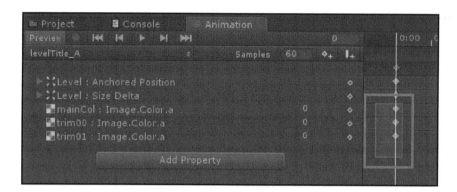

4. Press *Ctrl* (*command* on the Mac) and *C* on your keyboard to copy the keyframes.

5. Click on the record button in the **Animation** window to stop recording the animation.

6. Scrub to **1:50** and press *Ctrl* (*command* on the Mac) and *V* on your keyboard to paste.

7. Move your mouse cursor to the **Animation** window. Click and press *F* on the keyboard to get a full view of the timeline. Move the cursor back and forth to see the level text animating into the scene and the center strip glowing red.

When our Level 1 scene starts, we will see the title and the red bar before the animation, which we don't want. Therefore, we need to set the Level 1 text and red bar to the same values as the first frame of our animation:

1. Select the `mainCol` game object and set the **Image** component's alpha to zero.

2. Set the `trim00` **Image** component's alpha to zero.

3. Set the `trim01` **Image** component's alpha to zero.

4. Set the **Rect Transform Left** property value to −2000 and the **Right** property value to 2000.

The following screenshot shows the default position and alpha settings of the previous steps:

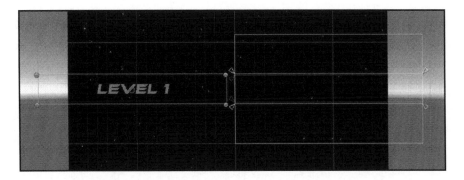

5. Save the scene.

Let's remind ourselves briefly of what we have covered so far before we move on to the final section. We took our `mainCol`, `trim00`, and `trim01` game objects and changed their **Image** component **Color** alpha values over a series of keyframes using the animation timeline.

Let's now move on to the next section where we will copy our art, text, and, in some cases, animation into other scenes. From there, we will tailor the components to each scene.

Copying and pasting art, text, and animation into other scenes

Finally, we can copy all of the hard work of our `level1` scene (including its animation) and paste it into the `level2` and `level3` scenes and amend each level number. To do that, follow these steps:

1. In the **Hierarchy** window, select **Canvas** and press *Ctrl* (*command* on the Mac) and *C* on your keyboard.
2. In the **Project** window, load up `level2` in `Assets/Scene`.
3. Click in an open space of the **Hierarchy** window and press *Ctrl* (*command* on the Mac) and *V* on your keyboard to paste the `level1` scene's `Canvas` game object and all of its content.
4. Select the `Level` game object in the **Hierarchy** window (within `Canvas` and `LevelTitle`).
5. Change the **Text** component's **Text** field from `Level 1` to `Level 2`.
6. Save the scene.

7. Repeat the process for scene `level3`:

Well done! Another big chapter has been conquered. We have started to make our game shine with some sweet art that we made ourselves. Let's recap what we have achieved.

We took some plain gray scenes and made them more presentable and fit with our sci-fi game. This was all thanks to the Unity Editor, as we were able to achieve this with no scripting. The main components we covered were as follows:

- **Text**: We imported a custom font and tweaked it within the component itself.
- **Image**: With any sprites, we set our colors to create a series of red stripes with transparency.
- **Animator Controller**: Held states for when the **Image** and **Text** components were to be animated.
- **Animation**: Each keyframe for a mixture of components was set in a single timeline animation.

Finally, we took what we created from one scene and simply copied and pasted the game objects and their components to the existing scenes to act as a template for the UI (and also its animation, if required). We then changed each of the scene's UI text (**Game Over, Killer Wave, Level 1,** and so on) to suit that particular scene.

Summary

This chapter was about taking our game project and polishing its current content with regard to the existing UI. It is also required with your Unity Programmer Exam to understand what tools and components we have to help us to create our game with regard to the *Working in the art pipeline* core exam skill.

We also took our **Text** and **Image** components and created one piece of animation from multiple game objects. These animations were called from the **Animator Controller** state machine.

In your future projects, you will have the option to keep your UI presentable while putting your game loop together.

In the next chapter, we will extend our current UI skills by making our shop scene more flexible with a range of screen ratios. Additionally, we will create a UI to sit at the bottom of our in-game levels.

Creating a 2D Shop Interface and In-Game HUD

9

n this chapter, we will be paying attention to our shop interface and how we can improve it visually, as well as its functionality. The current shop works well, but we could make it support multiple screen ratios. We could also introduce Unity's Event system and Button components, as well as a few other new functionalities.

The other area we will be visiting in this chapter is the in-game **Heads Up Display (HUD)**. This is fairly common in games where we have the game's information displayed at a particular location of the screen. We will be displaying our player's lives, score, and a mini-map to show where our enemies are. This can be seen in the following screenshot:

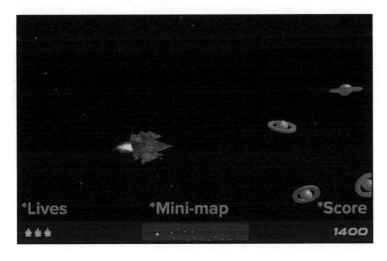

The other half of this chapter will be about improving the 2D visuals of our shop scene so that there are choices in terms of the upgrades we can buy and so that we can also expand the size of the shop dynamically. Also, your shop scene will support any landscape ratio, unlike what it did previously. The following screenshot shows what our shop looks like in different ratio sizes:

In the previous screenshot, notice that the 3:2 screen ratio cuts off some of the screen (you will especially notice this from each screen's selection grids spacing) compared to our 1920 x 1080 (16:9) screen ratio. By the end of this chapter, our shop scene will look like the one shown in the following screenshot, no matter what landscape ratio our game will be in:

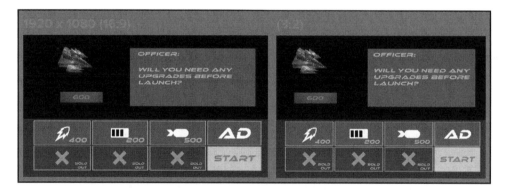

In this chapter, we will cover the following topics:

- Setting up our HUD
- Making our shop scene support alternative screen ratios
- Applying and modifying our shop scripts

Let's start by reviewing the core exam skills that will be covered in this chapter.

Core exam skills covered in this chapter

The following are the core exam skills that will be covered in this chapter:

- *Working in the art pipeline:*
    - *Understand materials, textures, and shaders, and write scripts that interact with Unity's rendering API.*

- *Developing application systems:*
    - *Interpret scripts for application interface flow such as menu systems, UI navigation, and application settings.*
    - *Interpret scripts for user-controlled customization such as character creators, inventories, storefronts, and in-app purchases.*
    - *Analyze scripts for user progression features such as scoring, leveling, and in-game economies utilizing technologies such as Unity Analytics and PlayerPrefs.*
    - *Analyze scripts for 2D overlays such as heads-up displays (HUDs), minimaps, and advertisements.*
    - *Identify scripts for saving and retrieving application and user data.*

- *Programming for scene and environment design:*
    - *Identify methods for implementing Game Object instantiation, destruction, and management.*

- *Optimizing for performance and platforms:*
    - *Identify optimizations to address requirements for specific build platforms and/or hardware configurations.*
    - *Determine common UI affordances and optimizations for XR platforms.*

- *Working in professional software development teams:*
    - *Recognize techniques for structuring scripts for modularity, readability, and reusability.*

Technical requirements

The project content for this chapter can be found at `https://github.com/PacktPublishing/Unity-Certified-Programmer-Exam-Guide/tree/master/Chapter09`.

You can download the entirety of each chapter's project files at `https://github.com/PacktPublishing/Unity-Certified-Programmer-Exam-Guide/archive/master.zip`.

All the content for this chapter is held in this chapter's `unitypackage` file, including a `Complete` folder that holds all of the work we'll carry out in this chapter.

Check out the following video to see the Code in Action: `https://bit.ly/3eAcKZh`.

Setting up our HUD

With side-scrolling shooter games, it is common for us to have some form of recording of how many lives the player has, what their score is, a time limit, power-ups, and more. For us, we are going to apply a typical HUD to show a similar set of information. Knowing about HUDs is a requirement of your Unity Programmer Exam.

By the end of this section, we will have created a HUD for our game that will consist of the following:

- Lives
- Mini-map
- Score

Before we add our HUD, we need to decide where it will sit on top of our game screen. As an example, we will pick a game so that we can briefly study how its HUD information is displayed.

We will be looking at a game called **Super R-Type**, which can be found at `https://github.com/retrophil/Unity-Certified-Programmer-Exam-Guide/blob/master/Reference/superRtype.jpg?raw=true`. Here, at the bottom of the screen, we can see that its HUD is made up of four parts, as follows:

- Skill level
- Lives
- Power bar
- Score

Behind these details is a black background so that the scene doesn't interfere when it comes to reading the HUD.

So, in this section, we'll start by declaring the HUD space and give it a dark background. To do this, follow these instructions:

1. In the Unity Editor, navigate to `Assets/Scene` in the **Project** window.
2. Open the `level1` scene.
3. With `level1` loaded, go to the **Hierarchy** window, right-click on the `Canvas` game object, and select **UI | Image**.
4. A game object called `Image` will appear in the **Hierarchy** window as a child of the `Canvas` game object.

   From the previous chapter, we should know that a game object containing an **Image** component must be a child of `Canvas`.

5. Right-click the `image` game object and select **Rename** from the drop-down. Name the game object `background`.

So far, we have created the game object that holds an **Image** component.

Now, let's move on and size this game object into place so that it can be used as a background for our HUD. Follow these steps:

1. With our `background` game object still selected, alter the **Rect Transform** settings in the **Inspector** window to the following:

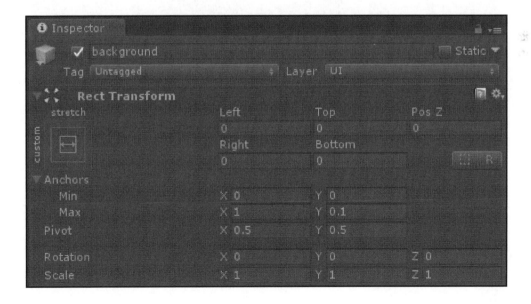

Our `background` game object should be scaled to the same proportions and centered as a white bar at the bottom of the screen, as shown in the following screenshot:

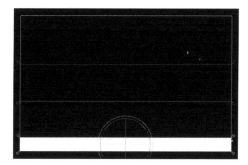

Now, let's darken this `background` game object so that it blends in with our game.

2. With the `background` game object still selected, in the **Inspector** window, click the **Color** field and change its color settings to **R**: 12, **G**: 13, **B**: 13, **A**: 210, as shown in the following screenshot:

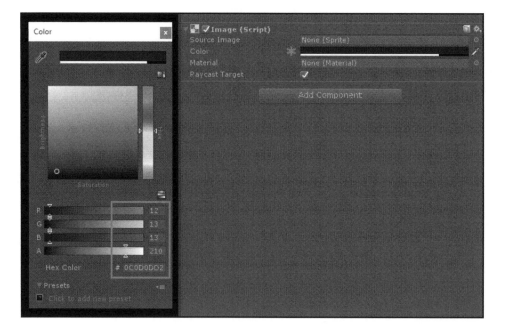

The `background` game object has changed color from its default white to a dark transparent dark color.

The area for our HUD has been set. The following subsections will go through each segment of our HUD and explain how to create the following:

- **Display lives**: We'll be adding **Image** components to the bottom left of the HUD to every life our player has from the `GameManager` script. Each life will be grouped neatly.

- **Display score**: The script already keeps track of the player's score, so all we need to do is use a **Text** component to keep the information up-to-date.

- **Mini-map**: The mini-map will work visually similar to a radar, where the player will be able to see the wave of enemy opponents approaching them. This mini-map will be made using a second camera on a wider angle and will only able to see colored dots instead of the actual ships themselves.

Now, we can begin filling the HUD with data that we have already made in our script, starting with the player's lives.

Displaying the player's lives

The player starts the game with three lives. The two typical ways of displaying the number of lives to the player are by displaying a number count or showing a little icon for each life they have. Let's go for the latter as we can use a couple of Unity components we haven't used before.

This section will also include some extra code that will be put into our `GameManager` script. This code will run a check to see how many lives the player has. With each life that's found, a game object will be created that holds an image.

Adding a Horizontal Layout Group component to our game object

All game object lives that will be created will be stored in a game object called `lives`. Let's continue working on the HUD and add the `lives` game object:

1. In the **Hierarchy** window, right-click the `Canvas` game object and select **Create empty** from the drop-down list. A new empty game object will be created.
2. Right-click the new game object and select **Rename** from the drop-down list.
3. Next, position the `lives` game object by adding the **Rect Transform** properties shown in the following screenshot:

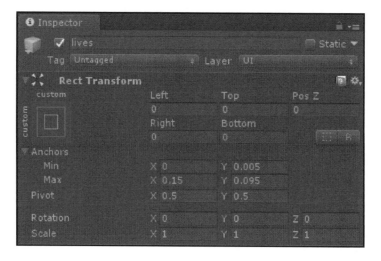

The last thing we need to do to the `lives` game object is give it a **Horizontal Layout Group** component. This component will make it so that when we create an image to represent each life the player has, we'll display a spaceship image.

The **Horizontal Layout Group** component will put each spaceship image in a stacked order. To add this component, do the following:

1. With the `lives` game object still selected, click the **Add Component** button in the **Inspector** window.
2. The **Add Component** down window will appear. Type `Horizontal Layout Group` until you see it on the list. When you do, select it.

The following screenshot shows the **Horizontal Layout Group** component when it's been added to the lives game object. We will need to alter some values to each life image so that they aren't too large.

3. Change the **Horizontal Layout Group** property values to the ones shown in the following screenshot (you may need to click the arrow next to **Padding** to expand its content):

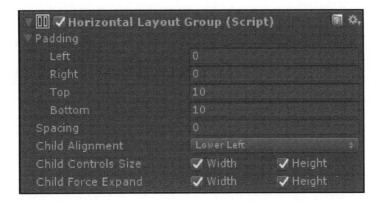

So far, we have created a game object called lives that will store and automatically order each player ship image.

In the next section, we are going to create a game object that will house each player's ship image. As an example of what's to come in the next two sections, the following screenshot demonstrates our lives game object holding each life game object:

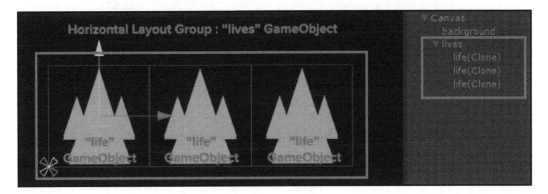

Now, let's move onto making a game object called life that will store a space ship icon.

Creating images to represent our life count

In this section, we are going to create a game object that will hold an **Image** component that will be a symbol of the player ship. We will also be sizing it specifically so that it's uniformed with the other lives it sits with.

Let's start by creating a game object that holds an **Image** component:

1. In the **Hierarchy** window, right-click the `Canvas` game object and select **UI** and then **Image** from the drop-down list.
2. Select the game object, right-click it, and select **Rename** from the drop-down list.
3. Rename the newly created game object to `life`.
4. Add an image and color to the **Image** component, as shown in the following screenshot:

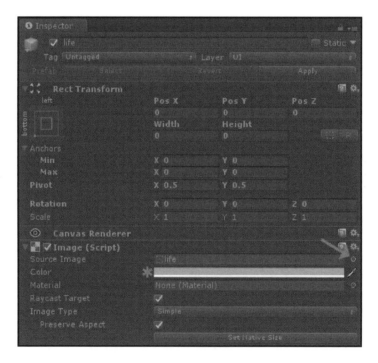

5. To add a source image to the `life` game object, click the **remote** button to the side of **Source Image** (denoted by an arrow in the previous screenshot).

6. From the drop-down list, start typing `life` until you see it appear and click it.

   Our ship icon should look like the one shown in the following screenshot. If it doesn't, it may have a **Default** texture type and will need to be changed to a **Sprite**. We covered how to change this in `Chapter 5`, *Creating a Shop Scene for our Game*:

   I'm going to change the color of the icon slightly as it's possibly a bit too distracting for the player.

7. With the `life` game object still selected, click the **Color** field, and change the color settings to an aqua grey (**R**: 153, **G**: 177, **B**: 177, **A**: 255).

8. Make sure to tick the **Preserve Aspect** box in the **Image** component so our life doesn't lose its dimensions.

That's our `life` game object created. The final thing we need to do to it is turn it into a prefab. As a reminder, the benefits of a prefab are that we have a game object with its components, preferences, and settings all stored, and that it can be created as many times as required.

To turn this `life` game object into a prefab, do the following:

1. In the **Project** window, navigate to `Assets/Resources/Prefab`.

2. Click and drag the `life` game object from the **Hierarchy** window into the `Prefab` folder. That's our prefab created.

We can now delete the `life` game object in the **Hierarchy** window as we will be creating this game object with code in the next section.

Coding our UI life counter

In this section, we are going to revisit the `GameManager` script and take the information about the player's life count and display it in the form of our UI system.

The following screenshot shows a section of the **Hierarchy** window that holds the level1 scene's Canvas game object. Within Canvas is the HUD background game object at the top, followed by the lives game object. Finally, with our code (which we will write shortly), we have created three life game objects within our lives game object:

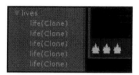

To instantiate the life game objects so that they show the same amount as our player's lives, do the following:

1. In the **Project** window, navigate to the Assets/Resources/Script/GameManager folder.
2. Double-click the file to openGameManager.

The GameManager script already has an Awake() function, which is the first thing the script tries to activate once the script becomes active. What we don't currently have is a Start() function that gets called after Awake().

We can create a Start() function in GameManager and make it call a method that we are going to make shortly, called SetLivesDisplay, and send it our playerLives variable, which is the count of the player's lives.

Like any function, we can place it anywhere within the class, as long as it's not inside another method/function. I typically keep my Awake() and Start() functions near the top of the GameManager class. To call the custom method in the Start() function, do the following:

1. Enter the following code into the GameManager script:

```
void Start()
{
    SetLivesDisplay(playerLives);
}
```

Now, we'll fill in the content for the SetLivesDisplay method.

I have put my SetLivesDisplay near the bottom of the GameManager script, but like the Start and Awake functions, put them wherever you wish in the GameManager script.

2. Enter the following code:

```
public void SetLivesDisplay(int players)
    {
```

This method is set to `public` because our `ScenesManager` script will need to access it for loading whatever level the player is on. We have our `SetLivesDisplay` method set to `void` as we aren't returning anything while in the method. As I mentioned previously, we take in the `playerLives` integer but we will refer to it as `players` while in the method.

Let's continue by adding some code inside the `SetLivesDisplay` method. This is where we will be checking, adding, and visually removing lives if the player dies.

3. Enter the following code inside the `SetLivesDisplay` method:

```
if (GameObject.Find("lives"))
    {
        GameObject lives = GameObject.Find("lives");

        if (lives.transform.childCount < 1)
        {
          for (int i = 0; i < 5; i++)
          {
            GameObject life = GameObject.Instantiate(Resources
              .Load ("Prefab/life")) as GameObject;
            life.transform.SetParent(lives.transform);
          }
        }
    }
```

In the previous code, we ran a check to find a game object called `lives`. If we find the game object, we store its reference in a game object called `lives`. We then ran a check to see `if` our `lives` game object is holding any game objects. If `lives` isn't holding any game objects, we are assuming this is the beginning of the level and that we need to create some lives. Inside the `if` statement, we ran a `for` loop with a limit of 5 counts. Inside this `for` loop, we `instantiate` our `life` prefab and let it sit inside the `lives` game object.

4. Continue writing inside the SetLivesDisplay method, which is where we manage the count of each life prefab, and make it shows the actual amount of lives the player has:

```
//set visual lives
for (int i = 0; i < lives.transform.childCount; i++)
{
    lives.transform.GetChild(i).localScale = new
Vector3(1,1,1);
}
//remove visual lives
for (int i = 0; i < (lives.transform.childCount -
players); i++)
{
    lives.transform.GetChild(lives.transform.childCount -
i
        -1).localScale = Vector3.zero;
}
    }
}
```

There are two main parts to the code we just wrote. The first for loop is set by the count of how many game objects sit under the lives game object. Each game object under lives gets scaled to 1.

The second for loop takes the count of game objects under lives and subtracts it against the player's int variable that is brought into the parameters of this method. Inside this second for loop – depending on how big the player's int variable is – each life prefab is shrunk to zero. Scaling the life prefab to zero doesn't affect the **Horizontal Layout Groups** spacing, leaving the lives counter to not fluctuate based on the number of lives shown.

5. Save the script.

GameManager is now capable of creating a life meter at the bottom of the level1 scene. We now need to add some functionality so that ScenesManager loads the number of lives when the level is loaded.

To get the `ScenesManager` script to load the player's lives when a level starts or when the player dies, do the following:

1. In the **Project** window, navigate to the `ScenesManager` script, `Assets/Resources/Script/ScenesManager`.

2. Double-click the `ScenesManager` script to be able to start coding.

3. In the `ScenesManager` script, we will add a `Start()` function that will contain a known Unity delegate, `sceneLoaded`, which is called from Unity's own `SceneManager`. This delegate will subscribe to when our game scene changes. For more information about the `sceneLoaded` delegate, go to `https://docs.unity3d.com/ScriptReference/SceneManagement.SceneManager-sceneLoaded.html`.

4. Within the `ScenesManager` script, enter the `Start` function, along with the name of the function we are hooking into the delegate:

```
void Start()
{
    SceneManager.sceneLoaded += OnSceneLoaded;
}
```

Still in the `ScenesManager` script, we will add the Unity recognized function, which will automatically take `Scene` and `LoadSceneMode` types, even if we aren't going to do anything with them.

Inside the function, we are calling the `GameManager` script's `SetLivesDisplay`, along with the number of lives the player has.

5. Enter the following code we just discussed inside `ScenesManager`:

```
private void OnSceneLoaded(Scene aScene, LoadSceneMode aMode)
{
GetComponent<GameManager>().SetLivesDisplay(GameManager.player
Lives);
}
```

6. Save the script.

Let's check what we have made:

1. Go back into the Unity Editor while still being on the scene we are working on (`level1`).

2. Press **Play** – three lives should be displayed. If the player dies, the life count will drop to two.

The following screenshot shows the game being played, alongside the player's life on the bottom-left:

In this section, we have hooked up the player's lives so that they can be displayed in the bottom-left corner of the HUD. We have applied components such as **Horizontal Layout Group** and **Layout Element** to set the player's lives images in uniform order and size. We also made the code apply and update the player's lives whenever the scene loads up.

Next, we will focus on the other side of the HUD and display the player's score.

Displaying the player's score

In this section, we will be applying the player's score on the right-hand side of the HUD, which we are currently filling up with information about the player.

We will continue to work in the Canvas game object and add another game object called score. Here, we will add a **Text** component and update a small section of the ScenesManager code to load the score display. Let's get started:

1. While still in level1 scene, right-click the Canvas game object in the **Hierarchy** window.
2. From the drop-down list, select **UI | Text**.
3. Right-click the new Text game object and select **Rename** from the drop-down list.
4. Rename the game object score.

With the `score` game object renamed and located inside the `Canvas` game object, the next thing we need to do is to size and move the `score` game object into position.

5. With the `score` game object still selected, alter its **Rect Transform** properties in the **Inspector** window so that they look like the ones shown in the following screenshot:

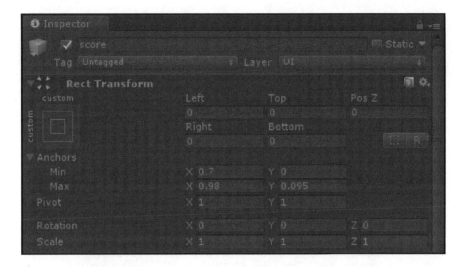

With the `score` game object in the correct position and scale, we can now customize its **Text** component settings.

With the `score` game object still selected, make the following changes to its **Text** component in the **Inspector** window:

1. Change the **Text** field from **New Text** to 00000000. The length of the zeros in the **Text** field will help us specify the size of the board.
2. As shown in the following screenshot, we have selected the same custom text we used for the game's level scene titles. Click the **remote** button to the right of the **Font** field and select **ethnocentric rg it** from the drop-down list.
3. Set the **Alignment** buttons to **Align Right** and **Middle Center**. This will position the text and minimize any space on its right-hand side.
4. Have **Best Fit** ticked so that our `score` text font size will set its own font size.

5. Change the **Best Fit** properties to the following: **Min Size** to 0 and **Max Size** to 60. This will set the limits for the **Best Fit** text.

    The last property to change is the **Color** of the text. We will set this to the same color as our player's lives.

6. Click the **Color** field property and change its RGBA values to **R**: 153, **G**: 177, **B**: 178, **A**: 255.

The following screenshot shows what our **Text** component properties have been set to:

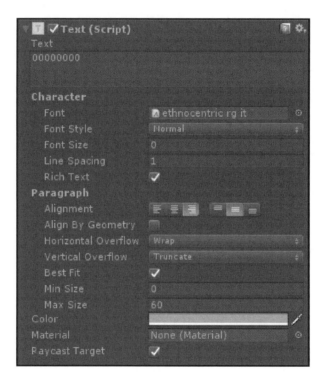

If we check the **Game** window, we should see that the score in the right-hand corner is a good size, as shown in the following screenshot:

The final phase for our `score` game object is to update our `ScenesManager` script by adding an `if` statement to check if the `score` game object is in the scene.

To update the `ScenesManager` script so that it supports our new score game object, do the following:

1. In the **Project** window, navigate to the `Assets/Resources/Script/ScenesManager` folder.

2. Double-click the `ScenesManager` script and scroll down to where we entered the `OnSceneLoaded` function.

3. Inside the `OnSceneLoaded` function, enter the following code:

```
if (GameObject.Find("score"))
{
GameObject.Find("score").GetComponent<Text>().text =
    ScoreManager.playerScore.ToString();
}
```

As briefly mentioned in the newly added piece of code, we are checking if the `score` game object is in the scene. If `score` is present in the scene, then we grab its `Text` component and apply the player's score integer to it from the `ScoreManager` script.

4. Save the script.

Speaking of the `ScoreManager` script, we need to load this script back up so that its `ResetMethod` resets the `score` UI at the start/end of each game. Follow these steps to do so:

1. In the **Project** window, navigate to the `ScoreManager` script located in `Assets/Resources/Script` and open the file.

   Inside the script, we need to bring in the `UnityEngine.UI` library so that we can make changes to our game's visual score.

2. At the very top of the `ScoreManager` script, enter the following code:

   `using UnityEngine.UI;`

3. Within the `ResetScore` method, add an `if` statement that checks that the `score` UI game object is in the scene and updates. The following code shows the complete `ResetScore` method in the `ScoreManager` script:

```
public void ResetScore()
 {
     playerScore = 00000000;
     if (GameObject.Find("score"))
```

```
    {
        GameObject.Find("score").GetComponent<Text>().text =
            playerScore.ToString();
    }
}
```

At the top of the `ScoreManager` script, we will make the `playerScore` variable `public` so our script can gain access to it:

```
public static playerScore;
```

4. Save the script.

5. Go back into the Unity Editor and click the **Play** button to play `level1`.

Our `score` game object will now update when we destroy the enemies, as shown in the following screenshot:

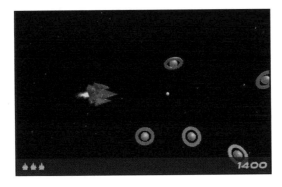

In this section, we took the existing `ScoreManager` code that was originally displaying the player's score and made it into a **Console** window in the Editor. Now, it sends the `score` variable to the new HUD score in the `level1` scene, which will update when an enemy is destroyed.

The final piece we need to create for the HUD is the mini-map, which will give us a visual of the enemies in our level.

Creating a mini-map

In this section, we are going to fit a mini-map inside the HUD display to show a larger scope of the level. This will display the player, along with the enemies nearby, in a radar style. The following screenshot shows a radar in the middle of the HUD that represents the player, along with the enemies around them and other enemies that are due to enter the player's screen:

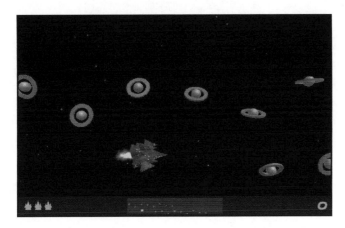

We will break down the mini-map into three sections:

- **Radar Camera**: The second camera in the scene.
- **Layers**: This makes the second camera recognize only a particular set of game objects.
- **Render Texture**: This displays the final results in an animated image on the HUD.

Let's start by creating an extra layer so that we can expose certain game objects to our radar camera.

Creating and adding layers to our player and enemy game objects

In this section, we will add an extra game object to our player and enemy game objects so that our second camera will only see the attached sprites. These will look like blips on a radar.

To add our radar blips to the game objects, do the following:

1. At the top right of the Unity Editor, click the **Layers** button, followed by **Edit Layers...**, as shown in the following screenshot:

2. The **Inspector** window will change and show the **Tags & Layers** properties. From here, we can click to expand the **Layers** tab.

3. Click on one of the available layers near the top and enter `Radar`, as shown in the following screenshot:

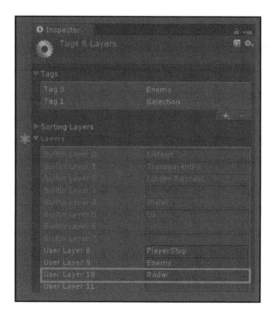

Now, we can add a radar point to the player and enemies. Let's make a start by bringing the player into the scene and updating its prefab so that it will be recognized by the radar camera. To do this, follow these instructions:

1. In the **Project** window, navigate to the `Assets/Resources/Prefab/Player` folder.

2. Drag and drop `player_ship` into the **Hierarchy** window at the bottom, in an open space.

3. In the **Hierarchy** window, right-click `player_ship`, select **2D Object**, and then select **Sprite**. This will create a new game object that will have a **Sprite Renderer** component attached to it.

4. Right-click the `New Sprite` game object and select **Rename** from the drop-down.

5. Rename `New Sprite` to `radarPoint`.

6. With `radarPoint` still selected, click its **Default** layer in the **Inspector** window and select **Radar** from the drop-down list, as shown in the following screenshot. We can also set our **Transform** property values:

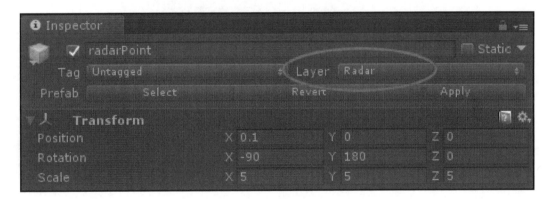

With the **Transform** properties set, we can now drop the radar dot sprite into the **Sprite** field and change its color:

1. Click the **remote** button to the right of the **Sprite** field in the **Sprite Renderer** component.

2. Start typing **knob** in the drop-down list until you can see it and select it, as shown in the following screenshot:

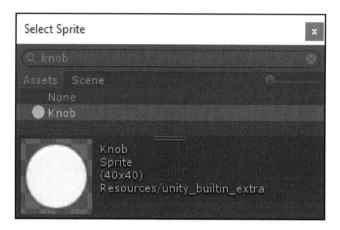

3. We can now change the color of the sprite by clicking the **Sprite Renderer Color** field and give it the following color properties: **R**: 0, **G**: 245, **B**: 255, **A**: 255.

4. Select player_ship in the **Hierarchy** window and click the **Apply** button near the **Inspector** window to update the player_ship game object's prefab settings.

5. Select the player_ship game object in the **Hierarchy** window and press *Delete* on your keyboard.

   We have now set the player ship so that it's ready to be detected by the radar camera.

   The next thing to do is repeat the same methodology for the enemies, which are located in Assets/Resources/Prefab/Enemies/enemy_wave.

6. Without going through the same instructions, the following screenshot shows our enemies' radarPoint game object with a bright red color value (**R**: 255, **G**: 0, **B**: 0, **A**: 0). If you get stuck, just follow the same steps for the player ship's radarPoint:

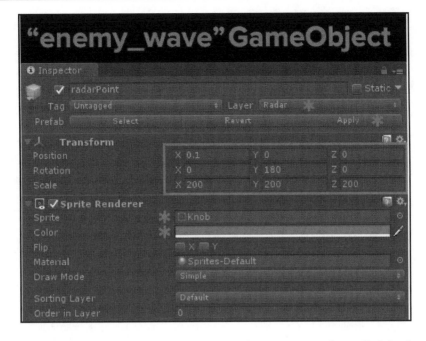

Click **Apply** in the **Inspector** window once you have finished making changes to your prefab.

Once we have finished making our changes and applied them to the prefab, we no longer need the enemy_wave game object as we have saved its details in the prefab.

7. Delete enemy_wave from the **Hierarchy** window.

We have effectively created a tracker (radarPoint) and attached it to the player and enemies for our level.

The next step is to add a **Render Texture**, which will work with a second camera in our scene. The feed from the second camera will be fed into a **Render Texture**. This **Render Texture** will then be placed at the bottom middle of the screen and display our player and enemy location.

Adding and customizing our Render Texture

Render Texture is typically used to hold moving images while in **Play Mode** (at runtime). We are going to use this **Render Texture** to hold the second camera's feed. This will work like a little TV screen in the center of our HUD.

To create and customize **Render Texture**, we will do the following:

1. In the **Project** window of the Unity Editor, navigate to the `Texture` folder, that is, `Assets/Resources/Texture`.
2. Right-click in an open space area and from the drop-down list, select **Create**, then **Render Texture**, as shown in the following screenshot:

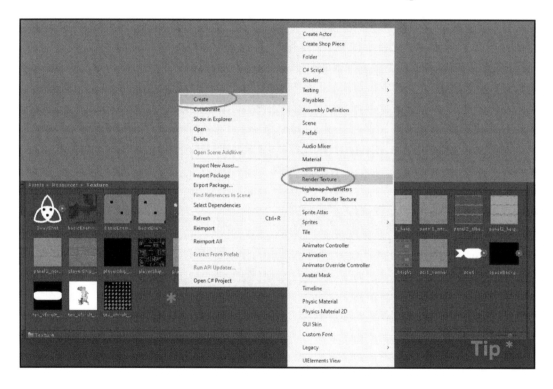

If you don't have an open space to right-click, as *step 2* suggests, you can change the size of the icons to gain space.

Change your icon size with the slider to the bottom right corner of the **Project** window.

3. Click the name of the file slowly twice and rename it `radar`.
4. With the `radar` **Render Texture** selected, we will need to change its size to one that will fit the HUD and, ideally, make it less blurry.
5. In the **Inspector** area, change the **Size** fields from `256, 256` to `236, 46`.
6. Change **Filter Mode** from **Bilinear** to **Point**.

The last part of setting up **Render Texture** is to place it into the HUD. Follow these steps:

1. Still in the `level1` scene, right-click the `Canvas` game object in the **Hierarchy** window and select **Create Empty**.
2. Select the new empty game object in the **Hierarchy** window, right-click it, and select **Rename** from the drop-down list.
3. Rename the game object `radar`.

   The radar game object will work as housing for anything related to the game object.

4. This game object will now need to be positioned and sized in the HUD. To do that, change the `radar` game object's **Rect Transform** properties in the **Inspector** window to the ones shown in the following screenshot:

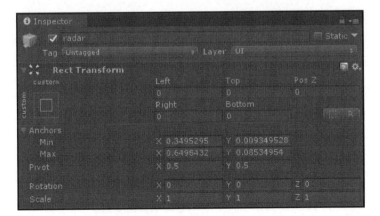

Moving and resizing the `radar` game object will give us a letterbox window for **Render Texture** to sit inside, as shown in the following screenshot:

We can now add another game object that will be a child of the `radar` game object we've just made. This game object will store **Render Texture**:

1. Right-click the `radar` game object in the **Hierarchy** window. From the drop-down list, select **UI** and then **Raw Image**.
2. Right-click the new game object called **Raw Image**, select **Rename** from the drop-down, and rename the game object `radarImage`.
3. With the `radarImage` game object still selected, change its **Rect Transform** settings to the ones shown in the **Inspector** window, as shown in the following screenshot:

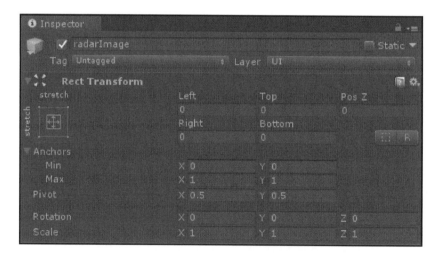

Next, we need to apply **radar Render Texture** to the **Raw Image Texture** field:

1. With `radarImage` still selected in the **Hierarchy** window, click the **remote** button next to the **Texture** field in the **Raw Image** component.
2. Start typing `radar` in the search bar at the top of the new window until **radar Render Texture** appears and select it.

That's our **Render Texture** made and set. Now, we can pass this into the second camera. But before we do that, we need to add the camera!

Adding and customizing our second camera

In this section, we will be adding a second camera so that we can only see the radarPoint game objects.

Let's start by setting up a second camera in our level1 scene:

1. In the **Hierarchy** window, right-click in an open space and from the drop-down, select **Camera**.
2. Right-click the newly created **Camera**, select **Rename** from the drop-down list, and rename it RadarCam.
3. With RadarCam still selected, change its **Transform** settings in the **Inspector** window to the ones shown in the following screenshot:

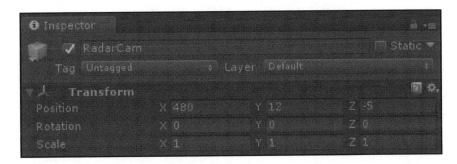

Still in the **Inspector** window and with our RadarCam selected, we need to change its **Camera** component settings to the following:

- **Clear Flags**: **Solid Color**. We don't require anything in the background for the second camera, so something basic like a solid color would work fine.
- **Background**: **R**: 255, **G**: 0, **B**: 0, **A**:50. This will give our radar a red tint.

- **Culling Mask**: Click the parameter field labeled **Everything**. Do the following:
  - Select **Nothing** from the drop-down list to remove all layers.
  - Select the field again and select **Radar** (shown in the following screenshot). By doing this, all our camera will see will be the game objects that relate to that layer:

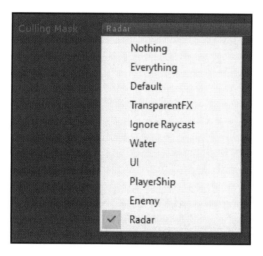

- **Projection**: **Orthographic**. The radar camera is 2D, so there is no need to have a perspective view.
- **Size**: 150. The size of our camera view will be larger than the main view the player is in.
- **Target Texture**: Click the **remote** button and select the radar's **Render Texture** from the new window that appears. This will send the feed from RadarCam to the radar's **Render Texture**.
- Our **Main Camera** (not the RadarCam) won't need to see the **Radar** layer. Select **Main Camera** from the **Hierarchy** window and deselect the **Radar** layer from its **Culling Mask**.
- Also, with RadarCam still selected, click the silver cog next to its **Audio Listener** component and remove it. We already have one camera that listens for audio in our scene.

- Finally, we need to make it so that `RadarCam` is apart of **Main Camera** so that it's part of the same functionality. Click and drag `RadarCam` into **Main Camera** in the **Hierarchy** window.
- Click **Apply** in the **Inspector** window to update the **Main Camera** prefab and save the scene.

Now, if we click **Play** in the Unity Editor, we will see the radar in the HUD with its red tint showing red dots for enemies and a neon blue for the player, as shown in the following screenshot:

This mini-map was all achieved without any code and made use of two new components: **Render Texture**, which will hold the second camera's feed, and a **Raw Image** component, which will display the final output.

In this section, we created a functioning HUD that has three main segments: player's live, a mini-map, and the player's score. We used the two fundamental UI tools that Unity offers to create a UI display. However, we also introduced three new components, as follows:

- **Horizontal Group Layout**: Spaced the player's lives equally
- **Render Texture**: Transfers the second cameras feed
- **Raw Image**: Displays the feed from the render texture

The following screenshot shows the final HUD:

Because we have updated our `level1` scene, we need to update `level2` and `level3`. The quickest way to do this would be to delete `level2` and `level3` and duplicate `level1`, as we did before, which leaves us to update the level number in the `Text` component. We did this in the previous chapter, right at the end, so please check that if you need some guidance.

Now, we will move on and improve the existing shop scene by removing the pre-made polygons for UI components. This will also introduce us to using UI event triggers and making our code smaller and more efficient.

Making our shop scene support alternative screen ratios

In this section, we are going to take our current shop scene and make it compatible with various screen ratios. Currently, our shop visuals are made out of polygons, which look fine, but, for example, our selection grid of buttons at the bottom of the screen has the risk of being clipped off at the edges. We can also change the way we select our buttons by using Unity's **Button** component, which works within the **Canvas**:

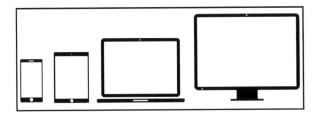

Because of these UI changes, this will cut our code down and make it more efficient as we will be relying on click events. We will cover these later in this section.

Let's make a start by replacing the selection grid at the bottom of our shop scene.

Upgrading our shop selection

In this section, we are going to remove all of the shop buttons and replace them with a **Horizontal Layout Group** set of buttons to add the player's lives to the HUD. Each of the new selection buttons will contain a Unity pre-made script called button that has its own raycast system. This raycast system will give us an easier way of adding and customizing our buttons when it comes to adding or extracting buttons to/from the selection grid.

In the next section, we will support this change by removing our 3D assets so that we can replace them with Unity's own 2D buttons.

Preparing our shop scene to go 2D

Let's start by removing the old selection grid at the bottom and our BUY ? button as that follows the same suit from our shop scene:

1. If you haven't loaded the shop scene already, locate it in the **Project** window in Assets/Scene.

2. Double-click **shop** to load the shop scene.

3. In the **Hierarchy** window, hold *Ctrl* (*command* on Mac) on the keyboard and select all of the game objects shown in the following screenshot:

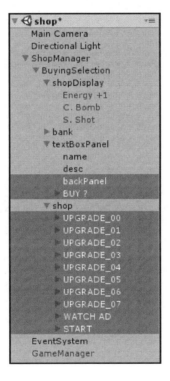

Press *Delete* on the keyboard. We haven't lost any of our sprite images, scripts, or any other type of information. We are simply removing polygons, 3D materials, and colliders (physics-based components). We are now going to move the same information we have into Canvas.

To create a `Canvas` with its own background, do the following:

1. In the lower part of the **Hierarchy** window, right-click and from the drop-down list., select **UI**, followed by **Canvas**.
2. Right-click the `Canvas` game object in the **Hierarchy** window and from the drop-down list, select **UI**, followed by **Image**.
3. Right-click the new game object called `Image` and select **Rename** from the drop-down list.
4. Rename `Image` to `backGround`.
5. With the `backGround` game object still selected, change its **Rect Transform** properties to the ones shown in the following screenshot:

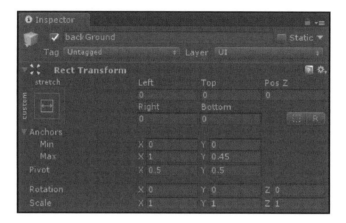

6. We can now give `backGround` some color. With the `backGround` game object still selected, click the **Color** field in the **Image** component in the **Inspector** window and set it's values to **R**: 255, **G**: 0, **B**: 0, **A**: 63.

The following screenshot shows the `backGround` game object positioned and scaled with a red tint:

We can now move onto the next section, where we will add three game objects that will control the position and scale of the button game objects.

Adding layout group components

In this section, we will add game objects that will support the spacing of the buttons we add to the grid. The benefit of this is that we can control the properties of each section of the buttons, as shown in the following diagram:

Next, we will make an empty game object and add a **Horizontal Layout Group** to it, which will keep our top row buttons in order:

1. Right-click the `Canvas` game object and from the drop-down list, select **Create Empty**.
2. Rename the new game object `gridTop`.
3. With `gridTop` still selected, change its **Rect Transform** settings to the ones shown in the following screenshot:

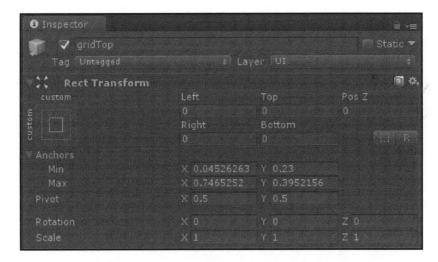

Now that our `gridTop` is positioned correctly, we can add a **Horizontal Layout Group** to it:

1. With the `gridTop` game object still selected, click the **Add Component** button in the **Inspector** window and type `Horizontal Layout Group` into the search bar at the top of the drop-down list until you see **Horizontal Layout Group**. When this group appears in the list, select it.
2. Give **Horizontal Layout Group** the following settings:

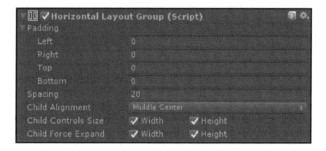

`gridTop` will now automatically order the top row of upgrade buttons.

We now need to repeat the process for the bottom row, without repeating the entire procedure again. Follow the same steps for `gridTop` but make the following changes:

1. Name the next game object in **Canvas** `gridBottom`.
2. Give the game object the following **Rect Transform** settings:

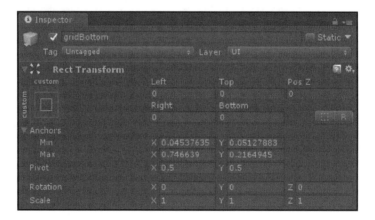

3. Then, like before, we need to add a **Horizontal Layout Group** with the same settings as `gridTop`.

4. We then repeat this process but this time, for our "AD" and "START" buttons, we will be adding a **Vertical Layout Group**.

5. Like before, create an empty game object and store it in the `Canvas` game object.

6. Name a new game object called `gridOther`.

7. Give `gridOther`'s **Rect Transform** the following settings:

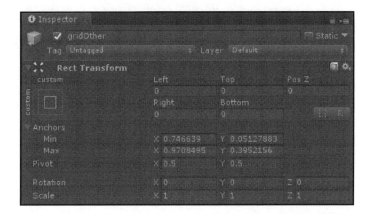

8. As mentioned previously, we will add a **Vertical Layout Group** component to the `gridOther` game object and give it the following settings:

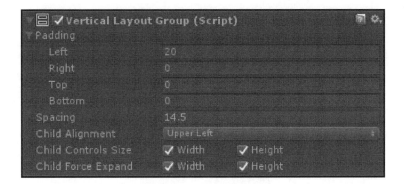

Our new reworked selection grid now supports the creation of multiple self-scaling buttons. In the next section, we will demonstrate how to create multiple buttons that scale themselves to fit in the selection grid.

Adding UI buttons

In this section, we are going to create a button that won't need any sizing changes to be made to it as the layout groups we placed in the previous section will take care of this.

To create a **UI** button for our new selection grid, right-click the `gridTop` game object in the **Hierarchy** window and do the following:

1. From the drop-down list, select **UI** and then **Button**.
2. Right-click the newly created `Button` game object and name it `00`.

We will get a button that will be stretched and out of place, but don't worry – this is normal. Later, when we add more buttons to this and the other rows, the buttons will snap into place and scale in size automatically.

By default, the button comes with an **Image** component with rounded-off edges. For cosmetic purposes, this doesn't suit our scene. We can remove this by doing the following:

1. Click the cog icon to the top right of the **Image** component.
2. From the drop-down list, select **Remove Component**.

The button no longer has any color.

Next, we are going to fill this game object with five game objects. In brief, their names and properties are as follows:

- `outline`: Adds a border to the button
- `backPanel`: The color of the button when it's not selected
- `selection`: The color of the button when it is selected
- `powerUpimage`: The picture on the button
- `itemText`: The cost or sold out message

The following image shows all of these game objects combined to create our new shop button:

The other way of changing a button's condition is by using Unity's **Button** component states. For more information about this and the `Button` script, check out: `https://docs.unity3d.com/2017.3/Documentation/Manual/script-Button.html`.

Adding the outline game object

Let's start by adding our `outline` for our new shop button:

1. Right-click the `00` game object in the **Hierarchy** window and from the drop-down, select **UI | Image**.
2. Select the `Image` game object, right-click it in the **Hierarchy** window, select **Rename**, and change its name to `outline`.
3. With `outline` still selected in the **Hierarchy** window, update its **Rect Transform** and **Image Color** fields to the following:

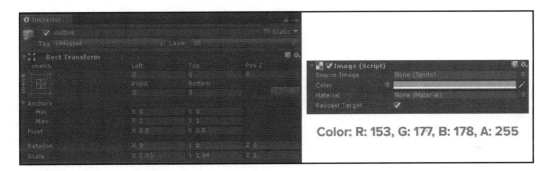

The shop button will now have a colored `outline`. Now, let's move on and look at the button's `backPanel`.

Adding the backPanel game object

Let's add `backPanel` to the `00` game object:

1. In the **Hierarchy** window, right-click the `00` game object and from the drop-down, select **UI | Image**.
2. Right-click the newly created `Image` game object and name it `backPanel`.

3. With `outline` still selected, in the **Inspector** window, change its **Rect Transform** so that it has the following values:

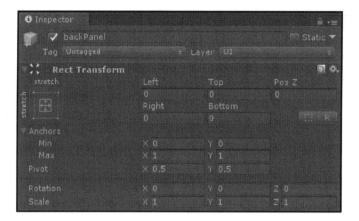

With the `outline` game object still selected, we can change the **Image** component's **Color** properties in the **Inspector** window. By clicking the **Color** field, we can change the `outline` game object's settings to **R**: 40, **G**: 39, **B**: 36, **A**: 255. That's the second game object that we've applied that gives us our default color.

We'll add the `selection` game object to the `00` game object next.

Adding the selection game object

To create the `selection` button, follow the same steps provided in the previous section. However, note that there are two differences:

1. Name this game object `selection`.
2. Give the **Image** component's **Color** field the following values: **R**: 144, **G**: 0, **B**: 0, **A**: 255.
3. Create and apply a **Tag** called "Selection."

 We covered creating and applying tags back in Chapter 2, *Adding and Manipulating Objects*.

The following screenshot shows our `selection` game object's **Tag** and **Rect Transform** property values:

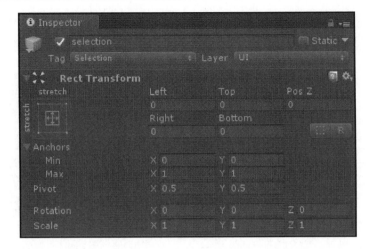

That's the third game object that we've applied to our 00 game object. Our buttons will light up and stay red until a purchase is made or a different button is pressed. We'll add the powerUpImage game object to our 00 game object next.

Adding the powerUpImage game object

To create the powerUpImage button, follow the same steps provided in the previous section, but make two changes:

1. Name this game object powerUpImage.
2. Drag and drop the powerup sprite into the **Source Image** field of the **Image** component.
3. Tick the **Preserve Aspect** box.

That's our fourth game object that displays each button's icon.

We'll add the itemText game object to the 00 game object next.

Adding the itemText game object

To add the itemText game object to our 00 game object, do the following:

1. In the **Hierarchy** window, right-click the 00 game object and from the drop-down list, select **UI**, followed by **Text**.
2. Right-click the newly created Text game object and name it itemText.

3. With `itemText` still selected, in the `Inspector` window, change its **Rect Transform** and **Text** components so that they have the following properties:

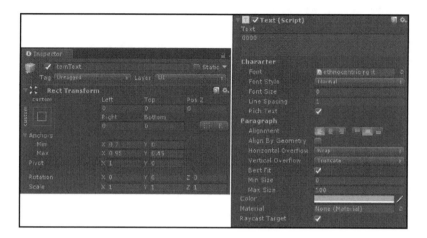

That's the fifth and final game object we need to add to our weapon upgrade button.

In the **Hierarchy** window, our `00` game object should be in the order shown in the following screenshot. If the order isn't the same, simply click and drag either one into position:

In this section, we stripped out the old `shop` scene setup where we were selecting items in the shop with a raycast system. We replaced the old selection grid with a 2D interface with **Button** components. These buttons were grouped with Unity's Horizontal and **Vertical Layout Group** components. The benefit of these two groups is that if we add more or fewer buttons to the grid, the buttons will reorganize their position and scale automatically.

We need to make a slight modification to the `ShopPiece` script that was originally attached to each game object button previously.

Once we have applied and modified the script, we will check what the buttons look like in the new selection grid.

Applying and modifying our shop scripts

Let's briefly recall the purpose of the ShopPiece script. Each button in the selection grid will be given information from a scriptable object that will customize the button's name, description, value, and image. Because the buttons have changed from being 3D assets to 2D ones, we need to alter and add some more code to make this work.

To modify ShopPiece so that it's compatible with our new 2D button, do the following:

1. In the **Project** window in the Unity Editor, navigate to the Assets/Resources/Script folder.
2. Double-click the ShopPiece script to open the file.

   The first line of code will allow our new code support to grab references from the **Text** component on the 00 game object.

3. Enter the following piece of code at the top of the ShopPiece script:

   ```
   using UnityEngine.UI;
   ```

   The second modification to make will be to replace the content of the Awake function. The original code accessed SpriteRenderer, which was used for accessing the sprite on each polygon button. The other piece of code we are replacing applied changes to the TextMesh component, which displays 3D text.

4. To update our Awake function, select the code within the Awake() function and delete it. Our Awake() function should look as follows:

   ```
   Awake()
   {

   }
   ```

   We can now enter the first if statement that applies our scriptable object icon image to our button's image.

5. Within the `Awake()` function, add the following `if` statement:

```
if (transform.GetChild(3).GetComponent<Image>() != null)
{
   transform.GetChild(3).GetComponent<Image>().sprite =
      shopSelection.icon;
}
```

The `if` statement grabs s reference from the second child in the `00` button and checks to see if it has an **Image** component. If it does (and it should), we apply the scriptable object icon to it.

6. The other `if` statement updates the text of the button/ Within the `Awake()` function, just after the first `if` statement, add the following piece of code:

```
if(transform.Find("itemText"))
{
GetComponentInChildren<Text>().text =
shopSelection.cost.ToString();
}
```

The `if` statement makes sure the `00` button has `itemText` (it should). When the `itemText` game object is found, its **Text** component receives the scriptable object price of the weapon.

7. Save the script.
8. Back in the Unity Editor, select the `00` game object in the **Hierarchy** and click the **Add Component** button.
9. Start typing `ShopPiece` in the drop-down list until you see it. When you do, select it.
10. With the `00` game object still selected, in the **Inspector** window, click the **remote** button in the `ShopPiece` component.
11. Select any weapon upgrade scriptable object from the list.

The following screenshot shows the `ShopPiece` script with a scriptable object applied to it:

We are now in a position to check what our button looks like with the four game objects we've applied and with its modified `ShopPiece` script.

In the next few sections, we are going to duplicate a series of the new shop buttons. These shop buttons will automatically fit in the allocated game object space we have put them in. Then, we will clear up any of the old UI and replace it with our new interface. Finally, we will comment out the old raycast system from our code and add our new interface code.

Reviewing the button's results

In this section, we will be reviewing the new 00 button in the gridTop game object. The button is too big and spreads across the majority of the **Canvas**, as shown in the following screenshot:

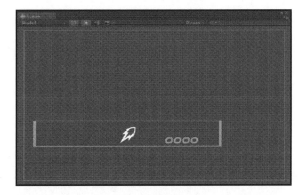

But if I select the 00 game object in the **Hierarchy** window and press *Ctrl* (*command* on Mac) and *D* to duplicate the game object a few times, the button will divide equally, as shown in the following screenshot:

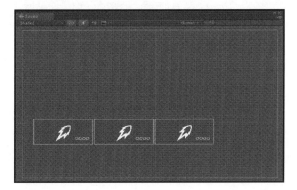

The button divides well and can be duplicated several times (not in **Play Mode**) to fill the top and bottom grids. To fill up and name the grids, to do the following:

1. In the **Hierarchy** window, select the 00 game object and press *Ctrl* (*command* Mac)and *D* three times.
2. Rename the three new duplicate game objects 01, 02, and 03 respectively.
3. Select 01 in the **Hierarchy** window and click the **remote** button in its ShopPiece component in the **Inspector** window.
4. Select a different scriptable object from the list to change the weapon upgrade.
5. Select game object 02 and select a different weapon in the ShopPiece component.

Now, we need to fill up the bottom row with buttons. To do that, follow these steps:

1. Click and drag the 03 game object from the **Hierarchy** window into the gridBottom game object.
2. With 03 still selected, press *Ctrl* (*command* Mac) and D twice.
3. Rename our newly created game objects to 04 and 05.

The following screenshot shows the top and bottom rows filled up:

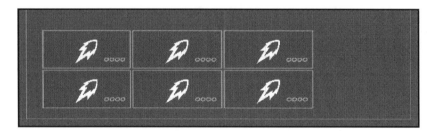

Because we don't have any more items to sell in our shop, the bottom three buttons look odd, so let's replace these with some sold-out signs. This can easily be achieved with our scriptable object assets.

To create a sold-out sign for our bottom row in our shop, we need to do the following:

1. In the **Project** window, navigate to Assets/Resources/Script/ScriptableObjects, right-click in an open space, and select **Create | Create Shop Piece.**
2. Rename the Create Shop Piece file to SoldOut.
3. Select SoldOut and give it the following property values:

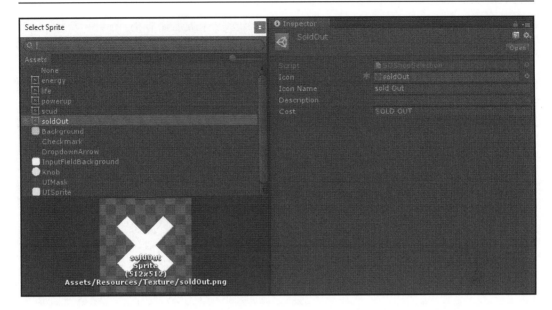

Lastly, apply the SoldOut file to game objects 03, 04, and 05 in the **Hierarchy** window in the Shop Piece component field's **Shop Selection** in the **Inspector** window.

Now, we need to repeat a similar process for our advert and start buttons.

Creating the advert and start buttons

To recreate the advert button, select either one of the buttons we duplicated in the **Hierarchy** window and do the following:

1. Press *Ctrl* (*command* Mac) and *D* to duplicate another button and drag it into the gridOther game object in the **Hierarchy** window.

2. Rename the duplicate game object AD.

3. Because the AD game object doesn't need a powerUpImage, we can delete it.

4. Expand the AD game object by clicking the arrow to the left of its name in the **Hierarchy** window and select the itemText button.

5. Apply the following settings to the **Text** component in the **Inspector** window:

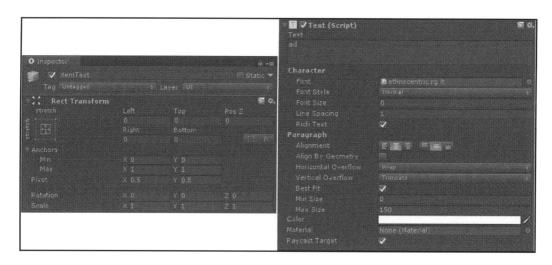

6. Repeat a similar process for the **START** button game object, except for its `itemText` and `selection` game object components (`selection` hex color: `FFC300FF`), as shown in the following image:

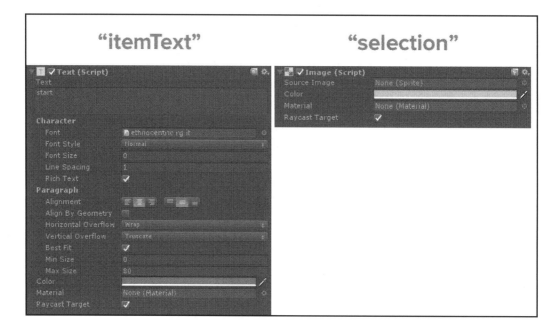

The following screenshot shows the **Hierarchy** window of the `gridOther` game object and its content, including the two buttons:

Now that our selection grid visuals are completed, we can move onto the description panel and partially convert it from 3D into 2D.

Adding the BUY? button

To add the 2D `BUY?` button to the description panel, do the following:

1. Right-click the `Canvas` game object in the **Hierarchy** panel and select **UI**, followed by **Button**, from the drop-down list.
2. Right-click the newly created `Button` game object and select **Rename** from the drop-down list.
3. Rename the `Button` game object `BUY?`.
4. With the `BUY?` button still selected in the **Hierarchy** window, set its **Rect Transform** properties to the ones shown in the following screenshot:

Now that the BUY? button is in place and scaled correctly, we can alter the aesthetics for the **Image** and **Button** components. In the **Image** component, select the **remote** button for the **Source Image** field and select **None** from the list to remove the curved edges for the button.

Next, we will make it so that the BUY? button changes colors when it's highlighted and pressed in the **Button** component. Follow these steps to do so:

1. In the **Button** component, select the **Normal Color** field and change its values to **R**: 255, **G**: 0, **B**: 0, **A**: 255.

2. Select the **Highlighted Color** field and changes its values to **R**: 255, **G**: 195, **B**: 0, **A**: 255.

3. When the cursor moves over the BUY? button, it will turn yellow and when pressed, it will turn to red.

Finally, for the BUY? button, we need to alter its **Text** component, as follows:

1. In the **Hierarchy** window, select the arrow next to the BUY? button to expand it.

2. Then, select the BUY? game object's child, called Text.

3. Enter the following values for the Text game object's **Text** component in the **Inspector** window:

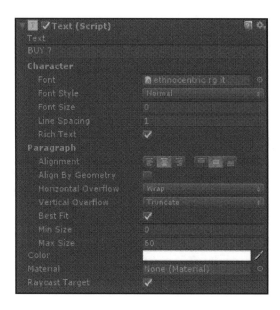

The following screenshot shows our BUY ? button positioned and styled:

In this section, we applied Unity's different state settings for our button without adding any extra code. Next, we will add a simple rectangle image to replace the polygon quad.

Replacing our textBoxPanel game object

In the previous section, we changed our BUY ? button so that it is 2D and part of the **Canvas**, which also means the BUY ? button will now be moved, scaled, and adjusted to the ratio of the screen instead of remaining static. Because of this, we have the risk of our BUY ? button moving outside of the static textBoxPanel it sits in, as shown in the following screenshot:

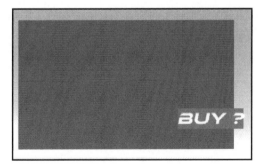

Also, the PlayerShipBuild script has a reference to textBoxPanel, so we can't delete the game object without altering our code. To fix this dilemma, we can remove the 3D components of textBoxPanel, leaving it as an empty game object to house other game objects within it.

To remove the components from the `textBoxPanel` game object, do the following:

1. In the **Hierarchy** window, start typing `textBoxPanel` in the search bar until it appears.
2. Select `textBoxPanel` and remove the two components in the **Inspector** window for **Quad (Mesh Filter)** and **Mesh Renderer** by selecting and clicking their cogs and selecting **Remove Component**.
3. To bring back our full game object content in the **Hierarchy** window, click the cross at the top of its window, to the right of the search bar.

The following screenshot shows the locations of both cogs:

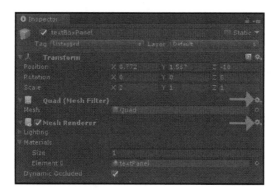

Now, we can create the 2D panel game object to replace the `textBoxPanel` game object's visuals, as follows:

1. In the **Hierarchy** window, right-click the `Canvas` game object and select **UI**, followed by **Image**, from the drop-down list.
2. Select the newly created game object, right-click it, and select **Rename** from the drop-down list.
3. Rename the game object `panel`.
4. Move the `BUY?` game object below the panel game object in the **Hierarchy** window so that the `BUY?` button sits on top of the `panel` in the **Scene** window. The following screenshot shows the order of the two game objects:

5. With the `panel` game object still selected, give its **Rect Transform** the following values in the **Inspector** window:

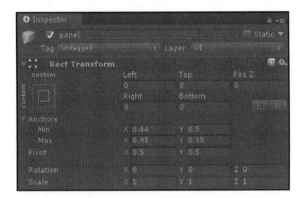

We can change the color of our `panel` game object by clicking its **Color** field within its **Image** component in the **Inspector** window and giving it the values highlighted in the following screenshot:

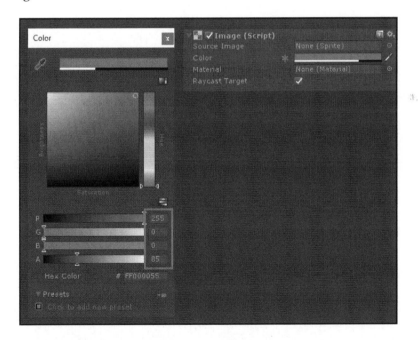

Finally, we can amend our `textBoxPanel` and `bank` balance fonts so that they fit in with the shop buttons.

To amend our bank balance, we need to do the following:

1. In the **Hierarchy** window, expand **ShopManager** | **bank** and select the `bankText` game object.
2. With `bankText` selected, update its **Text Mesh** component in the **Inspector** window so that the **Font** field takes our new **ethnocentric rg it** font.
3. Change the **Color** field to red (**R**:255, **G**: 0, **B**: 0, **A**: 255).
4. Add a few digits in the **Text** field to check the results, as shown in the following screenshot:

To change our `texBoxPanel`, we need to do something similar. Here, we will select its two child game objects in the **Hierarchy** window, `name` and `desc`, and update their **Text Mesh** components to the following:

1. Add the **ethnocentric rg it** font to the `name` and `desc` game object's **Text Mesh Font** fields.
2. Give them a white **Color**.

    In the `name` game object's **Text Mesh Text** field, add the following:

    ```
    officer:
    ```

    Apply the same changes to the `desc` game object but add the following text to the **Text** field:

    ```
    will you need any
    upgrades before
    launch?
    ```

The following screenshot shows a section of the **Game** window and its updated font:

Now, all of our shop's visuals have been amended and will support various screen ratios. By doing this, we also introduced Unity's own **Button** component.

We have now reached the point where we can open a template script of `PlayerShipBuild` from our chapter's project files folder. This script will be a replica of the current `PlayerShipBuild` script we have been making but with highlighted code we will add to the project to support our `shop` scene's functionality.

Upgrading the PlayerShipBuild script

In this section, we are going to replace the current `PlayerShipBuild` script with the one from this chapter's project files folder. The replacement script will contain the same code as your current script but with code to show what we will be adding and removing step by step.

Let's rename our current `PlayerShipBuild` script to something else before we begin working on our new replacement script. To rename the current `PlayerShipBuild` script, do the following:

1. In the **Project** window of the Unity Editor, navigate to the `Assets/Resources/Script` folder.
2. Double-click the `PlayerShipBuild` script.
3. With the `PlayerShipBuild` script open, rename the class name at the near top of the script from `PlayerShipBuild` to `PlayerShipBuild_OLD`.
4. Save the script and return to the `Assets/Resources/Script` folder in the **Project** window.
5. Click the `PlayerShipBuild` script slowly twice so that you're provided with the option to rename the filename.
6. Change the filename to `PlayerShipBuild_OLD`.

   Now, we need to disconnect the `PlayerShipBuild_OLD` script from the `shop` game object.

7. In the **Hierarchy** window, at the top, type `shop` into the search bar until you see the `shop` game object. When you do, select it.
8. With the `shop` game object selected, click the cog in the **Inspector** window in the `Player Ship Build_OLD` component (not **Transform**).
9. Select **Remove Component** from the drop-down list.

With that, we have renamed and detached the script from the scene. Now, we can bring in the new replica `PlayerShipBuild` script from this chapter's project files folder.

To hook up the new replica `PlayerShipBuild` script from our project files folder, do the following:

1. In the **Project** window of the Unity Editor, navigate to the `Assets/` folder.
2. Select the `PlayerShipBuild_NEW.txt` script inside the folder and drag it to the `Assets/Resources/Script` folder. Rename it and its file format from `.txt` to `.cs`. This will replace some of our old raycast scripts with the same name, `PlayerShipBuild.cs`, as shown in the following screenshot:

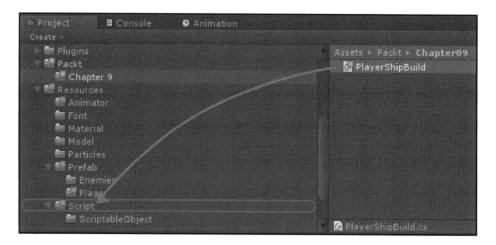

We can now apply this replica script to the `shop` game object in the scene. Let's get started:

1. Select the `shop` game object in the **Hierarchy** window, as we did before.
2. Click the **Add Component** button in the **Inspector** window and start typing `PlayerShipBuild`. When you see the `PlayerShipBuild` script, select it from the drop-down list.
3. With the `shop` game object still selected, we can now configure the attached `PlayerShipBuild` script.
4. To configure the script, set **Visual Weapons Size** to 3, click each **remote** button to the right of each field, and add the following highlighted assets:

Our new `PlayerShipBuild` script is now in place. This means we can now open the script and check through and reveal new sections of the code while explaining the fundamental parts of the old code's removal.

Each of the following **Removing Old...** subsections will do the following:

- **//REMOVE(number)**: Refer to what part of the code we are talking about
- **Reason for removal**: Specify why in the new `PlayerShipBuild` script its code has been removed
- **Replacement**: What has the previous code been replaced with

Removing the old shop scene's code

In this section, we are going to go through the newly installed `PlayerShipBuild` script and review parts of the code I have commented out so that it won't be acknowledged when it's compiled and executed in Unity.

We will be turning off the ability to raycast a 3D object, which we coded in Chapter 5, *Creating a Shop Scene for our Game*. Because we have swapped the intractable game objects from 3D to 2D, we are no longer required to shoot and identify game objects as Unity will take care of this with its own **Button** component.

To review the code we have commented out, go to the **Project** window and double-click the `PlayerShipBuild` script located where we left it (`Assets/Resources/Script`).

 `Commenting`, `Comments`, `UnComment` are words that refer to when a piece of code has two forward slashes in front of it. These will be ignored when our code is read by the compiler (when we run our code).

We are going to review each piece of code in separate sections so that it's clear when the changes we are going to make in `PlayerShipBuild` will be applied.

Reviewing code – REMOVED 01

Each main chunk of code begins with `//REMOVED`, followed by a number. Here are the reasons why we have removed the particular piece of code for `//REMOVED 01`:

- `//REMOVED 01`: This piece of code creates a raycast and returns a game object called `target`.

- **Reason for removal**: We no longer need to rely on getting references for each game object we shoot a ray at.
- **Replacement**: The **Button** component comes with an `OnClick` event, which is typically used to load a method when it's selected.

Let's continue scrolling down the `PlayerShipBuild` script until we get to `//REMOVED 02`.

Reviewing code – REMOVED 02

In this section, we are going to review what we have commented out in `//REMOVED 02`:

- `//REMOVED 02`: This piece of code will take a reference from a raycast selected game object and turn on that selection game object to show that a selection has been made.
- **Reason for removal:** The game object served no benefit apart from serving a cosmetic purpose.
- **Replacement:** The buttons still highlight when selected with the `selection` game object.

Let's continue scrolling down the `PlayerShipBuild` script until we get to `//REMOVED 03`.

Reviewing code – REMOVED 03

In this section, we are going to review what we have commented out in //REMOVED
03:

- //REMOVED 03: This part of the code checks for the player pressing the fire
  button; if they do, the code will shoot out a raycast to check if it made
  contact with a collider.
- **Reason for removal:** We no longer need this because game objects are
  identified in an if statement.
- **Replacement:** The OnClick event system holds a reference to what game
  object is selected.

Let's continue scrolling down the PlayerShipBuild script until we get
to //REMOVED 04.

Reviewing code – REMOVED 04

In this section, we are going to review what we have commented out in //REMOVED
04:

- //REMOVED 04: This script checks what the name of the raycast game
  object is. Once it's identified through a series of if statements, it runs the
  method applicable to it.
- **Reason for removal:** This section of the code would have checked for
  specific names our raycast would have made contact with. We no longer
  use the raycast system now.
- **Replacement:** Each button has its own event trigger that runs its own
  method.

Let's continue scrolling down the PlayerShipBuild script until we get
to //REMOVED 05.

Reviewing code – REMOVED 05

In this section, we are going to review what we have commented out in `//REMOVED 05`:

- `//REMOVED 05`: Every frame, it checks whether the player has made a selection in the shop.
- **Reason for removal:** Selection is now based on events; we no longer need to check every frame through the `Update` method.
- **Replacement:** The event trigger system.

In the previous sections, we reviewed and amended the way we interacted with the old shop scene's raycast system.

The next phase is to apply methods that can be called directly via an event when a button is pressed in the `shop` scene.

Adding methods to our PlayerShipBuild script

In this section, we are going to build two main parts so that we can set up our script for 2D UI selection. Thankfully, we have done most of the work for this chapter and all that remains is to make parts of the script `public` so that our code can be accessed from other sources; that is, our event trigger (`OnClick()`).

The second thing we are going to do is make our `AttemptSelection` method receive the `game` object button so that it will replace the previous `target` game object.

To confirm this, the `target` game object was originally used to store ray hits from our raycast system. If you would like to know more about raycast systems, check out `Chapter 5`, *Creating a Shop Scene for our Game*, if this sounds hazy.

Let's start by making the `PlayerShipBuild` script's methods available to the public:

 By default, the accessibility levels for our methods/functions and classes are set to private unless stated otherwise. For more information about accessibility levels, check out the following link: https://docs.microsoft.com/en-us/dotnet/csharp/ language-reference/keywords/accessibility-levels.

1. Open the `PlayerShipBuild` script and add `public` to the following methods:

    - **public** void WatchAdvert()
    - **public** void BuyItem()
    - **public** void StartGame()

    These methods are now open to other scripts and the Unity Editor via the **Inspector**. We will cover this in the next section, but before we do that, we need to amend our `AttemptSelection` method.

    `AttemptSelection` will be given the same treatment with regards to being a `public` method, but it will now also take a game object in parameters, which will be the button our script is attached to.

2. Scroll to the `AttemptSelection` method and add a `public` accessibility level, including a game object with the reference name `buttonName`:

    ```
    public void AttemptSelection(GameObject buttonName)
    {
    ```

    Inside this `AttemptSelection` method, we check `buttonName` instead of what we did before by checking `target`. We then follow the same procedure of turning off any buttons highlighted, then apply the `buttonName` game object reference to another game object called `tmpSelection`, which was originally sat in the `Select` method.

3. Update `AttemptSelection` with the following code:

    ```
    if (buttonName)
        {
            TurnOffSelectionHighlights();
            tmpSelection = buttonName;
    ```

Continuing with the next line of code inside our method, we set the button's child `selection` game object to active (switch it on). The following screenshot shows the child number of the `selection` game object in the **Hierarchy** window:

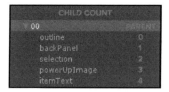

4. Enter the following code:

```
tmpSelection.transform.GetChild(1).gameObject.SetActive(true);
```

5. Inside the `AttemptSelection` method, we now need to change the old `target` game object's name to the new `buttonName` game object. The code in bold in the following snippet shows where you need to change the names:

```
UpdateDescriptionBox();
//not sold
if (buttonName.GetComponentInChildren<Text>().text != "SOLD")
{
    //can afford
    Affordable();

    //can not afford
    LackOfCredits();
}
else if (buttonName.GetComponentInChildren<Text>().text ==
"SOLD")
{
    SoldOut();
}
}
}
```

6. Scroll back up to the `CheckPlatform` method and paste in your own `gameId` string values.

7. Save the script.

Remember that if you get stuck with this part, you can always check the `Complete` folder for this chapter, where you'll have access to the completed files.

So far, we have removed multiple chunks of code and replaced them with a minimal amount that now supports the event triggers from the Unity Editor. This will help with performance and improve the readability of our code. In the next section, we are going to let each of the UI buttons know what methods to run when a selection is made.

Applying trigger events to call methods

In this final section, we are going to make it so that when the player presses a button in the shop, they will get access to it immediately, instead of our script shooting a ray and checking if and what collider it has made contact with to get access to its method. We will be doing this using Unity's Event system to run methods directly.

To make a button run a method directly, follow these steps:

1. In the Unity Editor, select the first shop scene button in the selection grid called 00 in the **Hierarchy** window, as shown in the following screenshot:

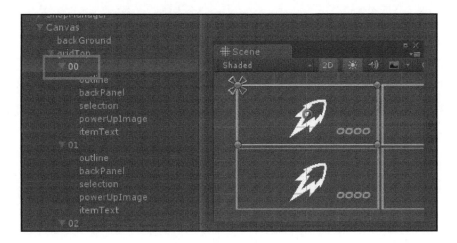

2. With 00 selected, scroll down the **Inspector** window until you come across the **Button** component. Within the **On Click ()** panel, click the + icon, as shown in the following screenshot:

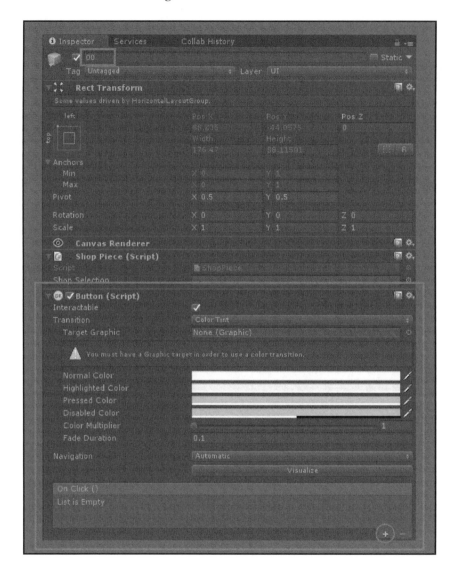

3. The **On Click()** panel will update from where we need to apply our shop game object to the field that currently says **None (Object)**.

4. Click and drag the `shop` game object from the **Hierarchy** window into the **None (Object)** field, as shown in the following screenshot:

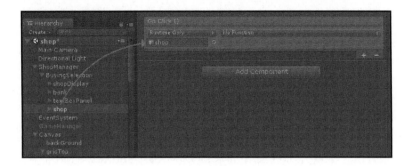

The **On Click ()** panel has updated with the `OO` game object. Now, we need to direct what function from `OO` it should load.

We will call the `AttemptSelection` method by making a request when we tap/click one of the `shop` scene's buttons.

To make our `OO` button load the `AttemptSelection` method, do the following:

1. Click the **No Function** field, followed by our`PlayerShipBuild` script and the `AttemptSelection(GameObject)` public method, as shown in the following screenshot:

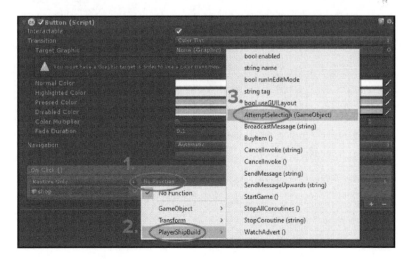

The last field to add within the **On Click ()** panel is the button we want to put through `AttemptSelection`.

2. Click the remote button on the far right and type the game object we have selected, that is, `00`. When you see it in the list, click it.

So, when the player presses the `00` button, our **On Click ()** event will run the `PlayerShipBuild` script from the `shop` game object. Then, it will run the `AttemptSelection` method, taking the `00` game object as a reference in parameters.

3. Set up the **On Click()** panel for game objects `01` and `02`. Once completed, each **On Click()** panel will look as follows for all three game objects:

Things are slightly different for our `START` and `AD` game object buttons (sat in the **Hierarchy** window).

To make our `AD` and `START` game object buttons work in the game, do the following:

1. Apply the `shop` game object to the `AD` game object's `OnClick` event in the **Inspector** window, as we did with the last few game object buttons.
2. Do the same for the `START` game object button.

Update each of the START and AD game object's OnClick events, as follows:

- AD **game object**: Select PlayerShipBuild, followed by the WatchAdvert method.
- START **game object**: Select PlayerShipBuild, followed by the StartGame method.

The very last button to change is the **BUY?** button. Follow the same principles that we used before and select the BUY? game object button in the **Hierarchy** window:

1. Apply the usual shop game object to its **On Click()** panel.
2. Set the script to PlayerShipBuild, followed by BuyItem.

Note that we don't apply event listeners to our bottom row of buttons (Sold Out) as there is no reason to press these buttons.

Our shop scene is now ready to test. Save the scene and press **Play** in the Unity Editor to try out our new shop buttons. It would also be worth testing different landscape views in the **Game** window to see the UI buttons pop into shape when a landscape ratio is selected.

The following screenshot shows the steps you have to follow to change the ratio. Do this by clicking the **Game** tab in the Unity Editor, followed by making a selection from two fairly common ratios:

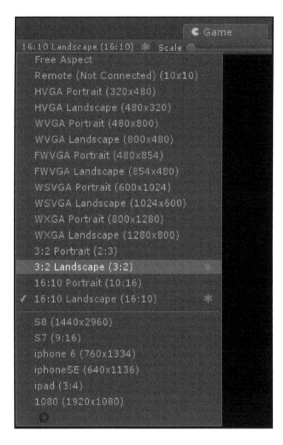

In this section, we reevaluated our code and took out the old raycast system, which involved selecting 3D game objects to run methods. We replaced this with Unity's Event System, complete with **Button** components that were dynamically organized with the Horizontal and Vertical Layout Group components.

Now, the UI is more robust since it contains different screen ratios. This will make our game more compatible with a variety of mobile and tablet screens that are old and current, as well as portable devices that haven't been released yet. This helps future-proof our application without any embarrassing ratio issues occurring.

Summary

In this chapter, we looked into two different parts of our game: the in-game HUD and rebuilding our shop scene. Both of these used Unity's UI components but in different ways.

In the in-game HUD section, we read up about what a HUD is and how we can incorporate one into our game. By doing this, we learned how to use **Horizontal Layout Group**, for ordering images correctly, **Render Texture**, for taking a feed from a second camera, and **Raw Image**, for displaying a feed from **Render Texture**.

Most importantly, as required by the Unity Programmer Exam, you need to understand what a HUD is and how to build elements into it such as a mini-map.

In the second part of this chapter, we reviewed our current shop scene's interface and code. We took it apart and rebuilt its interface as a Unity Event system that ran methods directly instead of casting a ray to call a method. We also made the interface support multiple ratios.

With the skills covered in this chapter, you should feel more confident in reviewing and understanding code that could be made more efficient.

In the next chapter, we will continue working on our in-game level so that we can pause the game, add and change the volume of our music and sound effects manually, and more.

10
Pausing the Game, Altering Sound, and a Mock Test

In this chapter, we are going to add background music to our game. Then, we will make our music fade in when the level starts, fade out when the level is completed, and stop if the player dies. After that, we will be using all the UI skills we have learned so far to create a pause screen and add some slider components to it (which will be used in the next chapter for volume controls). With the pause screen built, we will make our game pause by freezing the player, the enemies on the screen, bullets, and moving textures. Also within the pause screen, we will be giving the player the option to resume play or quit so that the game goes back to the title screen with the use of Event Listeners, which we learned about in Chapter 9, *Creating a 2D Shop Interface and In-Game HUD*. Finally, we will be extending our mini mock test to 20 questions to cover what we have learned from this chapter, as well as previous ones.

By the end of this chapter, we will be able to make changes to the `AudioSource` component directly within our script. We will know how to make every game object stop moving on the screen for our pause screen. Finally, we will know how to add a more fulfilling experience by adding a toggle and sliders.

The following topics will be covered in this chapter:

- Applying and adjusting level music
- Creating a pause screen
- Adding a game pause button
- Mock test

In terms of the Unity Programmer Exam, the next section will label the core objectives that will be covered in this chapter.

Core exam skills covered in this chapter

The following are the core exams skills that will be covered in this chapter:

- *Programming core interaction:*
  - *Implement behaviors and interactions of game objects and environments.*
  - *Identify methods to implement inputs and controls.*
- *Developing application systems:*
  - *Application interface flow such as menu systems, UI navigation, and application settings.*
- *Programming for scene and environment design:*
  - *Determine scripts for implementing audio assets.*

Technical requirements

The project content for this chapter can be found at `https://github.com/PacktPublishing/Unity-Certified-Programmer-Exam-Guide/tree/master/Chapter10`.

You can download the entirety of each chapter's project files at `https://github.com/PacktPublishing/Unity-Certified-Programmer-Exam-Guide/archive/master.zip`.

All the content for this chapter is held in this chapter's `unitypackage` file, including a `Complete` folder that holds all of the work we'll carry out in this chapter.

Check out the following video to see the Code in Action: `https://bit.ly/2Za9TQ7`.

Applying and adjusting level music

In this section, we are going to look at adding background music to our game levels. We will also be updating our scripts so that our music volume changes at different points of the game.

In the following sections, we are going to do the following:

- Add music to each level.
- When the player completes the level, make the music fade out.
- If the player dies, make the music instantly stop.
- Music will not play on other scenes, only level scenes.

So, let's make a start and add our game music to the level1 scene.

Updating our GameManager prefab

In this section, we are going to update the GameManager game object so that it holds a new game object (called LevelMusic) as a child in the **Hierarchy** window. We will then assign the LevelMusic's AudioSource component and an MP3 to play. This kind of setup is ideal for a simple game; otherwise, we potentially run the risk of adding another manager, which is fine for a bigger and more complicated game.

To create a game object and add a music file to it, we need to do the following:

1. In the Unity Editor, open the bootUp scene from the **Project** window (Assets/Scene/bootUp).
2. Right-click the GameManager game object in the **Hierarchy** window and select **Create Empty** from the drop-down list.
3. Right-click the newly created GameObject and rename it LevelMusic.

    Next, we need to attach an **Audio Source** component to LevelMusic.

4. Right-click the `LevelMusic` game object from the **Hierarchy** window, then select **Audio**, followed by **Audio Source**. The following screenshot shows how to create this:

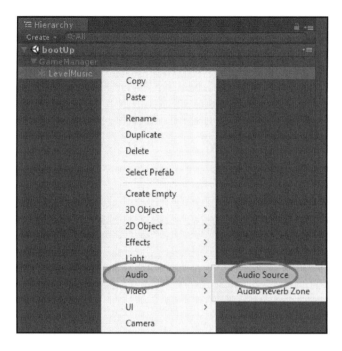

5. With the `LevelMusic` game object still selected, we can now drag our `lvlMusic` MP3 file from `Assets/Resources/Sound` in the **Project** window into the **AudioClip** parameter, as shown in the following screenshot:

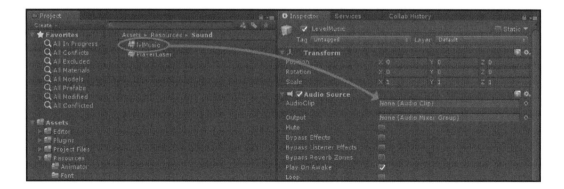

6. Now is a good time to save our `GameManager` prefab by selecting it in the **Hierarchy** window and clicking **Apply** in the top-right corner of the **Inspector** window.

   If we now click **Play** to play the game from the `level1` scene, the game will start to play music. This is because, by default, the **Audio Source** component is set to **Play On Awake**. This is good, but it won't stop playing until the scene changes, which is enough for most games. However, we want to add control to the music's volume via scripting.

In the next section, we are going to update the `ScenesManager` script and control when and how our music will be played.

Preparing states for our game music

In this section, we are going to ensure that our game music is no longer set to its default **Audio Source** setting of **Play On Awake**. We want the music to be aware of when to play, when to fade the volume down, and when to stop. These three states for the music are connected to the actions of when a game level starts, when the player completes a level, and when the player dies. So, it would be a fair judgment of the three music states to add the music code to the `ScenesManager` script as it is relatively connected.

To add our three music states (play, stop, and fade down), we need to do the following:

1. In the **Project** window, open the `ScenesManager` script (`Assets/Resources/Script`).

2. At the top of the `ScenesManager` script where we have entered our global variables, just below the scope of our `public enum Scenes` property, enter the following `enum`, along with its three states:

   ```
   public MusicMode musicMode;
   public enum MusicMode
   {
     noSound, fadeDown, musicOn
   }
   ```

We covered enum's back in the *Setting up our scene's manager script* section in Chapter 3, *Managing Scripts and Mock Test*; the principles are the same as labeling our states. For our `enum`, we have assigned it a data type name of `MusicMode`.

Now that we have our three states labeled, we need to put these into action. We need to make our three states carry out their intended actions:

- noSound: No music is playing.
- fadeDown: The music's volume will fade to zero.
- musicOn: The music will be playing and will be set to its maximum volume.

At various points of the game, we will want these states to be triggered, and the best way of accessing these short sets of states is to use a switch case to funnel out each outcome.

Now, we need to add a switch statement for our three music states.

Still inside the ScenesManager script, we are going to add an IEnumerator that will act on either state. We covered StartCoroutine/IEnumerator in the *Setting up our EnemySpawner script* section in Chapter 2, *Adding and Manipulating Objects*.

So, because we are adding an IEnumerator, we also need to add an extra library to suppose this functionality:

1. Inside the ScenesManager script, at the very top, add the following library:

   ```
   using System.Collections;
   ```

   Our script now supports coroutines and IEnumerators.

   I'm going to place my IEnumerator just outside of the scope of the Update function and name it MusicVolume, where it takes the MusicMode data type and we will refer to it as musicMode:

   ```
   IEnumerator MusicVolume(MusicMode musicMode)
     {
   ```

   Inside the scope of the MusicVolume IEnumerator, we will make a start with our switch statement and take in the reference of one of the three states that would have been sent through from the musicMode reference:

   ```
   switch (musicMode)
     {
   ```

If `musicMode` contains the `noSound` state, then we use `GetComponentInChildren<AudioSource>()` to grab the only child game object that holds `AudioSource`, which is the newly created `LevelMusic` game object.

We then use the `Stop` function to stop the music and then break out of the case:

```
case MusicMode.noSound :
    {
        GetComponentInChildren<AudioSource>().Stop();
        break;
    }
```

The next case is if `musicMode` holds the `fadeDown` state. Here, we grab the reference of the `LevelMusic` game object and reduce its `volume` value over time:

```
case MusicMode.fadeDown :
    {
        GetComponentInChildren<AudioSource>().volume -=
            Time.deltaTime/3;
        break;
    }
```

The third and final case is `musicOn`; inside the case, we first make a check to see if an audio clip has already been loaded into the `AudioSource`. If there is no audio clip, we discard the rest of the case; otherwise, we `Play` the music loaded in and set it to full volume (with `1` being the highest):

```
case MusicMode.musicOn :
    {
        if (GetComponentInChildren<AudioSource>().clip !=
null)
        {
          GetComponentInChildren<AudioSource>().Play();
          GetComponentInChildren<AudioSource>().volume = 1;
        }
        break;
```

To close the `switch` statement, we add our `yield return` with a fraction of a second delay to give our game time to change the settings from the `switch` statement:

```
        }
    }
        yield return new WaitForSeconds(0.1f);
}
```

Now that we have created our `enum musicMode` states and set up what each of them will do when triggered in the `IEnumerator`, we can move on to implementing the coroutines to make changes to the music.

Implementing our game's music states

In this section, we are going to continue making changes to our `ScenesManager` script and add `StartCoroutines` to specific parts of our code with the `musicMode` state, which is where our music's volume is going to change. So, for example, if the player dies in the game, we want the music to stop immediately by using the `noSound` state.

Let's make a start on this by loading our music into the game level:

1. In the `ScenesManager` script, scroll down to the `GameTimer` method. For the first case, which checks if the player is on level 1, 2, or 3, add the following `if` statement:

   ```
   if (GetComponentInChildren<AudioSource>().clip == null)
   {
     AudioClip lvlMusic = Resources.Load<AudioClip>
       ("Sound/lvlMusic") as AudioClip;
     GetComponentInChildren<AudioSource>().clip = lvlMusic;
     GetComponentInChildren<AudioSource>().Play();
   }
   ```

   Our `if` statement makes a check to see if the audio clip of our LevelMusic's `AudioSource` is empty (null). If it doesn't have an audio clip, the `if` statement will carry out the following roles:

   - Grab our audio file (`lvlMusic.mp3`) from its folder and store it as an `AudioClip` data type.
   - Apply the audio clip to the `AudioSource` component.
   - Run the `Play` function from `AudioSource`.

Now that our music plays when we start a level, we need to make it so that when a level is completed, the music fades out. This part is fairly simple as we are in the correct method to fade the game music out when a level is completed.

2. Scroll down to the `//if level is completed` comment and add the following line of code to fade the game music out when a level is completed:

```
StartCoroutine(MusicVolume(MusicMode.fadeDown));
```

3. The last thing to do within the `switch` statement is to add a line of code that resets the audio clip to `null` as a failsafe:

```
default :
{
  GetComponentInChildren<AudioSource>().clip = null;
  break;
}
```

Now, if our `GamerTimer` method is called and none of the cases (our player isn't on level 1, 2, or 3) apply, our player is likely to be on the title, game over, or boot up scene, which means we will not play any level music.

Now, we will look at how to use StartCoroutines.

Using StartCoroutine with our music states

Now, we need to learn how to stop and start the music, typically when the level is about to start or abruptly ends (typically when the player dies). Still inside `ScenesManager`, go back to the methods that will need updating so that they can support the music settings. Follow these steps:

1. The first method we will be updating is `ResetScene`. Within the scope of the method, enter the following code:

```
StartCoroutine(MusicVolume(MusicMode.noSound));
```

This will make a call to the `MusicVolume IEnumrator` to turn off the music. The following code block shows how the `ResetScene` method looks after it's been updated:

```
public void ResetScene()
{
   StartCoroutine(MusicVolume(MusicMode.noSound));
   gameTimer = 0;
   SceneManager.LoadScene(GameManager.currentScene);
}
```

2. The next method we are going to update is the `NextLevel` method. We can start the music at any time, irrespective of where the player is. We can play it whenever we want with the following code:

```
StartCoroutine(MusicVolume(MusicMode.musicOn));
```

The following code block shows what the `NextLevel` method looks like when the code has been updated:

```
void NextLevel()
{
   gameEnding = false;
   gameTimer = 0;
   SceneManager.LoadScene(GameManager.currentScene+1);
      StartCoroutine(MusicVolume(MusicMode.musicOn));
}
```

Now, we'll move on to the `Start` function, which works as a failsafe for starting a scene and to see if it should be playing music.

Whenever the `ScenesManager` script is active, it will automatically attempt to play music from our `LevelMusic` game object's `AudioSource` component.

If `AudioSource` doesn't contain a valid `AudioClip` (no MP3 found), then our code will presume the level the player is on doesn't require music.

3. The following code block shows the `Start` function in its entirety with the added `StartCoroutine`:

```
void Start()
{
   StartCoroutine(MusicVolume(MusicMode.musicOn));
   SceneManager.sceneLoaded += OnSceneLoaded;
}
```

4. The last method to update is `OnSceneLoaded`. When a level is loaded, we will attempt to turn the music on. The following code block shows the `OnSceneLoaded` method with the added `StartCoroutine` at the top:

```
    private void OnSceneLoaded(Scene aScene, LoadSceneMode
aMode)
  {
    StartCoroutine(MusicVolume(MusicMode.musicOn));

    GetComponent<GameManager> ().SetLivesDisplay(GameManager.
        playerLives);
    if (GameObject.Find("score"))
    {
      GameObject.Find("score").GetComponent<Text>().text =
        ScoreManager.playerScore.ToString();
    }
  }
```

5. Save the script and the `bootUp` scene.

Our code is complete for manipulating music for our level scenes.

In this section, we updated our `GameManager` so that it holds a second game object called `LevelMusic`. This `LevelMusic` game object will hold an `AudioSource` component that can be manipulated when the player starts a level, completes a level, or dies via the `ScenesManager` script.

In the next section, we will add a pause screen to our game and learn how to adjust the volume of our music and sound effects, and much more.

Creating a pause screen

Currently, we aren't able to pause the game, nor do we have an options screen that can manipulate the settings of the game. In this section, we are going to combine these ideas so that our game is capable of pausing and we will also be able to change the volume of the music and sound effects.

In this section, we are going to do the following:

- Add the pause button to the top corner of the screen.
- Create a pause screen.
- Add the option to resume the game.
- Add the option to quit the game.

- Add a slider for music and sound effects.
- Create and hook up **Audio Mixer** to both sliders.

The end result of the pause screen can be seen in the following screenshot:

Let's make a start by focusing on the visuals of the pause screen. Then, we will hook up the sliders and buttons.

To start with the pause UI visuals, we need to do the following:

1. Load up the `level1` scene from the **Project** window (`Assets/Scene/level1`).

   With the `level1` scene loaded, we can now focus on creating some game objects in the **Hierarchy** window for our pause screen.

2. Right-click on the `Canvas` game object in the **Hierarchy** window and select **Create Empty** from the drop-down list.

3. Select the newly created game object, right-click it, select **Rename** from the drop-down, and rename it `PauseContainer`.

   `PauseContainer` now needs to be scaled to the size of the game screen so that whatever is a child of this game object can be scaled to the correct scale and position.

4. To make `PauseContainer` fully scaled to the game screen's proportions, ensure `PauseContainer` is still selected in the **Hierarchy** window and set its **Rect Transform** properties in the **Inspector** window to the properties shown in the following screenshot:

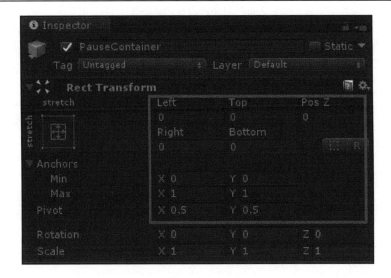

That's our `PauseContainer` created and set to hold two main game objects. The first game object will house all of the individual pause screen's buttons and sliders. The second game object is for the pause button in the top-left corner of the screen and will make the game pause and bring the pause controls up.

The following screenshot shows our game with the pause button in the top-left corner of the screen:

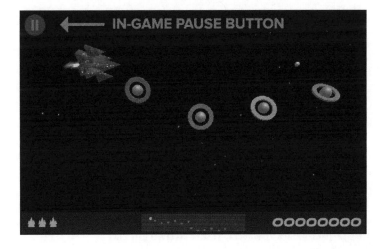

But let's stay focused on the pause screen and its content before we work on the in-game pause button. To create a `PauseScreen` game object that will house the game objects, we need to repeat a similar procedure for `PauseContainer` in terms of our **Rect Transform** properties.

To create and house a `PauseScreen` game object in `PauseContainer`, do the following:

1. Right-click the `PauseContainer` game object in the **Hierarchy** window.
2. Select **Create Empty** from the drop-down.

   The new game object will be a child of the `PauseContainer` game object. Now, let's rename the newly created game object to `PauseScreen`.

3. Right-click **GameObject**, select **Rename** from the drop-down menu, and name it `PauseScreen`.
4. With `PauseScreen` still selected in the **Hierarchy** window, give its **Rect Transform** the same settings as `PauseContainer` has. Use the previous **Rect Transform** image as a reference.

We can now make a start by filling our `PauseScreen` game object with its own game objects.

Let's start dimming the screen so that the player isn't distracted when the game is paused.

To create a dim effect, do the following:

1. In the **Hierarchy** window, right-click the `PauseScreen` game object and select **Create Empty**. Then, rename the game object `blackOutScreen`.
2. Apply the same **Rect Transform** properties that you applied to the last two game objects.

   Now, we need to add the **Image** component so that we can cover the screen with a semi-transparent black.

3. With `blackOutScreen` still selected, click the **Add Component** button in the **Inspector** window and type `Image`. Once you see the **Image** component from the drop-down list, select it to add it to`blackOutScreen`.
4. The last thing to do for the `blackOutScreen` component's image property is to set its **Color** settings to the ones shown in the following screenshot:

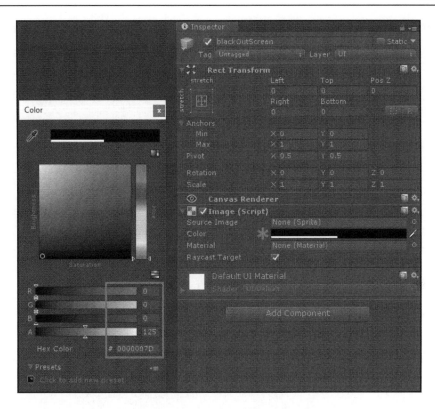

We will now have a sheet of semi-darkness across the screen.

Now, let's add the **Pause** text. To do that, follow these steps:

1. In the **Hierarchy** window, right-click the PauseScreen game object and select **Create Empty**. Then rename the game object PauseText.

2. This time, give the PauseText's **Rect Transform** properties the following values:

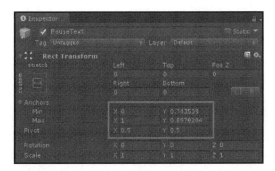

Next, we need to add the **Text** component and set its properties for the
PauseText game object, as follows:

1. With PauseText still selected, click the **Add Component** button in the
   Inspector window and begin to type Text until you can see it in the drop-
   down list. Once you do, select it.
2. Change the settings of the **Text Component** to the ones shown in the
   following screenshot:

If you require more information on **Text Component**, check out
the *Applying text and images to your scenes* section in Chapter
8, *Adding Custom Fonts and UIs*.

The following screenshot shows what the **Hierarchy** and **Scene** views currently look like:

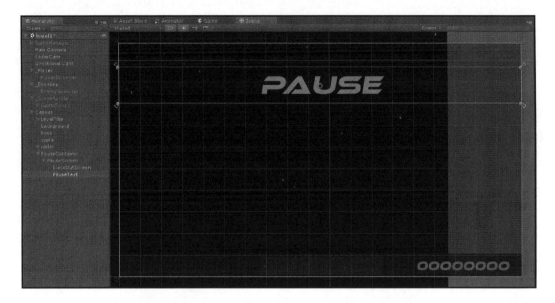

We have our pause title customized and centered. Now, let's move on to some sliders for the **Music** and **Effects** volume settings. We'll make a start on the **Music** slider and then duplicate it to the other side of the screen for the **Effects** slider.

Volume UI slider

In this section, we are going to give the pause screen its title name and create and customize the pause screen volume sliders for our game's music and its sound effects.

To create, customize, and position the **Music** slider, follow these steps:

1. Right-click the `PauseScreen` game object in the **Hierarchy** window. Then, from the drop-down, select **UI**, followed by **Slider**, as shown in the following screenshot:

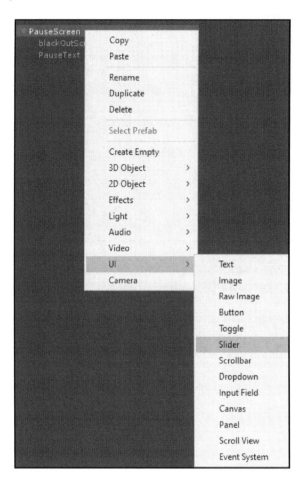

2. Select the newly created `Slider` game object, right-click it, and rename it `Music`.

3. Next, position the `Music` slider by changing its **Rect Transform** properties to the ones shown in the following screenshot:

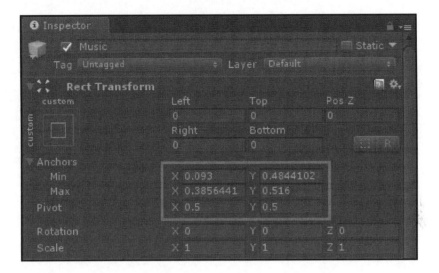

We will now change the color of the `Music` slider's bar to make it look more suited for the pause screen. We'll do this by changing it from light gray to red.

To change the color of the slider, do the following:

1. Click the arrow to the left of the `Music` game object in the **Hierarchy** window to expand the slider's content. Do this again for the `Fill Area` game object.

2. Select the `Fill` game object from the drop-down of the `Music` game object, as shown in the following screenshot, just as it would in the **Hierarchy** window:

3. With `Fill` still selected, in its **Inspector** window, change the **Image** component's **Color** value to red, as shown in the following screenshot:

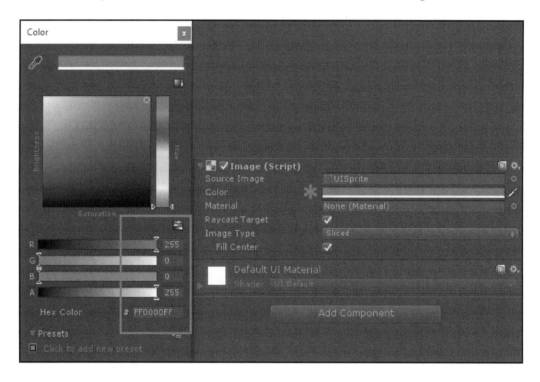

If you still have the `Fill` game object selected, you can view the red by adjusting the **Value** slider at the bottom of the **Slider** component in the **Inspector** window, as shown in the following screenshot:

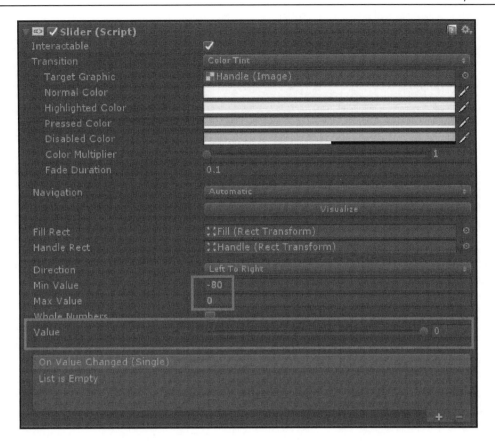

Also, in the previous screenshot, we need to set the slider's **Min Value** to -80 and its **Max Value** to 0. The reason for this is that in the next chapter, these will match the same values as the Audio Mixer's.

The Music slider is set to the right size; we just need to tweak the handle so it isn't so stretched and is easier to click or drag with our finger. Follow these steps to do so:

1. In the **Hierarchy** window, expand all of the game object arrows so that we can get access to the Handle game object. Then, select it.

2. In the **Inspector** window, tick the **Preserve Aspect** box under the Image component to stop the Handle game object from looking so stretched.

3. With Handle still selected, change its **Scale** in **Rect Transform** to 3 on all axes.

The following screenshot shows what our handle looks like now:

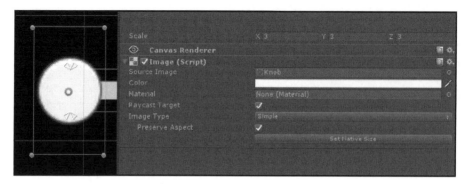

The `Music` slider is now set. This means we can move on to the text so that we can label the slider for the player. To give the slider its own UI text, we need to do the following:

1. In the **Hierarchy** window, right-click the `PauseScreen` game object and from the dropdown list, select **UI**, followed by **Text**.

2. Right-click our newly created `Text` game object and select **Rename** from the dropdown list. Rename the game object `MusicText`.

3. With the `MusicText` game object still selected, change its **Rect Transform** to the following values to position and scale the text in the correct location:

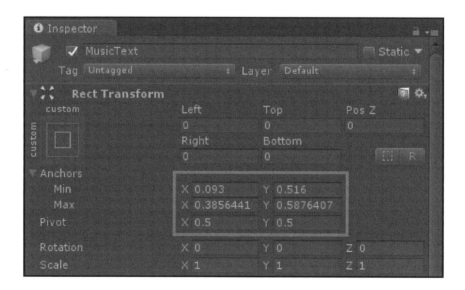

4. With the `MusicText` game object still selected in the **Inspector** window, update the **Text** component values to the following property values:

Our pause screen is starting to take shape. The following screenshot shows what we currently have:

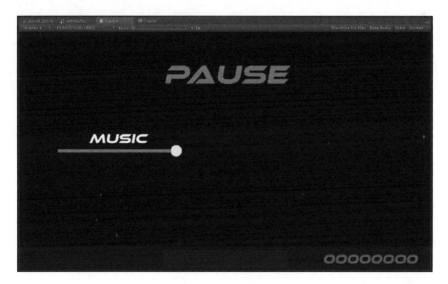

We can now copy and paste over our music text and slider to the other side of the screen and tweak some of its property values so that it will be identified as the sound effects volume bar.

To duplicate and tweak the music text and slider, do the following:

1. Hold *Ctrl* (*command* on Mac) and select `MusicText` and `Music` from the **Hierarchy** window so that they are highlighted. Then, press *D* on the keyboard to duplicate the two game objects.
2. Select the `Music (1)` game object, right-click it, select **Rename** from the drop-down, and change its name to `Effects`.
3. Select the `MusicText (1)` game object, right-click it, select **Rename** from the drop-down, and change its name to `EffectsText`.
4. With `EffectsText` still selected, update its **Rect Transform** in the **Inspector** window with the following property values:

With `EffectsText` still selected, we can now pay attention to renaming the text. The rest of EffectsText's **Text Component** properties can remain the same. Simply change the **Text** field from `MUSIC` to `EFFECTS`, as shown in the following screenshot:

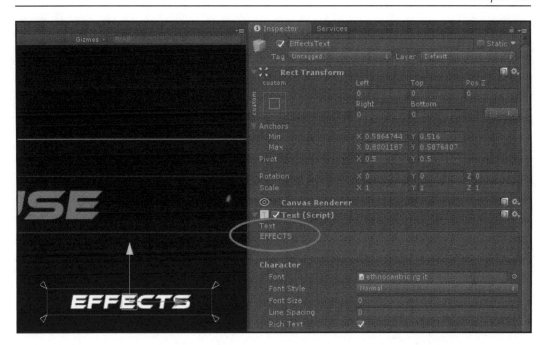

Next, we can move our **Effects** slider over so that it sits below the **EFFECTS** text in our scene view. To do this, follow these steps:

1. Select the `Effects` game object in the **Hierarchy** window. In the **Inspector** window, change its **Rect Transform** properties to the ones shown in the following screenshot:

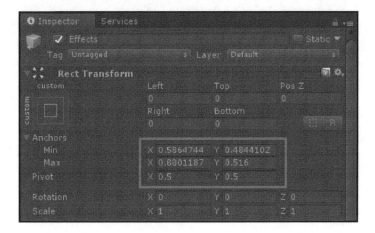

We are nearly done with our pause screen in terms of its visual elements. The last two things we have to configure are the **Quit** and **Resume** buttons. As with the slider game objects, we can make one, copy and paste it to create a second, and then edit them.

To create and customize a **Quit** button, do the following:

1. Right-click the `PauseScreen` game object in the **Hierarchy** window and select **UI**, then **Button**, from the dropdown list.
2. With the newly created `Button` game object, we can rename it to `Quit`; right-click the `Button` game object in the **Hierarchy** window, select **Rename** from the drop-down, and rename the game object from `Button` to `Quit`.

   Now, we can put the `Quit` game object into the correct location and resize it within our `PauseScreen` game object.

3. With the `Quit` game object still selected, change its **Rect Transform** properties in the **Inspector** window to the ones shown in the following screenshot:

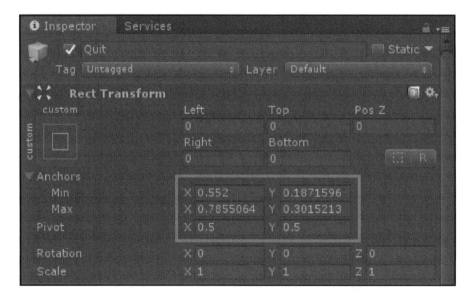

The `Quit` game object will now be in the bottom right of the pause screen:

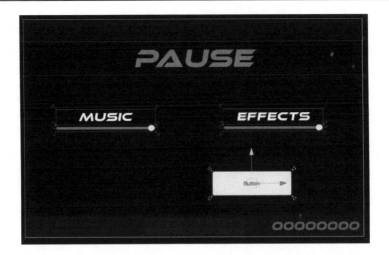

Next, we can customize it by changing the button's sprite, color, and text. We'll start with the buttons sprite by taking off the curved corners that we can see in the previous screenshot.

With our `Quit` button still selected, we can remove the single sprite by doing the following:

1. In the **Inspector** window, click the remote button in the **Image** component at the top right (denoted as **1**).
2. A new window will appear. Select **None** at the top from the drop-down (denoted as **2**):

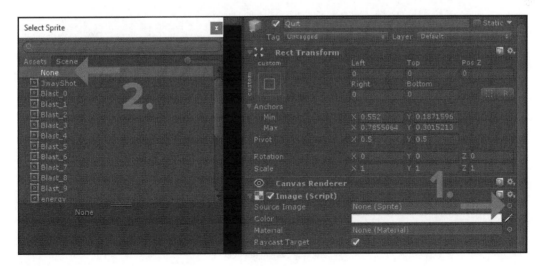

Next, we'll change the color of the buttons, as follows:

1. With the Quit game object still selected in the **Hierarchy** window, we can change the **Normal Color** property on **Button Component** in the **Inspector** window.

2. Select the color field titled **Normal Color**. Then, in the new popup window, change the RGBA settings to red so that it has a slight transparency. The values for it are **R**: 255, **G**: 0, **B**: 0, **A**: 150.

The third thing we need to do to the button is change its text.

3. With our Quit game object still selected in the **Hierarchy** window, select the drop-down arrow to the left of its name in the **Hierarchy** window.

4. Select the Text child game object from the Quit game object and give the **Text** component in the **Inspector** window the following property settings:

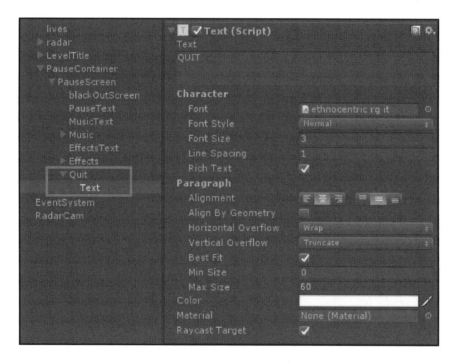

We will be left with a button that looks more fitting for our game:

The last thing to do in this section is duplicate the Quit game object we have just created and rename the text RESUME. The **Resume** button will be used to cancel the pause screen and let the player continue playing the game.

To create the Resume game object, we will need to do the following:

1. Select the Quit game object in the **Hierarchy** window.
2. Press *Ctrl* (*command* on Mac) and *D* on the keyboard to duplicate the game object.
3. Rename the duplicated game object from Quit (1) to Resume.
4. With Resume still selected, change its **Rect Transform** property values in the **Inspector** window to the ones shown in the following screenshot:

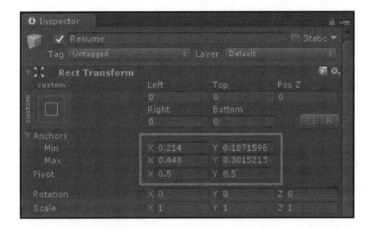

All that's left for the Resume game object is to rename its text from QUIT to RESUME by expanding the **Resume** selection by clicking on its an arrow on the left in the **Hierarchy** window. Follow these steps:

1. Select the Text game object in the **Hierarchy** window.
2. In the **Text** component in the **Inspector** window, change the text from QUIT to RESUME, as shown in the following screenshot:

The pause screen is now visually complete and can support various screen ratios thanks to the use of our **Anchors** from our **Rect Transform** properties. Earlier, we mentioned that we will have a pause button in the top left corner of the game screen so that we can pause our game and load up the pause screen that we've just made.

Everything we did in this section was all achieved within the Unity Editor without the use of any code. In this section, we covered the following topics:

- How to access our pause screen
- How the pause screen would overlay the levels in our game
- Applying a semi-transparent blackout to dim the game as the pause screen's background
- Creating sliders for our music and effects
- Applying custom text to various points
- Using Unity's **Button** component to give the player the option to quit or resume the game

Now, let's make the pause button. After that, we can start looking at hooking all these sliders and buttons up with our code.

Adding a game pause button

At the beginning of the previous section, we briefly spoke about the **in-game pause button**. This button will appear at the start of a level and once pressed, the player, enemies, and bullets that have been fired will freeze in time. In this section, we will only be focusing on the visuals, just as we did with our pause screen in the previous section.

The pause button will act slightly different from the previous buttons we have made. This time, the button will be an **on** or **off** type button. The game object for this will be a toggle as it is more suited to our needs. To make a `toggle` game object, do the following:

1. Select the `PauseContainer` game object in the **Hierarchy** window, right-click it, and select **UI** from the drop-down list, followed by **Toggle**, as shown in the following screenshot:

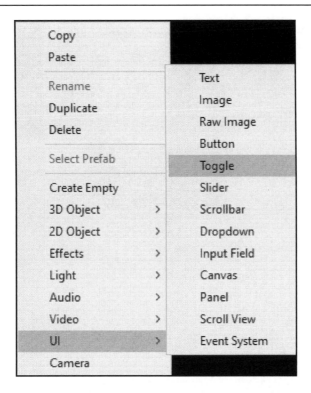

2. With the `Toggle` game object still selected in the **Hierarchy** window, right-click it, select **Rename** from the drop-down list, and name it `PauseButton`.

Currently, our `PauseButton` looks nothing like how we want it to and resembles a tick box, as shown in the following screenshot. However, we can fix this and make it look like a normal-looking **pause** button but with the functionality of a toggle (on or off):

To alter the current look of the `PauseButton` game object so that it looks like the prospective one in the preceding screenshot, we need to do the following:

1. In the **Hierarchy** window, click on all of the arrows within the `PauseButton` game object to expand its content, as shown in the following screenshot:

2. Select the `Label` game object in the **Hierarchy** window and press *delete* on your keyboard.

   The **Toggle** label will be removed.

3. Next, we will set our game object into its correct position and scale. Select `PauseButton` in the **Hierarchy** window and give its **Rect Transform** the following properties in the **Inspector** window:

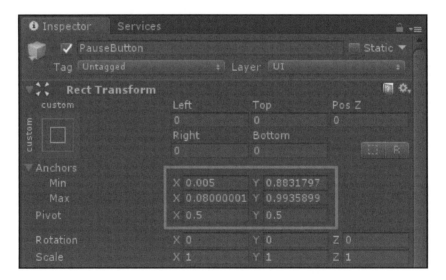

The toggle will now be placed and scaled to the top-left corner of the game canvas, as circled in the following screenshot:

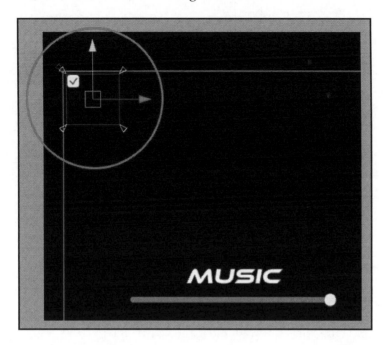

Notice how our **Anchors** (the four white arrows) are positioned but the small white tick boxes' scale hasn't been affected. This means the child of the PauseButton game object that holds another game object titled Background doesn't have its **Rect Transform** scaled correctly. The following screenshot shows the Background game object selected in the **Hierarchy** window:

4. To correct the `Background` game object's **Rect Transform** properties, we need to select the `Background` game object and give it the following values in the **Inspector** window:

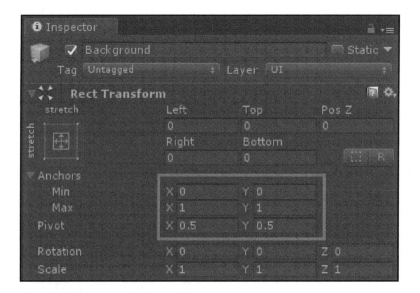

The `Background` game object is now the same size as the `PauseButton` game object with regards to the **Anchor** size.

We can now start tweaking the size and filling the **Background** with a suitable image. We'll replace the white-square-with-its-tick with a dark circle. Follow these steps to do so:

1. With `PauseButton` still expanded in the **Hierarchy** window, select the `Background` game object if you haven't done so already.
2. Select the small remote button to the right of **Source Image** in the **Image** component in the **Inspector** window.
3. From the drop-down that appears, replace its current selection with `UISprite` and change it to **Knob**. Its selection is shown in the following screenshot.

The square has now become a circle. Now, we can alter its color so that it matches the rest of our game's UI.

With the `Background` game object still selected, select its **Color** field and change its RGBA values to **R**: 92, **G**: 92, **B**: 92 and **A**: 123, as shown in the following screenshot:

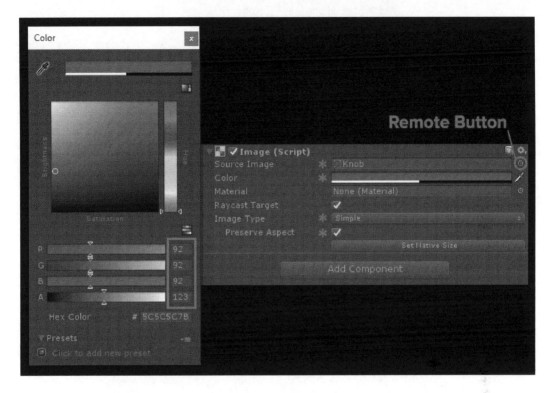

Next, we can make the gray oval shape into a circle.

Still in the **Image** component, set **Image Type** to **Simple** and tick the **Preserve Aspect** box, as shown in the previous screenshot.

Image Type offers different behaviors to an image; for example, **Sliced** works well as a progress bar/timer to increment how much of the image can be seen over time.

Preserve Aspect means that no matter which way the image is scaled, it will remain in its original form – there will be no squashed or stretched looking images.

Here is a close-up view of `PauseButton` in the **Scene** view:

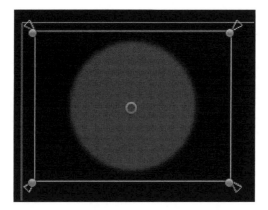

Now, we need to replace the tick image with a large pause symbol. Follow these steps to do so:

1. Select the `Checkmark` game object from the **Hierarchy** window (the child of the `Background` game object) and in the **Inspector** window, give its **Rect Transform** the following settings:

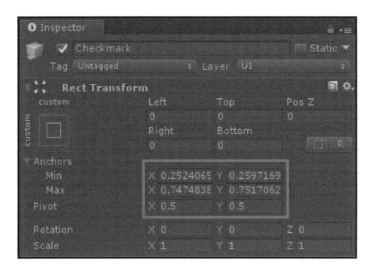

2. With the `Checkmark` game object still selected in the **Hierarchy**, go to the **Image** component and change **Source Image** from `Checkmark` to `pause` by clicking on the **remote** button and selecting the **pause** sprite from the drop-down list.

3. Select the **Color** field and give it the following RGBA values: **R**: 152, **G**: 177, **B**: 178, **A**: 125.

4. Change **Image Type** to **Simple** if it isn't already.

5. Tick the **Preserve Aspect** box, as shown in the following screenshot:

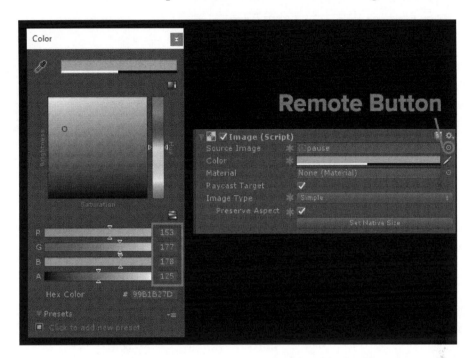

The **Scene** window should look something like this, with our pause button in the top-left:

Finally, to make it so that the `toggle` button actually does something when we click on it, we need to make sure we have an **EventSystem** in our **Hierarchy** window. This is very simple to do; follow these steps:

1. In the **Hierarchy** window, right-click an open space.
2. Select **UI**, followed by **Event System.**
3. Save the scene.

In this section, we mixed our UI images, buttons, text, and sliders on one screen that supports various landscape variations.

In the next section, we are going to move on to the scripting side of what each of the UI components we made in the pause screen will do when the player presses the buttons or moves the slider.

Creating our PauseComponent script

The `PauseComponent` script will have the responsibility of managing anything to do with accessing and altering the conditions the pause screen gives the player. Here, we will follow a series of subsections that will take us through setting up individual segments of the `PauseComponent` script. Before we do that, though, we need to create our script. If you don't know how to make a script, then revisit the *Setting up our camera* section in `Chapter 2`, *Adding and Manipulating Objects*. Once you've done that, rename the script `PauseComponent`. For maintenance purposes, store our script in the `Assets/Resources/Script` folder in the **Project** window.

Now, let's move on to the first subsection of the `PauseComponent` script by applying logic to the in-game pause button.

PauseScreen basic setup and PauseButton functionality

In this section, we are going to make the pause button appear when the player has control of the game in the level. When the player presses the pause button, we need to make sure that all the moving components and scrolling textures freeze. Finally, we need to introduce the pause screen itself.

If we start the level in its current state, we will see that the `PauseScreen` game object overlays the screen. This looks great, but we need to turn it off for the time being. To turn off the `PauseScreen` game object, do the following:

1. In the Unity Editor, open the newly created script `PauseComponent` by double-clicking the file held in `Assets/Resources/Script`.

2. With the script open, add an extra library at the top to support the pause button's functionality, including the usual `UnityEngine` library and the name of the class, along with its inheritance of `MonoBehaviour`:

```
using UnityEngine.UI;
using UnityEngine;

public class PauseComponent : MonoBehaviour
{
```

3. Add the following global variable to the `PauseComponent` class:

```
[SerializeField]
GameObject pauseScreen;
```

`[SerializeField]` will keep the `pauseScreen` variable accessible in the editor as if it was `public`. The second line is a `GameObject` type that will store the entire `PauseScreen` game object.

4. Save the script.

5. Back in the Unity Editor, select the `PauseContainer` game object from the **Hierarchy** window. In the **Inspector** window, click **Add Component** and type `PauseComponent` until you see it in the drop-down list.

6. Now, drag and drop the `PauseScreen` game object from the
   Hierarchy window into the empty game object slot titled `PauseScreen`, as
   shown in the following screenshot:

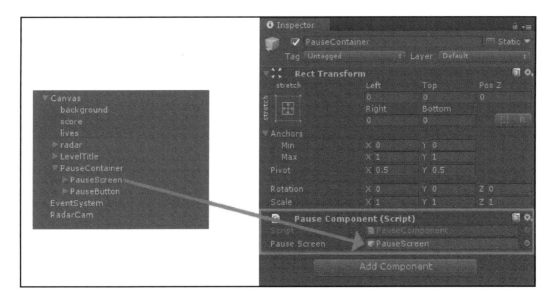

Back in the `PauseComponent` script, we can now turn off the `PauseScreen` game
object at the beginning of the level and back on when the player presses the pause
button. To turn `PauseScreen` off, we can do the following:

1. In the `PauseComponent` script, create an `Awake` function and inside it, turn
   the `pauseScreen` game object off, as shown in the following code:

```
void Awake()
{
    pauseScreen.SetActive(false);
}
```

2. Save the script.

   We can now test it in the editor when we press the **Play** button at the top of
   the screen. The game will run without the pause screen being shown. Now,
   we can focus on introducing the pause button to the player within a few
   seconds as the level begins.

Let's start by creating a method that will turn off/on the visuals and the interactability of the pause button for the player:

1. Go back into the `PauseComponent` script and create a method that takes one `bool` parameter, as shown in the following code:

    ```
    void SetPauseButtonActive(bool switchButton)
    {
    ```

    With our `PauseComponent` script being attached to the `PauseContainer` game object, we can easily access any of the game objects and their components. The other two main game objects attached are `PauseScreen` and `PauseButton`. The next few pieces of code we will add to our `SetPauseButtonActive` will relate to the visuals and interactivity of the `PauseButton` game object.

2. To change the visibility of our `PauseButton`, we need to access its `Toggle` component's `colors` value and store it in a temporary `ColorBlock` type. Enter this line of code inside the `SetPauseButtonActive` method:

    ```
    ColorBlock col = GetComponentInChildren<Toggle>().colors;
    ```

    Next, we need to check the condition of the value by looking at the `bool` parameter the method is receiving. If the `switchButton bool` is set to off, then we are going to set all colors related to the toggle to zero, which is black and zero alpha (completely transparent).

3. Enter the following code just after the line of code we entered previously:

    ```
    if (switchButton == false)
    {
      col.normalColor = new Color32(0,0,0,0);
      col.highlightedColor = new Color32(0,0,0,0);
      col.pressedColor = new Color32(0,0,0,0);
      col.disabledColor = new Color32(0,0,0,0);
      GetComponentInChildren<Toggle>().interactable = false;
    }
    ```

    The preceding code shows that we run a check to see whether the `bool` parameter is `false`.

If `switchButton` does contain a `false` value, then we step into the `if` statement and set the `col` (the color of the pause button) `normalColor` property to all zero. This means that it doesn't display this button at all. Then, we apply the same value to all of the other possible color states for the pause button. We also need to set the `Toggle intractable` value to `false` so that the player can't accidentally press the pause button either.

The image on the left shows the code we've just entered. The image on the right is the `Toggle` component with the properties we have changed in our `if` statement:

If `switchButton` is set to `true`, we set the values from all zeros to their chosen color values and make the `PauseButton intractable`.

4. Enter the following code just after the preceding code that we just wrote:

```
else
{
    col.normalColor = new Color32(245,245,245,255);
    col.highlightedColor = new Color32(245,245,245,255);
    col.pressedColor = new Color32(200,200,200,255);
    col.disabledColor = new Color32(200,200,200,128);
    GetComponentInChildren<Toggle>().interactable = true;
}
```

The last two lines after this piece of code are applying the `col` value back to the `Toggle` component.

The second line of code turns the pause symbol on or off. If this wasn't set, then the pause button would appear/disappear without affecting the two white pause stripes.

The last two GetComponentInChildren lines are added after the preceding code, which reapplies the color back to the `Toggle` component and the pause symbol to on or off with the use of the `switchButton` variable:

```
GetComponentInChildren<Toggle>().colors = col;
GetComponentInChildren<Toggle>()
    .transform.GetChild(0).GetChild(0).gameObject.SetActive
        (switchButton);
}
```

Now, all we need to do is make use of the method we've just written. Originally, we wanted the pause button to not be in view at the start of the level until the player has control of their ship. To turn off the pause button, we need to revisit the `Awake` function and do the following:

```
void Awake()
{
    pauseScreen.SetActive(false);
    SetPauseButtonActive(false);
    Invoke("DelayPauseAppear",5);
}
```

Here, I have added two extra lines of code in the `Awake` function. `SetPauseButtonActive(false)` turns the pause button off with the method we've just made, while the `Invoke` function will delay for 5 seconds until we run the `DelayPauseAppear` method. Inside `DelayPauseAppear` is `SetPauseButtonActive(true)`, which is the time our player gains control.

5. Add the extra method that we mentioned in the `Invoke` function to turn the pause button on, as follows:

```
void DelayPauseAppear()
{
    SetPauseButtonActive(true);
}
```

6. Save the script.

Back in the Unity Editor, press **Play**; our game will start normally and after 5 seconds, the pause button will appear in the top-left corner. If we press the pause button, it will break and nothing extra will happen. This is because we haven't made the pause button do anything when it is pressed.

Let's return to the PauseComponent script and add a small method that can run when the pause button is pressed. To add a pause method that freezes the game and brings up the pause screen we built earlier, do the following:

1. Reopen the PauseComponent script and enter the following method:

    ```
    public void PauseGame()
    {
      pauseScreen.SetActive(true);
      SetPauseButtonActive(false);
      Time.timeScale = 0;
    }
    ```

2. Within the PauseGame method, we set the following:

    - We set the pause screen game object's activity to true:
        - Turn off the pause button (because we have the QUIT button to use instead).
        - Set the game's timeScale to zero, which will stop all moving, animating objects in the scene. For more information about timeScale, check out the official Unity documentation here: https://docs.unity3d.com/2017.3/Documentation/ScriptReference/Time-timeScale.html.

    timeScale can also be found in **Time Manager** in the Unity Editor. This is located at the top of the **Editor** window, under **Edit | Project Settings | Time**.

    You also have other useful properties such as **Fixed Timestep**, where you can change its value to make our physics simulation more precise. For more information about **Time Manager** and its properties, check out the following link: https://docs.unity3d.com/Manual/class-TimeManager.html.

3. Save the script and return to the editor.

Now, we need to attach the new `PauseGame` method to the `PauseButton` event system, as follows:

1. Select the `PauseButton` game object from the **Hierarchy** window.
2. At the bottom of the **Inspector** window, click the plus (**+**) sign to add an event:

3. Next, drag `PauseContainer`, which contains our `PauseComponent` script, to the empty field (denoted as **1**). Then, click the **No Function** field and select `PauseComponent` from the drop-down (denoted as **2**).
4. Lastly, select the `PauseGame ()` public method (denoted as **3**).

The following image shows the marked out steps we have gone through in selecting the `PauseGame ()` method:

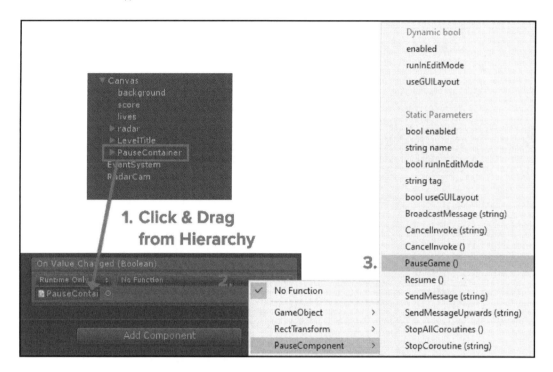

Now would be a good time to try and see if the pause screen appears when we press the pause button. Press **Play** in the Unity Editor and in the **Game** window, press the pause button in the top left corner when it appears. The pause screen will appear; we won't be able to escape from this until we code in the logic for our **Resume** and **Quit** buttons.

So far in this section, we have given the player the ability to pause the game. In the next section, we will make it so that the player will be able to resume or quit the game from the pause screen.

Resuming or quitting the game from the pause screen

In this subsection, we will continue to extend the `PauseComponent` script by adding two methods:

- `Resume`
- `Quit`

Let's make a start by adding the logic for the **Resume** button; follow these instructions:

1. If the `PauseComponent` script isn't open already, go to the **Project** window and locate the file at `Assets/Resources/Script`. Double-click the file open it.

    Inside the `PauseComponent` script, scroll to a point where we can add a new method – it doesn't matter where, as long as it's inside the `PauseComponent` class and not interfering with other methods.

2. Now, we are going to add a `Resume` method where the player wishes to close the pause screen, the game animation continues, and the pause button in the top-left corner reappears. To make all of this happen, add the following code:

    ```
    public void Resume()
    {
      pauseScreen.SetActive(false);
      SetPauseButtonActive(true);
      Time.timeScale = 1;
    }
    ```

    This code is similar to the code shown in the previous section, it's just in the opposite order (instead of the value being set to true, it's now false and vice versa to bring back the original settings).

3. Save the script and return to the Unity Editor.
4. In the Unity Editor, select the **RESUME** button from the active `PauseScreen` game object. Make sure the **Hierarchy** window also shows that **Resume** is selected.
5. At the bottom of the **Inspector** window, click and drag the `PauseContainer` game object from the **Hierarchy** window into the **None (Object) On Click ()** event system.

6. Select the **No Function** field and select `PauseComponent`, followed by **Resume ()**. The following screenshot shows the `On Click()` event system set up correctly for the `Resume` game object button:

Let's test the **Resume** button before moving on to the **Quit** button. Press **Play** in the Editor. Once the pause button appears in the top-left of the **Game** window, click it.

7. Finally, click the big **Resume** button. We will be brought back to the game playing out.

8. The last button to hook up in our pause screen is the **Quit** button. Reopen the `PauseComponent` script and add the following method to the script:

```
public void Quit()
{
    Time.timeScale = 1;
GameManager.Instance.GetComponent<ScoreManager>().ResetScore()
;
GameManager.Instance.GetComponent<ScenesManager>().BeginGame(0
);
    }
}
```

The code we've just entered resets the game; the `timescale` value goes back to `1`. We reset the player's score from `ScoreManager` directly and also directly told `ScenesManager` to take us back to scene zero, which is our `bootUp` scene.

9. Save the script before ending this section.

This is similar to the **Resume** button in regards to setting up an event to our script.

10. Select the **QUIT** button from the pause screen and make sure that, at the bottom of the **Inspector** window, you follow the same steps that you followed for the **Resume** button.

When we get to applying the **QUIT** button's function, change the field from **No Function** to the Quit method.

The following screenshot shows the Quit game object's button setup:

Before we wrap up this chapter, we need to ensure that the player and enemies behave how we expect them to when the game is paused.

Pausing player and enemies

So, we have reached the point where we can press our in-game pause button and watch our game freeze in time. To make sure the scene is saved, including new and edited scripts, let's test the pause screen:

1. Press **Play** in the Unity Editor.
2. When the pause button appears, press it.

The game pauses, but our enemies appear to float off. Also, when we press the fire button for the player, its player bullet light glows on the ship.

Let's fix the enemy floating first:

1. This is an easy fix – we need to change the update time for our EnemyWave script.
2. Stop playing. Then, in the **Project** window, navigate to Assets/Resources/Script and double-click the EnemyWave script.
3. Find the line that states the following:

   ```
   void Update()
   ```

4. Change this to the following:

   ```
   void FixedUpdate()
   ```

5. Save the EnemyWave script.

More information about `FixedUpdate` can be found here: `https://docs.unity3d.com/ScriptReference/MonoBehaviour.FixedUpdate.html`.

Now, let's reinforce the player's behavior so that all of its functionality is frozen when the game pauses. To freeze our player, we need to reopen its script:

1. In the **Project** settings window, navigate to the `Assets/Resources/Script` folder.
2. Double-click the `Player` script.
3. Scroll down to the `Update` function and wrap the player's `Movement` and `Attack` methods with the following `if` statement:

```
void Update ()
{
  if(Time.timeScale == 1)
  {
    Movement();
    Attack();
  }
}
```

The preceding code runs a check to see if the game's `timeScale` is running at full speed (1) and then carries on with the `Movement` and `Attack` methods.

4. Save the `Player` script.

Great! We now have the ability to pause our game, continue our game, or quit it. Don't worry about adding this pause screen to the rest of the levels as we will do this in the next chapter. Speaking of the next chapter, we will look at how we can change the **Music** and **Effects** sliders. For now, let's reflect on what we have covered in this chapter.

Summary

By completing this chapter, our game has improved even more and now has a pause screen, just as you would expect from any game. We also learned how to freeze time with the `timeScale` value. We did revisit some things we covered in previous chapters such as Event Listeners and UI positioning and scaling, but we also used other UI components such as toggles and sliders and modified them to suit our pause screen. Other things we covered included bringing in some MP3 music and making it so that the script knew when to fade in, out, and stop the volume.

In the next game you create outside of this book, you will know how and when to add background music to not just play when it's playing but how to attach your audio to a state machine. With state machines, you can make it possible for your music to be played, stopped, and faded out when particular moments occur, such as the game's screen being paused. Now, you will be able to take the UI components you've learned about in this chapter and create your own menu/pause screen. By doing this, you can run events to close or resume your game. You also know how to pause your game completely and/or slow time down with the `timeScale` function.

In the next chapter, we will be looking at Unity's Audio Mixer to control the volume of our player's bullets and music and hook it up to our pause screen volume sliders. We will also look into different types of data that need to be stored, such as our game remembering the volume settings so that we don't have to adjust the sliders every time we start our game.

I wish you the best of luck with your mini mock!

Mock test

1. If we want to keep a private variable visible in the **Inspector** window, which attributes should you put above the variable in your code?

   A) `[Header]`
   B) `[SerializeField]`
   C) `[AddComponentMenu]`
   D) `[Tooltip]`

2. You have created a pinball game for a mobile device; the game mechanics all work well but you also need to apply a pause screen. Obviously, when the player presses pause, the entire game should freeze. The way you are going to achieve this is by setting Unity's `timeScale` to zero.

   Which time property isn't affected when we set `Time.timeScale` to 0?

   A) `captureFramerate`
   B) `frameCount`
   C) `realtimeSinceStartup`
   D) `timeSinceLevelLoad`

3. In your `BuildSettings` window is a list of scenes. You know that the first scene is your title scene and that the rest that follow are your game's level scenes. Your game designer hasn't settled on the names of the scenes and keeps changing them. As a programmer, you can select the scenes to load by using what `SceneManager` method?

   A) `GetSceneByBuildIndex()`
   B) `GetActiveScene()`
   C) `SceneManager.GetSceneByName()`
   D) `SceneManager.GetSceneByPath()`

4. If you have a pause screen that can be enabled or disabled, which is the best UI component to switch between the two?

   A) `Toggle`
   B) `Button`
   C) `Slider`
   D) `Scroll Rect`

5. If you have a game object that holds an **Image** component and its child is a **Text** component, what property in `RectTransform` can you change that will affect the **Image** component but not the font of your **Text** component?

   A) Anchors Min and Max
   B) Width and Height
   C) Pos X and Pos Y
   D) Scale X and Y

6. You have created a UI button that displays an image of coins on it when you have money in your account and an image of an empty brown bag when your account is empty.

    What should the Transition field of the button be set to in the Unity Inspector to support these image changes?

    A) Color Tint
    B) None
    C) Animation
    D) Sprite Swap

7. While entering some UI details at the bottom of the screen to show your player's lives and what level they are on, you notice you need the text to be a specific size. You can change the text to any size you want, but you also need to accommodate the ratio of the screen.

    What's the best way of amending the font to make sure it doesn't appear squashed?

    A) Decrease Font Size
    B) Turn on Best Fit
    C) Set Vertical Overflow to Truncate
    D) Set Horizontal Overflow to Overflow

8. You have started working on a game that relies on time being stopped, rewound, and fast forward, but only for your enemies, with the use of the `Time.timeScale` functionality. Some of your enemies aren't being affected by the change of time.

    What property value could potentially cause this in the enemy's **Animator** component?

    A) Set Update Mode to Animate Physics
    B) Set Culling Mode to Cull Completely
    C) Set Culling Mode to Always Animate
    D) Set Update Mode to Unscaled Time

9. You have a selection of game objects that are tomato plants. Each tomato on the tomato plant has a script attached named `Tomato`.

    In order to avoid the tomato plants appearing repetitively, some of the artists have turned off the `tomato` game objects so they can't be seen.

At the start of the scene, we need to count how many tomatoes are in the scene, including the hidden ones.

Which command would get a reference to all `Tomato` scripts?

A) `GetComponentsInChildren(typeof(Tomato), true)`
B) `GetComponentInChildren(typeof(Tomato), true)`
C) `GetComponentsInChildren(typeof(Tomato))`
D) `GetComponenstInParent(typeof(Tomato), true)`

10. Which static `Time` class property would be used to freeze time?

A) `timeScale`
B) `maximumDeltaTime`
C) `captureFramerate`
D) `time`

11. Which of the following would be the most useful for labeling in a state machine?

A) Enum
B) String
C) Float
D) Int

12. Which of the following is related to triggering an event?

A) A particle effect is running
B) The player is idle on the menu screen for 20 minutes
C) The player presses a UI button
D) The player moves the mouse cursor

13. You have created a game where your player must sneak around and avoid the enemy. In one of the missions, your player has to listen out in the warehouse where the enemy is (listening for footsteps, talking, and so on).

What audio property would you add for this game?

A) Add an Audio Source component to each enemy, set its spatial blend to 3D, and play a sound.
B) Use an Audio Mixer Snapshot to add a low pass filter when enemies are nearby.
C) Measure the distance between each enemy and the player and play a sound if the distance drops below a certain threshold.

D) Add an Audio Source that plays music in the background and increase or decrease its volume based on the distance of the closest enemy.

14. Within your **Audio Source** component, which property will make the sound go from 3D to 2D?

    A) `CustomRolloff`
    B) `SpatialBlend`
    C) `ReverbZoneMix`
    D) `Spread`

15. You have started adding music and sound effects to your game. When testing, you notice that the background music cuts out when some sound effects are played.

    Which property in the **Audio Source** component will fix this so that your music doesn't cut out?

    A) Increase Priority
    B) Increase Volume
    C) Increase MinDistance
    D) Decrease SpatialBlend

16. You have been asked to make a UI menu screen. You have made a **Canvas** and set its **Render Mode** to **Screen Space - Overlay**.

    In the **Canvas Scaler** component, which property in UI Scale Mode will make UI elements retain the same size in pixels, regardless of screen size?

    A) **Constant Pixel Size**
    B) **Scale with Screen Size**
    C) **Constant Physical Size**
    D) **Disable Canvas Scaler**

17. When ticking the Preserve Aspect checkbox in an **Image** component, what does this do?

    A) Sets the aspect of the camera to match the perspective of the image.

    B) Makes the image match the same aspect ratio as the cameras'.

    C) The image retains its original dimension.

    D) Has no effect on **Image** components, only Sprite Renderers.

18. Can a Sprite Renderer be used instead of an **Image** component within the **Canvas**?

    A) No. Even though a Sprite Renderer can work in 2D/3D spaces, it's not intended to be used with the **Canvas** and therefore will not work.

    B) Yes, but Sprite Renderer has fewer features and is an older version of the **Image** component.

    C) Depending on the Unity project, if your scene is in 2D mode, yes.

    D) Yes, when being used to animate sprite sheets.

19. What does the **Graphic** property do in the **Toggle** component by default?

    A) Holds the graphic for the **Toggle** component.

    B) Turns the `Toggle` button on or off.

    C) Makes the graphic active or inactive when the player presses it during runtime.

    D) Holds the **CheckMark** image.

20. What does **Interactable** do when disabled on the **Toggle** component?

    A) Hides the game object.

    B) It changes the color of the Toggle and has no effect when pressed.

    C) Disables the Toggle from working at runtime.

    D) Destroys the Toggle's `parent` game object.

11
Storing Data and Audio Mixer

In this chapter, we will be looking at common ways of storing, sending, and monitoring data for our game. This will also involve us making use of Unity's ready-made Audio Mixer for us to store the player's volume settings for the game.

As you may recall, in the previous chapter, we had begun making our own pause screen from scratch. We will be carrying on with this in this chapter. We still need to work on the music and sound effects slider on the pause screen. We will hold all Audio Source controls for each sound to be played in the Audio Mixer. The Audio Mixer will act as a central point for all sound and can also be manipulated via scripting, which we will also be doing in this chapter. If our game had more sound effects and more music, an Audio Mixer controlling the game's sound from one place would help us avoid not getting tangled up with all the different audio source components attached to game objects.

We will be making use of storing the volume settings with Unity's own PlayerPrefs, which stores data locally on the platform playing the game. This is also known as persistent data because we can turn off the machine that holds the volume information and when the machine is turned back on, the data remains on the system. We will also be making use of JSON, which acts the same as PlayerPrefs but can also offer more functionality and security (data on a device could contain sensitive information such as passwords, credit card details, and so on) for storing and sending data. This can be beneficial for converting objects (our script content) into data (computer memory) and sending vast amounts of information to databases online.

At the start of this chapter, we also mentioned monitoring data. In this chapter, we will be looking at two online services that Unity offers via online browser dashboard. The first is Unity Analytics, which offers a series of events that can be spliced into the code of a game to measure activity from a released game. This can be useful to see how successful a game is with its consumers (how many players, how far into the game do they get, and plenty more events). The other online service Unity offers is Remote Settings, which acts similarly to PlayerPrefs in terms of storing and setting data, not just for volume controls but anything that involves data in general. The difference between PlayerPrefs and Remote Settings is that the values we can change via Remote Settings will be made on the server-side. You can imagine how powerful this would be if we wanted to make a game easier/harder by changing values online instead of rolling out updates to our consumers. In this chapter, we will make it so that if we play our game with an internet connection, we will be rewarded with an extra life.

In this chapter, we will be covering the following topics:

- Using the Audio Mixer
- Storing data
- Exploring Unity Analytics and Remote Settings

Let's get started!

Core exam skills covered in this chapter

The following are the core exam skills that will be covered in this chapter:

- *Programming core interactions:*
    - *Implement and configure game object behavior and physics.*
- *Developing application systems:*
    - *Interpret scripts for application interface flow such as menu systems, UI navigation, and application settings.*
    - *Analyze scripts for user progression features such as scoring, leveling, and in-game economies utilizing technologies such as Unity Analytics and* `PlayerPrefs`.
    - *Identify scripts for saving and retrieving application and user data.*

- *Programming for scene and environment design:*
    - *Determine scripts for implementing audio assets.*
- *Working in professional software development teams:*
    - *Recognize techniques for structuring scripts for modularity, readability, and reusability.*

Technical requirements

The project content for this chapter can be found at `https://github.com/PacktPublishing/Unity-Certified-Programmer-Exam-Guide/tree/master/Chapter11`.

You can download the entirety of each chapter's project files at `https://github.com/PacktPublishing/Unity-Certified-Programmer-Exam-Guide/archive/master.zip`.

All this chapter's downloads can be found in the `Complete` folder. You will need to create your own `Packt` folder to hold all the downloadable content that will be provided in this chapter.

Check out the following video to see the Code in Action: `https://bit.ly/381EUK5`.

Using the Audio Mixer

As the game grows, it's useful to have a mixer channel that focuses on all the allocated volume levels and sound effects. Otherwise, if not for a separate mixer channel, we would be clicking on various game objects and adjusting each of their components in the **Inspector** window.

For our game, we are going to keep this simple and create three **Audio Groups** with no added effects. Let's take a look at what each Audio Group will focus on:

1. **Master Audio Group**: Controls the master for the entire game
2. **Music Audio Group**: Controls the music of each level
3. **Effects Audio Group**: Controls the sound effects of the bullets firing from our player's ship

The following screenshot shows **Audio Mixer** and the setup for the three Audio Groups:

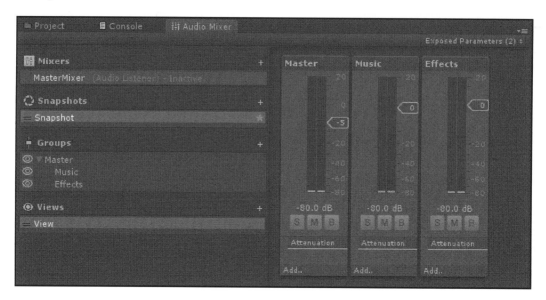

If you would like to know more about the layout of **Audio Mixer**, check out the documentation at: `https://docs.unity3d.com/ Manual/AudioMixerOverview.html`.

Let's now start by creating the **Audio Mixer** within the Unity Editor, by following these steps:

1. In the **Project** window, go to `Assets/Resources/Sound` and right-click on an open space within the folder.
2. From the drop-down menu, select **Create**, followed by **Audio Mixer**. The following screenshot shows the selection being made:

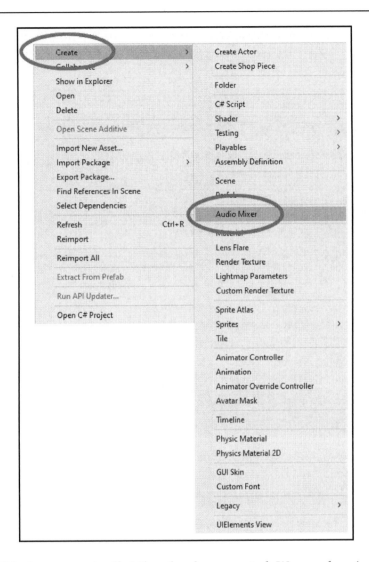

3. With that, a new **AudioMixer** has been created. We are also given the opportunity to rename this file, so let's rename it `MasterMixer`.

Before we hook up the mixer to the `LevelMusic` and `Player_Bullet` game objects (because these are the two game objects making the sounds), we need to go into the **Audio Mixer** and create **Music** and **Effects** mixers first (we only have the master Audio Group on its own at the moment).

Let's have a closer look at our **Audio Mixer**. To view the **Audio Mixer** with our MasterMixer, double-click the MasterMixer file in the **Project** window. We will be presented with the following screen:

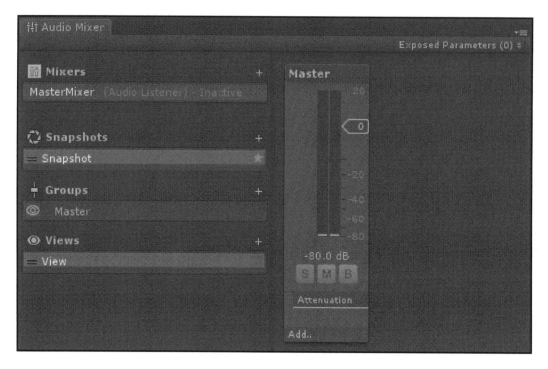

The previous screenshot shows our setup for the **Audio Mixer**. It consists of four categories:

- **Mixers** (top left): In this category, we only have one Audio Group and that's MasterMixer.
- **Snapshots**: Consider this a save state for our mixer. We can have multiple snapshots, such as a physical Hi-Fi where we can select different saved presets (Rock, Disco, Classical, and so on). Snapshots are used in the same way as presets; it saves us time so that we don't always have to adjust the mixer settings.

- **Group**: Within our `MasterMixer` will be our two groups – one for **Music** and the other for **Effects**. We will create these soon.
- **Views**: Used to save different Audio Mixer UI layouts.

Don't worry too much about the details as we are going to focus mainly on **groups**. There is more we can do with Audio Mixers. Check the official Unity documentation here to find out more at `https://docs.unity3d.com/2017.4/Documentation/Manual/AudioMixer.html`.

To add two extra volume mixers next to our **Master**, we need to do the following:

1. Right-click **Master** under the **Groups** section and select **Add child group**. We will gain a new mixer, as shown in the following screenshot:

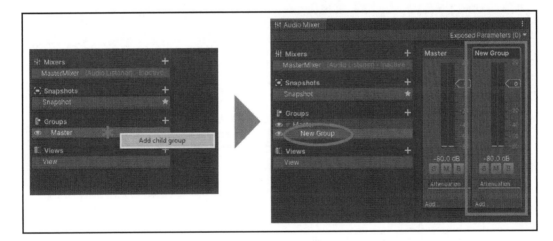

2. Right-click **New Group** (circled in the previous screenshot) and select **Rename** from the drop-down menu.
3. Rename `New Group` to `Music`.
4. Repeat *steps 1-3* to create another Audio Group and rename it `Effects`.

The following screenshot shows what the **Audio Mixer** window will look like now, with all three ASVs:

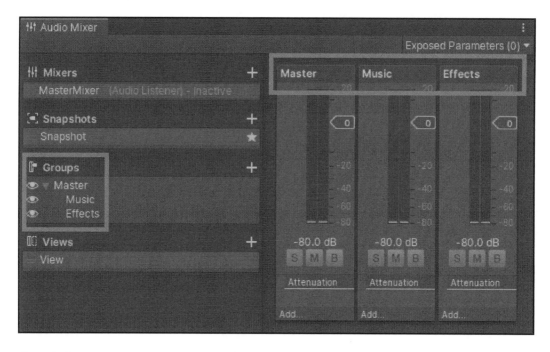

Great! Now, we can move on to hooking these audio groups to the game objects we want to affect. The first one is our LevelMusic game object, which is a child of the GameManager game object.

To update our LevelMusic game object's **Audio Source** component, do the following:

1. Load up the bootUp scene from the Unity Editor.
2. In the **Hierarchy** window, expand the GameManager game object and select the LevelMusic game object.
3. Back in the **Project** window, click the arrow to the left of **MasterMixer** to expand its content.
4. Click the **Music** child group and drag it into the **Output** field of LevelMusic's **Audio Source**, as shown in the following image:

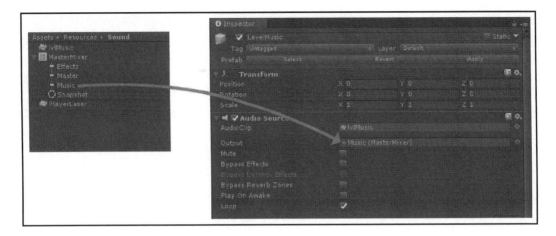

5. Click **Apply** in the **Inspector** window to update the GameManager's prefab settings.

Now, we need to do something similar for our `player_bullet` prefab. To update it's **Audio Source** with the **Effects** mixer, do the following:

1. In the **Project** window, go to the `Assets/Resources/Prefab/Player` folder. There, you should find our `player_bullet` game object.

2. Select `player_bullet` (denoted as **1** in the following screenshot) and drag and drop the **Effects** group from **MasterMixer** (denoted as **2**) into `player_bullet` for **Audio Source Output** (denoted as **3**).

   The following screenshot shows what the `player_bullet` game object's **Audio Source** should look like in the **Inspector** window:

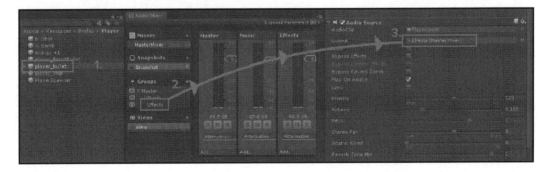

Now, the Audio Mixer is nearly ready to be connected to our pause screen's **Music** and **Effects** sliders. We need to do one more thing before we move on to the next section, and that is make the audio group's volume accessible so we can make it communicate with the pause screen's audio sliders. To ~~do~~ this, we need to set our Audio Mixer's Attenuation Volume property to open or **expose** it to our scripts.

To expose and name our audio groups, we need to do the following:

1. In the **Project** window, go to **MasterMixer** and expand its content so that we can see its groups.
2. Select the **Music** group.
3. In the **Inspector** window, we are presented with the **Music** group's properties. We want to expose **Volume** so that we can alter it with our script.
4. Right-click **Volume** (just under **Attenuation**) and select **Expose 'Volume (of Music)' to script**, as shown in the following screenshot:

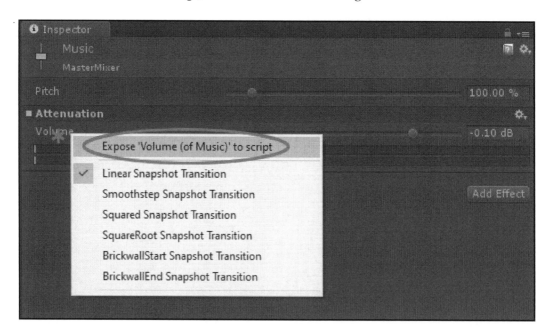

Now, we also have the option to give the exposed volume a reference name instead of its default name of `MyExposedParam`.

To change the reference of the exposed **Music Volume**, do the following:

1. Back in the **Project** window, double-click the `MasterMixer` file.
2. As you may have noticed, in the top-right corner of **Audio Mixer**, we are notified that we have **Exposed Parameters(1)** (denoted by **1** in the following screenshot). The **1** is the **Music Volume** that we just exposed.
3. Click **Exposed Parameters(1)** (denoted by **1**).
4. Right-click the **MyExposedParam Volume (of Music)** (denoted by **2**).
5. Select **Rename** from the drop-down menu (denoted by **3**).
6. In the parameter that appears, rename it `musicVol` (denoted by **4**).

The following image shows the stages we just spoke about in the preceding steps:

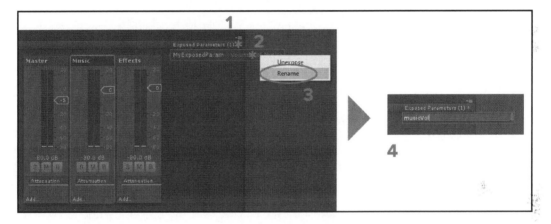

I hope you understood this process well, because I want you to do it again but with the **Effects** group. Also, when it comes to naming the **Effects** reference in the last step that we just discussed, rename it `effectsVol`.

Finally, we will have our exposed volume references named like so in our **Audio Mixer**:

Nice work! Before we move on to the next section, let's briefly recap what we have covered so far in this section:

- We introduced the Audio Mixer and its benefits.
- We created Audio Groups for our Mixer.
- We attached the Audio Mixer to our game object's Audio Source.
- We exposed the Audio Mixer to our scripts.

In the next section, we are going to code our pause screen's **Volume** and **Effects** sliders.

Attaching Audio Mixer to UI sliders

In this section, we are going to write two methods (`SetMusicLevelFromSlider` and `SetEffectsLevelFromSlider`) that attach our pause screen's **Music** and **Effects** sliders to the Audio Mixer that we created in the previous section.

Let's start by adding the **Music** slider to our Audio Mixer via the script, as follows:

1. In the **Project** window, go to the `PauseComponent` script, which should be located in `Assets/Resources/Script`, and open it.

   Because we are going to access the Audio Mixer, we need an extra Unity library to let this happen.

2. At the top of our `PauseComponent` script, add the following line of code:

   ```
   using UnityEngine.Audio;
   ```

3. Now, add a global variable that will store a reference for our **Audio Mixer**:

   ```
   [SerializeField]
   AudioMixer masterMixer;
   ```

4. We also need to add two more global variables for the **Music** and **Effects** sliders. Add these below the `masterMixer` variable, as follows:

   ```
   [SerializeField]
   GameObject musicSlider;
   [SerializeField]
   GameObject effectsSlider;
   ```

5. Save the script and return to the Unity Editor.
6. Load up the `level1` scene where we started creating our pause screen.
7. Select the `PauseContainer` game object from the **Hierarchy** window.
8. In the **Inspector** window, we will now have three empty parameters in `PauseComponent`. Here, we can drag the two sliders from the **Hierarchy** window and our **MasterMixer** from the **Project** window, as shown in the following screenshot:

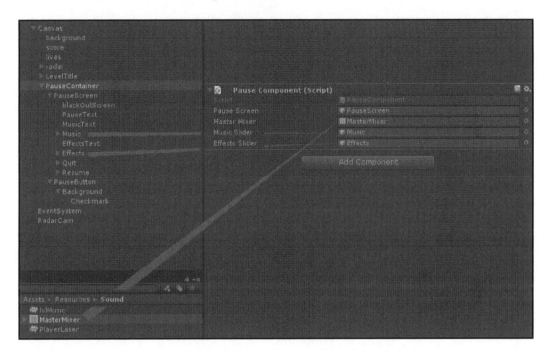

Now that our three global references (music slider, effects slider, and master mixer) are hooked up to their parameters, we can return to our `PauseComponent` script and code in a method for each of the pause screen's volume sliders.

To add functionality so that our **Music** slider controls the **Music** mixer, do the following:

1. In the `PauseComponent` script, add a `public` method within the `PauseComponent` class:

```
public void SetMusicLevelFromSlider()
{
masterMixer.SetFloat("musicVol",musicSlider.GetComponent<Slide
r>
        ().value);
}
```

The `public` method we have just entered, `SetMusicLevelFromSlider`, will work as an event from the **Music** slider. Inside the method, we have a reference to our `masterMixer`. Within this variable, we call its `SetFloat` function, which takes two parameters. The first is the reference name of the mixer (we called this `musicVol` earlier in this chapter), while the second is what value it is receiving to be changed. We are sending the value from our pause screen's **Music** slider.

2. Save the script and return to the Unity Editor.

Next, we need to attach our **Music** slider's event to the `SetMusicLevelFromSlider` method. To make the **Music** slider communicate with the method, follow these steps:

1. Still in our `level1` scene, in the **Hierarchy** window, select the `Music` game object.
2. In the **Inspector** window, click the **+** button at the bottom of the **Inspector** window to allow an event to be attached to the **Slider** component (denoted by **1** in the following image).
3. Drag the `PauseContainer` game object from the **Hierarchy** window to the **None (Object)** parameter (denoted by **2**).
4. Click the **No Function** drop-down menu and select the method we just coded in `SetMusicLevelFromSlider` (denoted by **3**).

The following image references the previous instructions for the `Music` game object in the **Inspector** window:

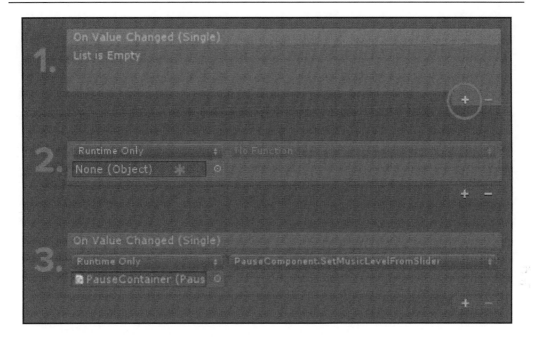

If we press **Play** on the Unity Editor and then, in the **Game** window, press the game's pause button when it appears, we will be able to turn the music up and down with the **Music** slider.

Now, we need to repeat this in a similar fashion for our **Effects** slider volume to work:

1. Return to the `PauseComponent` script and enter the following method:

   ```
   public void SetEffectsLevelFromSlider()
   {
   masterMixer.SetFloat("effectsVol",effectsSlider.GetComponent
        <Slider>().value);
   }
   ```

   As we can see, the code is virtually the same as the code for `SetMusicLevelFromSlider`, apart from the variable names.

2. Save the script.

3. Return to the Unity Editor and repeat the same procedure for dragging the `PauseComponent` game object but this time with the `Effects` game object and selecting `SetEffectsLevelFromSlider`, as shown in the following screenshot:

Finally, test to see if the **Effects** slider works when we run the game.

This will obviously only work in `level1` as `level2` and `level3` don't have the extra game objects. In the next chapter, we will be making a new `level3`, so if you can hold on until then, it'll save going through the process of removing and adding scenes again.

In this section, we covered the following functionality for the `PauseComponent` script:

- Ensuring it recognizes Audio Mixer
- Ensuring that the **Music** and **Effects** UI sliders alter Audio Groups

In the next section, we are going to start looking at how to store our data. We will use the pause screen one more time to show the benefit of our game remembering our volume settings.

Storing data

In this section, we are going to cover how we are going to store our data, such as the game's volume settings so that when we play our game, we don't have to keep setting the volume settings to where they were before. We want the game to remember them for us.

There are multiple ways we can store data. The ones we are going to cover are the two most common choices for Unity development. They are as follows:

- **PlayerPrefs**: This is short for **Player Preferences**. We can use this to store strings, floats, and integers on the device we are playing our game on. We will be using `PlayerPrefs` shortly to save our volume settings so that when we turn our game off and back on, it will remember our settings. `PlayerPrefs` is easily accessible from outside the game with a text file reader. When it comes to development, make sure you don't use `PlayerPrefs` to store sensitive information such as credit card details or things that would give a player an unfair advantage such as storing lives, energy, score, in-game credit, and so on. For more information about `PlayerPrefs`, check Unity's description at `https://docs.unity3d.com/2017.4/Documentation/ScriptReference/PlayerPrefs.html`.

- **JSON**: This is short for **JavaScript Object Notation** and is typically used when sending and receiving data from our device to another application or even from a server online somewhere in the cloud. One of the benefits of JSON over `PlayerPrefs` is that it uses data types such as `int`, `float`, and `string`, just like `PlayerPrefs`, but also `object` (our classes act as blueprints so that we can make objects), `array`, `bool`, and `null`.

It's wise to use this form of **application programming interface** (**API**) for transferring game data (lives, levels, player progress, energy, and so on), but don't store highly personal details locally with regards to in-game credit, bank details, personal addresses, and emails, unless you are using some form of encryption.

 An API basically tells us how applications communicate with each other.

For more information about JSON with Unity, check the documentation at `https://docs.unity3d.com/2017.4/Documentation/Manual/JSONSerialization.html`.

In the following sections, we are going to cover these two ways of storing data on the basis they are officially covered by Unity and are likely to be mentioned in your exam:

- PlayerPrefs and volume settings
- JSON and storing game stats
- Adding JSON variables

Let's make a start by looking at how to use `PlayerPrefs` and revisit our pause screen one last time.

PlayerPrefs and volume settings

As we know, our game has volume controls for its music and sound effects on the pause screen. To make our game remember these volume settings, even when the game has been turned off and back on again, we need to do the following:

1. In the **Project** window of the Unity Editor, go to `Assets/Resources/Script`.
2. Double-click the `PauseComponent` script.
3. Scroll down to the `SetMusicLevelFromSlider` method and add the following extra line of code at the bottom but within the method's scope. The following code shows what the method now looks like with the added code:

```
public void SetMusicLevelFromSlider()
{
  masterMixer.SetFloat("musicVol",musicSlider.GetComponent
    <Slider>().value);
PlayerPrefs.SetFloat("musicVolume",musicSlider.GetComponent
    <Slider>().value;    // << NEW CODE LINE
}
```

In the preceding code, we used the `value` from our music `<Slider>` component and applied its `float` value to the `PlayerPrefs` `float` with `musicVolume` as our key (the reference name to identify the `PlayerPrefs` value).

4. Do the same for the `effects` method:

```
public void SetEffectsLevelFromSlider()
{
masterMixer.SetFloat("effectsVol",effectsSlider.GetComponent
    <Slider>().value);
PlayerPrefs.SetFloat("effectsVolume",effectsSlider.GetComponen
t
    <Slider>().value;  // << NEW CODE LINE
}
```

That's our `PlayerPrefs` file ready to store the music and effects volume. The next thing to do is reapply the music/effects volume the next time we load the level from our `PlayerPrefs`.

To grab the music volume setting from our `PlayerPrefs`, do the following:

1. Reopen the `PauseComponent` script.
2. Within the `PauseComponent` class, enter the following code at the bottom of the `Awake` function:

```
masterMixer.SetFloat("musicVol",PlayerPrefs.GetFloat("musicVol
ume"));
masterMixer.SetFloat("effectsVol",PlayerPrefs.GetFloat("effect
sVolum e"));
```

In the preceding code, we are reapplying our saved `PlayerPrefs` values for our music and effects volume (which are both floats) to our Audio Mixer's Audio Groups.

The volumes that we want the mixers to have are now set. The last thing we need to do is to set both volume sliders to their UI positions.

3. To update the **Music** and **Effects** sliders visually, we need to add the following code within our `PauseComponent`:

```
float GetMusicLevelFromMixer()
{
  float musicMixersValue;
  bool result = masterMixer.GetFloat("musicVol",
    out musicMixersValue);
  if (result)
  {
    return musicMixersValue;
  }
  else
  {
    return 0;
  }
}
```

The preceding code is a method that returns a `float` value called `GetMusicLevelFromMixer`.

Let's go through the steps of this `GetMusicLevelFromMixer`:

- In this method, we create a `float` variable called `musicMixersValue`.
- The line after `musicMixersValue` checks to see whether the `masterMixer` instance contains an Audio Group called `musicVol`. We know it does because we set it earlier when we exposed each of the volume settings from the **Audio Mixer**, as shown in the following screenshot:

- So, if `masterMixer` does contain a `float` value with the name (key) of `musicVol`, we will store it in a `float` named `musicMixersValue`.
- `masterMixer.GetFloat` will send a `true` or `false` value if `masterMixer` does or does not contain a `float` that is also stored in a `bool` value, respectively.

- If the `bool` value is `true`, the `float` value from `masterMixer` is returned from the method; otherwise, it will return `0`.

Next, we need to call this `GetMusicLevelFromMixer` and make it so it sends its value to the music slider. Let's code this in now.

4. Within the `PauseComponent` script, at the top, in the `Awake` function, add the following code below the two `masterMixer` coded lines:

```
musicSlider.GetComponent<Slider>().value =
GetMusicLevelFromMixer();
```

In the preceding piece of code, we are sending the result from our `GetMusicLevelFromMixer` to the value of our `musicSlider` when the level starts.

That's our music slider set. Now, we need to repeat this process for our effects slider. The process is the same, apart from using the effect slider's variables, so without repeating the same process, I want you to do the following:

1. Create a `GetEffectsLevelFromMixer` method using the same code pattern as `GetMusicLevelFromMixer` but using `effectsVol` instead of `musicVol`.

2. Assign the results of `GetEffectsLevelFromMixer` to the `effectsSlider` variable in the `Awake` function. Use the `musicSlider` variable for reference.

Give it a go – if you're struggling, check out the `Complete` folder in this book's GitHub repository.

Save the script and return to the Unity Editor. Play the first level, change the volume, quit the game, and return to the first level to see if our volume has been saved for the music and effects sliders.

Now, we will move on and learn how to store and send data in a slightly different away.

JSON and storing game stats

JSON is great for creating, storing, and updating information across our game. As we mentioned earlier in this chapter, JSON is typically used for sending data from our game to a server online where the JSON data can be delivered to another set of data.

The best way JSON was explained to me is with an analogy of me being at a restaurant, sitting at a table (my game); the waiter (JSON) comes over and takes my order, then sends it to the kitchen (the online server). Finally, the waiter returns with my food.

With regards to coding JSON, we are storing variables into a single class, then serializing the class (object) into data (system memory or file). From there, we can transfer this data to an actual file or upload it to a server on a database. This whole process can also be reversed, where we take the data and return it as an object. This is called deserializing.

Now, let's move on to coding some JSON values.

Adding JSON variables

The objective of working with JSON is to create a simple way of storing and updating data with JSON. In our project, we will provide a simple example of storing statistical data for our game. When the player completes the game, we will store data and put it in JSON format.

The three variables we are going to store are as follows:

- livesLeft: How many lives the player has left
- completed: When the player has completed the game
- score: Stores the player's score

Let's make a start by creating a new script that will receive our game's three statistical updates. These will then be converted into JSON format. Follow these steps:

1. Create a new script (if you don't know how to do that, revisit the *Updating our camera properties via script* section in Chapter 2, *Adding and Manipulating Objects*).
2. Call the new script GameStats.
3. Before we open the GameStats script, I recommend that you keep your files stored in the Assets/Resources/Script folder location.
4. Next, we can open the GameStats script and code in the following variables:

```
public class GameStats
{
    public int livesLeft;
    public string completed;
    public int score;
}
```

Notice how the GameStats script doesn't require a library or need to inherit MonoBehaviour. We don't require either of these extra functionalities.

> When the player completes the game, we will take these three readings and store them in JSON format. From there, we can convert this data into a JSON file. This process is known as **serialization**.

Serialization/Deserialization:

These two terms are basically referring to the direction that data is stored in.

Serialization: This refers to converting an object from our script and turning it into bytes (a file, in our case).

Deserialization: As you can probably imagine, deserialization is the opposite of serialization. This means we are taking our raw data (file) and converting it into objects.

5. Save the script.

Next, we need to write some code that will update the player's lives, time and date, and score. We are going to do this when we play through the game and complete level 3. In this case, we need to go to our `ScenesManager` and update the code.

To update our `ScenesManager` so that it takes a reading of our player's stats and converts them into JSON format, we need to do the following:

1. In the Unity Editor, go to where our `ScenesManager` script is. This should be in the `Assets/Resources/Script/ScenesManager.cs` file.
2. Double-click the file to open it in our IDE and scroll down to the point where we check to see if the game has ended. This is located in the `GameTimer` method.

The following screenshot shows where in the `ScenesManager` script we need to add our new method:

```
//if level is completed
StartCoroutine(MusicVolume(MusicMode.fadeDown));
if (!gameEnding)
{
    gameEnding = true;
    GameObject.FindGameObjectWithTag("Player").GetComponent<PlayerTransition>().LevelEnds = true;
}
else
{
    GameObject.FindGameObjectWithTag("Player").GetComponent<PlayerTransition>().GameCompleted = true;
}

    Invoke("NextLevel", 4);
    }
}
break;
```

In the preceding screenshot, there is a star (*) marking where we are going to enter the name of our new method, along with a `string` parameter, which will be the name of the level we have completed.

3. Enter the following method name, where the * is in the previous screenshot:

```
SendInJsonFormat(SceneManager.GetActiveScene().name);
```

4. Next, we need to create the `SendInJsonFormat` method. Scroll down to a point in the `ScenesManager` script where we are still inside its class but not another method and enter the following:

```
void SendInJsonFormat(string lastLevel)
{
  if (lastLevel == "level3")
    {
      GameStats gameStats = new GameStats();

      gameStats.livesLeft = GameManager.playerLives;
      gameStats.completed = System.DateTime.Now.ToString();
      gameStats.score = ScoreManager.playerScore;
      string json = JsonUtility.ToJson(gameStats,true);
      Debug.Log(json);
    }
}
```

In the previous code, we go through a series of steps:

- We have our `SendInJsonFormat` method, which takes a `string` parameter.
- Inside the `SendInJsonFormat` method, we set an `if` statement that checks if the `lastLevel` string contains the `level3` value.

If `lastLevel` is equal to the `level3` string, we go through the following steps inside the `if` statement:

1. We create an instance of the `GameStats` class we made earlier in this chapter.
2. We access its `livesLeft` public variable and apply the static `playerLives` variable from the `GameManager` class.
3. The next variable shows the date and time we completed the game at. We send the command from the `System` library, which gives us the date and time, and we cast this as a `string` (`ToString()`). We send this result to the `gameStats` instance into the `string` variable.
4. The last variable we send data is the player's score. We get this from the `playerScore static` variable from our `ScoreManager` class.

Now that we have applied the three variables to our `gameStats` instance, we can use Unity's `JsonUtility` class to send our `gameStats` into the `ToJson` function.

We can also make the JSON data readable by adding `true` to the parameter so that when we send a `logout` command to the console to see that this has worked correctly, we can read the results.

5. Save the script and jump back into the Unity Editor and complete the game from the `bootUp` scene to the `gameOver` scene.

The following screenshot shows the console log when I played through the game and completed level 3:

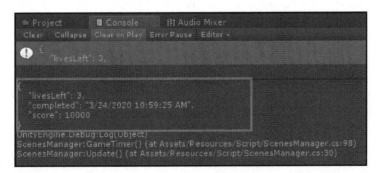

As you can see, we have the data from our script but displayed in JSON format.

This information can be saved to a physical file or can be sent to a server to keep a record of our player's gameplay, or/and deserialize the results later on with our project (check out the following tip if you are interested in this). The point is that we are storing and carrying data that can be sent away for us or another system to pick up, store, and alter.

> At this point, we have successfully taken the variables from our class (object) and converted them into JSON data format (serialization).

> Now, imagine if we altered our data (changed its values) and wanted to bring that data back into our game's code and into a class. The reverse method would be `GameStats loadJsonData = JsonUtility.FromJson<GameStats>(json);`.

> This would update our `GameStats` variables from the JSON file. You can imagine that this would be handy for saving and loading data in games.

Next, we will take the most current JSON data file and send it to the device (the machine we play the game on). To make and store a JSON file containing our custom-made stats, do the following:

1. Return to the `ScenesManager` script.
2. Scroll to where we created the `SendInJsonFormat` method.
3. Within the method's `if` statement, at the bottom, inside the scope of the `if` statement, add the following two lines of code:

```
Debug.Log(Application.persistentDataPath +
"/GameStatsSaved.json");
System.IO.File.WriteAllText(Application.persistentDataPath +
   "/GameStatsSaved.json",json);
```

The preceding code block shows that we don't necessarily need to add `Debug.Log` and shows us where the next line of code is creating and storing our JSON file. Each platform will store data in different folders. For more information on the locations for different platforms, please refer to Unity's own documentation about persistent data at `https://docs.unity3d.com/ScriptReference/Application-persistentDataPath.html`.

My system is a Windows PC, so `Debug.Log` will display the following location on my system:

The second line of the code we just entered is using a system library and uses a function (`Application.persistentDataPath`) that will refer to our device's local storage. Then, after the function, we add the name we want to use to refer to our JSON file (`/GameStatsSaved.json`), along with the format type, which is `json`.

4. Save the script.
5. Return to the Unity Editor, play all the way to the end of the game, and go to the location that is displayed on the console screen. The following screenshot shows the location of the file that our game has made:

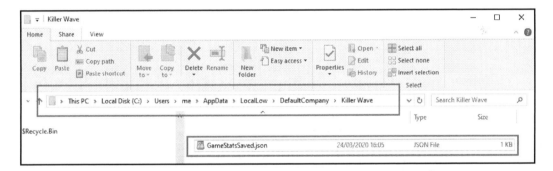

6. Double-click the file to view its content. As you will see, this is where our game's stats are kept, as shown in the following screenshot:

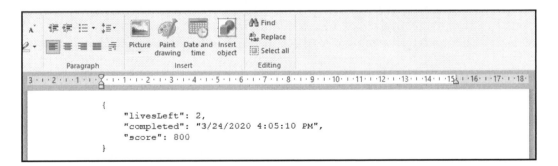

With this, we are now aware of how to store non-sensitive data such as our game's volume (`PlayerPrefs`), as well as how to create, store, and send other types of data in JSON format.

In the next section, we will look into Unity Analytics so that we can look at Analytic Events, which will display statistics about our game. We will also be trying Unity's Remote Settings, which acts in a similar way to `PlayerPrefs` in terms of storing the same type of data but in Unity's server online instead of the player's device. These tools give us, as developers, an advantage in terms of how well our game is received and how we can tweak our game from the cloud.

Exploring Unity Analytics and Remote Settings

In the ever-growing Unity Dashboard, we are going to take another look at the analytical system (we last visited the *Analytics Dashboard* in `Chapter 6`, *Purchasing In-Game Items and Advertisement*, where we made it possible for players to view adverts and gain credits to purchase items). This time, we will be looking into two main things:

- **Analytic Events**: This gives developers the ability to see what players are doing in their game (not in a **Big Brother** sense but in a statistical way). As soon as we turn on Unity's Analytics, this will give Unity the green flag to take readings regarding how many times our game has been installed, how many people are playing our game now, and how long people have been playing our game for. These **Core Events** will collect all international data and store the results in our Unity account online for you to view in a series of graphs. We can add other analytical events to our game that will specifically pinpoint particular phases in our game that we can inject into our code. We will look at these events in more detail later in this chapter.

- **Remote Settings**: Apart from monitoring the results, we can also manipulate our game from our Unity account online. For example, we could change an integer on our remote settings value that would change the number of enemies that spawn from a certain point, change the speed of the game, or even the color of the title of our screen. We wouldn't need to create another build of the game as we will be changing all the results online when our game automatically connects to the server.

It's worth mentioning that, as it stands, Unity's Analytics and Remote Settings are supported by the following platforms:

- iOS
- Android

- Tizen
- Universal Windows Platform
- Mac, PC, and Linux standalone
- WebGL 5.3 integration and onward

With all this said, let's now move on and go into the specifics of the four major event types Unity covers.

Analytic events

In this section, we are going to briefly cover the primary events Unity has to offer. For the exam, it's likely you will be asked general questions about specific problems in terms of how a developer records or sends data with Unity's event system.

Here are the names of Unity's analytical events:

- Core Events
- Standard Events
- Custom Events
- Transaction Events

Let's break them down one by one so that if you do want to know more, you at least know where to start.

Core Events

As soon as we turn on Analytics in the Unity Editor, we will also be turning on Core Events. From there on, the Unity Analytics Dashboard will collect and eventually display the following data:

- New installs
- **Daily active users (DAU)**
- **Monthly active users (MAU)**
- Total sessions
- Sessions per user
- Time spent in-app
- User segments for country and platform

When this event is active, we will receive information such as how many people have installed our game, how many are actively playing our game on a daily basis, how long a player has been playing our game, and more. All of this information is given to us on the dashboard. But first, we need to turn Unity's Analytics on.

In the Unity Editor, load up the **Services** panel by clicking **Window** at the top, followed by **Services**:

1. Make sure **Services** is selected.
2. Turn **On** Analytics.
3. Then, press **Play** on the Unity Editor, then **Play** again. This will send data to Analytics to wake it up on the Unity Dashboard.

The following screenshot shows **Analytics** being turned on and activated:

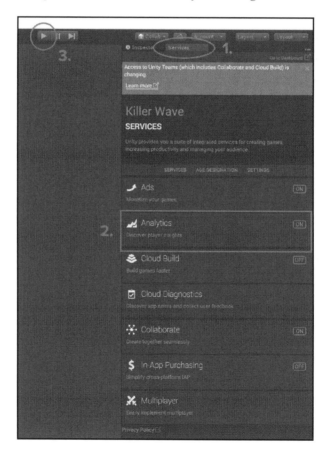

After some time has passed (a day), you can check to see if your Core Event results are coming through. To check these results, do the following:

1. In the Unity Editor, select **Account** in the top-right corner, followed by **Go to account...**. Your default internet browser will load up your Unity account.
2. Click the **Dashboards** link.
3. Now, you'll be provided with your game's Core Events:

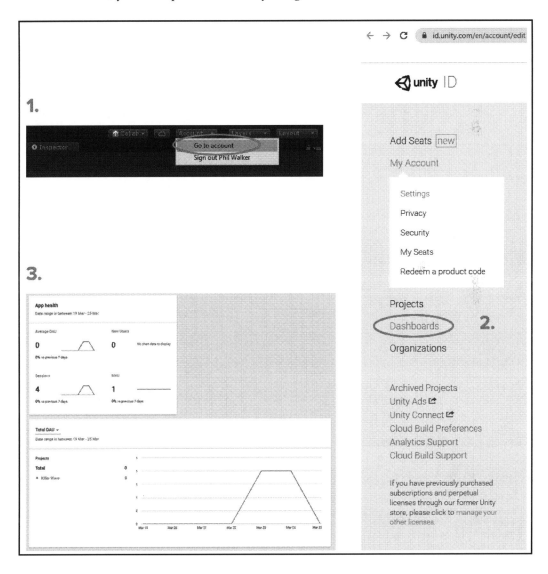

If you would like to know even more about Core Events, check the official Unity documentation here: https://docs.unity3d.com/ 2017.3/Documentation/Manual/UnityAnalyticsCoreEvents.html

Now, let's move on to Standard Events.

Standard Events

Standard Events holds five groups of events. Inside each of these groups are common events that a majority of games will likely run checks on. We will briefly discuss each group; here are their names:

- Application events
- Progression events
- Onboarding events
- Engagement events
- Monetization events

Let's go through each of these events and then provide an overview of these events as a whole.

Application

The events held in this group notify us when a player has opened something such as a menu and/or performed functions on the UI; other events include starting a cutscene or skipping one.

Progression

These sets of events have a range of purposes that can notify us when the player starts their game, when the game's over, and whether they completed or failed the level. From here, we can see the results of our player's progress and when they have left the game completely.

Onboarding

Onboarding events are targeted toward how players handle the tutorials we give them. Did they choose the tutorial or skip it? How far did they get through the tutorial? Was it completed?

Engagement

These events are used to monitor whether our player is still engaging in our game or whether they are skipping parts; are the players clicking our game's notifications or ignoring them? Are players completing the tasks required for achievements? When given the option to share a message from the game on social media, did they?

Monetization

The last event group is monetization. This is where we can check when the player chooses to visit a store and whether the player bought something. If so, what did they buy? Did the player pay real money or watch an advert? If they watched an advert, did they skip it?

 If you want to find out more about Standard Events and the implementation of these events, check out the official documentation from the Unity site at `https://docs.unity3d.com/2017.3/Documentation/Manual/UnityAnalyticsStandardEvents.html`.

Custom Events

If none of the events offered from the Standard Event group are available, we can make our own custom events. So, for example, if we wanted an analytics result for something specific, Custom Events would support this. However, these events carry less analytical support compared to Standard Events.

Transaction Events

Whenever a transaction is made, we can make a detailed record of what the user bought, how much was it bought for, and what currency was used.

 For more information about all of these events, check the official Unity documentation at `https://docs.unity3d.com/Manual/UnityAnalyticsEvents.html`.

Next, we're going to create our own event and send the data to the Analytics Dashboard before we manipulate it from the server-side with Unity's Remote Settings.

Remote Settings

In the last part of this section, we are going to use one of the Unity Dashboard's tools known as Remote Settings. This will allow us to send information from the Unity Dashboard to our game. In this case, we are going to give our players four lives when they are online instead of the usual three.

Let's start by installing Remote Settings from the Asset Store:

1. Within the Unity editor, select the **Asset Store** tab, or select **Asset Store** from the top of the Unity Editor by going to **Window | Asset Store**.
2. Once the Asset Store has loaded, in the search bar at the top of the store, enter `Remote Settings` and select it.
3. Next, we need to download the asset by clicking the **Download** button, as shown in the following screenshot:

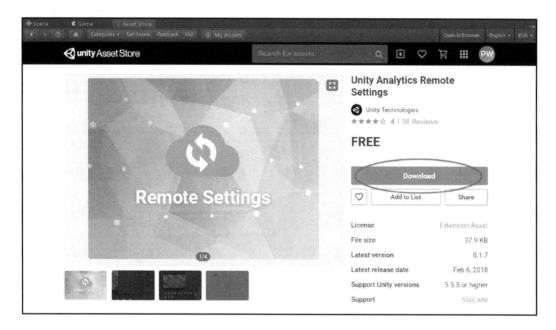

Once the Remote Settings asset has downloaded, the **Download** button will change to **Import**.

4. Click the **Import** button. A window will eventually appear with a list of assets that will be installed into our project.

5. Click the **Import** button in the bottom-right corner of the asset list:

Now that we have the assets for Remote Settings installed in Unity, we can start scripting our player so that they receive an extra life when they have an internet connection. Let's get started:

1. In the Unity editor, create a new script called `RemoteSettingsStartup` in the **Project** window under `Assets/Resources/Script/`.

2. Double-click the script to open it and enter the following code:

```
using UnityEngine;

public class RemoteSettingsStartUp : MonoBehaviour
{
  void Awake()
  {
    if (Application.internetReachability ==
        NetworkReachability.ReachableViaLocalAreaNetwork ||
          Application.internetReachability ==
NetworkReachability.ReachableViaCarrierDataNetwork)
    {

      RemoteSettings.Updated += () =>
      {
        GameManager.playerLives = RemoteSettings.GetInt
          ("PlayersStartUpLives",GameManager.playerLives);

      };

    }
  }
}
```

The code that we have entered into our `RemoteSettingsStartUp` script is split into two fundamental parts within an `Awake` function. The first is an `if` statement that checks to see if we are on the `bootUp` scene. The second `if` statement checks for internet connectivity. If there is an internet connection, we update our player's lives through the `RemoteSettings` integer value we set on the Dashboard; all of this is wrapped in a lambda.

What is a delegate lambda expression?

A delegate basically holds methods. We can add or take methods away and run them in our code. The benefit of this is that it is still carried as one identity. If you would like to know more about delegates, check out the official Unity documentation at: `https://learn.unity.com/tutorial/delegates`.

A lambda expression is a method without an identity, so it works like a normal method but has no name. These unnamed methods can't be called by any other part of our code. If you would like to know more about lambda expressions, please check the official Microsoft documentation at: `https://docs.microsoft.com/en-us/dotnet/csharp/programming-guide/statements-expressions-operators/lambda-expressions`.

3. Save the `RemoteSettingsStartUp` script.

Now that we are updating our player's lives via our new `RemoteSettingsStartUp` script, we need to revisit the code where we set the player's lives, way back when we created the `TitleComponent` script.

Let's remove its `Start` function as we no longer need to update the lives this way:

1. In the **Project** window, navigate to `Assets/Resources/Script`.
2. Double-click the `TitleComponent` script and remove the `Start` function and its content.
3. Save the `TitleComponent` script.

Within the `OnRemoteSettingUp` method, we call the `RemoteSettings` class and refer to its `GetInt` function. From there, we pass on a custom `string` name I made up called `PlayersStartUpLives`. In the next parameter, we add the `GameManager.playerLives` `static` variable to the integer section. Finally, we put whatever result we get from Unity's Remote Settings Dashboard back into the `GameManager.playerLives` variable.

So, if we have an internet connection, we check our `PlayerStartUpLives` key and grab the integer name that has been assigned on the Dashboard (which we will set up next) and return it to `GameManager.playerLives`.

Now, let's set up our Remote Settings in the Unity Editor and the Unity Dashboard:

1. Back in the Unity Editor, load up the `bootUp` scene from our **Project** window (`Assets/Scene`).
2. Select the `GameManager` game object in the **Hierarchy** window and click the **Add Component** button in the **Inspector** window.
3. From the drop-down menu that appears, type in the name of the script, that is, `RemoteSettingsStartUp`, and click it to add it to the list of `GameManager` components. The following screenshot shows what our `GameManager` game object will now contain in the **Inspector** window:

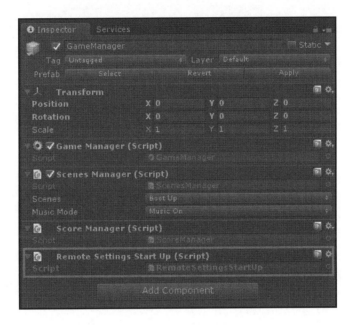

Next, we will enter the Unity Dashboard to add our Remote Settings value. To do that, we need to do the following:

1. Click the **Account** button in the top-right corner of the Unity Editor.
2. Then, click **Go to account**, as shown in the following screenshot:

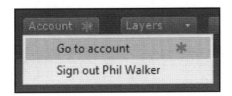

Your default internet browser will load up your Unity account.

3. Click the **Dashboards** link on the far left in the browser.
4. Click the **Projects** link (**1** in the following screenshot).
5. Then, select your game project, as shown in the following screenshot (**2**):

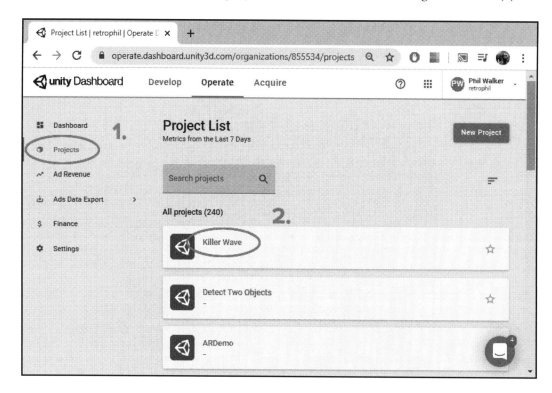

6. Ensure **Operate** is selected.
7. Click **Optimization** and then **Remote Settings**, as highlighted in the following screenshot:

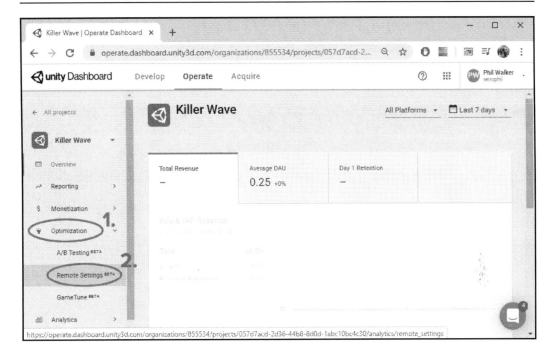

We are now in the **Remote Settings** panel on the dashboard. From here, we can add our player's lives.

8. First of all, make sure the drop-down menu option that's selected is **Development** (**1** in the following screenshot) since we haven't released our game yet.

9. Next, click **ADD NEW KEY-VALUE** (**2**), as shown in the following screenshot:

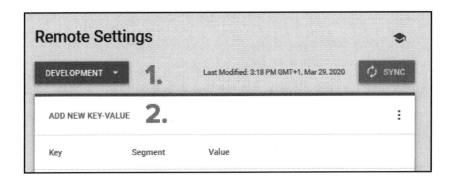

10. Now, we need to enter three fields. The first field's name has to be exactly the same as the one we used to name our key in `RemoteSettings` in our `RemoteSettingsStartUp` script, as shown in the following screenshot:

```
GameManager.playerLives = RemoteSettings.GetInt("PlayersStartUpLives",GameManager.playerLives);
```

11. The next field is the type of value we want to enter. As you can tell from the previous screenshot, we are using the `GetInt` function. So, from the drop-down menu, select **Integer**, as shown in the following screenshot:

12. Finally, enter the number of lives we wish to give the player when they start the game for the first time.

The following screenshot shows all three fields that we've entered:

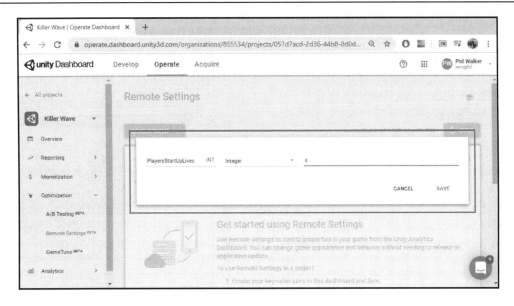

13. Click the **SAVE** button.
14. To send this update, click the **SYNC** button in the top-right corner:

15. A window will pop up. Just click the **SYNC** button in the window, unless you wish to type a reference in the text field.

Return to the Unity Editor and **Play** the bootUp scene. You should now start the game with four lives. If that doesn't work, try stopping and playing it again as there might be a delay. This will only happen once or twice, but it will work normally after that:

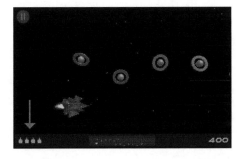

If you disable your internet connection and start the game, our player will only start with the standard three lives. We can, of course, add other Remote Settings to our game; the player's lives are merely an example, but as you can imagine, we could add other things, such as a setting that increases the speed of our enemies or alters the points system of our game.

As a brief recap, in this section, we covered the main segments of Unity's Analytics, which covered a series of useful event tools that can be used to explore and measure each player's progression through a game on one of the selected platforms on the market. This analytical data is available on the Unity Dashboard, which allows us to see how well the game is received by our consumers. We took a brief look at the categories of events Unity has to help us generalize common questions we would like to ask about our game. After looking into Analytics, we learned how to use Remote Settings and how to start manipulating our game without the need to roll out downloadable content packs for our players.

Now, let's summarize this chapter.

Summary

This chapter covered a variety of topics, including understanding Unity's Audio Mixer, which is where we can control the sounds in our game, and altering levels with our script. Then, we moved on and looked at storing data with PlayerPrefs and custom storage in JSON format in order to recognize the differences between the two ways of storing data. For JSON, we converted our data from object-based data into bytes and stored the results in a file (serialization). We then moved on to Unity Analytics, which is where we can mark events in our game so that we can keep track of our players and know what they're doing. Finally, we looked at Unity's Remote Settings, which play a similar role to PlayerPrefs, but allows the server-side updates to our game without the need for us to create a new installation build.

In future projects, you will likely make use of the coding we covered in the last two chapters regarding storing and reapplying data such as music and sound effect volume sliders. Hopefully, you will also be able to go further with this data by using other components in your projects so that your game can send out data to Unity's Dashboard to keep you connected with your players.

In the next chapter, we are going to look at pathfinding and how to improve the overall performance of our game.

12
NavMesh, Timeline, and a Mock Test

In this chapter, we are going to cover two main functionalities that Unity offers developers in issuing **AI** to our game objects and for animation that supports logic.

Unity has a ready-made system for our game objects to issue a path-finding algorithm where a game object can be given an area to patrol. This can be very handy in a series of games that use enemy soldiers to walk up and down a corridor looking for the player. A soldier could react depending on the behavior given to them.

The other functionality we will be covering is the **Timeline** component, which is used for animation in scenarios such as cutscenes in games/films. You may be thinking that we already covered an animation system back in `Chapter 4`, *Applying Art, Animation, and Particles*. Yes, you are right, but for a more complex animation that holds multiple game objects and animations, the transitions and states could get complex pretty easily. Also, **Timeline** supports a series of tracks that work specifically with our code and we can add our own custom animation tracks to our timeline.

These two main features will be assigned to our Killer Wave game project. The **Navigation Mesh (NavMesh)** controls a flock of small **Non-Player-Character (NPC)** robots that will move away from our player's ship like they're panicking to stay alive.

Timeline will be used to apply a mid-level cut scene where our player will see the end-of-level boss rush past them and lights in the scene will flash red.

Finally, we will end with the last mini mock test, which will include questions covering the content from this chapter and previous ones.

The following topics will be covered in this chapter:

- Preparing the final scene
- Developing AI with NavMesh
- Exploring the timeline
- Extending the timeline

Let's start by reviewing what skills are covered in this chapter.

The core exam skills covered in this chapter

Programming core interaction:

- *Implementing behaviors and interactions of game objects and environments*
- *Identifying methods to implement camera views and movement*

Working in an art pipeline:

- *Knowledge of materials, textures, and shaders: The Unity rendering API*
- *Knowledge of lighting: The Unity lighting API*
- *Knowledge of two-dimensional and three-dimensional animation: The Unity animation API*

Programming for the scene and environment design:

- *Determining scripts for pathfinding with the Unity navigation system*

Technical requirements

The project content for this chapter can be found at `https://github.com/PacktPublishing/Unity-Certified-Programmer-Exam-Guide/tree/master/Chapter12`.

You can download the entirety of each chapter's project files at `https://github.com/PacktPublishing/Unity-Certified-Programmer-Exam-Guide/archive/master.zip`.

All the content for this chapter is held in the chapter's `unitypackage` file, including a `Complete` folder that holds all of the work we'll carry out in the chapter.

Check out the following video to see the Code in Action: `https://bit.ly/3g1QlV6`.

Preparing the final scene

In this section, we are going to prepare our new `level3` scene in two parts—the first part of our game will have some three-dimensional art assets for the player to potentially collide with. Also, the environment will be used for our new fleeing enemies. The second part of this section is used to upgrade our camera's behavior so that instead of it being static, we now require it to move across the level. The player will also be given the same fixed speed as the camera.

By the end of this section, we will have an environment set up as in the following screenshot:

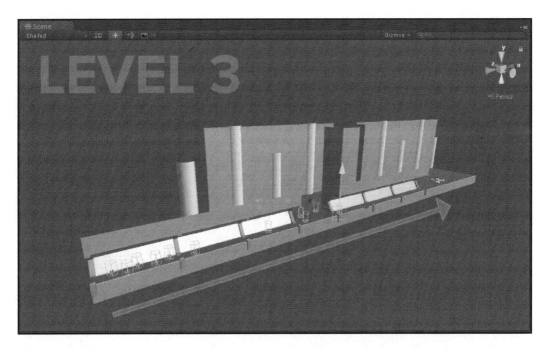

The arrow going from left to right in the previous screenshot shows the path of the camera. Once it reaches a particular point, it will stop and the level will end shortly after.

It is worth mentioning that within the `level3Env` prefab is a game object that holds a script called `BossTrigger`. This game object contains a box collider, a rigid body, and a `BossTriggerBox` script.

The purpose of the `BossTrigger` game object is to active the **Timeline** animation when the camera moves into the `BossTrigger` collider. We will discuss this further in *Exploring the timeline* section of this chapter.

Let's continue by moving our `level3` file's environment into the scene:

1. From the **Project** window, navigate to `Assets/Scene` and double-click on the `level3` scene file.
2. From the **Project** window, navigate to `Assets/Resources/Prefab`.
3. Click and drag the `level3Env` prefab into the `_SceneAssets` game object in the **Hierarchy** window.
4. Select `level3Env` from the **Hierarchy** window, and in the **Inspector** window, update its **Transform** property values the following:

   - **Position**: **X**: `2500`, **Y**: `17`, and **Z**: `-24`
   - **Scale**: **X**: `0.55`, **Y**: `0.55`, and **Z**: `0.55`

The following screenshot shows our scene setup, which is ready for our player to fly in:

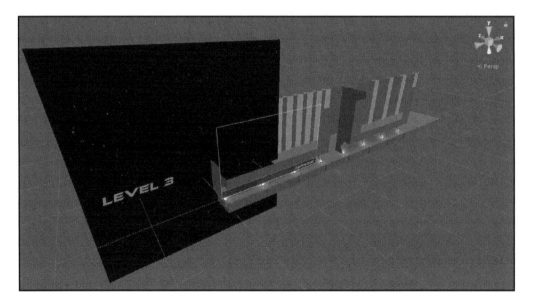

So, we need to make some changes to our `level3` scene so that it acts in a way that the camera supports the new environment and the environment itself doesn't have extra assets that we don't need, such as the animating texture quad for the background and the prefab particle system for the stars flying past.

Alter the `level3` scene in the **Hierarchy** window by doing the following:

1. Thankfully, the two assets mentioned sit within the `GameSpeed` game object in the **Hierarchy** window. All that we need to do is delete the `GameSpeed` game object.

2. We won't be using any directional lighting in our scene, so also remove `Directional Light` from the **Hierarchy** window.

3. Also, for the sake of running our `level3` scene without going through the entire game loop, we can drop our `GameManager` prefab from the `Assets/Resources/Prefab` folder location into the **Hierarchy** window.

Our **Hierarchy** window for `level3` will now look like the one in the following screenshot:

We now need to make it so that the **Camera** component supports a far clipping-plane value. To do this, we need to do the following:

1. Select the main camera in the **Hierarchy** window.

2. In the **Inspector** window, change the **Clipping Planes Far** component property of **Camera** to `1300`.

So, we have adjusted the clipping plane of the camera to show all of the `level3` file's environment, removed the `GameSpeed` game object that helps art assets for our previous levels, and added `GameManager` to `level3` to make development easier. We now need to turn our focus toward making the camera actually move instead of creating the illusion it is moving, as with `level1` and `level2`.

I have created a small script that will make it so that the camera moves from one point to another; everything inside the script demonstrates elements of code that we have already covered throughout this book. So, there's no need for you to create the script, but understanding it is obviously the main purpose.

We are going to attach the script to the main camera in our scene to control its movement. Follow these instructions:

1. Select the main camera from the **Hierarchy** window.
2. Click the **Add Component** button in the **Inspector** window and type `CameraMovement` until you see the script appear in the dropdown.
3. Select the **CameraMovement** script.
4. Click on **Add Component** again and type `box collider` into the drop-down list. When it appears, select it and check its **Is Trigger** box.
5. In brief, this script will translate along its *x*-axis after 6 seconds when active. When the script reaches a particular point, it will stop; it will also make sure the player stops traveling with it.

Let's modify our `Player` script to act on the movement of the camera for `level3`:

1. In the **Project** window of the Unity editor, navigate to `Assets/Resources/Script` and double-click on the `Player` script to open it.
2. Inside the `Player` script, at the top where we have our global variables, enter the private variable and its property:

```
float camTravelSpeed;
public float CamTravelSpeed
{
  get {return camTravelSpeed;}
  set {camTravelSpeed = value;}
}

float movingScreen;
```

The `camTravelSpeed` variable that we just entered will be used as an extra multiplier to set the pace of the player's ship when the camera moves along the *X*-axis.

The second variable, `movingScreen`, will hold the result of `Time.deltatime` multiplied by `camTravelspeed`. `movingScreen` will be used later when it comes to comparing the player's ship's *X*-axis.

3. In the `Start` function, add the following line at the bottom of its function:

    ```
    movingScreen = width;
    ```

Inside the `Start` function, we will add our `width float` measurement to `movingScreen` (this happens after `width` has been updated in the `Start` function) as this will be the starting position before it receives its increments from `Time.deltatime` and `camTravelspeed`.

Still inside the `Player` script, scroll down to the `Movement` method.

4. At the top of the `Movement` method, enter the following code, which will multiply our player's ship's speed:

    ```
    if(camTravelSpeed > 1)
      {
        transform.position += Vector3.right *
            Time.deltaTime * camTravelSpeed;
        movingScreen += Time.deltaTime * camTravelSpeed;
      }
    ```

In the code that we've just entered, we run a check to see whether `camTravelSpeed` has increased from our new `CameraMovement` script. If `camTravelSpeed` has been updated, we fall into the scope of the `if` statement.

Within the `if` statement, we increment the player's ship's *X*-axis to the right multiplied by `Time.deltatime` and `camTravelSpeed`.

The second thing we are doing is adding the `movingScreen` value that originally holds the current `width` of our playing area. However, because the screen is moving, we need to increment the playing area so that the player doesn't get left behind or go too far out of the camera view.

The last amendment we will be adding to our `Player` script is our horizontal movements, still in the `Movement` method.

5. Scroll down until you get to where the player can press the *right arrow* to move (`Input.GetAxisRaw("Horizontal") > 0`). Within the scope of the `if` statement, we can make an amendment to the second `if` statement to the following:

```
if (transform.localPosition.x < movingScreen+(width/0.9f)))
```

If the player presses the *right arrow* on their keyboard/joypad, we run a check to see whether the player's *x*-axis is less than the `movingScreen` float value; plus, we include a buffer to push the player further to the edge of the screen.

6. We can then do the same for when the player presses *left arrow* on the keyboard/joystick within the second `if` statement:

```
if (transform.localPosition.x > movingScreen+width/6)
```

Similar rules apply where we make use of the `movingScreen` variable, which is constantly incremented along with a slight buffer to keep our player's ship within the game screen.

7. Save the `Player` script.

Before we move onto the next script, we need to uncomment two lines of code in our new `CameraMovement` script, so that it can interact with the `Player` script.

Back in the **Project** window, open the `CameraMovement` script and uncomment the two following lines by removing the `//`. The first line to uncomment is:

```
// GameObject.Find("Player").GetComponent<Player>().CamTravelSpeed = camSpeed;
```

The second line to uncomment is:

```
//
GameObject.Find("PlayerSpawner").GetComponentInChildren<Player>().CamTravelSpeed = 0;
```

Now, these two lines of code can alter the speed of the player ship.

Next, we need to update our `GameManager` script so that it recognizes the difference between `level1` and `level2`, and `level3`, which has a moving camera.

So, let's move to the GameManager script and add two main elements—the camera speed and noticing the difference between scenes. Let's start by opening the GameManager script:

1. From the **Project** window, navigate to Assets/Resources/Script.
2. Double-click on the GameManager script to open it in your IDE.

   You may or may not have looked into the CameraMovement script that we attached to the main camera, but inside that script is a variable called camSpeed. This variable manipulates the camera's speed; in our GameManager script, we set the speed of the main camera.

   The main takeaway from this is that the CameraMovement script will manipulate the camera's speed from what is set in the GameManager script.

3. In the GameManger script, scroll down to the method titled CameraSetup.
4. We are going to make this method take a variable to alter the camera's speed. Change the CameraSetup method to take a float value in its parameter. The CameraSetup method will first look as follows:

   ```
   void CameraSetup()
   ```

   It will then change to this:

   ```
   void CameraSetup(float camSpeed)
   ```

5. Within the CameraSetup method, we need to transfer camSpeed to the new CameraMovement script:

   ```
   gameCamera.GetComponent<CameraMovement>().CamSpeed = camSpeed;
   ```

   Notice that the line of code we add to our CameraSetup method needs to be added after the main camera has been stored in a gameCamera variable.

   The last thing to do in the GameManager script is to update the LightandCameraSetup method so that when the CameraSetup method within it is called, it takes a value that sets the main camera's speed. So, in level1 and level2, we want the camera to continue to not move; in level3, we will need to apply speed to the camera.

6. Within `LightandCameraSetup`, replace its original `switch` statement with the following:

```
switch (sceneNumber)
{
  case 3 : case 4 :
  {
    LightSetup();
    CameraSetup(0);
    break;
  }
  case 5:
  {
    CameraSetup(150);
    break;
  }
}
```

So, before, our `switch` statement had all the cases run `LightSetup` and `CameraSetup` within cases 3, 4, and 5. But now, in the previous code, we have split the roles up. In cases 3 and 4, we run `LightSetup` as usual, and now, because `CameraSetup` now takes a `float` value, we set the camera speed to 0.

In case 5, which is the build number for our `level3` scene, we ignore `LightSetup` as we won't be using a directional light in this scene. We run `CameraSetup` but give it a value of 150, which will be the speed we set the `camSpeed` variable within the method:

1. Save the `GameManager` script.
2. Press **Play** to see how the `level3` scene plays out. The following screenshot shows what we have so far:

The previous screenshot shows a series of events of what happens after we press **Play** in the Unity editor. Let's go through each event, respectively:

- The `level3` scene before pressing **Play** (denoted by **1.**).
- The scene is in play mode and sets up the camera position and background (denoted by **2.**).
- The UI for the level is animated and the enemies start floating into the game window (denoted by **3.**).
- The player enters the level and the scene pauses for a few seconds before the player gets control of their ship (denoted by **4.**).
- The camera begins to move along with the radar camera, following the progress of the player and the oncoming enemies (denoted by **5.**).

In the next section, we will add our second enemy type (flee enemy), which will flee across the span of our new art.

Developing AI with NavMesh

In this section, we are going to introduce a new enemy that will attempt to flee with frenzy-type behavior from our player's ship. This enemy's behavior will be implemented with the use of Unity's built-in `NavMesh` functionality.

As you can imagine, this built-in feature from Unity could answer a lot of problems with regard to games with NPCs, similar to ones in the *Metal Gear Solid* game, where the player has to sneak around and not get detected by the enemy soldiers.

`NavMesh` gives the enemy soldiers a path to walk around, and then if they see the player, their behavior changes from `Patrolling` to `Attack`.

So, with our game, we are going to implement `NavMesh` but make it so that our enemies react differently to how they would in *Metal Gear Solid*. We will add multiple flee enemies in clusters to our third level scene. This chaotic, distracting behavior will make the final level more challenging for our players.

The following screenshot shows our fleeing enemy with a cylindrical radius around it. This radius is called the agent radius and can be altered to stop other obstacles and enemies from intersecting with each other:

Before we add these fleeing enemies to our scene, we need to tell the fleeing enemies where they can move around by baking a NavMesh first. To bake a NavMesh, follow these instructions:

First, we need to select the game object that we will use to bake, which also means we need to deselect game objects that don't need to be **Navigation Static**.

1. From the **Hierarchy** window, select the _SceneAssets game object.
2. From the **Inspector** window, from the top-right corner, we need to deactivate **Navigation Static** for _SceneAssests.
3. The following screenshot shows _SceneAssets selected and the static dropdown (denoted by **1.**), followed by **Navigation Static** being un-ticked (denoted by **2.**):

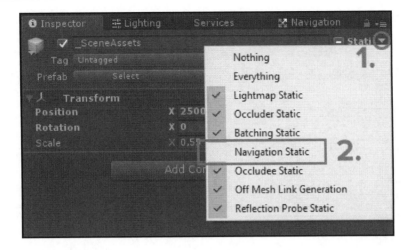

4. A window pops up asking whether we want to apply the changes to all the child objects. Select **Yes, change children**.

So, we have just deactivated all of our environment art assets in the level3 scene so that they are not recognized for navigation baking. We now need to turn on one of the child game objects within the _SceneAssets hierarchy:

1. From the **Hierarchy** window, click on the arrows next to the following fields to expand out its content until you get to the game object titled corridorFloorNav:

   - _SceneAssets
   - level
   - corridorFloor

   The following screenshot shows that from the **Hierarchy** window, we have selected corridorFloorNav (denoted by **1.**):

2. With corridorFloorNav selected, make sure its **Mesh Renderer** component is ticked in the **Inspector** window (denoted by **2.**).

3. Finally, select **Navigation Static** for this game object (denoted by **3.**):

We now need to check the **Navigation** window so that we can set it to bake our `CorridorFloorNav` mesh.

4. Select **Window** at the top of the Unity editor and then click on **Navigation**.

It's likely the **Navigation** window will appear at the top-right corner of the editor. If it doesn't and has appeared as a floating window somewhere in the Unity editor, simply click and hold on the **Navigation** tab and dock it next to the **Inspector** tab, as in the following screenshot:

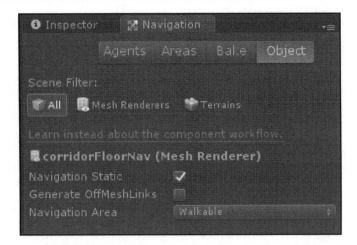

5. In the **Navigation** window, click on the **Bake** button at the top to give us our **Navigation** bake options.

 It's also worth noting that a game object that is manipulated in the NavMesh is referred to as an agent.

In this window, we are presented with a series of options for our navigation bake. This may look a little intimidating at first, but the blue cylinder is basically our agent (the fleeing enemy) and the following parameters are based on how flexible our agent is with the navigation path it'll be walking around. Let's briefly go through each of the options so that we are aware of its features before we bake:

- **Agent Radius**: This will create an invisible shield around our agent so that they can't clip into other agents, walls, doors, and so on.
- **Agent Height**: Similar to **Agent Radius**, this gives our agent an invisible height; this could be useful for the game object that the NavMesh is manipulating to pass through doors.

- **Max Slope**: We can alter, in degrees, how much of a slope our agent can walk up.
- **Step Height**: This is similar to the **Max Slope** property, but in this case, this controls how much our agent is allowed to move up a step/stairs.
- **Drop Height**: Enter a value for the maximum height the character can drop down from (associated with the **Off Mesh Link** component).
- **Jump Distance**: This specifies the value for the jump distance between the character and the object (associated with the **Off Mesh Link** component).

Information about the **Off Mesh Link** component can be found at `https://docs.unity3d.com/Manual/class-OffMeshLink.html`.

- **Manual Voxel**: Voxel is a three-dimensional measurement that is used to scale the accuracy of our navigation bake.
- **Voxel Size**: If the **Manual Voxel** option is ticked, this means we can give each agent tighter precision. The lower the number, the more accurate our agent will be; note that this will make the NavMesh take longer to bake.
- **Min Region Area**: This specifies a minimum area that a surface must have for it to be included in the NavMesh.
- **Height Mesh**: This checkbox will create a height mesh, which will improve the movement accuracy. This will also make navigation baking slower.

The following screenshot shows the navigation bake settings we just went through:

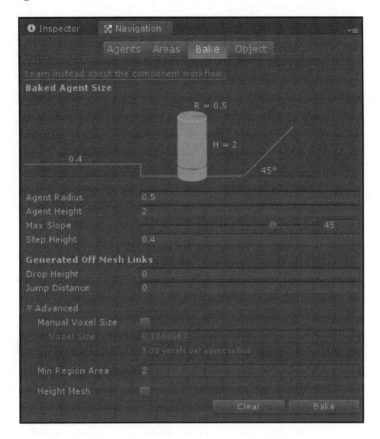

Thankfully, the **Bake** properties of our default setup window will work just fine as is.

6. Click on the **Bake** button at the bottom right of the **Navigation** window and wait until the meter at the bottom-right corner of the editor completes, as in the following screenshot:

Once the navigation bake has completed, corridorFloorNav in our **Scene** window will have a NavMesh sitting on top of its mesh.

If you can't see the navigation-baked mesh, make sure the **Show NavMesh** checkbox is ticked at the bottom-right corner of the mesh. The following screenshot shows our NavMesh and the **Navmesh Display** box:

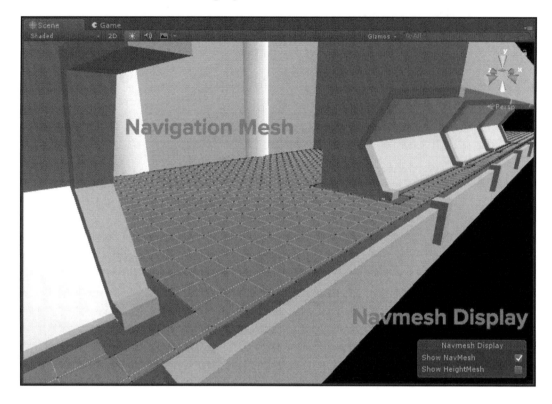

The last thing to do for this section is to turn off the corridorFloorNav game object's **Mesh Renderer** component. We only needed this component to be active for the NavMesh to be baked.

To turn off the corridorFloorNav game object's **Mesh Renderer** component, do the following:

1. Select the corridorFloorNav game object in the **Hierarchy** window.
2. In the **Inspector** window, uncheck the **Mesh Renderer** component.

The following screenshot shows the highlighted box that needs unchecking:

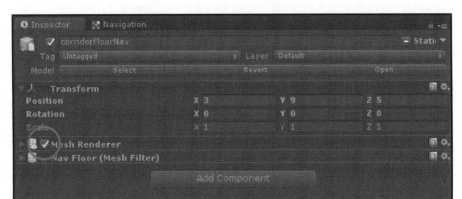

This is all that is needed to allow our fleeing enemies to move around.

> If you would like to find out more about the **Navigation** window, check out `https://docs.unity3d.com/Manual/Navigation.html`.

So far in this section, we have discussed the requirements of AI and how it is used in games and how we are going to implement, such methods applied to our fleeing enemies, with the use of the `NavMesh` system that Unity offers as standard.

Now that we have our NavMesh baked for our agents to move around on, we can look into setting up our `NavMeshAgent` component to give our agents a set speed, acceleration, stopping distance, and more in the next section.

Customizing our agents – NavMeshAgent

In this section, we will be continuing on from setting up our NavMesh but shifting the focus toward the agent (the fleeing enemy game object). The agent will be moving around the baked NavMesh.

It is necessary for the fleeing enemy game object to be able to react and move within the NavMesh, but also be able to move in a way that suits the behavior of what we're trying to achieve. For example, the enemy is to flee with an element of panic; so we need to consider characteristics such as when the enemy decides to move, how quickly the enemy would react, and how fast the enemy can move. These properties, and more, come from a component called `NavMeshAgent`.

`NavMeshAgent` is a required component that will be attached to each of the fleeing enemy game objects. The purpose of this component is to make it so that the game object is recognized as an agent and will stick to the NavMesh.

Before we add `NavMeshAgent` to the fleeing enemy, we need to create a prefab of the enemy so that we have a place where we can grab and clone copies of multiple enemies:

1. From the **Project** window, navigate to the `Assets/Resources/Model/`folder and drag `enemy_flee.fbx` to the bottom of the **Hierarchy** window.
2. Drag `enemy_flee` from the **Hierarchy** window to the **Project** window into `Assets/Resources/Prefab/Enemies`.

That's our fleeing enemy created; now, we can apply a material to it by doing the following:

1. Navigate to the `Assets/Resources/Prefab/Enemies` folder and select the `enemy_flee` prefab.
2. From the **Inspector** window, select the remote button of the **Mesh Renderer** component (denoted by **1**. in the following screenshot).
3. A dropdown will appear. Type `darkRed` in the search bar at the top if you can't see the material on the list.
4. Double-click on `darkRed` from the dropdown (denoted by **2**. in the following).
5. At this point, make sure the **Transform** component's **Position** and **Rotation** properties all have a 0 value and that the **Scale** property is set to 1.

The following screenshot shows the `enemy_flee` prefab with its update material and the correct **Transform** values:

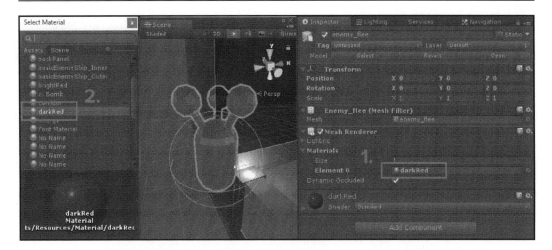

You may notice in the previous screenshot that `enemy_flee` has hard, shiny edges. We can make these appear smoother in our three-dimensional model import settings by doing the following:

1. From the **Project** window, navigate to the `Assets/Resources/Model` folder and select `enemy_flee`.

2. In the **Inspector** window, change the property value for **Normals** from **Import** to **Calculate**.

We can now adjust the **Smoothing Angle** value with the slider to change the smoothness between angles, as in the following screenshot:

In the previous screenshot, you can see three distinct stages in making the model look smoother. This can be done with any three-dimensional model imported into Unity.

3. Once you're happy with the **Smoothing Angle** value, click on **Apply** at the bottom-right corner of the **Inspector** window.

Coming back to `enemy_flee` in the **Hierarchy** window, as this is an enemy, we also need to give it an **Enemy** tag so that the player recognizes it as such if and when they collide with each other:

1. Click on the **Tag** parameter at the top of the **Inspector** window.
2. Select **Enemy**.

The following screenshot shows the **Enemy** tag selected for `enemy_flee`:

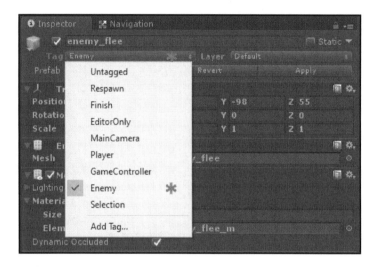

We are now ready to apply `NavMeshAgent` to the `enemy_flee` game object. With `enemy_flee` still selected, do the following:

1. Click on the **Add Component** button in the **Inspector** window.
2. A drop-down list will appear. Type in `nav` and select `NavMeshAgent` from the list.

`enemy_flee` now has `NavMeshAgent` attached to it. As previously mentioned, let's go through each of the properties. The following screenshot also shows the `NavMeshAgent` default values (these may differ to your default values, but don't be concerned as we will be changing the majority of the values):

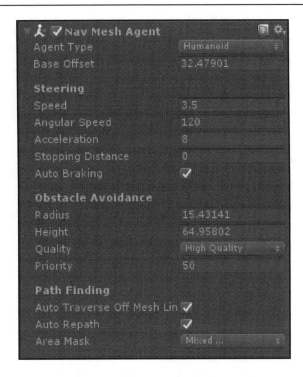

- **Agent Type**: By default, there is only one agent type. This holds a preset of the name of the agent, the radius, height, step height, and max slope. To find out more about these values, check the previous section.
- **Base Offset**: This will change the placement of the agent mesh that wraps around the fleeing enemy in the form of a cylinder that can only be seen in the **Scene** window.
- **Speed**: The maximum speed value, based on world units per second.
- **Angular Speed**: Sets how quickly the agent can rotate in degrees per second.
- **Acceleration**: Maximum acceleration based on world units per second squared.
- **Stopping Distance**: Agents will stop when they are at a particular measurement.
- **Auto Braking**: The agent will slow down gradually before reaching a complete stop.
- **Radius**: The agent's spatial area will increase the scale of the agent cylinder.

- **Height:** This will increase the height of the agent's cylinder.
- **Quality**: The ranges on the accuracy of obstacle avoidance.
- **Priority**: Agents of a lower priority will be ignored by this agent when performing avoidance.
- **Auto Traverse OffMesh Link**: If you want the agent to move between gaps, keep this checked; otherwise, custom animation will move the agent across the gap.
- **Auto Repath**: If the agent is no longer on the path they are walking, with this option checked, they will try and make their way back to the nearest point.
- **Area Mask**: With navigation baking, we can set which area this agent belongs to.

For `NavMeshAgent`, we will set its agents to a high speed, rotation, and acceleration value to make these enemies react fast to match their fleeing behavior.

3. Change the `NavMeshAgent` values for the `enemy_flee` prefab to the ones shown in the following screenshot:

4. Click **Apply** at the top-right corner of the **Inspector** section to confirm your prefab changes.

In this section, we created the fleeing enemy prefab and gave it a material. We also applied a `NavMeshAgent` component to our enemy so that it's calibrated and ready to react.

The following screenshot shows what the fleeing enemy looks like with its `NavMeshAgent` component wrapped around it, which can only be seen in the **Scene** window:

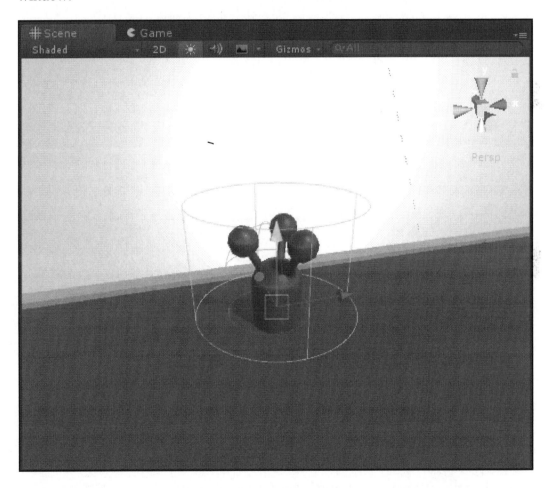

In the next section, we will give the fleeing enemy prefab a collider so that when the player makes contact with it, the player and the enemy are destroyed with the soon-to-come scripting.

Adding a capsule collider to our fleeing enemy

In this section, we are going to add a capsule collider to the fleeing enemy so that a collision can be detected from the player's ship when they collide with each other:

1. With the `enemy_flee` prefab still selected, scroll down to the bottom of the **Inspector** window and click on **Add Component**.
2. Start typing `Capsule` into the drop-down window until you see **Capsule Collider**.
3. Select **Capsule Collider** from the drop-down list. The fleeing enemy will now have a capsule collider wrapped around them.
4. Finally, tick the **Is Trigger** checkbox in the **Capsule Collider** component.
5. Click on the **Apply** button at the top-right corner of the **Inspector** window to save the `enemy_flee` prefab's settings.
6. Select the `enemy_flee` game object in the **Hierarchy** and delete it.

The following screenshot shows `enemy_flee` with its capsule collider; these values may differ to yours:

The fleeing enemy is nearly ready to be tried out in the game. We just need to add a script to tell the game object what to do when it gets within a certain distance to the player. We will cover this in the next section.

Creating our fleeing enemy script

In this section, we will be making it so that the fleeing enemy detects when the player is getting close to them. If the player is too close, we will make it so that the enemy begins to flee.

We will be taking a script that is partially made and import it into this chapter as the majority of the `EnemyFlee` script will contain a similar setup to our previous enemy that we made in `Chapter 2`, *Adding and Manipulating Objects*. Follow these steps:

1. From the **Project** window, navigate to `Assets/Resources/Script`.
2. Double-click on the `EnemyFlee` script to begin adding its navigation code.

The `EnemyFlee` script will contain similar-looking code to the `EnemyWave` script. The enemies in our game will carry the same properties, such as giving and taking damage when hit or dying, detecting a collision, inheriting its own scriptable object asset, and more. There's no real need to go through this process again. What we are interested in is how the `enemy_flee` game object acts.

To add the fleeing behavior to the `EnemyFlee` script, we need to do the following:

1. At the top of the script, add the AI library to give our script access to the **Navigation Agent** files:

   ```
   using UnityEngine.AI;
   ```

   In our script, we will need access to the `NavMeshAgent` component (which is attached to our `enemy_flee` game object). The AI library gives us this functionality.

2. Scroll down in the script to where our global variables are (`health`, `travelSpeed`, `fireRate`, and so on) and add the following variables that we will be using with our navigation setup:

   ```
   GameObject player;
   bool gameStarts = false;

   [SerializeField]
   float enemyDistanceRun = 200;
   NavMeshAgent enemyAgent;
   ```

   The first variable will be used to store the reference to the player's ship as we will be comparing its distance later on. The `bool` value will be used as part of a delayed start for our script. We will talk more about this later on as well.

   `enemyDistanceRun` will be used as a rule to "act" within the measured distance between the player and our fleeing enemy. We have also added the `SerializeField` attribute to this as it will be handy to change these values in the **Inspector** window while keeping this variable private.

Finally, we have `NavMeshAgent`, which will be required to receive data from the player and fleeing enemy results.

3. Create a `Start` function that will require a short delay to get a reference from the player ship. Enter the following code. We will go through each step to see why there is a delay and the standard `ActorStats` method:

```
void Start()
{
    ActorStats(actorModel);
    Invoke("DelayedStart",0.5f);
}

void DelayedStart()
{
    gameStarts = true;
    player = GameObject.FindGameObjectWithTag("Player");
    enemyAgent = GetComponent<NavMeshAgent>();
}
```

The `Start` function contains the `ActorStats` method, which will update our enemy's abilities (the health value, points added to the score, and more), similar to our `enemy_wave` game object. We will also run an `Invoke` function, which takes the name of the method we wish to run along with a parameter that determines when the method will be run.

We are running a short `0.5f` delay to give the player's ship time to be instantiated into the scene before we take a reference from it. We set a Boolean value to true to say the update function can run the content within it, which we will cover shortly. The final thing we do is take reference from the `NavMeshAgent` component attached to the game object.

We need to add a slight amendment to our speed value in our `ActorStats` method. Because we are affecting the `NavMesgAgent_speed`, we need to manipulate this directly.

To make the enemies' speed adjustable, add the following line of code within the `ActorStats` of the `EnemyFlee` script:

```
GetComponent<NavMeshAgent>().speed = actorModel.speed;
```

The enemy flee speed value is now hooked up.

4. Moving on to the last piece of our code, the Update function will be measuring and reacting to and from the distance of our fleeing enemy and the player. Enter the following Update function and its content and we will go through each step:

```
void Update ()
{
  if(gameStarts)
  {
      if (player != null)
      {
          float distance =
Vector3.Distance(transform.position,
          player.transform.position);
          if (distance < enemyDistanceRun)
          {
            Vector3 dirToPlayer = transform.position –
            player.transform.position;
            Vector3 newPos = transform.position +
dirToPlayer;
            enemyAgent.SetDestination(newPos);
          }
      }
  }
}
```

In the Update function, we run an if statement to check whether the gameStarts Boolean value is true; if it is true we then check to see if the player_ship is still in the scene. And if that is true we move on to the content in that if statement. Within this if statement, we use Vector3.Distance to measure the distance between the player's ship and the fleeing enemy. We then store the measurement as a float value called distance.

Next, we run a check to see whether the distance measured is less than the enemyDistanceRun value, which is currently set to 200.

If the distance variable's value is lower, then that means the player's ship is too close to the fleeing enemy, so we run the following steps for it to react:

5. Store the Vector3 variable, which minuses from the player's position to our own.

6. We then add this `Vector3` variable to the fleeing enemy's **Transform** position as a `newPos` position of `Vector3`, which will be the direction for the enemy flee to run in.

7. Finally, we send this `newPos` position to `NavMeshAgent`.

8. Save the `EnemyFlee` script.

We are now ready to attach the `EnemyFlee` script to our `enemy_flee` prefab. Let's do this now; then, we will be able to test the results:

1. Back in the Unity editor, navigate to the `Assets/Resources/Prefab/Enemies` folder in the **Project** window.

2. Select the `enemy_flee` prefab.

3. Click on the **Add Component** button in the **Inspector** window and type in `EnemyFlee`.

4. Select the `Enemy Flee` script from the drop-down list.

5. Create a new **Actor** (refer back to `Chapter 2`, *Adding and Manipulating Objects*). Name the Actor `BasicFlee_Enemy`, then store it in `Assets/Resources/Script/ScriptableObject`. Drag the Actor into the Actor Model area of the `EnemyFlee` script in the Inspector window, as shown in the following screenshot.

The following screenshot shows the scriptable object asset for the `EnemyFlee` script's **Actor Model** parameter on the right:

We now need to make it so that our `enemy_flee` script is recognized on the radar map in the game HUD, as with the `enemy_wave` game object. As a reminder, we made a `radarPoint` object before in `Chapter 9`, *Creating a Two-Dimensional Shop Interface and In-Game HUD*. So, in this chapter, we're going to speed things up and use a ready-made `radarPoint` object to attach to the `enemy_flee` game object. The only difference with the ready-made `radarPoint` game object is that I have attached a small script called `RadarRotation` that will make it so that the `radarPoint` sprite will always face the camera, regardless of which rotation the `enemy_flee` game object makes.

The `RadarRotation` script takes the current rotation in the `Awake` function, followed by reapplying the rotation on `LateUpdate`.

What is `LateUpdate`?

`LateUpdate` is the last function called in Unity's execution order game logic. The benefit to this is there is no fighting between the rotation of the `radarPoint` object and the `enemy_flee` rotation being called at the same time. If you would like to learn more about the execution order, check out `https://docs.unity3d.com/Manual/ExecutionOrder.html`.

To attach the pre-made `radarPoint` object to the `enemy_flee` prefab, we need to do the following:

1. Back in the **Project** window, drag and drop the `enemy_flee` prefab from `Assets/Resources/Prefab/Enemies` into the **Hierarchy** window.
2. Drag and drop the `radarPoint` object from `Assets/Resources/Prefab/Enemies` onto the `enemy_flee` prefab in the **Hierarchy** window.
3. Then drag and drop the `RadarRotation` script from `Assets/Resources/Script` into the **Inspector** window. This will make the `enemy_flee radarPoint` point towards the camera.
4. Once applied, select the `enemy_flee` prefab from the **Hierarchy** window and then click on **Apply** at the top-right corner of the **Inspector** window.

5. The following screenshot shows the `enemy_flee` prefab holding the `radarPoint` object, along with the `radarPoint` object in the **Inspector** window, as a reference to help avoid any errors:

5. Our `enemy_flee` prefab is now ready to be trialed out in **Play** mode. Drag, and drop `enemy_flee` from its current location to the _Enemies game object in the **Hierarchy** window. The following screenshot shows where `enemy_flee` now is in the **Hierarchy** window:

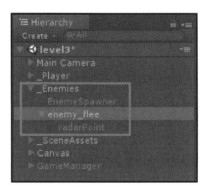

6. Set the `enemy_flee` prefab to somewhere near the start of the level. I have placed mine at the following **Transform** values:

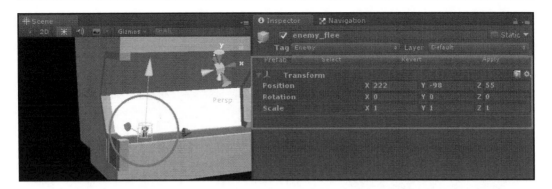

If you also have the EnemySpawner object in the scene close to the start of the level, push it back along the *X*-axis as far as 1000 to get it out of the way.

7. Click the **Play** button in the Unity editor and your enemy_flee object should now start panicking and moving around to try and escape from you!

Feel free to select the enemy_flee object in the **Hierarchy** window and press *Left + Ctrl* (*Command* on macOS) + *D* on your keyboard to spread a few fleeing enemies around to make the level more interesting, as shown in the following screenshot:

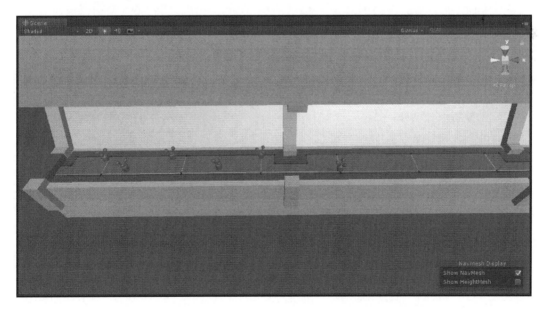

The following screenshot shows our new fleeing enemies trying to escape from the player in a pure panic!

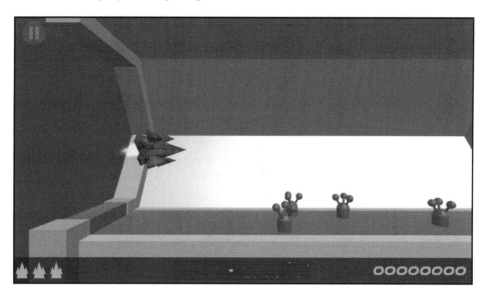

8. Save the scene.

That's the end of this section and hopefully, you now feel comfortable with this introduction to using the NavMesh and agents. As you can imagine, our fleeing enemy could have other events attached to it, such as shooting bullets at the player when at a safe distance, taking cover around a corner, and calling for help. Adding a series of events to an NPC would require a finite state machine to go through each appropriate event.

In this section, we introduced a new enemy that acted differently to our current wave enemy. We also became familiar with the ready-made path-finding algorithms offered by Unity, such as NavMesh.

We are going to move on to the next section where we will introduce the timeline, which works as an animator but can also be used with regard to blending logical behavior with our components, for example, to make a light blend into a different color by using scripting.

Exploring the timeline

Timeline is a component in the Unity editor that is intended to put a sequence of animations together that is attractive to industries such as film and TV. **Timeline** is also welcomed in games that may have cutscenes to help tell a story or introduce a player to level. Unity also has two other useful components—**Animator Controller** and **Animation Clips**—as you will know if you have been following this book as we covered these other components in `Chapter 4`, *Applying Art, Animation, and Particles*. They carry out the same tasks but as a scene becomes busier with a series of individual animation clips, things can get messy quickly in the animator controller, with the multiple states transitioning between each other.

The following screenshot shows the animator controller with multiple states and transitions:

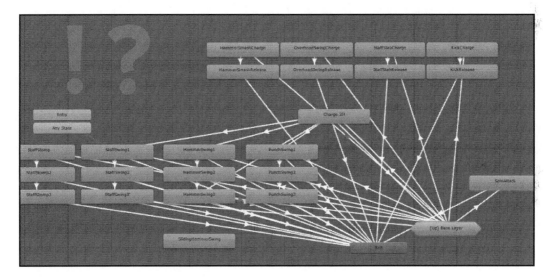

Timeline supports three tasks:

- Playing animations and clips
- Playing audio
- Turning game objects on or off

These three capabilities on their own limit **Timeline**—for example, if we want to change the color of light, **Timeline** wouldn't be able to change the individual property alone. To change the color of the light, we would need to change the light's property values in the **Animation** window itself. However, with some extra scripting to our timeline, we can introduce dragging and dropping game objects that hold components, such as a light component, where changes can be made on the fly.

In this section, we are going to start by animating a large robotic craft in the timeline. Then, we will discuss playables and how they can extend a timeline's functionality. Finally, we will implement additional tracks to the timeline to control the color of the lights and fade the level into darkness once the player reaches the end of the level.

Let's start by creating our `Timeline` game object and add a **Timeline** component to it in the next section.

Creating a timeline

In this section, we are going to get more familiar with the **Timeline** component and create some of our own animations with a large, flying robot. When setting up the timeline, we will also discuss the components and properties that are involved.

To add a timeline to our scene, do the following:

1. In the Unity editor's **Project** window, navigate to `Assets/Scene/`.
2. Double-click on `level3` to load the scene if it isn't loaded already.
3. Right-click in the **Hierarchy** window and select **Create Empty** from the dropdown to create an empty game object.
4. Click on `GameObject` twice slowly to rename it.
5. Rename `GameObject` to `Timeline`.

With our `Timeline` game object still selected in the **Hierarchy** window, we can now open our **Timeline** window.

At the top of the Unity Editor, click on **Window** and then **Timeline**; the following screenshot shows this:

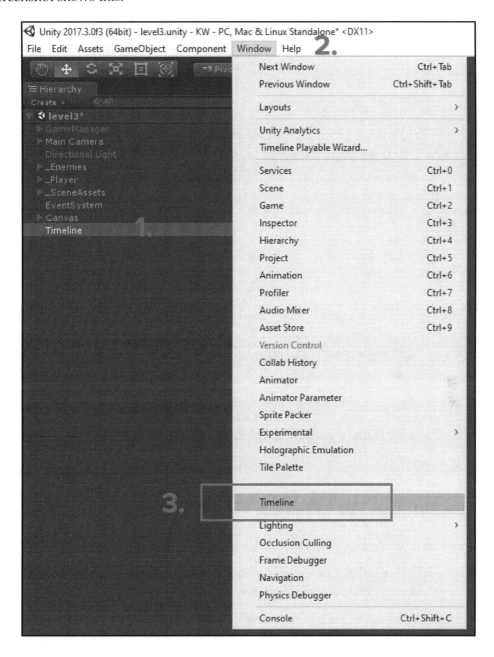

It's likely that the **Timeline** window will appear in the same window layout as your scene, which isn't ideal as we want to see our **Scene** while animating. To move the **Timeline** window to a better place, click on the name of the **Timeline** tag and drag it down to the bottom of the screen, where the **Console** and **Project** windows are. The following screenshot shows my current Unity editor layout proportions:

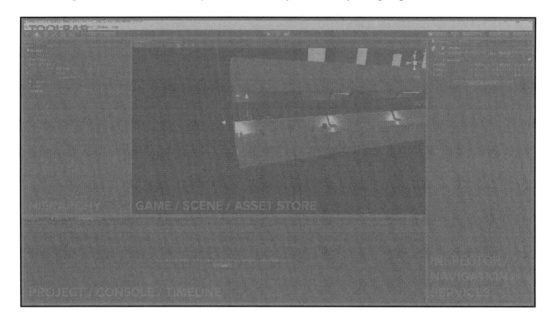

We can now continue to create our Timeline asset, where we will be creating our new animations for all of our game objects and their components.

To make a playable Timeline asset, do the following:

1. With the Timeline game object still selected in the **Hierarchy** window, click on the **Create** button in the **Timeline** window.
2. A window browser will appear to let us select where we want to save our playable file.
3. Choose the Assets folder.
4. Give the playable file a name (something relevant to what it's going to be used for; I'm naming mine level3) and click on the **Save** button.

Our Timeline asset has been created.

If you have been following along with this book, at first glance, the **Timeline** window will likely look like the **Animation** window we saw in `Chapter 3`, *Applying Art, Animation, and Particles*. If so, that's good! A good section of the controls and methodology will be familiar to you. One of the main differences of **Timeline** is that any of the game objects can be dragged into the **Timeline** window without needing to have any kind of hierarchical relationship between them.

The following screenshot shows our **Timeline** window holding the **Timeline** game object in its first **Timeline** track:

Also, in the **Inspector** window, our **Timeline** game object has gained some extra components. The following screenshot shows two of the added components—**Playable Director** and **Animator**:

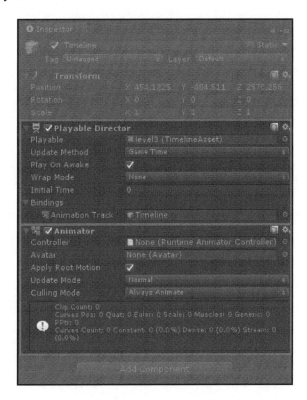

We worked with the **Animator** component in `Chapter 3`, *Applying Art, Animation, and Particles*, so for more details about this particular component, refer back to that chapter. Also, we don't actually do anything with the **Animator** component; it's just a required component for our **Timeline** setup.

The other component we gain when creating a `Timeline` asset file is **Playable Director**. It's the responsibility of this component to keep a relationship between the timeline and the game objects/components that are being manipulated. So, let's go through each of the properties under the **Playable Director** component to briefly get a general understanding of them.

First, we have **Playable**. When we click on the **Create** button in the **Timeline** window, we create a **Playable** file. This file holds all of the animations and game object/component instances relating to the timeline.

Then, we have **Update Method**. This parameter offers four properties that control how time affects the timeline. These properties are as follows:

- **DSP**: **Digital Signal Processing** (DSP) helps to improve accuracy between our timeline and it's audio to prevent it from going out of sync.
- **Game Time**: The time for the timeline will be sourced from the game's time. This also means the time can be scaled (that is, slowed down or paused).
- **Unscaled Game Time**: This option works the same as the **Game Time** property but it is not affected by scaling.
- **Manual**: This property uses the clock time we give it through scripting.

Next, we have **Play On Awake**. If this checkbox is ticked, our timeline will play as soon as the scene is active.

The next parameter is **Wrap Mode**. This property determines what happens when the timeline has finished playing:

- **Hold**: When the timeline reaches the end, it holds on to the last frame.
- **Loop**: The timeline repeats.
- **None**: The timeline plays, then resets back.

Initial Time adds a delay in seconds before the timeline begins.

Finally, we have **Bindings**. When a game object or component is dragged into the **Timeline** window, the **Bindings** list will update and show what object is connected to the timeline.

So far, we have discussed the timeline and introduced it to our scene. We have also gone through the components that are required to make the timeline work.

Now that we are more familiar with the timeline and the components that work in conjunction with it, in the next subsections, we are going to incorporate our large boss ship into our level3 scene and animate it through the timeline.

Setting up the boss game object in our scene

In this section, we are going to take a static UFO-looking game object from our imported Chapter 12 project files, drop it into the scene, and attach it to the timeline. From there, we will animate our UFO so that it spins and moves across the scene on two occasions.

To bring the large, boss UFO game object into our scene before animating it, we need to do the following:

1. Drag and drop the boss.prefab object from Assets/Resources/Prefab/Enemies into the _Enemies game object in the **Hierarchy** window.

   Next, we need to position the boss so that it's in our scene but out of view from the camera. That way, when it comes to animating the boss in the timeline, we can change its position and rotation when required.

2. Select the boss game object in the **Hierarchy** window and make sure that in the **Inspector** window, its **Transform** properties are set to the following:

   - **Position**: **X**: 0, **Y**: 0, and **Z**: -2000
   - **Rotation**: **X**: 0, **Y**: 0, and **Z**: 0
   - **Scale**: **X**: 1, **Y**: 1, and **Z**: 1

3. With the boss object still selected in the **Hierarchy** window, press *F* on your keyboard to see what it looks like in the **Scene** window.

The following screenshot shows the imported `boss` prefab, which contains a list of components and property values:

The `boss` object holds the following component and property values, as shown in the previous screenshot:

- Tagged as **Enemy** (denoted by **1.**).
- The **Transform** property values set to the ones detailed under *step 2* (denoted by **2.**).
- **Sphere Collider** set as a trigger with a **Radius** value of `80` (denoted by **3.**).
- `BossScript` makes the `boss` game object invincible to the player and if the player makes contact with the boss, the player will die (denoted by **4.**).
- Because the `boss` object is an enemy, it has a `radarPoint` object that is picked up on the radar (denoted by **5.**).

Before we move onto the next section, we need to add a `RadarRotation` script to the `radarPoint` game object which is a child of the boss game object. This script will make it so the `radarPoint` will always face the camera:

1. Expand the `boss` content in the **Hierarchy** window.
2. Select `radarPoint`, then drag and drop the `RadarRotation` script from `Assets/Resources/Script`, moving it from the **Project** to **Inspector** window.
3. Finally, select the **boss** game object in the **Hierarchy** window. Then drag and drop the `BossScript` from `Assets/Resources/Script` into the **Inspector** window.

Now that the `boss` object is in the scene, we can add it to the timeline in the next section.

Preparing boss for the timeline

In this section, we are going to take the `boss` game object from our **Hierarchy** window, drag it into the timeline, and animate it to fly past the player's ship at a particular point in the game. Finally, we will make it so that the `boss` object greets the player at the end of the level before jetting off after the player.

Further sections will continue to make use of the timeline, including using specialized **Playable** scripts from the Asset Store. But for now, let's get the `boss` object animated.

To animate the `boss` object in the timeline, do the following:

1. Select the `Timeline` game object and in the **Inspector** window, untick **Play On Awake** as we will be triggering the **Timeline** animation ourselves.

   To make it so that we trigger the **Timeline** animation, we need to apply a box collider to the main camera so that it is recognized when it collides with the `BossTrigger` game object that we mentioned toward the beginning of this chapter.

   To have the main camera recognized as a trigger, we need to do the following:

2. Select the main camera in the **Hierarchy** window.
3. Click on the **Add Component** button in the **Inspector** window.
4. Type in `Box Collider` and when you see it in the drop-down list, select it.
5. Tick the **Is Trigger** box under the **Box Collider** component.

Let's now continue setting up our **Timeline** window so that we can drag our `boss` game object into it:

1. Select the **Timeline** tab, which—as you will know if you have been following along with the previous sections—is found at the bottom of the Unity editor.

   The `Timeline` game object and the **Timeline** tab should now be selected. We can remove the `Timeline` game object from the **Timeline** window because we aren't going to animate the `Timeline` game object.

2. Right-click on the `Timeline` object in the **Timeline** window and select **Delete** from the dropdown.

The following screenshot shows the `Timeline` game object being deleted:

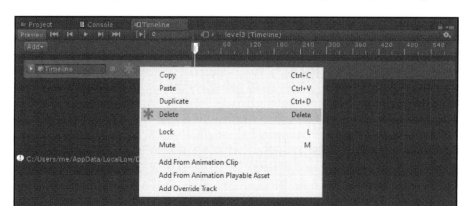

3. With the `Timeline` game object still selected in the **Hierarchy** window, click and drag the `boss` game object from the **Hierarchy** window down into the **Timeline** window.

A dropdown will appear with a choice of three selections:

- **Activation Track**: Turns a game object on or off
- **Animation Track**: Animates the game object
- **Audio Track**: Sets particular audio on or off

4. Because we want to animate our `boss` game object, we will choose **Animation Track**.

We will now have the `boss` game object in our **Timeline** window and our `boss` game object will gain an **Animator** component in the **Inspector** window.

The following screenshot shows what our timeline currently looks like:

Next, we will start adding keyframes to our **Timeline** window, which will affect our boss's position and rotation. Let's start by locking our **Timeline** window so that when we click on another game object, the **Timeline** window will remain active:

1. Select the Timeline game object in the **Hierarchy** window.
2. Select the **Timeline** window tab.
3. Click on the padlock button at the top-right corner of the **Timeline** window.

The padlock button is highlighted in the following screenshot:

Let's now move on to the next section, where we start adding keyframes to the timeline and make our boss game object move and rotate in two phases of the third level. Let's start with phase one.

Animating the boss in the timeline – phase one

In this section, we will be adding keyframes to the **Timeline** window for the boss game object. This will make it so that the boss game object will travel from one point to another while rotating on its center pivot.

To start adding keyframes for the boss game object, do the following:

1. With the **Timeline** window still locked, select the boss game object.

   We will now start recording our boss's position and rotation.

2. In the **Timeline** window, click on the record button next to the boss game object name; the button should begin to flash.
3. Make sure **Timeline Frame** is set to 0, as in the following screenshot:

4. In the **Inspector** window, change the boss's **Transform** property values to the following:

- **Position**: **X**: 1675, **Y**: 0, and **Z**: 600
- **Rotation**: **X**: 60, **Y**: −90, and **Z**: 0

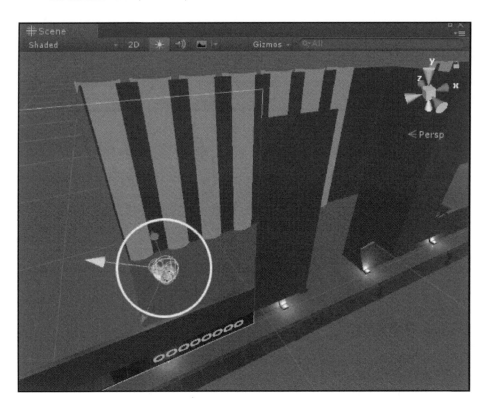

Now, to animate the boss object from one end of the corridor to the other, we need to add another keyframe for the boss. Do the following:

5. With the record button still flashing in the **Timeline** window, drag the timeline to frame 112 or change the value of the **Frame** parameter to 112.

6. Select the boss game object in the **Hierarchy** window and in the **Inspector** window, change the **Transform** property values to the following:

- **Position**: **X**: 3160, **Y**: 0, and **Z**: 600
- **Rotation**: **X**: 60, **Y**: −90, and **Z**: 20

The **Timeline** and **Animation** windows have the same navigation rules with regard to zooming and panning in either window: Holding down the middle mouse button and moving the mouse will pan.

Rolling the middle mouse wheel up or down zooms in and out. Hovering the mouse cursor over the animation bar and pressing *F* on the keyboard shows all the keyframes on the window.

7. Click on the record button next to the `boss` game object in the **Timeline** window to stop recording.
8. Click and scrub (scrub is an animator term for dragging) back and forth on the timeline's white arrow to see the `boss` game object move from left to right while rotating.

The following screenshot shows a bird's-eye view of the `boss` game object moving from left to right:

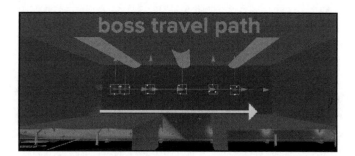

Later on, when we play the third level, we will see a moment where the `boss` game object rushes past the player in the distance. For now, we will continue by adding more keyframes to our **Timeline** window before moving on to looking at playables.

Let's move on to phase two of animating our `boss` game object.

Animating the boss in the timeline – phase two

In this section, we are going to animate our boss for a second time before the level ends as some form of resolution for the ending of this third and final level.

We are going to continue on from the same **Timeline** track that we started in the previous section.

So, let's continue animating our boss from where we left off:

1. Keep the **Timeline** window padlocked to stop the window from losing its display.
2. Select the boss object from the **Hierarchy** window.
3. Press the record button next to the boss object's name in the **Timeline** window so that the button flashes.
4. Enter 1012 into the **Frame** parameter.
5. With the boss object still selected in the **Hierarchy** window, we can now make changes to the **Transforms** property values. Set the boss object's position and rotation values to the following:

- **Position**: **X**: 4545, **Y**: 0, and **Z**: 600
- **Rotation**: **X** 60, **Y**: -90, and **Z**: 0

The following screenshot shows where our boss sits in phase two:

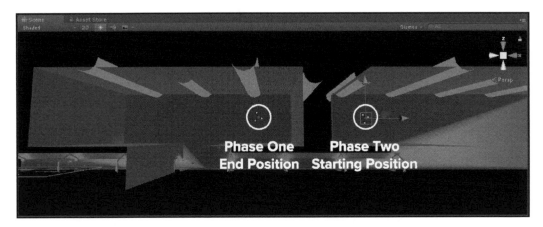

6. With the record button still flashing, move to frame 1180 in the **Timeline** window and set the boss game object to the following **Position** and **Rotation** values in the **Inspector** window:

- **Position**: **X**: 6390, **Y**: 0, and **Z**: 600
- **Rotation**: **X** 60, **Y**: -90, and **Z**: 20

7. Now, move to frame 1193 in the **Timeline** window and set the boss game object to the following **Position** and **Rotation** values in the **Inspector** window:

- **Position**: **X**: 6390, **Y**: 0, and **Z**: 207
- **Rotation**: **X**: 60, **Y**: 450, and **Z**: 0

8. Now, move to frame 1215 in the **Timeline** window and set the boss game object to the following **Position** and **Rotation** values in the **Inspector** window:

- **Position**: **X**: 5520, **Y**: 0, and **Z**: 50
- **Rotation**: **X**: 60, **Y**: 90, and **Z**: −40

9. Now, move to frame 1380 in the **Timeline** window and set the bossgame object to the following **Position** and **Rotation** values in the **Inspector** window:

- **Position**: **X**: 5510, **Y**: 0, and **Z**: 50
- **Rotation**: **X**: 60, **Y**: 90, and **Z**: 0

10. Now, move to frame 1400 in the **Timeline** window and set the boss game object to the following **Position** and **Rotation** values in the **Inspector** window:

- **Position**: **X**: 5510, **Y**: 0, and **Z**: 50
- **Rotation**: **X**: 60, **Y**: −70, and **Z**: −40

11. Now, move to frame 1420 in the **Timeline** window and set the boss game object to the following **Position** and **Rotation** values in the **Inspector** window:

- **Position**: **X**: 7540, **Y**: 0, and **Z**: 50
- **Rotation**: **X**: 60, **Y**: −70, and **Z**: 0

12. Press the **record** button next to the boss game object in the **Timeline** window to stop recording.

The following screenshot shows a birds-eye view of each of these positions with their **Timeline** frame numbers:

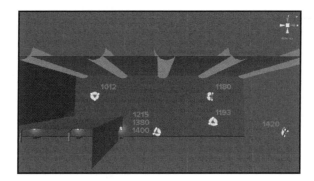

If you want to adjust the **boss** game object rotation more, it is recommended to have **boss** selected in the **Hierarchy** window. Make sure the local position is selected (denoted by **1** in the following image) and, with the Timeline still in record mode, rotate the Z axes several times (denoted with the number **2**):

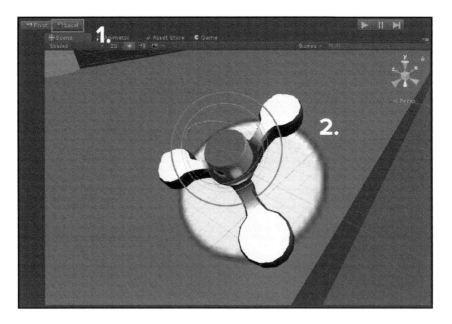

Finally, scrub backward and forward (move the **Timeline** indicator) in the **Timeline** to see the result you are given.

When you are happy, stop recording.

As you can see in the previous screenshot, the boss game object flies in from the left to the right toward where the player will be. The boss will stop rotating, pause, turn around, and zip off to the far right.

Let's press **Play** in the Unity editor and see the results of our level3 scene so far with the boss versus our player's ship throughout the level3 scene.

The player moves through the level and the boss animation is seen on two occasions. What we do see that we likely shouldn't is the large yellow dot of the boss even when the boss has moved on. It would be good if we can have it so that the boss disappears off the radar when we can't see the game object itself.

The following screenshot shows the boss object on the left screen that is not visible on the right screen but is still detected on the radar:

Let's make use of the timeline before ending this section to simply turn the radarPoint game object off and then on when we see the boss game object. Follow these steps:

1. Select the Timeline game object from the **Hierarchy** window.
2. Select the Timeline tab to see the **Timeline** content along with our boss animation.
3. Click and drag the boss's radarPoint object from the **Hierarchy** window into the **Timeline** window.
4. The **Timeline** dropdown appears. This time, select **Activation Track**.
5. Our **Timeline** window now has the radarPoint track.

Let's now add an activation clip to decide when the player should and shouldn't see the radarPoint object. Follow these steps:

Right-click on the track of the `radarPoint` object and select **Add Activation Clip**, as in the following screenshot:

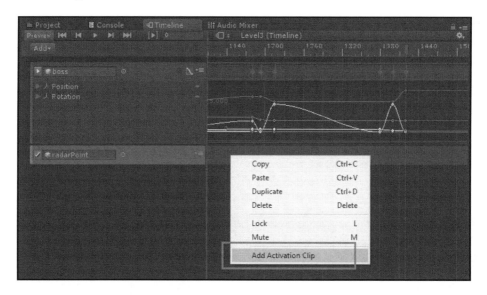

An **Active** clip will appear. This **Active** clip allows us to choose how long in the **Timeline** track we want this game object to be active. We want the `boss` game object to be active on two occasions—once when the boss moves past the player in the open-space area of the environment and once at the end when the boss approaches the player head-on.

For the first occasion, we need to set the **Active** clip between 35 and 95 on the timeline. We can do this by clicking and dragging its bar down to the 95 mark, as in the following screenshot:

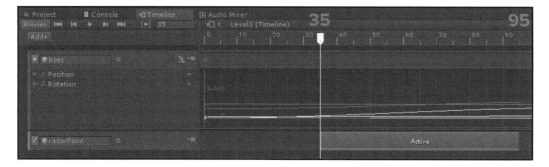

For the second occasion, we see the `boss` object to around `1020` to `1420`.

Repeat this process by doing the following:

1. Right-click and create an activation clip on the `radarPoint` track.
2. Scale the **Active** bar between the two **Timeline** points.
3. Save the scene.

We have now set the settings so that the `boss` game object and its `radarPoint` object are active at the same time.

We have successfully introduced a timeline to our scene and customized it so that it accommodates a new game object that needs to be animated throughout the third and final level of our game. In the next section, we are going to look further into extending the features of the timeline by introducing animating lights.

Extending the timeline

In this section, we are going to add more functionality to the timeline by increasing its standard track selection, as in the following screenshot:

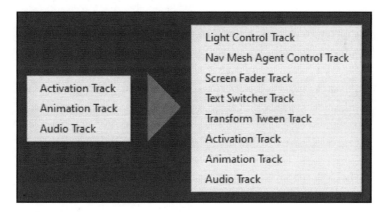

From this new extended track selection list shown in the previous screenshot, we will make use of **Light Control Track**.

It is possible to see a bigger selection from the drop-down list; this, however, is beyond the scope of this book. However, if you are interested, I will direct you to what to read to find out how to extend the list later on in this section.

In the next few sections, we will increase our tracklist with the aid of the Asset Store and download a free asset from Unity to increase our **Timeline** functionality. Then, we will animate the lights in our scene, which wouldn't have been possible before.

Adding Default Playables to the project

In this section, we will take a shortcut in scripting to extend the timeline's functionality by going to the Unity Asset Store and downloading a free package called **Default Playables**. We will discuss the main features of playables and what they entail, but it is too lengthy to discuss it as a scripting approach.

Playables organize, mix, and blend data through a playable graph to create a single output. To download and import **Default Playables** to our list, do the following:

1. Press *Ctrl* (*command* on macOS) + *9* on your keyboard to load the **Asset Store** window.
2. At the top of the **Asset Store** window, in the search bar, type `default playables` and press *Enter* on your keyboard.
3. Select the only selection from the thumbnail list—**Default Playables**.
4. On the **Default Playables** shop screen, click on the **Download** button.
5. Once downloaded, we can now import the asset into our project by clicking on the **Import** button, as in the following screenshot:

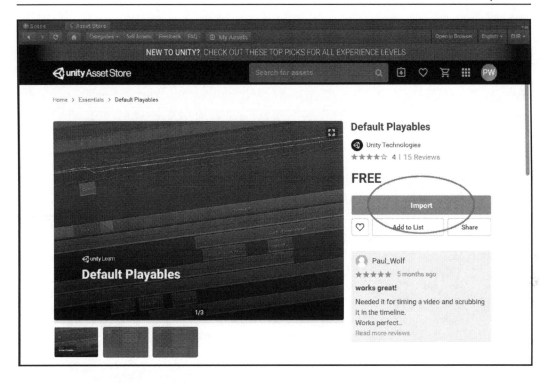

A window will appear with a list of scripts to import to our project.

6. Click on the **Import** button at the bottom right of the window to import all the files into our project.

We now have extra functionality added to our timeline, with an added folder in our Assets folder called DefaultPlayables. Also, as mentioned, to add even more functionality (such as timeline tracks) to the timeline, check out the file inside the DefaultPlayables folder named DefaultPlayablesDocumentation.

Let's now move on to the next section where we will make use of manipulating the lights in the scene.

Manipulating light components in the timeline

In this section, we will continue working on the same timeline and expand it to hold more tracks. In the last section, we introduced a free to downloadable asset from the Asset Store called **DefaultPlayables** to save us from writing code from scratch and to offer new playables. This asset gave us the ability to add new tracks to our timeline. To continue adding new tracks, we will manipulate the lights in our third level scene.

To add a light component to the timeline, we need to do the following:

1. Make sure the **Timeline** window is still locked, which we set in the *Preparing boss for the timeline* section.
2. Right-click in the bottom-left open-space corner of the **Timeline** window and select **Light Control Track**, as in the following screenshot:

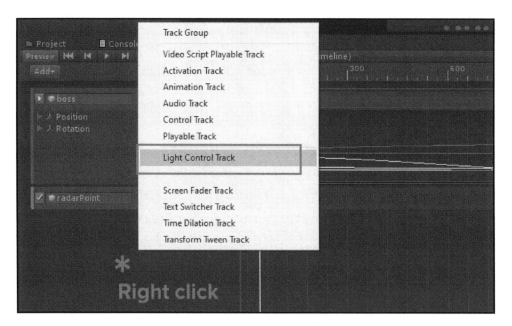

We now have an empty light component track added to our timeline.

3. Next, we can add an **Animation** clip by right-clicking on the timeline's track line and selecting **Add Light Control Clip Clip**, as in the following screenshot:

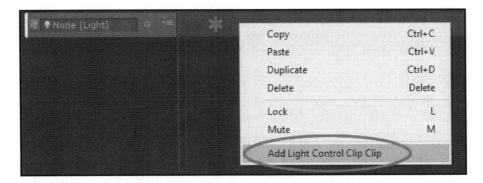

4. We now have a `LightControlClip` object in our timeline. Click on this clip and look at the **Inspector** window. There are a few options here, but we are going to focus mainly on **Color, Intensity**, and **Range**.

   These properties will directly change the values of the light that sits in the **None (Light)** parameter.

5. Set your **Light Control Clip** values to the ones shown in the following screenshot in your **Inspector** window:

6. Next, we will set the duration of this clip to `100`. We can do this by either changing the value of the **Duration** parameter in the **Inspector** window or by clicking on and dragging `LightControlClip` to the `100` mark, as in the following screenshot:

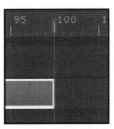

Because this light is going to flash white then red, ideally it would make sense to have a loop between the two transitions. However, for the sake of blending and filling up the timeline, we are going to do it this way.

7. Select `LightControlClip` and press *Ctrl* (*command* on the macOS) + *D* 25 times to spam the track line with light control clips.
8. Select the second `LightControlClip` object from the left and change its **Color** property from white to red.
9. Repeat this process for clips 4, 6, 8, 10, 12, 14, 16, 18, 20, 22, 24, and 26.
10. Now, zoom into the second `LightControlClip` object and move it 50% of the way across to its previous clip to create a blend between the color of the light, as in the following screenshot:

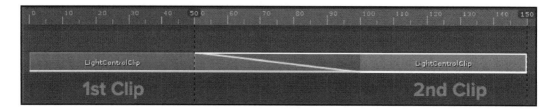

11. Continue moving each clip 50% of the way across to the previous clip's location to make it so that the lights flash white to red until the level finishes. The following screenshot shows the position of the third clip:

Once you've merged the clips, we can now duplicate our light track asset so that more than one light can flash.

12. Click on the track asset and press *Ctrl* (*command* on macOS) + *D* four times. The following screenshot uses the * symbol to highlight where to click, along with the duplicates made:

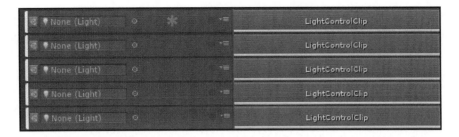

As these are all of the same types of tracks, we can put them into a track group to keep our timeline tidy.

13. Right-click in the open-space area at the bottom left of the timeline and select **Track Group** from the dropdown.

14. Our track group is made. Now, click and hold the top light track asset while holding down *Shift* and click on the bottom light track asset to select all of the light track assets. Still holding down the left mouse button, drag these track assets into the track group.

15. Click on the **Track Group** name and rename it to something relevant, such as Lights.

    You can use the **+** button to expand and collapse the group.

    The following screenshot shows the final result of the timeline lights:

16. Now that you know how to make a track group, follow the same process for the boss object and its radarPoint object and call the track group Boss.

    The final step is to drag and drop the five lights that will flash red and white into the **Game** window.

17. Either click on the small, round remote button next to **None (light)** or drag and drop `light00`, `light01`, `light02`, `light03`, and `light04` into each parameter.
18. Scrub or drag the **Timeline** indicator backward and forward on the timeline to see the selected lights flashing red.
19. Save the scene.

The following screenshot shows our player on the third level with a new set of AI enemies, a large boss flying in the background, and flashing lights:

Now would be a good time to apply the pause screen, if you haven't already, to all three scenes. Follow these instructions if you don't feel comfortable doing this on your own:

1. With the `level3` scene saved, load up `level1` from the `Assets/Scene` folder from the **Project** window.
2. In the **Hierarchy** window, hold down *Ctrl* (*command* on macOS) and select the `Canvas` and `EventSystem` game objects, then press *C* to copy them.
3. Load the `level3` scene back up.
4. Select the `Canvas` game object from the **Hierarchy** window and press *Delete* on your keyboard.
5. Press *Ctrl* (*command* on macOS) + *V* to paste `EventSystem` and `Canvas` from the level that contains the pause screen.
6. Expand `Canvas` and then the `LevelTitle` game object in the **Hierarchy** window.

7. Select the `Level` game object and change the **Text** property value from `level 1` to `level 3` in the **Inspector** window.

8. Save the scene.

9. Repeat this process for `level2`.

The following screenshot shows `level3` paused:

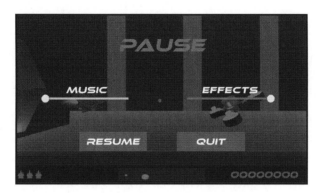

Let's move on to summarizing what we have covered in this chapter.

Summary

In this chapter, we introduced a new concept to our game to make it more interesting than just taking place in space. Our camera and player needed to be slightly tweaked for the final level to support side-scrolling, instead of them being static in one screen as is the case on the previous two levels. We also introduced a second enemy that would move around the floor, dodging other enemies in a panic-like state. The fleeing enemy used the navigation system that comes with Unity as standard and we gave the enemy a floor to run around on. Lastly, we introduced the **Timeline** feature, which is related to the original animation system we used in Chapter 3, *Applying Art, Animation, and Particles*. We also discovered how **Timeline** lets any game object or component be animated in it without needing some form of hierarchical link between the game objects. Also, we extended the timeline to cover other components, such as lights, which we can't animate alone with the **Timeline** feature.

The main takeaways from this chapter are the introduction of AI with a navigation system that can also be used for other behaviors in other games and the introduction of the timeline and its use to encourage creativity in projects, such as cutscenes, films, and TV animated sequences.

In the next chapter, we will look at polishing the visuals of our game and we will see what tools can help us in optimizing performance and testing for bugs.

Before you move on to the next chapter, try out the following mock test as this is the last mini mock test in this book before the big one.

Mock test

1. You are developing a game where your player is inside an office with other staff workers around them. When your player walks to a particular point, a trigger event is called to move the staff into another room with the use of **Playable Director**.

   You notice that when the game is paused and then un-paused, the audio and animation are out of sync with each other.

   Which property in the **Playable Director** component will likely fix this issue?

   A) Set the wrap mode to **Hold**.
   B) Set the update method to **DSP**.
   C) Set **Initial Time** to the current time (the time when the game is paused).
   D) Set the update method to **Unscaled Game Time**.

2. We have a set of playables linked within our playable graph. We need to remove one of these playables and its inputs.

   Which **PlayerGraph** function should we use?

   A) **DestroyOutput**

   B) **DestroyPlayable**

   C) **DestroySubgraph**

   D) **Destroy**

3. You have developed an eight-ball pool game. One of the testers has come back to you saying the frame rate of the game drops too low when one of the players breaks the balls up at the start of a game. All of the balls have rigid body sphere colliders.

How can we improve the drop in the frame rate?

A) Use a less expensive shader on the objects that are colliding with one another.
B) Set the maximum allowed timestep to a range of 8–10 fps to account for this worst-case scenario.
C) Change the rigid bodies so that they are kinematic.
D) Use box and capsule colliders instead of sphere colliders.

4. What does the `NavMesh` modifier do?

A) A `NavMesh` modifier determines what stage of the build process the NavMesh is baked at.
B) A `NavMesh` modifier describes the AI of each agent in the scene.
C) A `NavMesh` modifier allows NavMesh baking to occur outside the main thread so that it can be dynamically baked at runtime.
D) A `NavMesh` modifier adjusts how a game object behaves during NavMesh baking and can, for example, only affect certain agents.

5. Why does it help to only have the necessary boxes checked in the layer collision matrix?

A) Unchecking boxes will hide layers so that they're not rendered.
B) Checking boxes will indicate which collisions can be ignored.
C) Checking boxes will show which layers are colliding in the frame debugger.
D) Unchecking boxes will reduce the number of layer collisions the physics system needs to check.

6. When we create a `Timeline` asset for a game object, what component is created and added to our game object?

A) `PlayableBinding`
B) `PlayableDirector`
C) `PlayableOutput`
D) `PlayableGraph`

7. In your first-person shooter, which you are testing, you notice that when the alarm is sounded, the enemy guards come running toward the player. When you observe the enemy guards advancing, you close the door on them but notice that their arms and heads are coming through the door that you have closed.

What setting do you need to increase to stop these arms and heads coming through objects that they shouldn't?

A) **Step Height**
B) **Max Slope**
C) **Agent Height**
D) **Agent Radius**

8. You have got yourself involved in a classic Save the Mayor rescue game. Your player is a trained vigilante trying to eliminate potential attackers to harm the city's mayor. One of the attackers gets too close and you take a shot to warn them off. The attacker runs away but returns shortly after crawling towards the mayor.

    Which `NavMesh` agent property can simulate this cautious behavior?

    A) **Area Mask**
    B) **Auto Braking**
    C) **Stopping Distance**
    D) **Priority**

9. Congratulations—Save the Mayor was a massive success and you have been asked to start development straight away on Save the Mayor 2! Your vigilante is back and this time he can jump *and* run and jump across building rooftops.

    Yet again, you have applied the `NavMesh` agent so your vigilante can run and jump across buildings in a linear path. You have correctly hooked all your animation controls up but have noticed that your vigilante isn't animating when it comes to jumping between building rooftops.

    What setting or property do we need to change to solve this issue?

    A) Uncheck **Auto Traverse OffMesh Link** under the `NavMesh` agent component.
    B) Increase the **Obstacle Avoidance Priority** value in the `NavMesh` agent component.
    C) Uncheck the **Height Mesh** property in the **Bake** settings under **Navigation**.
    D) Increase the jump distance in the **Bake** settings under **Navigation**.

10. We are working on a third-person game and our character is using a finite state machine to react to their states. We currently have it set so that if we get too close to a particular character, they will attempt to run and hug you.

    What finite state machine component is the programmer working on?

    A) **Actions**
    B) **Transitions**
    C) **Events**
    D) **Rules**

11. Which of these tracks can the timeline not add without applying additional coding?

    A) **Activation Track**

    B) **Animation Track**

    C) **Light Control Track**

    D) **Playable Track**

12. One of the 3D artists has supplied you with a series of three-dimensional models to be applied to one of the startup scenes for the project you are currently developing.

    When importing the models into the scene, you notice that all the models have sharp edges. You have asked the artist to make the models smoother.

    Is there anything else that can be done on the developer-side to possibly fix these sharp three-dimensional model edges?

    A) Calculate the normals to a particular smoothing angle value.

    B) Import the files through Unity instead of dragging and dropping the files.

    C) Apply materials to each three-dimensional model.

    D) Make sure there is lighting in the scene.

13. What does `LateUpdate` do?

    A) Replaces the standard `Update` function when frames are overloaded.

    B) `LateUpdate` takes fewer resources to run, which makes it ideal for mobile platforms.

    C) An update is only called once on every frame. `LateUpdate` is called every three frames.

    D) `LateUpdate` is the last item in the execution order before rendering.

14. What are the advantages of using `GameObject.Find` (if any)?

    A) There aren't any; it's slow and demanding.

    B) If not called on every frame, it makes coding useful for referencing.

    C) `GameObject.Find` is deprecated.

    D) `GameObject.Find` searches through library asset data outside of the Unity project.

15. Do we have to import the `UnityEngine` library and `MonoBehaviour` with every script?

    A) No, as long as they are not applied to a game object.

    B) Yes, or the Unity engine rejects the script.

    C) Yes, as they act as a header to all scripts.

    D) Only `MonoBehaviour` must be inherited in all cases.

16. When moving from one scene to another, you notice the second scene is much darker even though it uses the same art and lighting as the scene before it.

    How do we make it so that the lighting acts how it should in the scene?

    A) Make sure all the lights are turned off before being turned on in the second scene.

    B) Keep all the lights on from the first scene when moving into the second scene.

C) Duplicate the lights from the previous scene over to the new one on load up.

D) Turn off **Auto Generate** in the lighting settings and manually generate the lights.

17. What are the benefits of `Debug.Log()`?

A) It is useful if developers want to know the value of a variable.

B) Sends string values to each variable.

C) There aren't any; it's deprecated, so we don't use it.

D) Logs information into Unity's database.

18. Is the Audio Mixer useful to developers?

A) No, it's specifically built for audio users; developers use the AudioSource.

B) Yes, as it can be used to hold all sound in one central point.

C) Only if the developer is skilled in handling audio alone.

D) Yes, it helps the performance of the audio.

19. Why do some developers prefer JSON over PlayerPrefs?

A) PlayerPrefs was released before JSON, which gives it a bigger following.

B) JSON can be used with more data types and is a more compatible API.

C) Both are good; it's just a matter of personal preference.

D) JSON is owned by Unity, so it incorporates a lot of features.

20. Why would we use a trigger box instead of a collider?

A) Triggers and colliders carry out the same task.

B) Triggers have more functionality and cost less to run than colliders.

C) A trigger can call code when another collider/trigger enters it.

D) Triggers have different colored boxes.

13
Effects, Testing, Performance, and Alt Controls

In this final chapter, we are going to go through the process of checking, supporting, polishing, and preparing our game so that it's built and ready to be played on a device, making it platform-independent. Because our game will be ready to be played on various devices, we need the game to support as many screen ratios as possible. Back in Chapter 7, *Adding Custom Fonts and UI*, we made our game's UI support various screen ratios. The game, however, was built purposely for a 1920 x 1080 resolution, as discussed in Chapter 2, *Adding and Manipulating Objects*.

In this chapter, we will make our game run at different screen ratios to support the use of mobile devices. This will involve changing Unity's Canvas scale and updating our Player script controls to update its screen boundaries, touch screen capability, and our ability to tap to move our ship. Furthermore, we will make our game aware that it is being played on a mobile device and we'll make some changes, such as removing the **AD** button in the shop as adverts aren't supported on PC devices.

The PC version of Killer Wave will have more polished effects applied, such as post-processing, which will basically make our game more pretty with effects such as motion blur, chromatic aberration, color grading, and a few more effects on top. We will also be looking at reflection probes to create a mirrored effect for some of our art assets in the level3 scene.

In this chapter, we'll be covering the following topics:

- Applying physics with RigidBody
- Customizing for different platforms
- Preparing to build "Killer Wave" for mobile
- Applying PC visual improvements
- Adding global illumination and other settings
- Building and testing our game

The next section will specify the exam objectives that will be covered in this chapter.

Core exam skills being covered in this chapter

The following are the core exam skills that will be covered in this chapter:

- *Programming core interactions*:
    - *Implement and configure game object behavior and physics*
    - *Implement and configure inputs and controls*
    - *Implement and configure camera views and movement*

- *Working in the art pipeline*:
    - *Understand materials, textures, and shaders, and write scripts that interact with Unity's rendering API*
    - *Understand lighting, and write scripts that interact with Unity's lighting API*

- *Optimizing for performance and platforms*:
    - *Evaluate errors and performance issues using tools such as Unity Profiler*
    - *Identify optimizations to address requirements for specific build platforms and/or hardware configurations*

- *Working in professional software development teams*:
    - *Demonstrate knowledge of developer testing and its impact on the software development process, including Unity Profiler and traditional debugging and testing techniques*
    - *Recognize techniques for structuring scripts for modularity, readability, and reusability*

Technical requirements

The project content for this chapter can be found at `https://github.com/PacktPublishing/Unity-Certified-Programmer-Exam-Guide/tree/master/Chapter13`.

You can download the entirety of each chapter's project files at `https://github.com/PacktPublishing/Unity-Certified-Programmer-Exam-Guide/archive/master.zip`.

All the content for this chapter is held in this chapter's `unitypackage` file. This file includes a `Complete` folder, which holds all of the work we'll carry out in this chapter. So, if at any point you need some reference material or extra guidance, check it out.

Check out the following video to see the Code in Action: `https://bit.ly/2NvBSEK`.

Applying physics with RigidBody

Throughout this book, we have used colliders and trigger boxes to detect hits from a bullet or a selection made in the first rendition of our shop. We have also referred to applying a **RigidBody** component to some of these game objects with colliders to ensure a collision is detected. We haven't made use of **Rigidbody** any other way so far. However, in this section, we are going to make more use of **Rigidbody** by making a collision happen: the blocks will collapse from our `level3` boss game object going through them.

The following image shows the cargo art assets being smashed out of the way with the use of applying and tweaking **Rigidbody** components, which is what we will achieve in this section:

Let's make a start by setting up our `level3` scene with some pre-made assets:

1. In the **Project** window, navigate to the `Assets/Scene` folder.
2. Double-click the `level3` scene to open it.
3. In the **Project** window, drag and drop `physicsBarrier` from `Assets/Resources/Prefab` into the **Hierarchy** window.

4. Select the `physicsBarrier` game object in the **Hierarchy** window and make sure its **Transform Position** and **Rotation** property values in the **Inspector** window are set to zero. Note that **Scale** should be 1 on all axes.

The following image shows `physicsBarrier` in the `level3` scene. Notice the green outline, which shows this is our series of box colliders, which will contain our physics:

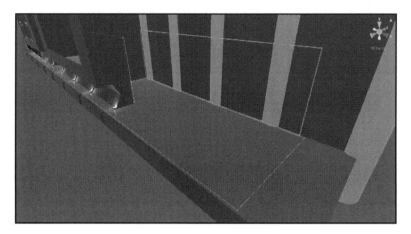

5. In the **Hierarchy** window, expand `physicsBarrier` to show its three children game objects.
6. Select all three of these child objects and set their **Rigidbody** component so that **Is Kinematic** is ticked.
7. The following screenshot shows all three game objects selected and the **Rigidbody** settings being updated:

Is Kinematic will ensure these three game objects aren't affected by the physics in the scene. Even if we did tick the **Gravity** box, the game objects won't begin to fall when the scene starts as expected. So, whatever happens in our scene regarding collisions, these three game objects will remain still and solid so that they cage all of the physics engine's reactions.

With a game object selected that holds a **Rigidbody** component, the following properties will alter the game object's behavior when it's manipulated by Unity's physics engine:

Mass: Game Objects mass in kilograms (Default value: **1**)
Drag: Air resistance, with zero being no resistance (Default value: **0**)
Angular Drag: Air resistance based on rotation (Default value: **0.05**)

More information about **Rigidbody** and its properties can be found here: `https://docs.unity3d.com/ScriptReference/Rigidbody.html`.

Now, we can bring our cargo boxes into the scene.

In the **Project** window, drag and drop the `cargoBulk` prefab from `Assets/Resources/Prefab` into the **Hierarchy** window. As with the `physicsBarrier` prefab, make sure the **Transform** property values are set to their default values.

The `cargoBulk` prefab should be in place and look like the one shown in the following screenshot:

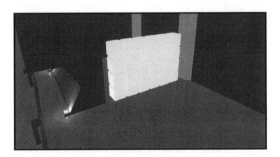

To reinforce `cargoBulk` so that it collapses at the right time, a script needs to be applied called `TurnOnPhysics`. This will set all of the cargo game objects from **Is Kinematic** that are `true` to `false` after `38` seconds, which is the time the boss is due to crash through the cargo boxes.

`physicsBarrier` and `cargoBulk` and their children game objects are all set as colliders. Currently, our boss is set as a trigger for when it is shot by the player. However, we don't want it to be a trigger here as the boss will move through the cargo boxes like a ghost.

We can make `boss` start as a non-trigger and then, at the end of the level, turn its trigger on with the use of **Timeline**. To alter the **Is Trigger** tick box, we need to do the following:

1. Select the **Timeline** game object in the **Hierarchy** window.
2. Right-click the `boss` **Timeline track asset** and from the drop-down, select **Edit in Animation Window.**

The following screenshot shows where to right-click and load the **Animation** window:

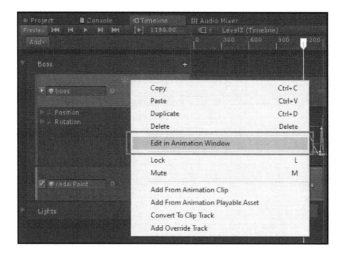

Our **Animation** window appears along with the keyframes from the `boss` game object that we placed in the previous chapter. We can add two keyframes to this window to turn on and then off with the **Is Trigger** box. To do this, follow these steps:

1. Drag **Animation Indicator** to the beginning of the animation track in the **Animation** window.
2. Click the **record** button.
3. In the **Hierarchy** window, select the `boss` game object and select the **Is Trigger** to be unchecked in the **Sphere Collider** component in the **Inspector** window.

4. Back in the **Animation** window, drag **Animation Indicator** all the way to frame `1193` (this will be the part where the `boss` game object has already burst through the blocks).

5. Select the **Is Trigger** box in the **Inspector** window so that it's ticked.

6. Finally, back in the **Animation** window, press **record** to turn it off and close the **Animation** window.

7. Save the scene and press **Play** in the Unity Editor to play `level3`.

However, after doing this, something doesn't seem right. By the time we reach the end of the level, the blocks have already collapsed and when the `boss` game object collides with them, the blocks appear to float away. This is because the game objects in our scene aren't scaled to real-world size, but the gravity is. To make things look heavier, we can change the gravity of the project, as follows:

1. At the top of the Unity Editor, go to **Edit** | **Project Settings** | **Physics**.

   Here, we have **Physics Manager**, which is where the gravity has been set to its default world scale.

2. Change the **Y** value of **Gravity** from `-9.81` to `-1000`.

Your project's gravity can also be changed through scripting, as shown here: `https://docs.unity3d.com/ScriptReference/Physics-gravity.html`.

3. Save the scene again. Now, if we press **Play**, our cargo blocks will remain and our `boss` game object will burst through them, as shown in the following screenshot:

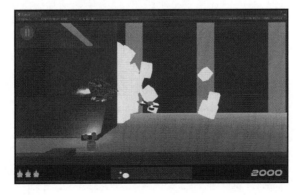

The **Physics Manager** contains global settings for your project's physics. One of the many useful settings at the bottom of the **Physics Manager** is **Layer Collision Matrix**. This holds all the names of the layers in your project that can and can not collide with each other. If you would like to know more about **Layer Collision Matrix**, check out the following link: `https://docs.unity3d.com/Manual/LayerBasedCollision.html`.

If you aren't happy with the way the `cargo` game objects react when they're hit by the `boss` game object, even by tweaking its **Rigidbody** property values (including the ones mentioned in the first tip, earlier in this section).

Every collider can have a physics material applied to it, which will affect the object's bounciness and friction.

Creating and applying a physics material can be done in three steps:

1. In the **Project** window, right-click and select **Create | Physic Material**.
2. Select **New Physic Material** and change its property values in the **Inspector** window (you can also rename the file so that it represents what physical material you're trying to achieve).
3. Select a game object with a collider. Then, click the **remote** button next to the **Material** field and select **New Physic Material**:

More information about **Physic Material** can be found at `https://docs.unity3d.com/Manual/class-PhysicMaterial.html`.

Our game now has some physic effects applied to it. Now, each time the boss crashes through the cubes, the reaction will be different each time and not like a fixed animation. This is because the movement is all based on the Unity engine's physics.

Now, let's move on and make our game more customized for multiple platforms.

Customizing for different platforms

Throughout this book, we have been developing and playing our game in the Unity Editor. In this section, we are going to start making some considerations regarding what will differ between the Android and PC versions of our game. For example, mobile devices have a touch screen, so it would be useful if our game could detect that it's being played on a mobile device and therefore implements the correct controls.

Also, our game has been developed with a strict 1,920 x 1,080 resolution, we have introduced flexibility with the shop scene's UI, and ensured it accommodates various aspect ratios. In this section, we will go further and make our game support various aspect ratios.

Let's get started and modify our `Player` script so that it supports touch screen movement and fires on mobile devices.

Navigating and firing the player's ship with the touch screen

In this section, we are going to revisit the `Player` script and add some functionality so that if and when our game is ported to an Android device, the player has touch screen capabilities.

To allow our player to auto-fire and navigate to a touch position, we need to do the following:

1. In the **Project** window, navigate to the `Assets/Resources/Script` folder and open the `Player` script.

    At the top of the `Player` script, we are going to add some new global variables to support the new control system.

2. Add the following code, along with the rest of the global variables, to the `Player` script:

    ```
    Vector3 direction;
    Rigidbody rb;
    public static bool mobile = false;
    ```

    The `direction` variable will hold the player's touch screen location, `rb` will hold a **Rigidbody** reference for our player's ship so that it can access other properties within, and the `mobile` variable is simply a `static` switch that lets the rest of the game know the player's controls.

    We need to make it so the game recognizes which platform the game is running on so that it can implement the player's mobile controls. Unity has a platform-dependent compilation that lets us choose from a list of directives so that we can determine what platform the game is running on.

3. Scroll down to the `Start` function in the `Player` script and add the following code inside the `Start` function's scope:

    ```
    mobile = false;

    #if UNITY_ANDROID && !UNITY_EDITOR
        mobile = true;
        InvokeRepeating("Attack",0,0.3f);
        rb = GetComponent<Rigidbody>();
        #endif
    ```

Within the `Start` function, we set our `mobile bool` variable to `false`. Then, we run a platform define directives check to see if we are running an Android device and not using the Unity Editor.

 If you would like to find out more about the other platform-dependent compilations, check out the following link: `https://docs.unity3d.com/Manual/PlatformDependentCompilation.html`.

If we are using an Android device, we fall into the scope of this special type of `if` statement and do the following:

1. We set the `bool mobile` variable to `true`.
2. Make it so our `Attack` method gets called every `0.3` seconds with Unity's own `InvokeRepeating` function, which acts as an auto-fire tool.
3. Assign the `player_ship` game object's **Rigidbody** to the `rb` variables.
4. Finally, we close the `if` statement.

   To make our `InvokeRepeating` method fire a bullet with the use of the `Attack` method at `0.3` seconds, we need to modify the `Attack` method's `if` statement.

5. Scroll down to the `Attack` method in the `Player` script and replace the `if` statement with the following:

   `if (Input.GetButtonDown("Fire1") || mobile)`

   By adding the `mobile` variable to the `if` statement's condition, we can check if the player is pressing the fire button or `if` the `mobile` `bool` variable is set to `true`.

   Now, we need to add more functionality to the `Update` function within our `Player` script, which includes two new methods we haven't coded in yet but will after the following code block.

6. Replace the current `Update` function in the `Player` script and its content with the following code so that it supports PC and mobile controls:

   ```
   void Update ()
   {
     if(Time.timeScale == 1)
     {
       PlayersSpeedWithCamera();
   ```

```
        if (mobile)
         {
           MobileControls();
         }
        else
         {
           Movement();
           Attack();
         }
      }
    }
```

Our refreshed `Update` function contains the following:

- An `if` statement to check if the game has been paused. If it has, we bypass the rest of the `Update` content. If you want to find out more about pausing the game, check out `Chapter 10`, *Pausing the Game, Altering Sound, and a Mock Test.*

- Within the `if` statement, we run a new method called `PlayersSpeedWithCamera`, which will contain code we have already coded. We're simply moving the code into the method so that it covers PC and mobile controls for when the camera has speed applied to it.

- Then, we have a second `if` statement that checks if the `mobile` `bool` variable is set to `true` or `false`. If `true`, we run our `MobileControls` method; otherwise, our PC `Movement` and `Attack` will run.

- As mentioned previously, we have two new methods (`PlayersSpeedWithCamera` and `MobileControls`). The first method is a simple cut and paste of code from the current `Movement` method, which we want to accommodate for PC and mobile controls. The second method will cover touch controls for when the player places their finger on the screen and the `player_ship` game object moves to that location.

7. So, let's start with the `PlayersSpeedWithCamera` method first. Still in the `Player` script, scroll down to the `Movement` method and select and cut the first `if` statement. The following is the code that I want you to cut:

```
if(camTravelSpeed > 1)
  {
     transform.position += Vector3.right * Time.deltaTime
         * camTravelSpeed;
     movingScreen += Time.deltaTime * camTravelSpeed;
  }
```

Then, create a new method in the `Player` script called `PlayersSpeedWithCamera` and paste the previous `if` statement code block inside the scope of the `PlayersSpeedWithCamera` method.

Now, the content of the `PlayersSpeedWithCamera` method will run for mobile and standalone platforms. If you would like to refresh yourself on the details of the camera's travel speed, take a look at Chapter 12, *NavMesh, Timeline, and Mock Test*.

Now, let's take a look at the second method called `MobileControls`, which can be found in the `Player` script.

8. Write the following method inside the `Player` script so that the player can navigate player_ship around the screen:

```
void MobileControls()
{
    if (Input.touchCount > 0)
    {
        Touch touch = Input.GetTouch(0);
        Vector3 touchPosition =
Camera.main.ScreenToWorldPoint
                                    (new
Vector3(touch.position.x,
                                    touch.position.y,300));
        touchPosition.z = 0;
        direction = (touchPosition - transform.position);
        rb.velocity = new Vector3(direction.x,
                                    direction.y,0)* 5;
        direction.x += movingScreen;
        if (touch.phase == TouchPhase.Ended)
        {
            rb.velocity = Vector3.zero;
        }
    }
}
```

Keep in mind that the `MobileControls` method is called on every frame in the `Update` function. Inside the `MobileControls` method, we do the following:

- Run an `if` statement to check if there has been more than one touch on the screen of the device. If a finger has touched the screen, we fall into the `if` statements scope.
- We assign a touch to a `touch` variable.

If you would like to know more about the `Touch` struct and its other properties. such as `deltaPosition`, which is useful for measuring swipe gestures, take a look at `https://docs.unity3d.com/ScriptReference/Touch.html`.

- Next, we take a ready-made function from Unity to convert the screen's touch position and store it in a world space position.

If you would like to know more about converting a point into world space, check out the following link: `https://docs.unity3d.com/ScriptReference/Camera.ScreenToWorldPoint.html`.

- Because we aren't affecting the player ship's Z axis, we set `touchPosition` on the Z axis to zero.
- Store the `Vector3` position of `touchPosition`, minus the `Vector3` position of the player's ship.
- Send the `player_ship` game object to the `Vector3` position that is stored in `direction`. Multiply it by 5 to make it move slightly faster.
- Apply whatever value is in the `movingScreen` variable to the `direction` X position.
- Finally, if the state of touch phase has ended (finger taken off the screen), apply a zero value to the `rb velocity` variable.

So, now, the player's ship automatically fires and can move around the screen thanks to its **Rigidbody** component. Now, we need to make it so that when either level ends, we stop the player from firing automatically and **Rigidbody** no longer has an effect on the player's movement. Otherwise, when the level ends, the player's ship won't stop firing and runs the risk of not being able to animate out of the level.

To fix our player from continuously shooting and being able to be moved at the end of the level, we need to do the following:

1. In the **Project** window, navigate to the `Assets/Resources/Script` folder and open the `ScenesManager` script.

2. Inside the `ScenesManager` script, scroll down to the `if` statement that checks if the game has not ended (`!gameEnding`) and add the following line of code within its `if` statement:

```
if (!gameEnding)
{
    gameEnding = true;
    GameObject player = GameObject.Find("Player");
// ADD THIS CODE
    player.GetComponent<Rigidbody>().isKinematic = true;
// ADD THIS CODE
    Player.mobile = false;
// ADD THIS CODE
    CancelInvoke();
// ADD THIS CODE

    if (SceneManager.GetActiveScene().name != "level3")
```

In the previous code block, we have added four new lines of code that will do the following:

- Cache a reference from our `player_ship` game object
- Access the `player_ship` **Rigidbody** component and set **isKinematic** to `true`
- Set the `mobile bool static` variable to `false`
- Run Unity's `CancelInvoke` function to stop all invokes running in our scene (stops auto-fire)

3. Save the `ScenesManager` script.

Now, we need to go into **Input Manager** and look at the **Fire1** button. Here, the left mouse button is set to the **Alt Positive Button** property. To fix this in the Unity Editor, do the following:

1. Go to **Edit | Project Settings | Input.**
2. Set **Alt Positive Button** to `mouse 0`.

Our game is now self-aware of what device it will run on and if the device does run on a mobile Android device, the touch controls will be implemented.

Now, let's widen the support for our game and ensure our game covers various screen ratios and screen boundaries on either platform.

Extending screen ratio support

In this section, we are going to do two things, The first is to make it so no matter what aspect ratio our game is running at, our player will be able to fly around. The second is to make it so the Text UI isn't affected by the different screen ratios.

So, let's start with our first task of making our game support multiple screen ratios during levels.

In the **Project** window, navigate to the `Assets/Resources/Script` folder and open the `Player` script. Now, follow these steps:

1. At the top of the script, where the global variables are, comment out the width and height floats; we are going to replace them:

   ```
   // float width;
   // float height;
   ```

2. Add the following `GameObject` array to hold our new points:

   ```
   GameObject[] screenPoints = new GameObject[2];
   ```

   The array we've just added will hold two points to represent our screen's boundaries.

3. Next, in the `Player` script's `Start` function, we need to comment out the following:

   ```
   // height = 1/(Camera.main.WorldToViewportPoint(new
   //     Vector3(1,1,0)).y - .5f);
   // width = 1/(Camera.main.WorldToViewportPoint(new
   //     Vector3(1,1,0)).x - .5f);
   // movingScreen = width;
   ```

4. .Add the following method name:

   ```
   CalculateBoundaries();
   ```

The method we've just entered does not exist yet, so let's add this new method now.

5. Still in the `Player` script, add the following method and its content to create our new screen boundaries:

```
void CalculateBoundaries()
{
    screenPoints[0] = new GameObject("p1");
    screenPoints[1] = new GameObject("p2");
    Vector3 v1 = Camera.main.ViewportToWorldPoint(new Vector3
        (0, 1, 300));
    Vector3 v2 = Camera.main.ViewportToWorldPoint(new Vector3
        (1, 0, 300));
    screenPoints[0].transform.position = v1;
    screenPoints[1].transform.position = v2;
    screenPoints[0].transform.SetParent(this.transform.parent);
    screenPoints[1].transform.SetParent(this.transform.parent);
    movingScreen = screenPoints[1].transform.position.x;
}
```

So, let's go through the steps of the `CalculateBoundaries` method and see what it does to our game:

1. First, it creates two new game objects and names them `"p1"` and `"p2"`.
2. We then make use of the `ViewportToWorldPoint` function, which will give us our game's world space positions for our screens boundaries.
3. Then, we apply our new `Vector3` variables, v1 and v2, to our array of game object's positions; that is, `"p1"` and `"p2"`.
4. Now that `"p1"` and `"p2"` represent the boundaries, we need to make them children of the `Player` script, which will update their **Transform Position** values.
5. Finally, we update the `movingScreen float` value with our `screenPoint` value for when the game has a moving camera.

Continuing with the `Player` script, we now need to update the `Movement` method's directional conditions so that they support our new game boundaries.

6. Scroll down to the `Movement` method and replace all four of the old `if` statements with the new ones:

```
if (transform.localPosition.x < width + width/0.9f)
//OLD

if (transform.localPosition.x <
    (screenPoints[1].transform.localPosition.x -   //NEW
screenPoints[1].transform.localPosition.x/30f)+movingScreen)

if (transform.localPosition.x > width + width/6)
//OLD

if (transform.localPosition.x <
    (screenPoints[1].transform.localPosition.x -   //NEW
screenPoints[1].transform.localPosition.x/30f)+movingScreen)

if (transform.localPosition.y > -height/3f)
//OLD

if (transform.localPosition.y >
    (screenPoints[1].transform.localPosition.y -   //NEW
        screenPoints[1].transform.localPosition.y/3f))

if (transform.localPosition.y < height/2.5f)
//OLD

if (transform.localPosition.y <
    (screenPoints[0].transform.localPosition.y -   //NEW
        screenPoints[0].transform.localPosition.y/5f))
```

Each of the new `if` statements in the previous lines of code will hold the same purpose of taking the value from the p1 or p2 game objects to get a restriction of the boundaries of the screen. This ensures the player ship doesn't go too far out of view.

The following screenshot shows the level1 scene with p1 and p2 representing the new gameplay boundaries in a different resolution from the usual 1920 x 1080 to show the flexibility our gameplay boundary now has:

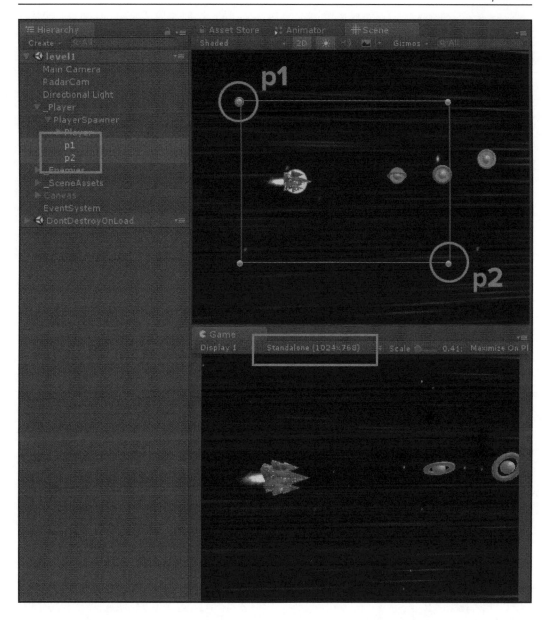

Lastly, we need to update our `PlayerSpeedWithCamera` method and set the `movingScreen` variable to zero if the game camera isn't moving to the right.

7. Inside the `Player` script, go to the `PlayersSpeedWithCamera` method and add the following `else` condition:

```
else
    {
        movingScreen = 0;
    }
}
```

8. Save the `Player` script.

   `CrossPlatformInput` for 2017.3:

   Unity offers an alternative controls package that is called instead of the `Input` class. It can offer support for alternative platforms with added components and tools such as a virtual joystick and buttons.

   If you are interested in finding out more about the `CrossPlatformInput` package, it can be downloaded from the Standard Assets package in the Asset Store.

Now, let's move on and look at the second part of this fix. Here, even though the gameplay window now supports various aspect ratios, some images and text will struggle to look as cosmetically pleasing. The following image shows what would happen to our game's pause screen if we changed the typical 1,920 x 1,080 resolution:

As you can see, the text and images lose their scale when they're in different aspect ratios. We can fix this by doing the following:

1. In the **Project** window, navigate to the `Assets/Scene` folder and double-click the `level1` scene.
   - Select the `Canvas` game object in the **Hierarchy** window. Then, in the **Inspector** window, change **UI Scale Mode** in **Canvas Scaler** to **Scale With Screen Size**, as shown in the following screenshot:

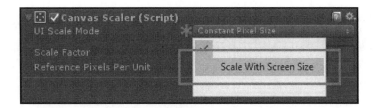

2. Change the **Reference Resolution** property to **X**: 1920 **Y**: 1080.

Now, our **Game** window, when shown at various screen sizes, will look more in proportion:

3. Save the level1 scene and update **Canvas Scaler** for all the scenes in the project.

With that, we've made our game more compatible in that it supports various aspect ratios for platforms other than a standard 1920 x 1080 resolution. Also, our game controls are self-aware of whether it's being played on a PC or Android device. We also made use of the Touch class to move our player around the scene.

In the next section, we are going to finalize our game for mobile before adding extra effects and general polish for the PC build.

Preparing to build Killer Wave for mobile

In this section, we will be finalizing our version of Killer Wave for Android. Before we build our game to Android, we need to apply some fixes that will only be necessary for the Android build.

The fixes we will be applying in this section are as follows:

- Adjust the lighting so that it suits our Android device
- Make it so that when pressing the pause button, our ship doesn't move to its location
- Make it so that our game stays in landscape mode
- Stop the screen from dimming when the device hasn't been touched for a while
- Set the game textures to a lower resolution
- Add prefab explosion to enemies and players

After we've applied these minor fixes, we will build the game for our Android device.

So, let's get started with our first task by altering the lighting.

Setting up the lighting for Killer Waves for Android

Each scene that contains a 3D model will require lighting to be generated. Unity Editor's lighting will differ from the lighting provided on an Android device.

With the current default lighting settings applied, the following image shows the difference between both platforms. The image on the left was taken on PC, while the one on the right was taken from a mobile device:

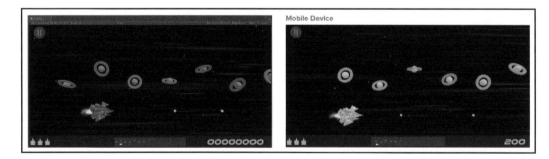

So, let's adjust the lighting so that both platforms have a similar level of brightness and contrast:

1. At the top of the Unity Editor, go to **Window** | **Lighting** | **Settings**.
2. Press the **Scene** button at the top of the **Lighting** window and apply the following values:

3. Untick **Realtime Global Illumination** and untick **Baked Global Illumination**.

   We will cover these two settings when we apply visual improvements, but for now, **Realtime Global Illumination** affects the indirect lighting that's applied to other objects to help create a more realistic, soft-colored light. **Baked Global Illumination** will have lights stuck on 3D assets to give the appearance of light shining on a surface, but the majority of our lights move, so this will not work as a baked light.

The following image now shows that the PC and mobile versions are starting to look similar:

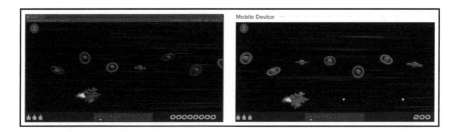

4. Now, we need to enable and adjust the emission of the following enemy materials in the **Project** window under `Assets/Resources/Material`:

- **basicEnemyShip_Inner**: **Emission** ticked, **Color**: `993600 (Hex)`, **Intensity**: `0.6`
- **basicEnemyShip_Outer**: **Emission** ticked, **Color**: `4C0000 (Hex)`, **Intensity**: `0.3`
- **darkRed**: **Emission** ticked, **Color**: `801616 (Hex)`, **Intensity**: `0.5`

We explained how to change the emission of an material back in `Chapter 2`, *Adding and Manipulating Objects*. Changes these values will give us the following output:

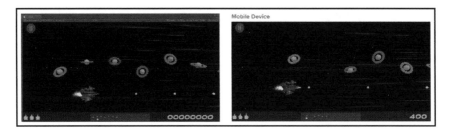

Our game now looks nice and bright on either platform. We'll fix the small issue with pausing the mobile version of the game next.

Stopping involuntary player controls

When it comes to playing the game on a mobile device, we will want to press the pause button. But if and when we do, the game will also consider the press as a movement command and the player's ship will move into the top left corner where the press was made.

So, to fix this minor issue, we will apply an extra condition to our `MobileControls` method, as follows:

1. In the **Project** window, navigate to the `Assets/Resources/Script` folder and open the `Player` script.

2. Inside the `Player` script, scroll down to the `MobileControls` method and replace the following `if` statement condition with the following one:

```
if (Input.touchCount > 0 &&
    EventSystem.current.currentSelectedGameObject == null)
```

The preceding code block will run a check to see whether a finger is touching the screen as before, but will also check there isn't a game object in the location when being pressed. If any of these conditions aren't met, then the player will not move.

3. Finally to enable the `EventSystem` scroll to the top of the `Player` script and add the following namespace:

```
using UnityEngine.EventSystems;
```

4. Save the `Player` script.

In the next section, we will do some final texture optimizations and apply a ready-made and well-earned explosion prefab.

Final optimizations for Killer Wave

In this section, we will be adding some optimization to our mobile version of the game by reducing the size of the textures. We will also add explosions to our enemies and player.

Let's start by reducing our textures and compressing them.

Reducing texture sizes and compression

To reduce the size of the `.apk` file that gets installed on Android devices, as well as the overall performance increase, we can reduce the size of the textures of our game through Unity and also apply compression, which lowers the size even more.

The trick is to reduce the size of the texture but not too much; otherwise, the textures themselves will begin to blur and look cheap.

In this section, we will be reducing the texture sizes of the following:

- `PlayerShip` and its extras (shop upgrades and thrusters)
- The background wallpaper texture of the stars in our two levels
- Shop button icons

Let's start by selecting and reducing the player ship's texture sizes and compress them:

In the **Project** window, navigate to the `Assets/Resources/Texture` folder.

Select all of the following filenames:

- `playerShip_diff`
- `playerShip_em`
- `playerShip_met`
- `playerShip_nrm`
- `playerShip_oc`

All these files have a texture size of 512 x 512, so let's reduce them to 256 x 256, compress them, and turn off any filtering by setting them to the values shown in the following screenshot of the **Inspector** window:

Do the same to the following textures, all of which can be in the same folder. However, this time, set the texture size from 1,024 x 1,024 all the way down to 64 x 64:

- `b. Shot_diff`
- `b_Shot_nrm`
- `c. Bomb_diff`
- `c. Bomb_nrm`

Continue doing this for the rest of the textures and see what the results look like in the game by playing between the `shop` and `level1` scenes. Do this at your own discretion.

 If you would like to know more about the textures that get imported into a project and how to adjust their quality levels, check out the following link: `https://docs.unity3d.com/Manual/ImportingTextures.html`.

Now, let's move on and add a ready-made particle explosion to each of our players and enemies by making some minor scripting tweaks.

Adding explosions to our players and enemies

The time has come to add a prefab explosion to our game objects to represent their destruction and their general effect on the boss when it's being shot at. We covered particle systems back in Chapter 4, *Applying Art, Animation, and Particles*. Here, we will apply some scripting so that when a `Die` method is called, we will instantiate our explode prefab.

To instantiate the explode prefab when an enemy dies, we need to do the following:

1. In the **Project** window, navigate to the `Assets/Resources/Script/` folder and open the `EnemyWave` script.

2. Inside the `Die` method, replace its content with the following to instantiate the `explode` game object:

```
GameObject explode =
    GameObject.Instantiate(Resources.Load("Prefab/explode"))
        as GameObject;
explode.transform.position =
this.gameObject.transform.position;
Destroy(this.gameObject);
```

In the previous code block, we added two extra lines above the current `Destroy` function. We covered this in detail in Chapter 2, *Adding and Manipulating Objects*. The two extra lines do the following:

- When the `Die` method runs, it will create the `explode` prefab from `Assets/Prefab`.
- The position of the `explode` prefab is updated with the same location as the enemies.

3. Save the `EnemyWave` script and repeat this process for the `EnemyFlee` and `BossScript` scripts.

   Finally, for our `Player`, we will add something similar but also add a delay for when the `player_ship` gets destroyed so that we can see the explosion before we reload the scene again.

4. Still in the same **Project** window, open the `Player` script, scroll down to the `Die` method, and replace its content with the following:

```
GameObject explode =
  GameObject.Instantiate(Resources.Load("Prefab/explode"))
    as GameObject;
  explode.transform.position =
this.gameObject.transform.position;
  GameManager.Instance.LifeLost();
  Destroy(this.gameObject);
```

In the previous code, we have updated the player's `Die` method so that it creates a prefab explosion and houses its position where the player's position is.

However, we need to add a delay in the `GameManager` script where the previous code block was introduced.

5. Save the `Player` script before continuing with the `GameManager` script.

6. Open the `GameManager` script so that you can add a delay to the scene when it's updated.

7. In the `GameManager` script, scroll down to the `LifeLost` method, select its content, *Cut* it (cut, not *Delete*, as we are going to paste it somewhere else), and replace the `LifeLost` method with the following code:

```
StartCoroutine(DelayedLifeLost());
```

Here, we are delaying the content from our `LifeLost` method. However, here, we will be using `StartCoroutine` to create the delay, as shown in the previous line of code.

8. Next, we will paste the content from the original `LifeLost` method inside the following code block:

```
IEnumerator DelayedLifeLost()
{
   yield return new WaitForSeconds(2);

// PASTE LIFELOST CONTENT HERE

}
```

In the preceding code block, we have added an `IEnumerator`. This will be executed from `StartCoroutine`, along with a 2-second wait.

9. Paste in the `LifeLost` content we cut earlier and then save the `GameManager` script.

The following screenshot shows our game object with particle explosions applied:

Now, the time has come to create a build of our Android build.

Setting up the build settings for Android

In this section, we are going to set up our **Player Settings** and build our Unity Project for an Android device. For testing purposes, I will be using a fairly old tablet and a recent phone to see if there are any differences in terms of the setup between the two devices.

Before setting up our **Player Settings**, ensure you have a copy of the Java Development Kit and Android Development Kit installed. To check this, do the following:

1. At the top of the Unity Editor, go to **Edit | Preferences**.
2. Then, click on **External Tools** in the **Unity Preferences** window.
3. The following screenshot shows these two development kits, along with **Download** buttons for them. If you don't have either, you'll need to install them:

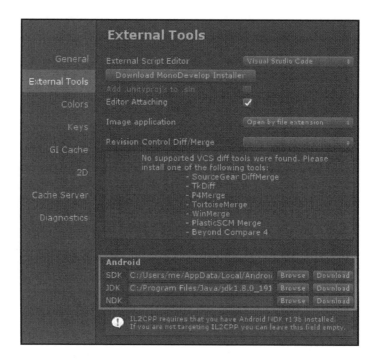

 If you require any more specific information about the development kit installation process, check out the following link: `https://docs.unity3d.com/Manual/Preferences.html`.

Now, let's continue to **Player Settings** and set up our game:

1. At the top of the Unity Editor, go to **File | Build Settings...**.
2. Make sure you have all of the scenes set up in **Scenes In Build**.
3. Select **Android** from **Platform list** and click **Switch Platform...**

4. Click **Player Settings...** to move on to the next stage of setting up for Android.
5. In the **Inspector** window, at the top of the window, update the **Company Name** and **Product Name** fields to whatever you wish.
6. Select the **Resolution and Presentation** tab and untick **Portrait** and **Portrait Upside Down**.
7. Select the **Other Settings** tab.
8. Scroll down to the **Identification** section. For the first **Package Name** in the list, clear the content of the field and type com., followed by the name of the company you entered and the name of the game. In the following screenshot, I have added a company name and the name of the game. Make sure you add the . in-between:

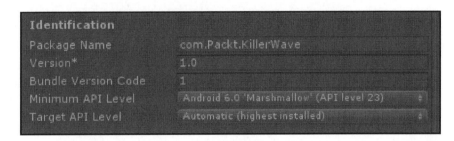

9. Also, set your **Minimum API Level** to 23 or above if your device can handle it. If it can't, when we go to build, you will receive an error in the **Console** window regarding changing the **Minimum API Level** value.
10. Go back to the **Build Settings** window and click the **Build** button.
11. You will be asked to give apk a name and location. Pick wherever and whatever you want to name the file and click **Save.**

> If you get a **Gradle build failed** error, try changing **Build System** in the **Build Settings** window to **Internal.**

12. Finally, ensure you have your Android device in USB debugging mode and copy apk over to the device.
13. Go to the location where apk has been copied on the device and select it to install and run it.

When testing the game on an Android device, you may find it distracting that your device's brightness dims when the screen isn't being touched.

We can fix this by adding the following code. ideally in the `Awake` function of the `GameManager` script. as this relates to the game's overall interaction:

```
#if UNITY_ANDROID
        Screen.sleepTimeout = SleepTimeout.NeverSleep;
#endif
```

This brings us to the end of building our game for mobile. In this section, we covered setting up our lighting settings so that they matched what we were seeing in the Unity Editor. After that, we cleared up some small fixes so that we wouldn't unintentionally move the player ship to where the pause button is when we press it on our device. We also reduced the size of our `apk` by reducing the size of the textures for our game. This also helps with the performance of Android devices when they're playing our game. Then, we added our explode prefab and made some fixes to our script to instantiate our explosions in the right place at the right time.

Finally, we went through the procedure of setting up our Unity build file and copied it over to the Android device so that it can be installed and run.

Congratulations if you have made it this far, built the game, and everything works as expected. If not or you met some issues along the way, don't worry – other Unity users will have had similar problems and they aren't too hard to find with some Googling. Now, we will start bug testing our game.

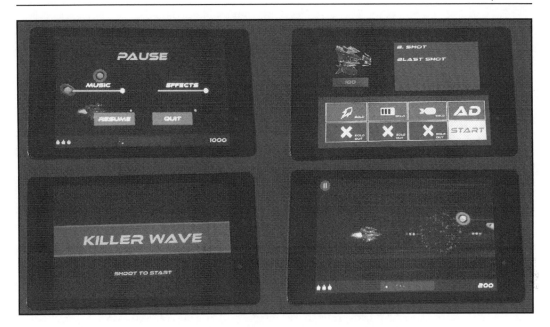

In the next section, we'll apply polish and shine to our PC version.

Applying PC visual improvements

In this section, we are going to focus on the PC version, where we will have more leg room to apply effects as it's likely the PC playing this game will be more powerful than a mobile device.

We will cover things such as post-processing, where we can create pretty effects to make our game shine even more. We can do this by applying effects such as blur motion, blurring to the edges of the screen, bending the screen to give it a dome screen effect, altering the coloring, and a few more.

We'll also be taking a look at lighting and reflections so that we have a slightly modified shop scene that will hold multiple lights and make the game stand out more. In the `level3` scene, we will be adding reflective assets to show off the use of these reflection probes on our art assets.

Let's start by discussing post-processing.

Post-processing

In this section, we will be installing and applying post-processing effects to our game. This will provide us with effects that are used in films, such as film grain, chromatic abbreviation, color grading, lens distortion, and more. Let's make a start by installing this package into our project.

Installing post-processing

In later versions of Unity, post-processing can be installed via the Package Manager. We don't have this in version 2017.3, so usually, we'd have to install the package via the Asset Store. However, the download for post-processing no longer exists. This leaves us with two options: either we install a new version of Unity and risk complications with converting our project into a higher version, or I provide a post-processing import package so that we can continue. I'll leave this choice up to you as you already how to install post-processing for your version of Unity. However, in this chapter's download content, there will be a `unitypackage` file named `PostProcessingv2_2017` that you can use to install this into our project.

To install the 2017 version of post-processing, we need to do the following:

1. Ensure your Unity Editor project is open.
2. Navigate to the location where you have downloaded the file and double-click it.
3. We will be presented with the **Import Unity Package** window. Select **All** and then **Import**, as shown in the following screenshot:

If you are carrying on from the previous section, your platform will still be aimed at Android devices, so we will need to change back to **Standalone**. Let's do that now:

1. At the top of the Unity Editor, go to **File | Build Settings....**
2. Select **PC, Mac & Linux Standalone**, followed by **Switch Platform**.

Our Unity project now has post-processing installed. With that, we can begin preparing some scenes for our standalone game.

Preparing and applying post-processing to our title and level scenes

In this section, we are going to make some changes to our title scene so that it supports our image and text being affected by post-processing. By the end of this section, our title scene will look more impressive, as shown in the following image:

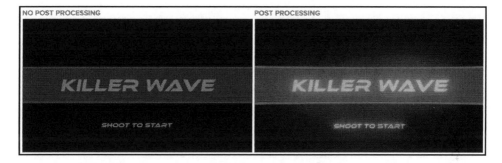

To apply post-processing to our title scene, we need to do the following:

1. In the **Project** window, navigate to Assets/Scene and open title.

   We now need to change some property values in the Canvas game object so that the post-processing changes come from the camera's feed, not just the Canvas itself.

2. In the **Hierarchy** window, select the Canvas game object.
3. In the **Inspector** window, change the Canvas component property's **Render Mode** to **Screen Space - Camera.**

4. Drag **Main Camera** from the **Hierarchy** window into the **Render Camera** property field.

Next, we will add two post-processing components to our **Main Camera** game object.

5. Select **Main Camera** in the **Hierarchy** window.

6. Click the **Add Component** button in the **Inspector** window.

7. Type `Post Process Layer` into the drop-down list. When you see its name in the list, select it.

8. In the **Post Process Layer** component, change the **Layer** property value to **Everything**. This means it will affect all the layers in the scene. This normally isn't recommended, but because there isn't very much in our scene, there isn't a lot to affect.

If you want to change the **Post Processing Layer** component from **Everything** to something else, you will need to create a new layer at the top-right of the **Inspector** window, as we did in Chapter 2, *Adding and Manipulating Objects*. Give it a name such as `PostProcessing` and change **Everything** to **PostProcessing** to remove the warning message in the **Post Processing Layer** component.

9. Click the **Add Component** button again and type `Post Process Volume` until you see it on the list. Then, select it.

10. At the top of the **Post Process Volume** component, tick the **Is Global** box.

11. In the **Project** window, drag and drop the **TEXT** asset from the `Assets/` folder into the **Profile** parameter into the **Inspector** window.

12. The **Game** window will have the **Profile** post-processing effect applied to it, which may or may not be too extreme for you. We can set **Weight** from `1` all the way down to `0`. I'm setting mine to `0.6`.

The following screenshot shows our title scene **Game** window, along with the two **Post Process Layer** and **Post Process Volume** components and the highlighted areas mentioned in the previous steps for reference:

13. Save the scene.

14. Repeat *steps 2-12* for the shop scene, but instead of applying the **TEXT** post-processing profile, use **SHOP** instead. The following image shows the final result this has had on the shop scene before and after post-processing has been applied (with the **Weight** property set to 1):

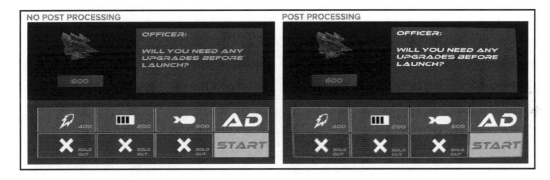

15. Now, repeat *steps 2-13* for the gameOver scene. The end result should look similar to the following:

16. Repeat *steps 5-13* but instead of applying the **TEXT** post-processing profile, add the **DEFAULT** post-processing profile.

The following image shows an example of the `level3` scene with and without the **DEFAULT** post-processing profile applied:

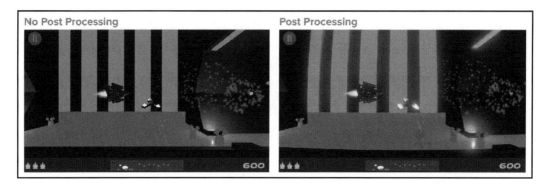

That's all of the scenes we need to implement for a post-processing profile. In the next section, we will briefly go through each of the effects that we have and can apply.

Post-processing effects (overrides)

In this section, we are briefly going to discuss the effects the post-processing package offers us. By the end of this section, you will be more familiar with the effects and be able to make your own post-processing profile.

Now that we've got to see what post-processing does to our game, we can talk about each of the effects. Let's start by loading up the `title` scene and altering what we have:

1. In the **Project** window, navigate to the `Assets/Scene` folder and load up the `title` scene.
2. Select **Main Camera** in the **Hierarchy** window.

Our main focus for this section will be the **Overrides** section in the **Post Process Volume** component:

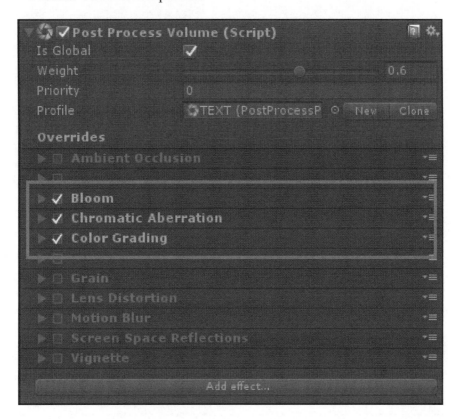

So, let's go through some of these **Overrides** for our **Post Process Volume** in the **Inspector** window. Then, I will provide a link that I encourage you to explore so that you can play around with some of the values.

Bloom

This effect creates fringes of light extending from the borders of bright areas in an image.

We can extend the content by selecting the arrow to the left of the **Bloom** tick box (top-left corner in the following screenshot):

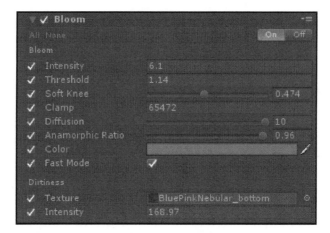

In the previous screenshot, we have turned all of the properties on. Simply deselect and select each property to see what influences (if any) are made to each of the properties. Also, try and change some of the values. Use the previous screenshot as a fallback if you feel you have gone too far with the effect.

An interesting property to take a look at here is the **Threshold** property, where if we lower its value to under `1.14`, the bloom effect will increase. However, if we make the value too low, we can overcook it and destroy the look of our game, as shown in the following:

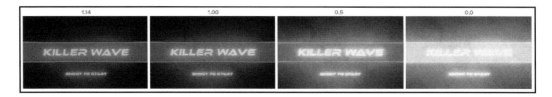

Hopefully, I have introduced enough curiosity for you to continue playing and experimenting with the bloom effect.

 More information about the **Bloom** effect can be found at `https://docs.unity3d.com/Packages/com.unity.postprocessing@2.1/manual/Bloom.html`.

Next, we'll look at **Chromatic Aberration**.

Chromatic Aberration

This effect mimics what a real-world camera produces when its lens fails to join all the colors to the same point.

The following screenshot shows our current settings:

This effect is more noticeable around the edges of the **Game** window. As an example, in the following image, I have moved the image and its text up so that we can see these two components begin to warp more obviously:

 More information about the **Chromatic Aberration** effect can be found at https://docs.unity3d.com/Packages/com.unity. postprocessing@2.1/manual/Chromatic-Aberration.html.

Next, we'll look at the final effect we applied to our `title` scene – **Color Grading**.

Color Grading

This effect alters the color and luminance of the final image that Unity produces. **Color Grading** has had the biggest range of properties throughout all of the post-processing effects. I've split these properties up into bulleted segments:

- **Mode:**

Here, we have a choice of three color grading modes so that we can alter the camera's final image. In the previous screenshot, Unity is giving us a warning regarding changing **ColorSpace** from **Gamma** to **Linear**. If you want to do this, it can be changed in **Edit** | **Project Settings** | **Player** | **Player Settings** | **Other Settings**.

- **Tonemapping:**

This hosts a selection of tonemapping algorithms that we can use at the end of the color grading process.

- **White Balance:**

This alters the temperature and tint of the final picture.

- **Tone:**

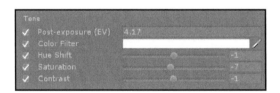

Here, you can adjust the **Saturation, Contrast, Hue Shift, Color filter,** and **Post-exposure (EV)** options which, similar to the **Bloom** effect's **Threshold**, can easily be overcooked and provide some powerful bright/dark results.

- **Channel Mixer:**

This changes each overall image's RGB channel.

- **Trackballs:**

Here, the three trackballs (**Lift** adjusts dark tones, **Gamma** adjusts mid-tones, and **Gain** adjusts highlights) affect the overall hue of the final image.

- **Grading Curves:**

Grading Curves are an advanced way to adjust specific ranges in hue, saturation, or luminosity in the final image.

 More information about the **Color Grading** effect can be found at https://docs.unity3d.com/Packages/com.unity.postprocessing@2.1/manual/Color-Grading.html.

That concludes looking at all three of the post-processing overrides for the title scene. If you would like to know more about the rest of the effects that are available, check out the following link, where you can read up on the other 11 effects that can be applied to a Unity scene: https://docs.unity3d.com/Packages/com.unity.postprocessing@2.1/manual/index.html.

Anti-aliasing modes

In this section, we are going to view the different types of anti-aliasing in the **Post Process Layer** component. As you may know, anti-aliasing smooths the rough edges of game objects in our game to get rid of staircase effects. Unity offers three different algorithms that smooth edges.

The following modes are offered:

- **Fast Approximate Anti-aliasing (FXAA)**: This is typically used with mobile platforms due to its quick algorithm. It is the most efficient technique but doesn't support motion vectors.
- **Subpixel Morphological Anti-aliasing (SMAA)**: This is high quality but is more demanding in terms of system performance.
- **Temporal Anti-aliasing (TAA)**: An advanced high demanding technique that uses motion vectors (a motion vector is a key element in the motion estimation process).

The following image shows the player's ship with different anti-aliasing techniques applied to it:

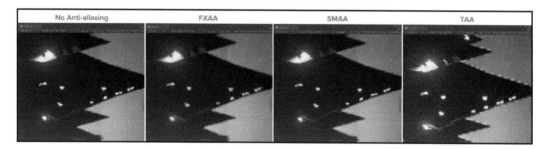

As you can see, the purpose of anti-aliasing is to take off jagged edges, but with our game, these edges aren't as noticeable since it's full of dark backgrounds.

 If you would like to apply anti-aliasing and find out more, check out the following link: https://docs.unity3d.com/Manual/PostProcessing-Antiali asing.html.

Next, we'll look at creating and applying our own post-processing profiles, which we created at the start of the *Applying PC visual improvements* section.

Creating and applying post-processing profiles

In the final section on post-processing, we will discuss creating a post-processing profile. From there, you can (if you want to – I encourage you to) create your own profile and apply it to the **Post Process Volume** component in the **Inspector** window. Finally, you will be able to add/remove your own effects to alter the final look of the standalone game.

So, to create and add our own effects, I suggest that we go back to a scene that we have already prepared – the `title` scene:

1. In the **Project** window, navigate back to `Assets/Scene` and open the `title` scene.
2. Select the **Main Camera** game object in the **Hierarchy** window.
3. Press the **New** button inside the **Post Process Volume** component (as shown in the following screenshot):

4. To add your own post-processing effects, click the **Add effect...** button (as shown in the previous screenshot) at the bottom of the **Post Process Volume** component and select an effect from the drop-down list.
5. Once you have applied the effect, click **All** to turn all the properties on (as shown in the following screenshot):

6. If you want to remove the effect, click in the top-right corner of the effect (above the **Off** button) and select **Remove** from the drop-down list (as shown in the previous screenshot).

7. It's as simple as that! If you want to see where the file is located, click on the **PostProcessProfile** field, as shown in the following screenshot:

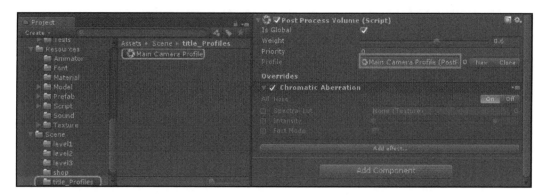

8. The location will ping yellow in the **Project** window (as shown in the previous screenshot), which is also where you can rename the file to something that resembles the use of the profile (right-click the file and select **Rename** from the drop-down).
9. If you don't like what you've created, you can delete the **PostProcessProfile** file from the **Project** window and click the small **remote** button to the right of the **Profile** parameter in **Post Process Volume** to add the **TEXT** profile once more (or whichever profile you want).

That was an extensive overview of the post-processing package that Unity has to offer. In this section, we imported the 2017 Unity package and added post-processing components to each of our game scenes. From there, we applied ready-made profiles to customize the scenes post-processing effects. We then lightly reviewed some of the effects that can be added to the **Post Process Volume** component, which was already in our scenes.

We ended this section by altering our scene's anti-aliasing properties. With this, we took the rough edges off our art assets.

I encourage you to make your own profiles, but if you feel like you need more profiles to play around with, you can purchase a compilation of profiles from the Asset Store for a small price.

In the next section, we are going to take a look at the lighting settings and apply some global illumination, lighting, and fog to our shop scene.

Adding global illumination and other settings

In this section, we are going to give our shop scene a background by adding art assets from the `level3` scene and adding a red emission material. We will activate the scene's real-time global illumination, which is where the red emission material will glow on the surface of the corridor. We will also be adding extra lights to our shop display and the player ship to make it stand out more. Finally, we will add some black fog to create some darkness creeping around the glowing lights.

The following image shows a comparison between the shop scene before and after we complete this section:

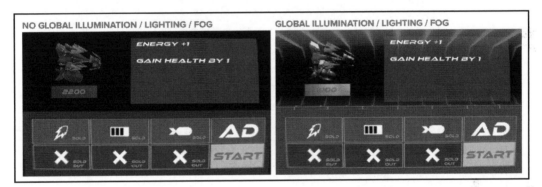

So, let's start this section off by adding the art assets we are going to use for the shop scene.

Adding art assets to our shop scene

In this section, we are going to drag and drop some pre-made art assets into our `shop` scene. From there, we can continue setting up our **Lighting** settings.

To apply the art assets to our `shop` scene, we need to do the following:

1. First, load up the `shop` scene itself from the **Project** window by going to `Assets/Scene`. Then, double-click the `shop` scene.
2. In the **Project** settings, navigate to the `Assets/Resources/Prefab` folder.
3. Drag and drop the prefab **Environment** into the **Hierarchy** window.

The scene, when viewed from the **Game** window, will look as follows:

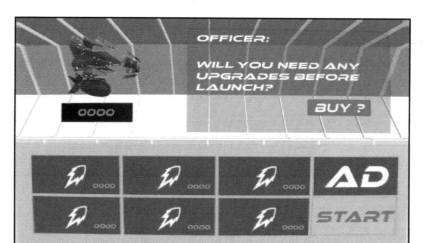

The art assets that we have brought into the shop scene should be marked as **static**. Specifically, it's **Lightmap Static** that needs to be marked so that we can generate the lights we need from our red emission strips, as shown in the previous screenshot.

4. The following screenshot shows the **Inspector** window with the **Environment** game object (and all its children) marked as **Static**:

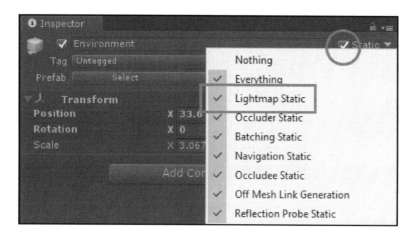

If we did have moving game objects in the scene that we wanted to be affected by the lighting of the scene, we would need to add **Light Probes** to update any indirect colors on that moving game object.

If you would like to know more about **Light Probes**, check out `https://docs.unity3d.com/Manual/LightProbes.html`.

Now, we need to disable any kind of light we currently have in our scene so that we don't dilute the effect we are trying to achieve:

1. If the **Hierarchy** window contains a **Directional Light**, select it and press *delete* on your keyboard.

   Now, we can set up our **Lighting** settings so that they support **Realtime Global Illumination**. To do that, we need to access our **Lighting** window and enter some values.

2. If the **Lighting** window hasn't loaded, in the Unity Editor, at the top of the screen, select **Window** | **Lighting** | **Settings.**

3. Select the **Scene** button in the **Lighting** window. Now, let's start turning off all **Environment** lights. Set your **Environment** settings to the ones shown in the following screenshot:

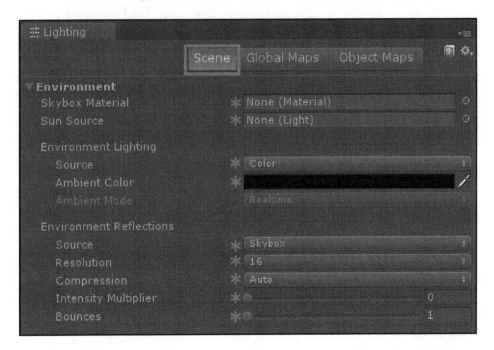

4. As shown in the previous screenshot, we have knocked out any kind of light that our scene might have had. Now, we can turn **Realtime Global Illumination** on, which is just below the **Environment** segment of the **Lighting** window:

5. Make sure **Baked Global Illumination** is unticked as we don't want our lights to be precomputed at runtime. This is because it uses up RAM and HDD/SSD space.

   Still inside the **Lighting** window's settings, we can lower some of the **Lightmapping Settings** values so that the map isn't as detailed and so that it is also quicker to generate light on slower systems.

6. Enter the values for **Lightmapping Settings** that are shown in the following screenshot:

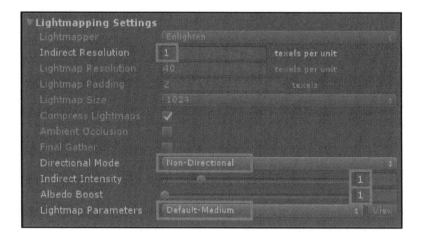

7. At the bottom of the **Lighting** window, make sure **Auto Generate** is unticked and click the **Generate Lighting** button.

8. Wait for the blue bar in the bottom-right corner of the Unity Editor to complete and disappear.

   We will be presented with the following output in the **Game** window:

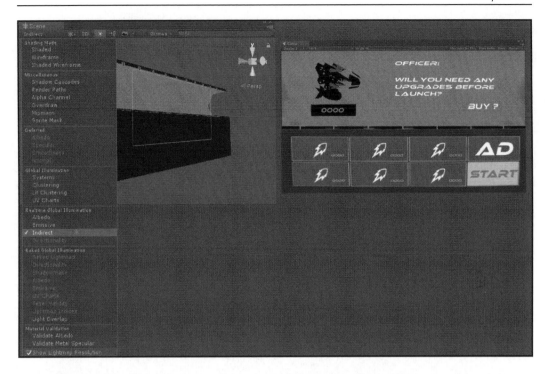

We can (if we want to) check the indirect lighting that we have created from our current **Lighting** settings by selecting the **Shaded** button below the **Scene** tab and selecting **Indirect** from the drop-down (don't forget to change it back to **Shaded** once you're done).

Our shop scene looks too bright red and has drowned the scene out. However, we nearly have what we want. Now, we can turn on some **fog** from the **Lighting** window to create a dark alley with the red emission bleeding through.

9. To add **fog** to the `shop` scene, in our **Lighting** window, near the bottom, we need to apply the following values:

Our **Game** window will now have a faded darkness in the background of our `shop` scene, as shown in the following screenshot:

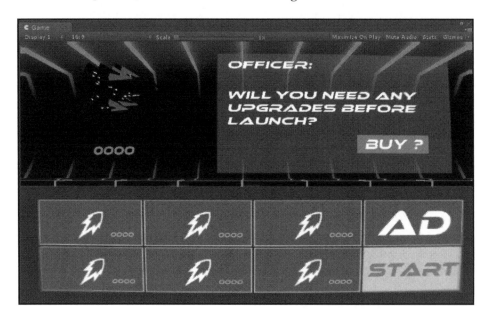

10. The final touch is to drag and drop the `shopLights` prefab from `Assets/Resources/Prefab` into the **Hierarchy** window to light up the player ship:

11. Save the `shop` scene.

With that, w have successfully removed the default lighting from our `shop` scene and applied **Realtime Global Illumination** from the emission material and added darkness (fog) to our `shop` scene's background.

In the next section, we will be discussing and implementing a small section of our `level3` scene so that we can start adding art assets with reflections.

Reflection probe

In this section, we are going to introduce the final art asset for our game. This asset will reflect the environment in the scene, as shown by the two-sphere statues in the following screenshot:

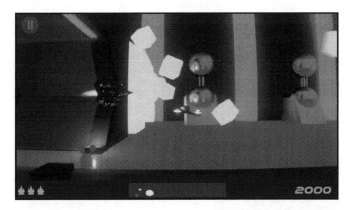

You can imagine how useful it would be to have a material that reflects its surroundings like a mirror. We are going to add the **shinySphere** art asset to our `level3` scene and calibrate its property values to get a decent result without affecting our systems resources.

So, let's start by loading up the `level3` scene:

1. In the **Project** window, navigate to the `Assets/Scene` folder and double-click on the `level3` scene.

    Now, we are going to place our **shinySphere** into the scene.

2. In the **Project** window, navigate to the `Assets/Resources/Prefab` folder.
3. Drag **shinySphere** into the **Hierarchy** window.
4. Select the **shinySphere** asset in the **Hierarchy** window and make sure its **Transform** values are set as shown in the following screenshot:

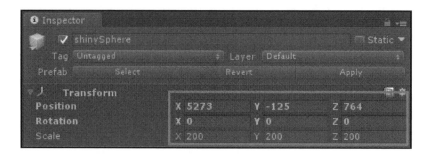

The **shinySphere** game object should now be in a location next to the cargo blocks at the end of the level, as shown in the following screenshot:

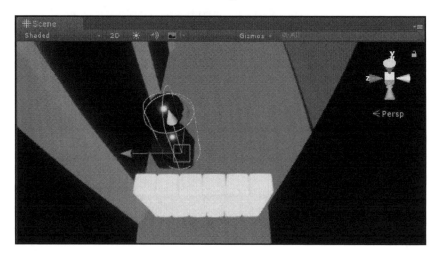

Before we add the second **shinySphere**, let's add a **Reflection Probe** to this game object, as follows:

1. In the **Hierarchy** window, expand the **shinySphere** game object and select the **spheres** child game object.
2. Right-click the **spheres** game object in the **Hierarchy** window and select **Light | Reflection Probe.**
3. The **spheres** game object now has a child game object called **Reflection Probe**. Select this game object.
4. In the **Inspector** window, we have the **Reflection Probe** component, along with its values. First, let's change the **Type** values to the ones shown in the following image to make our game object reflect its environment:

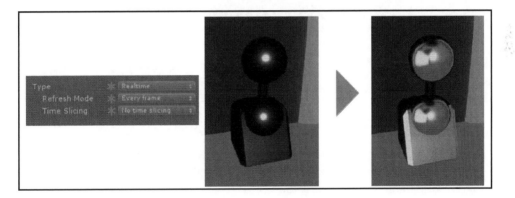

Our **shinySphere** will now update its reflection on every frame.

5. Next, we will alter the **Runtime settings** values to increase the accuracy of the reflection. Use the values shown in the following screenshot:

Box Projection will help improve the accuracy of the reflections given in the environment. If you would like to know more, check out the following link: `https://docs.unity3d.com/Manual/AdvancedRefProbe.html`,

6. The last property values to update can be found in **Cubemap capture settings**. Changes these values will change the final look of the reflections (simply estimate what color the **Background** property should be so that it suits your scene):

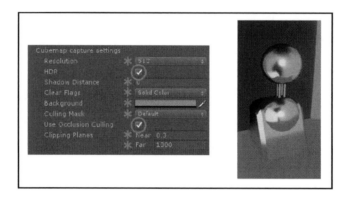

The reflection probe can create performance issues if it's not used carefully, depending on the platform the game is being pointed toward. For example, with the previous settings, the higher resolution will show a clearer reflection but will obviously require more resources.

 For more information about reflection probes and their performance, check out the following link: `https://docs.unity3d.com/Manual/RefProbePerformance.html`.

To duplicate the **shinySpace** game object in our `level3` scene, we need to do the following:

1. Select the **shinySpace** game object in the **Hierarchy** window and click **Apply** in the top-right corner of the **Inspector** window to update the prefab.
2. To copy and paste the **shinySpace** game object, right-click **shinySpace** in the **Hierarchy** window and select **Copy** from the drop-down list.
3. Right-click in the **Hierarchy** window (in an open space, near the bottom) and select **Paste** from the drop-down list.

4. Finally, move the **shinySpace** game object to the right of the X-axis.

5. Save the scene.

The following screenshot shows the two **shinySpace** game objects reflecting the environment:

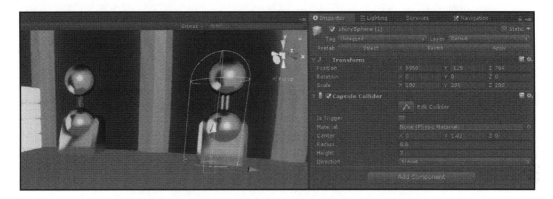

If, in any other future Unity Projects, you are required to create a shiny surface, marble floor, a brand new shiny car, and so on, making use of a reflection probe would cover these requirements.

With that, we have reached the point where our game is complete and we've covered everything specified in the Game Design Document. Now would be a good time to build our standalone version of the game and see how well it runs. Are there any bugs? How are we going to test our game? Let's move on and see how we can tackle such issues.

Building and testing our game

We have reached the point where we can build and run our game instead of just testing our game's scenes in the Unity Editor. This section will be about not only building the game, as we did earlier for the Android version of the game, but also to see if we have any bugs with our final build. We will also look for any potential issues along the way by using performance spikes in the profiler.

Let's start building our game and see how well it runs before we do any tests.

To build our game for PC, we need to do the following:

1. At the top of the Unity Editor, go to **File | Build Settings....**
2. Make sure all the scenes are in the **Scenes In Build** list and in the correct order.
3. **Platform** should be set to **PC, Mac & Linux Standalone**. If not, select it and select the **Switch Platform** button.

Next, we need to add the aspect ratios that this game is intended for in the **Player Settings...** window:

1. Select the **Player Settings...** button.
2. In the **Inspector** window, expand the **Resolution and Presentation** content.
3. Expand the **Supported Aspect Ratios** content.

Deselect the aspect ratios shown in the following screenshot:

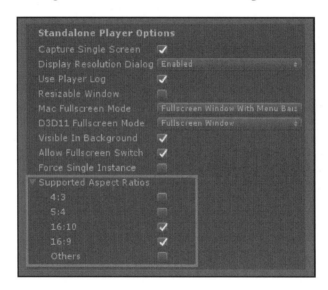

4. Back in the **Build Settings** window, press the **Build** button.

The following screenshot shows these references highlighted:

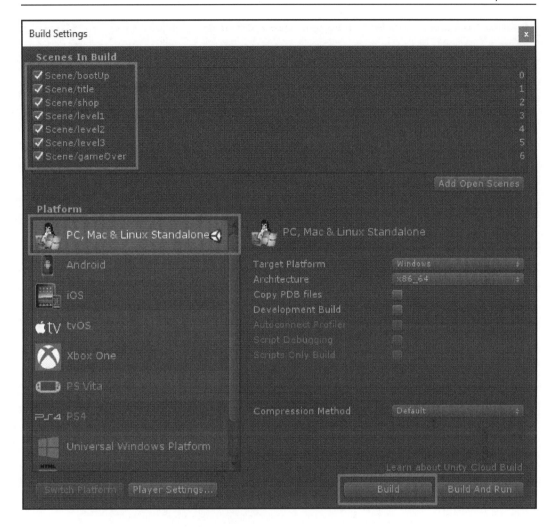

5. In the **Windows Explorer** window that appears, select a location where you wish to install the game and click the **Save** button.

6. Once the game has been built, run its .exe file.

The **Killer Wave Configuration** window will now appear. Run the game using a different screen resolution with and without **Windowed** selected to see if there are any scaling issues or/and if the player ship stays within the game screen's boundaries.

The following screenshot shows the supported resolutions I have on my machine:

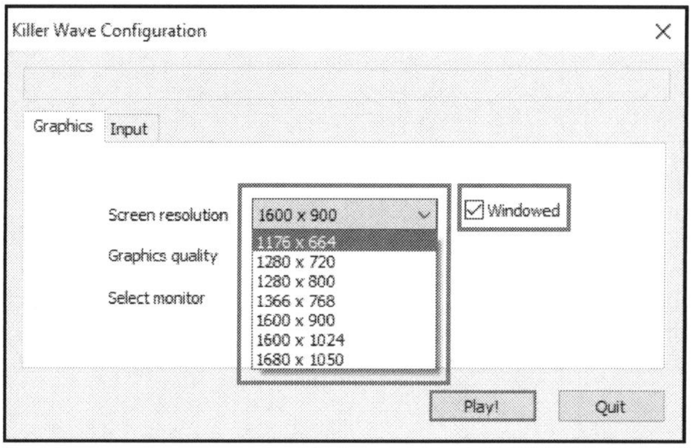

If you run into trouble with either screen resolution or the game's playing area, take a look at the various complete `unitypackage` files that have been supplied with this book.

Now, let's fix any potential issues that may arise in our game.

Tackling bugs

Imagine we have sent our game off to be bug tested and we get a response from several bug testers questioning bugs, the game's UI, and the performance of the game.

The following sections contain four reports that I want you to read and think about. We will go through the answers near the end of this chapter.

Let's start with the first bug report.

Bug report – "Standalone AD button"

It has been reported that when our bug tester plays the PC version of the game, they can't watch an advert in the shop scene.

How can we resolve this issue?

The following image shows the AD button in the `shop` scene:

Hint: Do we need the AD button in the standalone version of the shop scene? Is it supported by Unity?

Bug report – "Resetting player's lives"

A second report has been given to us suggesting that when the game is completed, the player's lives don't reset.

Why is this happening and how do we fix this issue?

The following image shows the player's lives counter on level 1:

Hint: Does this happen when you quit the game through the pause screen? Do the player's lives reset when all their lives are lost?

Bug report – "Slower systems on level 3"

When the Android version is played on slower systems, it has been reported that level 3 runs slower than levels 1 and 2.

What amendments can be made, if any, to fix this problem?

The following image shows where the game slows down:

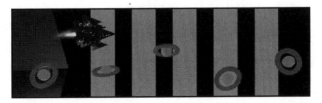

Hint: What changes could be made that won't upset standalone or more powerful performing Android devices?

Bug report – "Sometimes, the game ends too quickly"

Some bug testers have reported that, when starting a game, it ends earlier than intended, with the player ship animating out of the screen.

Why is this happening and how can this be amended?

The following image shows the tail end of the player ship's thrusters as it leaves the level too soon:

Hint: Which level does this happen on? Does it happen in the Unity Editor? Does it happen all the time? If not, what are you doing and what's different?

You may be able to solve some of these questions by Googling *key problems*. Others are more specific and you may need to add `Debug.Log()` to parts of your code holding variable names so that you can see what's changed after a certain point in the game. For example, does `GameManager.playerLives` debug a different value than it should at certain points in the game? If you're using Microsoft Visual Studio as your IDE, you may want to start adding breakpoints and step through your code to see what changes. If you don't know what breakpoints are, I suggest that you check out the following link: `https://docs.microsoft.com/en-us/visualstudio/debugger/using-breakpoints?view=vs-2019`.

To potentially help with these performance issues, we are going to check the **Profiler** out and see how it can help us with checking the performance of our game.

Understanding the Profiler

In this section, we will be checking out one of the Unity Editor's tools – **Profiler**. This handy tool will show us where our game may spike in demands for system resources or/and show where our game is using too many resources at once.

Let's open the **Profiler** window and see its default layout before going into any more detail about it:

1. At the top of the Unity Editor, select **Window** | **Profiler.**

The **Profiler** window behaves like any other new window in Unity. Typically, this **Profiler** should run well fullscreen on a second screen. Otherwise, dock the **Profiler** down with **Console**, as shown in the following screenshot:

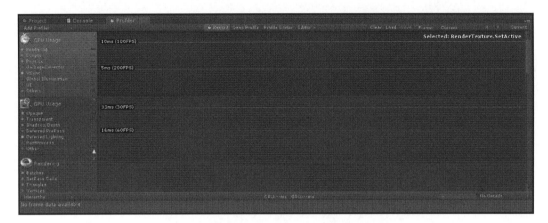

2. At the top of the Unity Editor, press the **Play** button. After about 5 seconds (roughly), press the **Pause** button (it doesn't matter which scene is running).

The **Profiler** window will come alive, showing a graph and table of information. This will be split into two sections, as shown in the following screenshot:

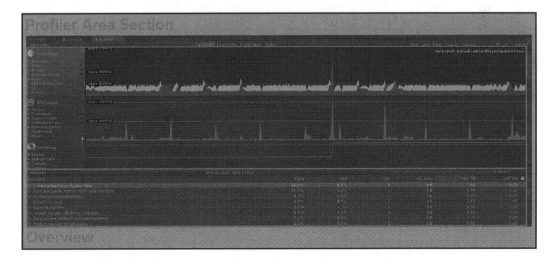

Let's take a look at these sections in more depth:

- **Profiler Area Section**: This shows where various methods are being recorded. In the previous screenshot, these are indicated by two graphs.
- **Overview**: This provides a detailed, broken down list of each profile.

In the top-left corner of the **Profiler** window is the **Add Profiler** button, which is where more methods can be added to the **Profiler Area** section. These methods are shown in the following screenshot:

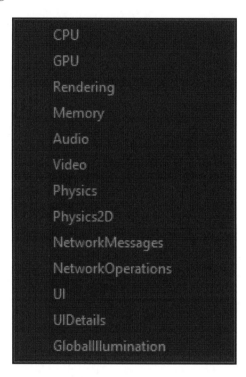

Also, in the **Profiler Area** section, we can click and scrub (drag) the mouse to see an indicator on the Profiler area. The Overview list will update with what resources are being used.

The following screenshot shows a highlighted spike, along with the indicator (denoted as i.). It is also updating the Overview list (denoted as ii.) to show what's causing the performance spike:

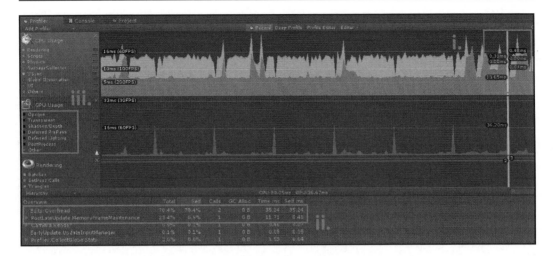

To see things clearer in the **Profile Area** section, we can turn off specific usages (denoted as iii.) so that we can drill down to what's causing a spike in our game.

It's also worth noting that, in the Overview window, at the top of the list, we have the two most important resources:

- **EditorOverhead**
- **PostLateUpdate.MemoryFrameMaintenance**

EditorOverhead takes a total of 70.4% resources and a **Self** of 70.4%, which means this resource alone takes most of your project's resources at this time. **PostLateUpdate**, on the other hand, takes a total 23.4%, but the resource alone only takes 0.9%, which means we can click the arrow to the left of it to expand each of the resources it houses, as shown in the following screenshot:

Overview	Total	Self	Calls
EditorOverhead	70.4%	70.4%	2
▼ PostLateUpdate.MemoryFrameMaintenance	23.4%	0.9%	1
LogStringToConsole	22.4%	22.4%	177

To amend this spike from the two hungry resources, we would have to remove any `Debug.Log()` being called in our game from either of the scripts we have written. This will likely fix the **LogStringToConsole** issue. If there is an issue with the code itself, this would need further debugging and likely Googling to solve.

Another way of checking this, and one that will likely solve second resource issue – **EditorOverhead** – is to run our game outside of the Unity Editor to remove any resources being used up. One way of tackling this is to build and run (denoted in iii.) our game as a standalone (denoted in i.) out as a **Development Build** and auto-connect it to the **Profiler** window (denoted in ii.), as shown in the following image:

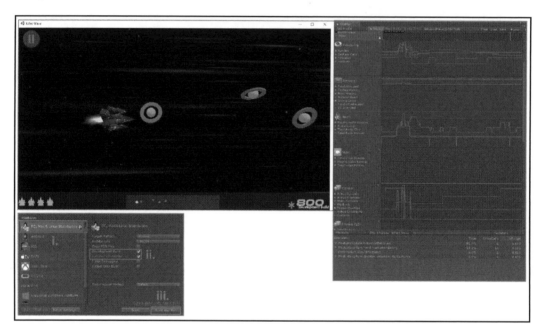

As you can see, we no longer have these two resource issues showing up in our **Development Build** (denoted by * in the preceding image).

 If you would like to know more about the **Profiler** window, check out the following link: `https://docs.unity3d.com/Manual/Profiler.html`.

As we have seen, the **Profiler** window is a helpful tool that helps us rectify any issues with memory leaks, garbage collection, and any other possible issues.

Now, we'll look at our last Unity tool, which we can use to see how the graphics pipeline is being used to display our game.

Frame Debugger

Frame Debugger can be used to show how each frame is created for our game in the Unity Editor. This can help us with any potential shader issues regarding how a piece of art is displayed. However, this is also a healthy reminder of how a scene is brought together and challenges potentially any unnecessary uses effects/materials.

To access the **Frame Debugger** tool, do the following:

1. At the top of the Unity Editor, select **Window | Frame Debugger.**

   Our **Frame Debug** window will appear.

2. Now, let's load up our `title` scene from the **Project** window (`Assets/Scene`).
3. Click on the **Enable** button at the top of the **Frame Debug** window to see how the frame is created.
4. The **Frame Debug** window will come alive and show us a list of tools and properties being implemented.
5. With the **Game** window in view, scroll the slider (highlighted in the following image) in the **Frame Debug** window from the right slowly to the left to see how this frame is created.

The following image shows the **Frame Debug** window with the **Enable** button highlighted, along with three steps (4,8,26):

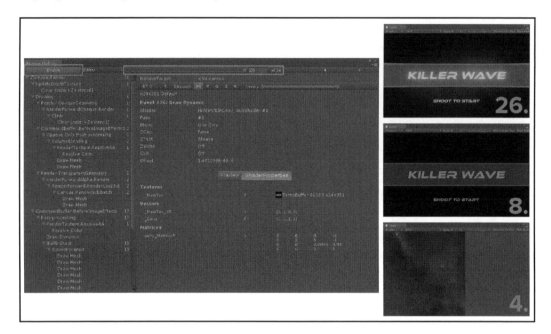

Notice that step 4 shows the image that has been applied to the **Bloom** texture to create the shiny glow in step 26.

After going through each of these steps and seeing all the maps, render targets, and all the other necessary steps to make a frame, it's also possible to select draw calls (a call to the graphics card) from the **Frame Debug** window, which will highlight the game object it's referring to.

In the following image, we have the shop scene with a total of 47 steps, as shown at the top of **Frame Debug.** If one of the draw calls are selected within the **Frame Debug** window (middle highlighted rectangle), it will ping which game object it is referring to in the **Hierarchy** window, as shown on the left-hand side:

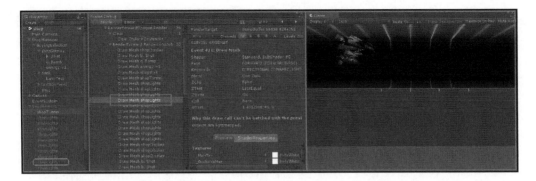

 If you would like to found out more about **Frame Debugger** and its capabilities, check out the following link: `https://docs.unity3d.com/Manual/FrameDebugger.html`.

Hopefully, you will be able to make great use of **Frame Debugger** and debug any graphical issues and understand the graphical pipeline more with Unity.

Before we summarize this chapter, we are going to go through each of the four bug reports from our game's bug testers.

Tackling bugs – answers

Typically, testing code happens when something has gone wrong. As programmers, we need to, for example, follow a value through a series of steps to see if it's the reason why the code is not doing what it's supposed to do. However, there are also different methods for carrying out testing and it's also good to think about checking yours or someone else's code after an update has been applied to the project's code.

As a programmer, you will likely hear of different types of methodology that are carried out and how much of a project's code should be tested.

Here are the more popular types of test you will carry out on your own and other projects:

- **Unit**: A unit test is typically the first test that's carried out whenever a new piece of code has been added to a project before you carry out further testing on a larger scale. These tests can be as small as checking a `for` loop or a method to making sure a small block of code is working correctly.

- **Integration**: This type of test is used when multiple sections of code (could be from other programmers) are brought together and tested to see if any issues are caused when the game is running.
- **Smoke**: These are tests that are carried out to determine whether the current build is stable or not. This type of test helps bug testers make a decision regarding whether to proceed or not with further tests. Smoke tests should be minimal and frequent between builds.
- **Regression**: When adding code to a project, there is always a chance that the existing code may clash with the new code that's been added. Here, you check the existing code to make sure that a change or addition hasn't created errors. These tests can be run manually for small projects or a suite of tests each time an update has been implemented for larger projects.
- **System**: Typically, a system test would be conducted after an integration test to check the project code as a whole for any defects and general code behavior.

Testing often helps you keep track of a project overall and to not be solely focused on one part of it. This is also why it's important to have some kind of plan; for example, we have our Game Design Brief. We could also be even more technical and have a UML diagram to help us see the connections between our scripts. So, we shouldn't think any differently about coding. Now that we have our code, we can hopefully improve it, make it more efficient, and remind ourselves of the SOLID principles.

Speaking of bug testing, have you thought of any solutions to the four bug reports that were made for our game back in the *Tackling bugs* section? Hopefully, you have, as we are going to go through each of them now.

Bug report – "Standalone AD button" solution

As you may recall, we have our shop scene, which features an AD button. When pressed, the player will watch an advert and receive shop credits as a reward. This works fine in the mobile version of the game, but it had been reported that this button does not work on the standalone version.

The short answer to this is that Unity doesn't support adverts for standalone builds. This leaves us to either looking for a solution to have an advert in our game, or we can turn off the AD button game object through either scripting or manually through the **Hierarchy** window. Either way, this is a simple quick fix as removing the AD button will automatically make the Start button resize, thanks to **Vertical Layout Group**. Some redesign would need to be implemented to solve this issue rather than it being solely a programmer problem:

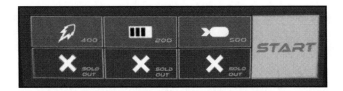

Bug report – "Resetting player's lives" solution

To make it so the player's lives reset correctly, we need to apply a fix in the TitleComponent script so that when our game restarts back to the beginning from either quitting or the player losing all of their lives, GameManager.playerLives is reset back to 3.

In the TitleComponent script, add the following code to reset the player's lives back to 3:

```
void Start()
{
  if (GameManager.playerLives <= 2)
      GameManager.playerLives = 3;
}
```

Save the TitleComponent script.

Bug report – "Slower systems on level 3" solution

The benefit of having multiple devices to run a series of tests is vital. If your game supports a low spec device, then you are also appealing to a wider audience. Reports for our game are coming in stating that the device struggles with lower-powered devices. To fix this, you need to ensure the following:

- Post-processing is disabled.
- Fewer enemies are in the levels on the screen at once. You can do this by changing the speed of EnemySpawner in the **Inspector** window.
- Remove any global illumination from scenes and apply basic lighting.
- Remove additional backgrounds from the shop scene.
- Change the CameraMovement script's Start function. Invoke from a 6-second
  wait to 7 seconds to give the device more time to load.

Bug report – "Sometimes, the game ends too quickly" solution

It has been reported that levels finish earlier when they should do, so instead of a level lasting 25 seconds, it has been reported to last only 5-10 seconds.

This is happening because the `BeginGame` method in the `ScenesManager` script is not resetting the `gameTimer` variable back to zero. Follow these steps to fix this bug:

1. Open the `ScenesManager` script.
2. Scroll down to the `BeginGame` method and at the top of the method, add the following line:

   ```
   gameTimer = 0;
   ```

3. Save the `ScenesManager` script.

Test your code, keep revisiting it, and keep polishing it. Continue to look at other ways of improving your script. Accept that the first few lines of code aren't going to be your best and that it's OK to revisit and keep optimizing your code.

 If you would like to continue looking into how to improve the code for the game you've created, check out the following link from Unity: `https://learn.unity.com/tutorial/fixing-performance-problems#5c7f8528edbc2a002053b595`.

That brings us to the end of this section, where we built our standalone version of our game and looked at potential issues that we needed to overcome that we picked up by our bug testers. After that, we look at the **Profiler** window, which we can use to monitor the performance of our game, and **Frame Debugger**, which shows what steps are followed to make a frame. We then spoke about how and when to test our game before looking at the bugs we were issued and how to correct them.

Now, let's discuss this chapter as a whole.

Summary

This chapter was about taking the game we have been developing throughout this book and putting it together as it reached its end. We spoke about how we could push our game further by adding physic collisions other than bullets or buttons. We set up collisions that got us more involved with tweaking the **Rigidbody** component to make our game objects behave in different ways. We did this by adding drag and affecting our scene's gravity.

We then moved on and discussed how we could improve our game's screen ratio by updating its **Canvas Scaler** and how it would make our UI look more stable under the different ratios. We also made our game playing area more flexible under the different resolutions using different Unity functions, such as `WorldToViewportPoint`.

At this point, our mobile version was ready to be built and tested so that we could see how well it ran with updated touch screen controls. We also looked into its optimization in terms of textures and compressed them to decrease the size of our game and make it run better overall.

After the mobile build, we looked at the PC version and made some more changes to improve the look of the game. We did this because the standalone machine was likely going to have a more powerful CPU, graphics card, memory, and more. Then, we added effects such as post-processing to change the look and feel of our game to look it more polished. We continued adding more polish to our game by adding global illumination and fogging effects from our **Light settings** window. This made our materials shine red and bleed through the foggy darkness to give them more of a futuristic feel. We also added reflective statues to our end level. These made use of the reflection probe component. After that, we discussed how to optimize it in terms of the size of its reflective texture.

Finally, we looked into building and testing our standalone version and also introduced some bug testing scenarios, where our bug testers found issues with things not working the way they should. We reviewed and addressed them together.

Making a game isn't easy, and there are many ways a game can be made. Someone will always have a better way than you and likely pick holes out of it. However, as mentioned in this chapter, a game can be made in sweeps and improved at each sweep; the worst thing to do is to try and make a perfect game the first time around. If you think like that, you'll end up with no game at all.

14

Full Unity Programmer Mock Exam

Welcome to the Full Unity Programmer Mock Exam. Here, we will provide a series of multiple-choice questions, similar to the ones you have been answering at the end of every few chapters in this book.

Try your best and see how it goes – the idea is to get **all** of the questions right. If and when you do complete the exam, you will be ready to go ahead with the real Unity Programmer exam. If, for any reason, you get the question wrong, go back through this book or Google to try and find the answer. Try to avoid skipping to the answer in the *Appendix*; use your knowledge more than muscle memory. It's important you understand the question so that you can answer it. These mock questions are only examples of what you will get in the exam.

I recommend reading every question at least twice; sometimes, exam questions will try to catch you out in how the questions are worded.

The exam is timed, but you should have enough time to answer each multiple-choice question. It's probably best to keep some personal time aside when you start and finish this mock exam. If you are struggling with a question, skip it and come back to it later. Sometimes, it's easier to do the exam questions in sweeps to get the easier ones out of the way. If you are still struggling, I have marked, in brackets at the end of each question, the chapter/appendix you can get more information from.

So, take your time, don't get caught out with the wording, and proceed... If you enjoy it, that's also a bonus!

Full mock exam

1. One of your junior programmers has asked for a global instance with a class that can be accessed anywhere in the code of the game. What design pattern would fulfill this requirement when you could have code that acts as a manager to all? (CH1)

   A) Prototype

   B) Abstract Factory

   C) Singleton

   D) Builder

2. You have been asked by your head of development to make it so whenever a player walks through a doorway, a light next to the door will turn on. You have made an `OnTriggerEnter()` script that enables a light and added a collider to your doorway with a `Rigidbody`. Your player has a collider and `Rigidbody` as well. When you run the game to test your code, the light doesn't turn on.

   What is most likely the cause of this issue? (CH2)

   A) The doorway's collider is not marked as a trigger.
   B) The light game object needs a trigger as well.
   C) You don't need multiple `Rigidbody` components.
   D) The doorway isn't connected up to the light.

3. What function allows us to take a `Vector3` or `Vector2` reading from any direction but keep its magnitude to just one? (CH7)

   A) `Normalize()`
   B) `MoveTowards()`
   C) `Lerp()`
   D) `Scale()`

4. We have been given our **Game Design Document** (**GDD**) and in it, it states that our **Player Character** (**PC**) will need to run and dodge multiple beach balls that are thrown at them. Granted, the beach balls can bounce off each other. Also in the scene are various static props and a trigger area for the PC to grab health.

Which objects in this scene would at least need a `Rigidbody` component? (CH2)

A) The PC and the beach balls
B) The PC and the invisible health area
C) The beach balls only
D) The beach balls and the invisible health area

5. Relating to the beach ball question; in the Layer Collision Matrix (**Edit |
Project Settings | Physics**) of our project, which of our collider's physics in
the matrix should be checked when it comes to them interacting with each
other? (CH13)

A) PC and beach ball, beach ball and beach ball, and PC and health area
B) PC and beach ball
C) Beach ball and health area, beach ball and beach ball
D) PC and health area

6. We have a mobile app that will need to support low performing tablets. In
our app, we will have a mini-game where the player will be able to throw
an unlimited supply of basketballs into a hoop. However, only 10
basketballs are in the view of the camera. Due to this, the programmer has
made a mini-game so that the same 10 basketballs will be used instead of
instantiating a new basketball on each throw.

The programmer is aware that the design pattern for reusing the basketball
assets has a name. What is this design pattern's name? (CH1)

A) Abstract Factory
B) Object Pool
C) Dependency Injection
D) Builder

7. You have been assigned to make an application that plays music as the
application starts. As the user goes through different scenes, the music will
not be removed or affected and continue to play. We've made a start by
creating a game object and added a script to it that plays the music.

What else do we need to do to make sure our music continues to play? (CH3)

A) Create two game objects that contain both music scripts on the starting scene only.
B) Each scene needs a music game object with a script.

C) Add `DontDestroyOnLoad(this.gameObject);` to the `Awake` function in the music script.
D) Instantiate the `music` game object on every scene.

8. While working on our project, we realize we have made a mistake in our code. Thankfully, we have been using Unity's Collaborate and all we need to do is go back a commit.

   Which window in the Unity Editor do we go to in order to achieve this? (CH1)

   A) Collab History
   B) Profiler
   C) Services
   D) Inspector

9. When it comes to excluding folders from Unity's Collaborate with the `.collabignore` file, which folder can we simply ignore? (CH1)

   A) Assets
   B) Editor
   C) All folders
   D) No folders

10. You have your own indie team and you have managed to recruit yourself a willing 3D artist to add to your project. You are using Collaborate as your version control and need to add them.

    To do this, we need to go to the Unity Dashboard and make a change in which section? (CH1)

    A) Unity Teams
    B) Users
    C) General
    D) Integrations

11. In Unity's Cloud Build, what should we check to find the latest build? (CH1)

    A) `cloudBuildTargetName`
    B) `buildNumber`
    C) `bundleID`
    D) `scmCommitID`

12. We have a mobile game that is gesture-controlled, and we want to make it so we swipe the screen from one side to the other to release an event.

    What's the best way of measuring our player's finger press location from and to the `Touch` struct? (CH13)

    A) `type`
    B) `phase`
    C) `deltaPosition`
    D) `fingerId`

13. Our head programmer is trying to find an easy way for our Flight Simulator game to cover controls for mobile, PC, and console.

    What's the easiest way of achieving this? (CH13)

    A) Make a Unity project that supports each game.
    B) Have a class for each platform.
    C) Import the `CrossPlatformInput` package from Standard Assets.
    D) Use `#define` directives for each possible platform to create a custom input manager.

14. In our flight simulator, we have just hooked up our horizontal and vertical controls with
    `Input.GetAxis("Horizontal")` and `Input.GetAxis("Vertical")`.
    The game designer has pointed out the controls are sluggish and we need the movements to be more responsive. (CH2)

    What settings do we need to alter in the Input Manager to improve/amend this?

    A) Invert
    B) Sensitivity
    C) Axis
    D) Gravity

15. Our head programmer has mentioned that our flight simulator game should be able to support various platforms. He points out that he's installed the new `CrossPlatformInput` package and wants you to replace "_____" with `CrossPlatformInputManager`. (CH13)

    A) `GetAxis`
    B) `Input`
    C) `Vertical`
    D) `Translate`

16. We are now making a side-scrolling platform game and we want it so that when we press the *A* button, we jump, but we also want it so that if we press the *up* arrow key, we also jump. In the Input Manager, where do we add the second button to jump? (CH2)

    A) Alt Positive Button
    B) Alt Negative Button
    C) Negative Button
    D) Positive Button

17. With our platform game, I have noticed the player will run left and right fine, but when I put the gamepad down, my player's character is slowly moving right. I believe I need to change a setting in the Input Manager, but which one? (CH2)

    A) Sensitivity
    B) Snap
    C) Gravity
    D) Dead

18. Another situation that has been pointed out from our game designer is that when we are playing our side-scrolling platform game, the character takes a while to pick up speed. Also, when the character is running full speed one way and then we change direction on the gamepad, there appears to be too much deceleration before the character picks up speed in the new direction.

    What do we need to change with our current input to make the direction more snappy? (CH2)

    A) `GetAxisRaw`
    B) `GetButtonDown`

C) GetTouch
D) GetKeyDown

19. Typically, when typing names of instance variables, what naming convention do we use? (CH2)

A) Positional notation
B) All caps
C) Snake case
D) Camel case

20. What would a declared class called AssetCollection look like if it is or acts like a singleton and won't be required to be attached to a game object in the Unity Editor? (CH3)

A) public class AssetCollection : MonoBehaviour { }
B) public static class AssetCollection { }
C) static class AssetCollection { }
D) public static class AssetCollection : MonoBehaviour { }

21. A bug fix has been issued to you where game designers have been altering a public int variable and making it too high in the Unity Editor. There is no reason for the variable to go over 100.

What attribute should the programmer use to restrict the game designer? (CH2)

A) [GUITarget]
B) [TextArea]
C) [Range]
D) [Header]

22. You have been assigned a task from your technical lead to store the 800 **non-player character** (**NPC**) prefabs. Either one of these prefabs can be picked and dropped into the game to roam around. This system needs to be user-friendly for our designers and ideally, all selections of NPC should come from the **Inspector** window. There is also a chance the number of enemies will increase from the original 800.

How will you prepare to issue these NPCs? (CH2)

A) Simply create a script to store a public array that will accommodate the creation of each prefab.

B) Create a Scriptable Object containing an array of referenced prefabs.

C) Make a class containing a private serialize field list of NPC prefabs and have each class of the NPC create an instance of an NPC at runtime.

D) Create all 800+ NPCs at runtime and store them out of the camera view.

23. What setting do we change in **Time Manager** if we want Unity to calculate its physics at a certain time in an update? (CH10)

   A) Maximum Allowed Timestep
   B) Fixed Timestep
   C) Maximum Allowed Particle Timestep
   D) Time Scale

24. Which collider is the most efficient? (CH2)

   A) Capsule
   B) Sphere
   C) Mesh
   D) Box

25. We are simulating a boulder falling through the sky, as well as a packet of crisps. We want the boulder to fall faster.

   What settings do we change in either of our game objects' `Rigidbody` components? (CH13)

   A) Decrease the packet of crisp's Mass and increase the boulder's Drag.
   B) Increase the packet of crisp's Angular Drag and increase the boulder's Mass.
   C) Increase the boulder's Mass and decrease the packet of crisp's Mass.
   D) Decrease the boulder's Drag and increase the packet of crisp's Drag.

26. When would we use a trigger instead of just a collider? (CH2)

   A) When a character is sitting in a health zone charging their energy.
   B) If two game objects collide but we only want to set our particle effects manually.

C) Only if we need to alter our `Rigidbody` settings during runtime.

D) Whenever multiple colliders are children of another collider.

27. You are making a sci-fi arcade shooter game. The gamer's view has a UI display wrapped around the screen with lots of vital details about your mission and your ship's health. In the lower corner of the screen, we have a 3D view of the condition of our ship. Whenever the ship takes damage, we can see the results in our 3D view, along with particle effects to emphasize the damage. Each possible damage point on the ship in the 3D view has a collider that reacts if a missile hits it.

    In testing, you realize the ship in the 3D view has enemy missiles bouncing off your colliders when they're supposed to be damaging your ship.

    How should the programmer solve this issue while retaining the functionality of both the in-game objects and the UI? (CH13)

    A) In the Layer Collision Matrix, turn off collisions between the 3D UI ship layer and the missile and asteroid layers.
    B) Increase the Mass of the missiles to get through the collider.
    C) Add a second collider to all the colliders on the ship to increase its probability.
    D) Add one main collider to go around the ship so that when a missile hits it, this will disable all the colliders inside for a split second.

28. You have moved studios and jumped on a new game project where you are in a desert defending a fort from 6,000 donkeys charging to destroy your civilization. Your only line of defense is throwing heavy wet bean bags to tire the donkeys out. To target each donkey, you use a raycast system that makes contact with the mesh collider on either donkey. Your head of development has now requested 20,000 donkeys to up the ante. We are now starting to notice the performance of the game has drastically dropped. Everyone in the team is making an effort so that all 20,000 donkeys are in the game.

    What changes can you make to improve the game's performance? (CH2)

    A) Make the donkeys slightly bigger so more space is taken up in the environment.
    B) Replace the mesh colliders with sphere colliders.

C) Create a special donkey layer mask so the rest of the environment is ignored.
D) Shorten your raycast's length.
E) Never go full donkey.

29. A member of your team has pushed a commit for a new segment to your game. At this stage, it's recommended to make sure the entirety of our game runs OK.

    Your head of development has requested that you test your game. Which test shall you perform? (CH13)

    A) Smoke
    B) Integration
    C) Regression
    D) System

30. You have been asked to check specific parts of someone else's code by creating custom methods to make sure the return type is what it should be.

    There is a name for the specific type of test you are performing. What is it? (CH13)

    A) Static test
    B) Accessibility test
    C) Unit test
    D) Backend test

31. What are some of the benefits of a unit test? (CH13)

    A) It will check the entirety of your code.
    B) All simple functions are exposed before the complex ones.
    C) If performed regularly, it only requires the latest code to be tested.
    D) Unit tests expose how efficient your code is between functions.

32. When using a `MinMaxCurve`, which property is the least expensive in terms of performance? (CH4)

    A) Optimized curve
    B) Random between two constants
    C) Random between two curves
    D) Constant

33. Which of the following will prevent a particle system from supporting Procedural Mode? (CH4)

    A) Disabling looping
    B) Set the `Simulation Space` property to `World`
    C) Uncheck the `Auto Random Seed` tick box
    D) Enabling Collision

34. An artist has approached you, requesting you to make a visual change to the sci-fi game you are currently working on. He has requested you to shrink a series of asteroids over time as they hurtle closer to a planet.

    The asteroids come from a particle system emitter; which module would suit the requirement from the artist? (CH4)

    A) Renderer
    B) Texture Sheet Animation
    C) Sub Emitters
    D) Size Over Lifetime

35. The whole development team have nearly finished creating their "Spitfire Battle of Britain" game and want to add particle effects to the back of each Spitfire plane as a final touch.

    One of the game designers has suggested smoke coming out of the back of the Spitfire should change randomly to emphasize the choppiness of the wind. You have programmed to the point where the particle effect is detecting wind, but what should you do to the particle smoke to show that the wind is affecting the smoke? (CH13)

    A) Change the Angular Velocity property in the Rotation by Speed module.
    B) Set the Multiplier property in the External Forces module to `0`.
    C) Increase the Strength property in the Noise module.
    D) Alter the curve of the Size property in the Size by Speed module.

36. In the indie game you are developing, you have set your scene up so that the Environment Lighting Intensity Multiplier is set to an intensity of `0.75`. When your player completes the level and moves onto the next scene, the lighting is set at `1.24`. You are using `LoadSceneAsync` with a `LoadSceneMode` of additive.

When you load up the next scene, what will the light intensity be set to? (CH3)

A) `1.24`
B) `0.75`
C) `1`
D) `0`

37. You have moved studios yet again and started working on a massive open-world game where your player can walk for miles and miles. Because of the complications of scenes being potentially too big, you have decided to break your scenes up into multiple segments. When it comes to a scene change, your player will be loaded through into the next scene.

    What function allows us to make a game object move over into another scene? (CH3)

    A) `CreateScene()`
    B) `MoveGameObjectToScene()`
    C) `MergeScenes()`
    D) `SetActiveScene()`

38. When it comes to storing data, which is the more likely choice for `PlayerPrefs`? (CH11)

    A) Purchase information
    B) Monitor resolution settings
    C) User email address
    D) Login passwords

39. Which type of variable can you save without emulating (natively) in PlayerPrefs? (CH11)

    A) Float
    B) Double
    C) Enum
    D) Array

40. Which system namespace would you use when serializing data to the device's local disk space? (CH11)

    A) Linq
    B) IO

C) Data
D) Collections

41. At the end of our sci-fi game, we save all of our stats in JSON format from our `PlayerStats` class to local disk space. But when we want to retrieve the JSON file from our storage, what do we replace the missing gap with? (CH11)

    `JsonUtility.FromJson<____>(stringFromFile);`

    A) `StatsInfo`
    B) `string`
    C) `array`
    D) `PlayerStats`

42. When retrieving an image from the internet, which UI component do we use to display the result? (CH9)

    A) Canvas
    B) Raw Image
    C) Image
    D) Panel

43. Which UI component stores a series of UI elements in a row at a fixed distance? (CH9)

    A) Vertical Layout Group
    B) Horizontal Layout Group
    C) Grid Layout Group
    D) Canvas Group

44. We have made it possible for our game to update several statistics from the Remote Settings section in the Unity Dashboard.

    Which of the following values are we allowed to use? (CH11)

    A) `char`
    B) `string`
    C) `List`
    D) `UInt16`

45. Which of these platforms can Unity Analytics be used for? (CH11)

    A) PS4
    B) Commodore Amiga 500
    C) Android
    D) Facebook

46. As soon as you connect your game to Unity Analytics, which event will automatically start giving you daily reports? (CH11)

    A) Core Events
    B) Standard Events
    C) Custom Events
    D) Transaction Events

47. When entering a value into Remote Settings, you use a divider : in-between each word; for example, `lives:53:score:200:time:50`.

    Why would the programmer be unable to save this Remote Settings entry? (CH11)

    A) Key names cannot contain the : character
    B) The value cannot be a string
    C) Statistics in Remote Settings is an illegal operation
    D) The key name cannot start with a letter

48. In our first-person shooter, we have just hooked up our marine's space cannon's Finite State Machine so that it fires the projectile.

    When the cannon is fired, there is a banging sound, particle effects fountain out from the cannon, and a beam fires outward.

    Currently, the only thing the beam can come into contact with is a wall, which has a collider attached to it.

    When the beam hits the wall, there is another particle that is triggered when the impact of the surface hits. During this explosion, we shrink then destroy the beam.

    Which event should we expect the beam to be destroyed in? (CH4)

    A) `OnStateExit`
    B) `OnStateEnter`

C) `OnStateMove`
D) `OnStateUpdate`

49. You are prototyping a third-person character for a SWAT team game, and we are going to need to get some fundamental controls up and running. Our character is currently set to run, lean, and shoot in all directions. Ideally, we want it so our character can shoot and jump, or shoot and lean. Currently, our Base Movement is set to Override Blending, while the other layers are set to Additive Blending.

In which order should the Animation Layers be set? (CH4)
A) Shoot, Lean, Base Movement
B) Base Movement, Shoot, Lean
C) Lean, Base Movement, Shoot
D) Shoot, Base Movement, Lean

50. We have an animation from a player that goes from standing to crouching. We want the animation between each animation to take exactly 0.8 seconds.

What properties do we need to focus on in the Animation transition? (CH4)

A) Transition Duration and Transition Offset
B) Fixed Duration and Transition Duration
C) Has Exit Time and Fixed Duration
D) Has Exit Time and Exit Time

51. When it comes to animating a face in Unity, which is the best blend tree to use? (CH4)

A) 2D Freeform Cartesian
B) Direct
C) 2D Simple Directional
D) 1D

52. In your latest indie game development, you have been focusing on the Animation Controller's transitions. The order of your transitions go as follows:
    1. Idle to Cry
    2. Idle to Skip
    3. Idle to Sneeze
    4. Idle to Laugh

Your animation transition properties are set to the following:

- Interruption Source: Current State
- Ordered Interruption: Ticked

Your current transition is set to **Skip**. At runtime, your character has begun to Skip, but as a tester, you also press all four buttons to trigger each of the animation states.

Which of the transitions will take priority? (CH4)

A) Idle to Laugh
B) Idle To Sneeze
C) Idle to Cry
D) Idle to Skip

53. You are creating a **First Person Shooter** (FPS) and you are currently working on the player's camera and making sure their weapon doesn't clip through objects when you get too close.

    All of the player's weapons are set to a layer called **FPS**. You then set your camera's Culling Mask in order to view everything apart from the **FPS** layer.

    Next, you create a second camera and set its Culling Mask to only render the **FPS** layer and its Clear Flags to what? (CH9)

    A) Depth Only
    B) Solid Color
    C) Don't Clear
    D) Skybox

54. Being an enthusiastic indie developer, you have decided to make a spiritual successor to the game "Desert Bus." You have nearly finished developing the game and decided to add some optimizations. You have decided to make it so that any of the smaller 3D assets such as pebbles, small plants, and insects should not be rendered at a far distance, only when close up. We should still be able to see the larger assets, no matter what distance we are from them.

    Which camera property would you use to help achieve this? (CH2)

    A) `farClipPlane`
    B) `layerCullDistances`

C) `cullingMatrix`
D) `useOcclusionCulling`

55. When writing a custom toon-shaded edge detection effect script, what should the camera's `DepthTextureMode` be set to? (Appendix)

   A) None
   B) `DepthNormals`
   C) `MotionVectors`
   D) `Depth`

56. We are currently developing a game where our player sees through Unity's main camera and has the capability to temporarily zoom in.

   What property of our camera allows us to zoom in? (CH2)

   A) `targetDisplay`
   B) `aspect`
   C) `lensShift`
   D) `fieldOfView`

57. You have introduced a multiplayer split-screen mode to your game. You are now dividing the screen into two rows.

   How should the programmer set the Viewport Rect options on the cameras? (CH2)

   A) Set both camera's **W** to `1`, **H** to `0.5`. Set Player 1 **Y** to `0.5` and Player 2 **Y** to 0.
   B) Set both camera's **W** to `1`. Set Player 1 **H** to `0.5` and Player 2 **H** to `1`. Set both cameras **Y** to `0.5`.
   C) Set both camera's **W** to `0.5`, **H** to `1`. Set Player 1 **Y** to `1` and Player 2 **Y** to `0.5`.
   D) Set both camera's **W** to `1`, **H** to `0.5`. Set Player 1 **Y** to `1` and Player 2 **Y** to `0.5`.

58. We have a physics-based object that we want to rotate around a particular point such as a door.

   Which type of joint will allow this type of movement? (CH2)

   A) Character
   B) Fixed

C) Hinge
D) Spring

59. We have been given a lamp asset from an artist and they have asked us to make it so the lamp's light flickers in the game.

Which property of our light do we need to manipulate in our script to achieve a flickering effect? (CH2)

A) `mode`
B) `spotAngle`
C) `range`
D) `intensity`

60. You are testing a scene and applying different lights to it. Within the scene, you have a series of game objects:

- Decorative lights
- The sun
- A car with its hazard lights on
- A garage

The car is parked in the garage. Around the inside of the garage, walls are decorative lights, and the sun is shining through the garage door.

You have enabled Global Illumination to increase the realism of the sun. As impressive as this looks, your scene now takes a high amount of memory usage.

How can we keep our scene looking as impressive but continue to keep the memory usage low? (CH13)

A) Set **Indirect Multiplier** to 0 on the sunlight.
B) Change **Light Mode** for the lights to **Baked**.
C) Set **Indirect Multiplier** to 0 on the decorative lights, that is, the car's hazard lights.
D) Disable **Realtime Global Illumination** in the **Lighting** settings.

61. An artist has asked us to change the glow of a neon sign from red to blue with our script.

Which property can we use to alter the glow of our sign? (CH4)

A) _EmissionColor
B) _Color
C) _SrcBlend
D) _EmissionMap

62. You have been requested to add a reflective marble effect to a shiny hallway with large white silver windows open. Outside of the building is a bright sunny background with grass, bushes, and trees all applied to a skybox. The hallway contains a series of reflection probes.

Which Reflection Probe option should be used on the hallway's Mesh Renderer component to create a shiny reflective surface? (CH13)

A) Simple
B) Blend Probes and Skybox
C) Blend Probes
D) Off

63. Our hallway floor looks shiny and reflective thanks to the reflection probes. We have also noticed that the walls don't appear to be in sync with the reflective floor.

What setting do we need to change regarding our reflection probe to fix this? (CH13)

A) Enable Box Projection
B) Increase Resolution
C) Increase the Importance
D) Enable HDR

64. Your artist has created 3D assets for a snow level and has also attempted to use assets from a previous game. The artist has made a wooden hut and put the asset into the game as well. The overall scene looks great but the overall colors in the scene don't sit with each other.

Which property from our post-processing stack would help uniform the colors in our scene to give our assets an overall icy look? (CH13)

A) User LUT
B) Grain
C) Chromatic Aberration
D) Vignette

65. We have a tech demo where the player walks down a sci-fi corridor and through the window, the sun shines through and lights up the corridor. We have applied a bloom effect from our post-processing stack. We want some of the game assets in the corridor to shine and glow like what should be expected from a bloom effect. An artist has informed you that all art assets have emission maps, but their levels vary.

Which property do we need to alter to make it so our bloom effects cover the lower-level emission maps? (CH13)

A) Decrease Threshold
B) Increase Intensity
C) Decrease Soft Knee
D) Increase Radius

66. What is the function that transitions two materials from one over to another at runtime? (CH9)

A) `SetColor`
B) `Lerp`
C) `SetFloat`
D `EnableKeyword`

67. We are making a first-person survival horror game. Our player has a flashlight for when they walk around a spooky house. Our designer has requested that the end of the flashlight produces a glass pattern on the surfaces the light projects onto.

What light property will support what the designer is asking for? (CH2)

A) `cullingMask`
B) `cookie`
C) `spotAngle`
D) `type`

68. You have reached the end of development for your PC VR game. You currently have your Camera component's Rendering Path set to Forward.

Which of the following post-processing properties would help lower the risk of nausea when using a VR application? (Appendix)

A) Depth Of Field
B) Section Multiplying

C) Motion Blur
D) Antialiasing

69. When developing a VR game, what level of motion for photon latency should a developer target to convince the player's mind they're in another place? (Appendix)

   A) 80
   B) 20
   C) 35
   D) 50

70. We are developing a mobile VR game with art assets that hold single-color materials and unlit shaders. Also, our camera component's Render Path is set to Forward.

   Which Anti Aliasing setting would improve the visuals of the game, but likely not impact the performance so that it's in an unplayable state? (Appendix)

   A) 4x Multi Sampling
   B) 8x Multi Sampling
   C) 12x Multi Sampling
   D) Disabled

71. Which window in the Unity Editor will provide a list of draw calls from our project and will also allow us to step through it frame by frame? (CH13)

   A) Profiler
   B) Frame Debugger
   C) Services
   D) Statistics

72. We have created a VR game where our player is inside a room with a locked door that will not open. The room contains a window and outside is a field of grass with mountains in the distance.

   Everything in the player's scene is 3D modeled and textured, and there is also one-directional light.

   When the player walks toward the window, the game begins to lag due to the spike in draw calls.

How can we improve the performance of our game? (Appendix)

A) Remove the 3D models in the distance and replace them with a rendered skybox.
B) Disable Generate Mip Maps in the Texture Import Settings for all textures in the distance.
C) Bake the lighting from the directional light and disable it in the level.
D) Add fog to occlude objects in the distance.

73. To help combat nausea in VR, what frames per second do developers need to aim for with their games? (Appendix)

A) 90 FPS
B) 30 FPS
C) 60 FPS
D) 75 FPS

74. In the Frame Debugger window, the developer selects a draw call for the geometry of a game object.

In which window does the object get highlighted? (CH13)

A) Curve Editor
B) Project
C) Hierarchy
D) Console

75. In the mobile build of your VR game, you come across an error that stops you from building to the device.

You check your current settings:

- Player Settings API Level is at 16.
- XR Settings has Virtual Reality Supported set to true.

What might be stopping your game from being built? (CH13)

A) The Depth Format in the Cardboard SDK settings is set to 24-bit.
B) The Scripting Runtime Version in Other Settings is set to .NET 4.x Equivalent.
C) The Stereo Rendering Method in the XR settings is set to Single Pass.
D) The Minimum API Level in Other Settings is set to 21 or higher.

76. A designer wants to change the parameters of your scripting of their game characters and save them locally to disk.

    What's the safest and easiest way to give the designer access? (CH11)

    A) Store the data as public variables in a MonoBehaviour.
    B) Save the data in a ScriptableObject.
    C) Save the data in PlayerPrefs.
    D) Create a web service with an API that can be read by the game.

77. If we are writing a script that depends on a particular component, which attribute do we add? (CH2)

    A) [Include]
    B) [Range]
    C) [SerializeField]
    D) [RequireComponent]

78. Which method will return a Touch struct? (CH13)

    A) GetKeyDown()
    B) touchSupported
    C) Input()
    D) GetTouch()

79. With regards to the Input class, what is the difference between GetMouseButtonUp and GetMouseButton? (CH13)

    A) GetMouseButton will return true if the mouse button is held down, while GetMouseButtonUp will only return true once during the frame where the mouse button is pressed.

    B) GetMouseButton will return an Int indicating which mouse button is being pressed, while GetMouseButtonUp will return true if any mouse button is pressed.

    C) GetMouseButton will return true if a mouse is connected, while GetMouseButtonUp will return true if a mouse button is pressed.

    D) GetMouseButton will return an array containing the available mouse buttons, while GetMouseButtonUp will return an index for the array indicating which mouse button is being pressed.

80. How can we improve performance with a particle system? (CH4)

    A) Reduce the number and size of the particles to reduce the number of pixels on the screen that need to be alpha blended.
    B) Increase the particle lifetime so that more particles can be reused in memory rather than generating new ones.
    C) Reduce the speed of particles to reduce the number of physics updates that are needed.
    D) Randomize properties between two curves rather than two constants to reduce the number of random numbers that need to be generated.

81. Which of the following methods would be ideal for a health bar that goes across the top of the screen? (CH8)

    A) `Horizontal`
    B) `Radial90`
    C) `Radial180`
    D) `Span`

82. You are developing a third-person game where your player will interact and talk to other characters. You are currently developing speech boxes that appear above each player's head when they're talking in the 3D world.

    Which canvas property would suit best a 3D environment for speech? (CH13)

    A) Screen Space Camera
    B) Pixel Perfect
    C) World Space
    D) Screen Space Overlay

83. Which would suit the use of an orthographic camera? (CH9)

    A) A first-person player perspective
    B) A map screen that shows an overview of the game world
    C) A 3D space battle
    D) An enemy AI

84. We are developing a strategy game where all players and NPCs are based outdoors. You need to create a day and night cycle, so in your scene, you have a skybox and a directional light.

How will you achieve this? (CH2)

A) Rotate the directional light
B) Adjust the shadow settings on the directional light
C) Update the TimeManager settings
D) Switch the skybox

85. Which of the following will change a material property for a single object? (CH4)

A) `Renderer.shader`
B) `Renderer.instance`
C) `Renderer.material`
D) `Renderer.sharedMaterial`

86. What's the best method to create a glowing lava lake? (CH4)

A) Create an emissive texture for the lava and animate the UVs on the material.
B) Create a screen space shader that applies a lava effect to the desired area.
C) Add dozens of point lights to areas where the lava is moving.
D) Create a particle effect to simulate the lava's movement.

87. Our game has a cutscene and we want it to play the music at a particular volume level.

What is the best way of achieving this? (CH10)

A) When the game plays the cutscene, switch to a different Audio Mixer Snapshot.
B) When the cutscene starts, change the volume on the Audio Source playing the music and attach a script component to cut out high frequencies.
C) When the cutscene starts, apply a Reverb Zone around the play area.
D) When the cutscene starts, apply changes to the player's stored volume controls in `PlayerPrefs`.

88. A VR game for low-performance machines uses a Forward Rendering Path. Which of the following will improve the game's overall visuals with a minor frame drop? (CH13)

A) Anti Aliasing
B) Real-Time Reflection Probes

C) Deferred Rendering
D) Spotlights

89. You have developed a mobile app that starts with a UI interface where the user can configure their experience. Once configured, the app goes into VR mode.

How do we make this app start in non-VR mode to begin with? (Appendix)

A) Place a Camera in the scene and set its FOV to null.
B) Change the build platform to PC instead of a VR platform.
C) Set `Time.timeScale` to 0 at the start of the game and add a script that searches for VR devices after the first frame is rendered.
D) Add `None` to the top of the VR SDK list.

90. If a VR device is rendering at 90 Hz, how many milliseconds should the programmer try to get that latency below? (Appendix)

A) 11
B) 12
C) 13
D) 14

91. You have developed a VR game that is getting reports from your testers stating that the game lags in certain parts. Your camera's Rendering Path is set to Forward. You have decided to not reallocate the memory of the eye texture at runtime to avoid any other performance conflicts.

If a frame rate drop is detected, we can set a property in our `XRSetting` class to help combat this issue.

Which property is the most effective? (Appendix)

A) `occlusionMaskScale`
B) `eyeTextureResolutionScale`
C) `renderViewportScale`
D) `useOcclusionMesh`

92. You have created a PC first-person shooter that offers two types of LAN game modes: Two-Player Co-Op and DeathMatch.

    Which property in the Network Discovery component should we use to make it so just one connection is attempted for either mode? (Appendix)

    A) Broadcast Subversion
    B) Broadcast Port
    C) Broadcast Key
    D) Broadcast Version

93. You have created an online multiplayer game; it's hosted on a web page with the `NetworkTransport` class.

    We need to test out our internet's latency by mimicking a similar result in a development build.

    Which of the functions in our `NetworkTransport` class will open and test a socket? (Appendix)

    A) `ConnectToNetworkPeer`
    B) `ConnectAsNetworkHost`
    C) `AddWebsocketHost`
    D) `AddHostWithSimulator`

94. If we apply a Network Proximity Checker to our game object, what else is also required? (Appendix)

    A) Network Transform
    B) Network Start Position
    C) Network Discovery
    D) Network Identity

95. We are writing a script that inherits `NetworkBehaviour`. We need to invoke a server method when the client's method is run.

    Which of the following attributes should we use on the line above the declaration of this method? (Appendix)

    A) `[ServerCallback]`
    B) `[SyncEvent]`
    C) `[Command]`
    D) `[ClientRpc]`

96. A programmer is creating a visual effect for an online multiplayer game that will spawn when a player jumps while having rocket boots equipped.

The designer has created a particle system and attached it as a child to an empty Game Object called `BoostEffect`.

The `BoostEffect` object has both a Network Identity and a `NetworkTransform` component on it.

The `BoostEffect` object is spawned on the network into the level at the location of the jump, but never moves or rotates after it is spawned. The effect does not interact with other players on the network but should be visible to them.

What property of the `NetworkTransform` component should the programmer change from the default value to optimize the impact this object will have on the connection between the players? (Appendix)

A) Decrease **Interpolate Movement Factor** to `0.01`
B) Increase **MovementThreshold** to `0.005`
C) Set **Network Send Rate** to `0`
D) Set **Transform Sync Mode** to **Sync Rigidbody 3D**

Appendix

This section will include added notes and other topics that don't quite fit in our Unity project for a number of reasons; topics such as **Virtual Reality (VR)** for a side-scrolling game that could work, but ideally would be better suited to a first-person view format to help with the potential issues that a developer may encounter.

Other topics, such as Unity's networking setup, are somewhat ill-timed as regards the Unity programmer exam as this topic is marked as deprecated and Unity is currently working on a new networking setup as of the time of writing this book. I, therefore, thought that this would be of greater benefit as general knowledge.

Finally, in the last topic, we will cover some random general knowledge pertaining to Unity that could also help you through the exam.

Developing for Virtual Reality

As you probably know, VR has been around commercially since the '90s, but it only became more widely recognized when Oculus and Vive headsets, which could be hooked up to a PC, became accessible. A short time thereafter, mobile phones were being turned into VR headsets as a cheaper alternative, examples including Google Cardboard and Samsung's Gear VR attachment headsets.

As a Unity Developer, we need to not only understand the technical limitations of these VR devices, but also understand how and why some people feel sick while others do not.

VR games/simulations can get rejected very quickly if, for example, the brain and the body know they are not inhabiting the world their eyes are telling them they are a part of.

 If you would like to know more about the health and safety aspect of using/developing a VR app, refer to the following link: `https://retrophil.codes/Self-Study-App-Cognitive-Behaviour-GearVR`

So, in terms of performance and VR applications, the frame rate is pretty important. Developers are encouraged to aim for a high frame rate of 90 to avoid a jerky disconnect with the world the user is in. Latency or, to be more precise, **motion to photon** (**MTP**) is required to be no higher than 20 milliseconds (the delay in updates when the user moves their head) with a display refresh rate of 90 Hz (displays refresh every 11 ms).

The following diagram shows the three aforementioned technical targets that need to be achieved when designing a VR app:

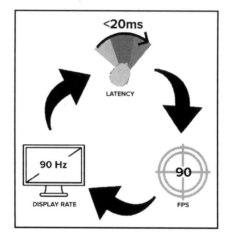

So, if we can hit those three targets consistently, the user will feel more immersed in their world. Keeping performance high means being careful with the platform's resources. For example, if, in the user's distance, there are plenty of 3D assets with materials and various textures applied that the players are never going to reach, we may as well replace those assets with a skybox to help maintain the fluidity of the VR app. Another technique designed to help keep the VR app running smoothly is by altering the texture of the display (`renderViewportScale`) at unavoidable parts in the VR app.

Did you know that you can create an application that has VR capability without having to start it in VR mode?

To achieve this, in the **Player Settings** window, set the **XR Settings** so that **None** is at the top of the **Virtual Reality SDKs** list

We, of course, can still make the user feel ill by overdoing things as regards post-processing effects and by adding aspects such as motion blur and depth of field, which may confuse the user, while removing aspects such as jagged edges on assets would naturally make the user feel even less like they are in a game/simulation. Meanwhile, even going as far as increasing the resolution by means of super-sampling, this method can be very expensive for a mobile device. If your VR app is basic (no textures, basic lighting, and few assets), you may be able to achieve this ... as long as your performance doesn't dip!

The main take-away from this is that VR needs to run as smoothly and convincingly as possible before filling and polishing a scene too soon.

Unity's current networking setup

As mentioned at the beginning of this Appendix, the original networking setup UNet is officially deprecated, as confirmed in the following links:

- `https://support.unity3d.com/hc/en-us/articles/360001252086-UNet-Deprecation-FAQ`
- `https://blogs.unity3d.com/2018/08/02/evolving-multiplayer-games-beyond-unet/`

This is also mentioned in Unity's programmer exam under the *Programming core interactions* section in `Chapter 1`, *Setting Up and Structuring Our Project*. The fact that it may be one of the questions that comes up in the exam means we need to prepare for this potential outcome with some general knowledge regarding Unity's networking setup. My advice would be to just get the gist from the manual itself (`https://docs.unity3d.com/Manual/UNet.html`) as I feel it's too much of a waste studying something that is no longer officially supported.

The following is a list of points and links that will help steer you toward acquiring some basic knowledge in terms of Unity's deprecated "UNet":

- LAN gaming:

  `https://docs.unity3d.com/Manual/class-NetworkDiscovery.html`

- Simulating online latency:

  `https://docs.unity3d.com/2017.3/Documentation/ScriptReference/Networking.NetworkTransport.AddHostWithSimulator.html`

- The visibility of game objects for network clients:

  ```
  https://docs.unity3d.com/Manual/class-NetworkProximityChecker.
  html
  ```

- Performing remote actions across the network:

  ```
  https://docs.unity3d.com/Manual/UNetActions.html
  ```

- The synchronization of movement and rotation:

  ```
  https://docs.unity3d.com/Manual/class-NetworkTransform.html
  ```

Closing suggestions for the game/exam

There is also a possibility in the Unity programmer exam that you will come across the odd question on shaders to establish how much you know with regard to creating shaders or knowing what different shaders can create. Learning about shaders is another book in itself, and it's also unlikely when you sit your exam that the majority of it will be devoted to shaders. Hence, if you don't know how to write shaders, do not concern yourself with the coding and focus more on the general practice and functions used. For example, a cel-shaded toon in an environment or custom post-processing effect could be achieved by using functions such as `Camera.depthTextureMode` to calculate the depth of a scene.

Knowing that these functions and methodologies exist will give you a better chance at answering them and, if you need more information on shaders in general, refer to the Packt book entitled *Unity 2018 Shaders and Effects Cookbook - Third Edition*, otherwise, I recommend skimming through the Shader reference manual provided by Unity: `https://dev.rbcafe.com/unity/unity-5.3.3/en/Manual/SL-SurfaceShaders.html`

In the next section, I'll go through the process of installing post-processing v2 on later versions of Unity.

Installing the post-processing package in Unity 2018.1+

Moving past Unity 2017.3, the installation of post-processing will differ with Unity 2018.1 and beyond. Unity at this point introduced a window that is responsible for adding new components and packages to your project. Some of these are currently in development, while others are being released and updated on a weekly basis.

One of these packages is the post-processing we employed in `chapter 13`, *Effects, Testing, Performance, and Alt Controls*, along with a number of updates.

If you are using version 2018.1 and above and want to install the post-processing package, perform the following steps:

1. At the top of Unity Editor, select **Window | Package Manager** (denoted by **1, 2**).
2. When the **Package Manager** window appears, make sure that **All packages** (denoted by **3**) at the top is selected.
3. When all the content appears (this can take a few seconds), scroll down and select the **Post Processing** package (denoted by **4**).
4. Then, click on the **Install** button (denoted by **5**).

The following screenshot shows the stages involved in in installing the post-processing v2 package:

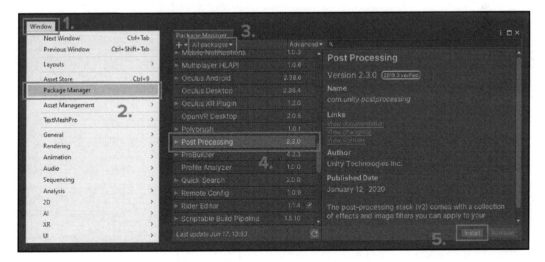

Rendering paths

Some of the mock questions in the Unity programmer exam may refer to **Forward** and **Deferred** graphic settings, but what are these, apart from a selection that can be made in our **Camera** component in the **Inspector** window?

The following screenshot shows alternative rendering paths in the **Camera** component:

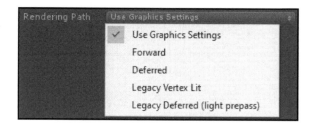

As we can see in the preceding screenshot, there are a variety of different rendering paths. Each of these will render our scene's surface and light in a slightly different way. Some will work faster than others, but will be devoid of other benefits, such as anti-aliasing.

 Refer to the following link to see the chart comparisons of either rendering path: https://docs.unity3d.com/Manual/RenderingPaths.html

Adding/optimizing Killer Wave

So we really have come to the end of the book, and the whole process of designing a game was a way of trying to cover as many objectives from the Unity programmer exam as possible in a variety of scenarios. There are parts in this tutorial series where obviously things could have been quicker or done better with regard to creating a project, but this book was never about making a game. It was about covering as much as possible while seeing your project develop.

Also, if you bought this book simply with a view to making a game and you haven't made one before, you've covered a range of tools and components that you can now use and, for sure, you could find employment as a Unity developer. The majority of the 30+ Unity projects I have worked on have all emanated from the skills I have demonstrated in this book. Hence, if you want to carry on with Killer Wave or rename it and change the concept to make the game more yours, go for it. You have an adequate foundation to continue, but where should you go next with the game?

Here is a list of things that you could work on in order to continue with Killer Wave:

Optimize the code:

- Use the Unity **Profiler** as often as possible and take the first, the most expensive resource used off the top of its list as discussed back in Chapter 13, *Effects, Testing, Performance, and Alt Controls*.
- As your game will likely get bigger and more complex, using functions such as GameObject.Find and Transform.Find are going to slow your game down even more. Reference these variables by other means, such as in the **Inspector**.
- Avoid any kind of if statement within a for loop.
- Any multiplications made with Vector3s and floats need to be done separately (keep all floats within parentheses to prevent code going back and forth between variables).
- The following code block shows an example of keeping Vector3's and floats separate:

```
transform.position = lastPos + wantedVelocity *
                    (speed * speedFactor *
Mathf.Sin(someOtherFactor) * drag                    *
fricition *Time.deltaTime);
```

- Cache transforms; Unity performs checks to establish whether a game object has been deleted with its own standalone transform. The following code block shows an example of caching a transform:

```
Transform _transform;

void Start()
{
_transform = this.transform;
}
```

- Use `transform.localPosition` instead of `transform.position` (if you can). Unity automatically stores all data as local positions internally.
- Reduce engine calls by caching variables.
- Remove `get` and `set` accessors, and keep variables as `public` to avoid accessing.
- Try to avoid `Vector` math and replace it with cache multiplied floats. This saves the creation of `Vector` and having to store values inside it.
- Store `Time.deltaTime` as a `static` float to avoid multiple engine calls.
- Use `for` loops instead of `foreach`, since `foreach` creates garbage.
- Use an `array` instead of a `List`.
- Try and keep the **GC Alloc** list at zero in the **Profiler**. Basically, don't generate garbage if possible so as to avoid performance spikes.
- Instantiate game objects in the first frame.
- Make an object pool of bullets instead of instantiating and destroying.
- Don't use `string` concatenations; in worst-case scenarios, use `StringBuilder`.
- Create your own `Update` / `FixedUpdate` managers instead of using those offered by Unity. This aids performance and you can create your own custom features to add to it.
- Use animated sprites instead of 3D assets.
- Avoid animating game objects with a large hierarchy.
- Create a loading screen if the scenes take too long to load.
- Make all final **Profiler** tests on the platform (**Development Mode** and/or **logcat** for Android) on which you intend to build your game/app.

Other game ideas:

- Create alternative scriptable assets for the current enemy.
- Make more items available in the shop.
- Add different enemy spawners.
- Make the cluster bomb do something!
- Fight the boss.
- Create level 4.

I hope these ideas/suggestions help and that the book, in general, helps you on your journey. The very best of luck!

Mock answers

The answers to the mock questions located at the end of some chapters can be found in the following sections.

Chapter 3

Questions	Answers
1	D
2	C
3	C
4	B
5	A

Chapter 7

Questions	Answers
1	C
2	B
3	B
4	B
5	A
6	D
7	B
8	B
9	D
10	D

Chapter 10

Questions	Answers
1	B
2	C
3	A
4	A
5	B
6	D
7	B
8	D
9	A
10	A
11	A
12	C
13	A
14	B
15	A
16	A
17	C
18	A
19	D
20	B

Chapter 12

Questions	Answers
1	B
2	C
3	B
4	D
5	D
6	B
7	D
8	C

9	A
10	C
11	C
12	A
13	D
14	B
15	A
16	D
17	A
18	B
19	B
20	C

Full mock

Questions	Answers
1	C
2	A
3	A
4	A
5	A
6	B
7	C
8	A
9	B
10	B
11	B
12	C
13	C
14	B
15	B
16	A
17	D
18	A

19	D
20	B
21	C
22	B
23	B
24	B
25	D
26	A
27	A
28	B
29	C
30	C
31	C
32	D
33	B
34	D
35	C
36	B
37	B
38	B
39	A
40	B
41	D
42	B
43	B
44	B
45	C
46	A
47	A
48	A
49	B
50	B
51	B
52	C

53	A
54	B
55	B
56	D
57	A
58	C
59	D
60	C
61	A
62	B
63	A
64	A
65	A
66	B
67	B
68	D
69	B
70	A
71	B
72	A
73	A
74	C
75	D
76	B
77	D
78	D
79	A
80	A
81	A
82	C
83	B
84	A
85	C
86	A

87	A
88	A
89	D
90	A
91	C
92	C
93	D
94	D
95	C
96	C

Other Books You May Enjoy

If you enjoyed this book, you may be interested in these other books by Packt:

Unity Game Optimization, Third Edition
Dr. Davide Aversa and Chris Dickinson

ISBN: 978-1-83855-651-8

- Apply the Unity Profiler to find bottlenecks in your app, and discover how to resolve them
- Discover performance problems that are critical for VR projects and learn how to tackle them
- Enhance shaders in an accessible way, optimizing them with subtle yet effective performance tweaks
- Use the physics engine to keep scenes as dynamic as possible
- Organize, filter, and compress art assets to maximize performance while maintaining high quality
- Use the Mono framework and C# to implement low-level enhancements that maximize memory usage and prevent garbage collection

Hands-On Game Development Patterns with Unity 2019
David Baron

ISBN: 978-1-78934-933-7

- Discover the core architectural pillars of the Unity game engine.
- Learn about software design patterns while building gameplay systems.
- Acquire the skills to recognize anti-patterns and how to avoid their adverse effect in your codebase.
- Enrich your design vocabulary so you can better articulate your ideas on how to better your game's architecture.
- Gain some mastery over Unity's API by writing well-designed code.
- Get some game industry insider tips and tricks that will help you in your career.

Leave a review - let other readers know what you think

Please share your thoughts on this book with others by leaving a review on the site that you bought it from. If you purchased the book from Amazon, please leave us an honest review on this book's Amazon page. This is vital so that other potential readers can see and use your unbiased opinion to make purchasing decisions, we can understand what our customers think about our products, and our authors can see your feedback on the title that they have worked with Packt to create. It will only take a few minutes of your time, but is valuable to other potential customers, our authors, and Packt. Thank you!

Index